IDENTITY AND AUTHORITY

Identity and Authority

Explorations in the
Theory of Society

Edited by

ROLAND ROBERTSON AND BURKART HOLZNER

St. Martin's Press · New York

All rights reserved. For information write:
St. Martin's Press, Inc., 175 Fifth Avenue, New York, N.Y. 10010
First published in the United States of America in 1980
Printed in Great Britain

Library of Congress Cataloging in Publication Data
Main entry under title:
Identity and authority
   Includes bibliographical references and index.
   1. Authority — Addresses, essays, lectures
   2. Identity — Addresses, essays, lectures
   I. Robertson, Roland   II. Holzner, Burkart
HM271.I33   301'.01   79–5439
ISBN 0–312–40448–4

In Memory of
Benjamin Nelson

Contents

Acknowledgements

This volume has developed through a number of stages, beginning with conversations between Burkart Holzner, Vytautas Kavolis and Benjamin Nelson within the context of the International Society for the Comparative Study of Civilizations (USA) in 1973. At that time the basic idea was to hold a special conference on the theme of identity in civilizational perspective, to which Holzner was to add the idea that it would be sociologically significant to consider identity in relation to authority. Early in 1974 Holzner and Roland Robertson decided to push ahead with this idea by holding a conference on identity and authority in Pittsburgh in 1975. That conference was held under the auspices of the Pittsburgh University Center for International Studies and the Department of Sociology at the University of Pittsburgh in April 1975. Planning and execution being primarily the responsibility of Robertson in consultation with Holzner. This volume is an outgrowth of that conference.

Not long before this book went to press we very sadly learned of the death of Benjamin Nelson. Both of the editors are proud to have been closely associated with him during the last few years of his life, the primary vehicle for the association being the International Society for the Comparative Study of Civilizations (USA), in which Ben Nelson was without doubt the leading light. We regard a number of aspects of the present volume as conforming to the kind of civilizational science which Nelson so strenuously and brilliantly advocated in his later years, although Ben Nelson certainly would not have regarded all of the present volume as conforming to his own views. In any case, we wish to dedicate this volume to the memory of Benjamin Nelson and to record the important role that he played in its gestation.

The editors are grateful to Carl Beck, Director of the Center for International Studies, for facilitating partial funding of the conference and to J. Edward Shoben, who at the time was Associate Provost at the University of Pittsburgh. Dr Shoben was instrumental in obtaining funds from the Provost's Fund and the Maurice Falk Medical Fund. We wish to give particular thanks to the Maurice Falk Medical Fund for providing financial assistance from an early stage and continuing that assistance in the production of this book. Phillip Hallen of the Maurice Falk Medical

Fund has shown considerable interest in our work, to the point of volunteering to facilitate additional assistance beyond our original request. Ms Josephine Stagno has performed admirably in a secretarial-organizational role, as have other secretaries in the Department of Sociology, University of Pittsburgh.

In addition to the contributors to the present volume other participants in the 1975 Pittsburgh Conference on Identity and Authority included Benjamin Nelson, Harold Isaacs, Omar K. Moore, Laurie Taylor, Geoffrey Guest and Toby Huff. We were glad to have the involvement of a number of our graduate students—Barbara Renchkovsky, in particular, being very helpful. Joni Klepin provided valuable assistance in proof-reading.

Introduction

Talk of 'crises' with respect to various aspects of modern societies has become commonplace in recent years. While we are not directly concerned with notions of crisis in this book, it is certainly worth noting at the outset that among the aspects of modern societies which are most frequently referred to in that connection are those evoked by the terms *identity* and *authority*. That is not to say that the two terms have been explicitly and frequently linked. Indeed it is one of the purposes of this book to provide for the systematic linking of the two terms and the empirical phenomena indicated by them. More specifically, we argue that the comprehension of the one requires the simultaneous invocation of the other. We believe that important advances will be possible by taking this complementarity seriously.

We have decided to point-up continuities and divergences among contributors in vignette form at the beginning of the essays. The first essay, a collaborative effort on the part of the editors, is the most abstract and general of all the contributions. It combines phenomenological, cultural-civilizational and sociological perspectives in order to gain purchase on the chosen theme in as wide ranging a manner as possible. In contrast to Robertson's last chapter which locates the theme of identity and authority within the contexts of classical and modern sociological theory, the first chapter in effect treats the topic analytically, almost *de novo*. We try to specify the anthropological ubiquity of identity and authority without discussion in the frame of the history of sociology—although we certainly invoke insights from the work of others as we proceed with what we call 'a problem analysis'. The latter is a very deliberately chosen phrase, signifying the delineation of a problem area from a number of angles.

The second chapter by Vytautas Kavolis is also general, in that its sweep is cross-civilizational and historical. Kavolis extracts his 'logics of selfhood and modes of order' from an impressive vista of mankind's collective experience. The perspective changes in Rainer Baum's paper, but the level of generality remains high. Baum, too, uses a highly comparative framework, but a very different one and for different purposes. Baum restricts himself to Western civilization in an attempt to show the resilience of four major types of societal identity-authority codes.

After the long paper by Baum the centre of attention switches to the USA, although the subsequent papers are by no means restricted in their relevance to modern America. Richard Fenn, in the fourth chapter, raises important issues about the disjunction between collective and individual levels of identity and about legitimation in modern societies, particularly the USA. John Marx in the next chapter sees a different disjunction — that between culture and social structure — which he presents in the context of his own analytic reconstruction of major patterns of change in Western history. His central argument emphasizes the contention that while social structure has become very stable the cultural resources for the construction of personal identity models have greatly expanded. In the sixth chapter, Guy E. Swanson concentrates upon the relationship between changes during the last few decades in the manner in which complex organizations have adopted what he calls 'government by objectives', connecting such changes to the concern with identity as the latter sharply developed during the late 1960s. Central to Swanson's discussion is the dependence of the latter on the former.

What unites the latter three papers is their concentration upon recent shifts in the mode of operation of modern societies, with particular reference to the relationship between large-scale organizations and societal macro-structures on the one hand, and individual modes of existence on the other. In comparison chapters one, two and three (Holzner and Robertson, Kavolis, and Baum) are pitched at higher levels of generality and cover more sociocultural and psychological 'space'. Thus the first papers tend to declare a much greater degree of *invariance* than the later ones — this being particularly true of Baum's contribution and certain aspects of that by Holzner and Robertson. This difference in level of generality does not by any means account for some important differences of conviction. In particular Baum's emphasis upon invariance in authority-identity codes as a mode of accounting for the very persistence of national societies cannot be fully reconciled with John Marx's claims about the increasing state of flux with respect to identity formation in some contemporary societies. It is — to repeat — very important to realize that some of the differences between Baum's pathbreaking paper and other contributions *are* accountable for in terms both of the differences in levels of generality *and a priori* decisions adopted by authors whether to focus upon change in empirical appearance or long-term continuity.

The last chapter by Robertson attempts to specify the significance of the link, identity-authority *via* discussion of the work of Durkheim, Weber, and especially Simmel; it traces the development of sociological ideas on the overall topic since the classical period of sociology. It is intended to show the place of the current effort in the larger intellectual context of thematizations in sociology.

R.R. and B.H.

1

Identity and Authority: A Problem Analysis of Processes of Identification and Authorization

Burkart Holzner and Roland Robertson

This, by intent the most abstract and general of the essays in this book, examines the scope and nature of the sociological, theoretical problem of the relation between authority and identity. What in some contexts may seem 'obvious' about this relation, is not taken for granted here; the attempt is made to penetrate to the grounds of the relation in conceptual terms. There are some brief references to the history of the matter, the reasons for the prevalence of concern with authority in the sociological, and with identity in the psycho-analytical traditions (with only occasional bridges), but the purposes of the essay are not historical: they are, rather, to present a map of the analytical territory.

The analytical point of departure is a phenomenological and logical examination of the principles of identity and difference. From this point on, however, the study uses an explicitly sociological frame. There emerge necessary relations, as that between the object determination of actors, and the sense of their authenticity. The reflective, indeed dialectic, process of authorization and identification is placed into the context of a conception of social structure. The core of the matter emerges in the discussion of social constitutions, solidarities and collective actors. This part of the essay deals with an area of theory construction—in an inevitably sketchy way—from which we feel a more comprehensive frame can be constructed, one that might encompass even the apparent diversities and divergencies of concepts in this volume.

Turning more explicitly to individual identity, meaning, and models of identity, the analysis pursues further the need for new constructs in sociology. A typological sketch illustrates certain of the analysed relations and concludes the essay.

The pattern of analysis in this essay should be seen as building upon, not attempting to overthrow, the sociological tradition and the gains in

*knowledge it has achieved. At the same time, we agree with Eisenstadt that
a broadening of analytical scope is indicated, and that efforts must be
made to understand the symbolic and social grounds for meaningfulness in
social action. * Nowhere does this issue appear in sharper focus than in the
problem of identity and authority.*

BACKGROUND

The social linkage of 'identity' and 'authority' may not on first consideration seem obvious, let alone of great theoretical import. In spite of
the interest which specific schools of sociology, particularly that of symbolic interactionism, have maintained in identity construction (Brittan
1973), sociology in a general sense has not shown much concern with
identity as a problem area. 'Identity' is not a core sociological concept in
spite of its frequent occurrence in the everyday vocabulary of sociologists.
Even in substantive areas, such as the study of ethnicity, where we *can*
observe the use of the term with great frequency, identity has not received
sustained analytic attention, in the sense of locating it in conceptual
contexts and sharpening it to much more than connotative significance.

Concern with identity within the sciences of man has been centred in
psychology, particularly in ego psychology and — more recently — attribution theory. But the most continuous concern with identity has been
among philosophers, a concern which has taken two major, although
certainly not unrelated, forms. The first has focused on the question of
identifying persons, selves and individuals and thus also the issue of at-
tributing identity (in the sense of entitivity) to humans as subjects and/or
objects. The second has had to do with the problem of the relationship between 'reason and reality'. Specifically the latter interest has frequently
centred upon Hegel's oft-called 'panlogism' which rendered the
relationship between reason and reality in terms of their being identical.
More generally, the problem of identity has — in roughly those same
terms — been an important theme in the modern philosophy of science,
with respect to the relationship between scientific language and operation,
on the one hand, and empirical reality, on the other. That these
philosophical interests in identity have permeated sociology cannot be
denied. But the fact remains that in the mainstream of sociology concern
with identity has been intermittent, tentative and discontinuous. Even the
fact that sociologists who have dwelt upon the theme of identity are social-

---

* S. N. Eisenstadt with M. Curelaru, *The Form of Sociology—Paradigms and Crises.* New
York: Wiley, 1966.

psychologically inclined (namely, many of the symbolic interactionists) emphasizes that the study of identity has been regarded by most sociologists as an extra-sociological issue.

Not so with the theme of authority, which has been a much more central sociological concept, constitutive of a range of *Problemstellungen* for at least half a century. Moreover, issues of power, authority and legitimacy were a central legacy of the direct pre-history of sociology—illustrated for example by the social contract theorists of the seventeenth and eighteenth centuries. But that observation highlights something of the *implicit* significance of the concept 'identity' in the same period. For contract theories are constructions of the relationship between persons (or sometimes social sub-systems) and wider systems, such as collective actors, including sovereigns of various kinds. In the main, social contract theories have involved conceptions of relationships between individuals and national societies.

One of the crucial variables distinguishing one such theory from another concerns the conception of the individual and, in a broader sense, conceptions of actors rather than the overall system, the national society. Thus the long-standing debate about the nature of individual and collective actors has been in an important sense one concerning identity and processes of identification. It is not too much to say that the *leitmotif* of the contract-theory debate has been the problem of the relationship between individual and collective identities: how should the boundaries between individuals be drawn? Can collective actors be identified and legitimated, and if so, how and under what circumstances should this be done? What collective actors should be granted effective existence in the interstices between the individual and the wider society?

It can be safely said that the forces shaping the long development of our modern conception of the *identifiable individual* (and the identifiable self and collectivity) *were* in many significant respects of a political nature. For example, the crystallization of the concept of the person in the Roman Imperial period was grounded in politico-legal considerations (Mauss 1968).[1] And even when the vicissitudes of the concept of the ego (the more general term for analysing conceptions of individuality) were largely dictated by moral-religious factors, in an important respect these were still in the broadest sense of the term political, since these factors were bound-up with questions of *authority*, with the 'official' monitoring of individual actions, both in intra-individual and inter-individual terms.

In fact it is safe to state that in Western civilizational contexts the question of the ego had strong political significance—was indeed connected directly to matters of *authority*, involving the politically-based use of forensic and casuistic methods (Nelson 1965) for regulating the individual in reference to religious tradition—until the Reformation. The ensuing processes of differentiation, particularly in dominantly Protestant societies, was the ground upon which the ego began to depart from transparent affiliation with external authority—most notably with respect to the notion of *conscience*—and where in an important respect the question of identity in its modern form of 'the problem of identity' began.[2] That, for example, is the ground upon which the idea of the *convertibility* of men and women has grown—convertibility involving at its root the proposition that men and women can change their modes of identification of self (Robertson 1978: 186–222).

It may well be that the rather wide—but never complete—acceptance of the idea that the problem of order is a pivotal sociological one was responsible for the crystallization of *explicit concern* with the notion of authority (*via* political authority in Weber, and moral authority in Durkheim), and *the muting* of the problem of identity (Cf. Wrong 1977:31–70, 81–94). On the other hand, it has become increasingly clear that the central concern of much classical sociology was indeed, implicitly at least, the problem of personal identity (in a non-psychological sense). The latter argument focuses upon the abiding concern with the individual in the works of such sociologists as Durkheim and Simmel, the early Marx and, in diffuse terms, Max Weber. Each of these in their different ways took the notion of individual*ism* very seriously and they were, in different respects, concerned to strike an optimal balance between the demands of 'society' and the rights and needs of the individual.

Durkheim and Simmel, in particular, spoke at length of the rise of individualism as a prominent substantive theme of industrial societies. Each in turn addressed the contingent problems of superordination and subordination. Marx and Weber, on the other hand, took the oppressiveness of modern authority more as their starting points and then worried about the degrees to which and ways in which individuals could create and maintain freedom of manoeuvre and integralness relative to circumstance. Their views on this were, of course, very different (as were those of Durkheim and Simmel)—Marx dwelling (at least in his early work) upon the possibility of simultaneously cancelling the problem of authority and maximizing individual meaning and control, Weber in a less optimistic mode arriving at an ambiguous subscription to a position which wavered between, on the one hand, the inevitable suppression of what we would now call personal identity and, on the other hand, the possibility of what has sometimes been called existentialist-like resistance to the controls of authority.

That the individual/society problem is not exactly the same as the identity/authority problem is clear. But the similarities of concern are numerous; and we propose that the identity/authority relationship is the form in terms of which the individual/society relationship can be fruitfully re-focused. The problem of the relationship between *the individual and society* (political and/or civil) is too artificial for many sociological purposes. It becomes a more realistic sociological problem when woven into the more specific identity/authority theme. In brief, to us identity constitutes the form of presentation of the actor, both in internal and external relationships. Similarly authority is the mode of presentation of society and other collectives to constituent 'units'. There is, of course, considerable variation — historically and anthropologically — in degrees of phenomenal experience in these matters; an issue which will receive attention as our discussion progresses.

We argue that the terms identity and authority are mutually implicative. No conception of authority makes sense unless we speak also of the ways in which units are identified and identify themselves. By the same token, identity implies authority in that identification of self and others involves the problems of *authorship* and *authorization*. Moreover, authority is bound-up with the issue of collective identity. More specifically, authority problems are frequently attendant upon the differentiation of identities into personal, special or 'local' aspects, on the one hand, and collective or 'cosmopolitan' aspects on the other hand.

In what follows we will tend to focus more upon identity and processes of identification than upon authority at a number of points, mainly because that has been the most neglected of the two concepts in sociology, at least as regards explicit analysis. Thus matters of authority will often be treated contingently; although it must be emphasized from the outset that we do not propose in empirical terms that authority is necessarily more dependent upon identity matters than *vice versa*.

A SUMMARY OF THE PROBLEMS

In sociological analysis the study, on the one hand, of meanings and attributions and, on the other hand, of social structure are often dealt with as if they were so different as to require divergent approaches. Much of phenomenological sociology, for example, has de-emphasized — indeed frequently ridiculed — analysis of social structure, whereas many social-structural and social-ecological investigations are couched in terms which make it difficult to link them with interpretations of meaningful interactions (e.g., Heap and Roth 1973; Cf. Holzner 1974, 1972). By discussing the concept 'identity', especially in its relation with 'authority', in this problem analysis we are forcing a reconsideration of these matters. Even a cursory consideration of 'identity' reveals its reflexive and dialectic structure. Identities have an objective and a subjective aspect at the same time, similar in a sense to the way in which George Herbert Mead uncovered the reflexive and dialectic structure of the self and captured it in his notions of the 'I' and the 'me'. The reflexivity of identity in this sense should lead into questions concerning reflexivity in social structure.

It is well known, not only since Freud, that the developmental structuring of personalities necessarily includes a coming to terms with and a changing of objects of authority and relations with authority. The studies in social psychology stimulated by the seminal inquiry *The Authoritarian Personality* (Adorno *et al.* 1950) have shown this again and again.[3] Political beliefs, cognitive styles, patterns of prejudice, the patterning of hostility — all these have been linked to the complex emotional dynamics of authority and personality in an individual's development. In fact, the conception of such dynamics has often been popularized in many Western societies into the notion that authority is *necessarily* oppressive and distorts personality development.

In our perspective the relationship between authority and identity departs from the conceptions advanced in the psychoanalytic traditions or those espoused by the Frankfurt School. In one sense this departure centres on substantive disagreements that cannot be adumbrated here. In another respect we are concerned to address the more *cognitive* aspects of identification. Running the risk of being charged with 'cognitive inflationism' (Martins 1972, 1974; Wrong 1977:47–54) we nevertheless feel that it is precisely the cognitive aspects of processes of identification which have been badly neglected by sociologists (Cf. Warner 1978; Gonos 1977). From our sociological standpoint 'identity' centres upon images, knowledge and assessment of positions, performances, and attributes of social objects. It is a concept much different from the concept personality. We believe that 'personality' is a theoretical construct which, while of undoubted utility, may have been over-extended in sociological analyses. In any case, the level of what is often called 'personal identity' we place between the constructs of personality and social structure (Cf. Schneider 1968; Schneider and Smith 1973). In a similar mode of modifying some of the conventional wisdom we locate authority between the levels of social structure and culture. Such analytic relocations are necessary if only to encompass, at least in principle, *all* action-systemic, societal and civilizational circumstances; for there are circumstances in our purview where the degree of differentiation is so low as not to give rise to identity and authority phenomena in the sharpness that they exhibit in much of the modern world. It is through these procedures that we hope our treatment of identity and authority may provide a new context for understanding the relationship between individual and society, especially as it is reflectively mediated and symbolically constructed.

We do not claim here to present a theory of identity construction. Instead, we work modestly to explore, so to speak, the lie of the land — to sketch a map of the territory of concepts and issues surrounding our focus. This is what we mean by a 'problem analysis'. On the other hand, we do not proceed in the style of a review of the literature. (Aspects of that approach are presented in the last chapter.) This would require us to be elaborately critical of many different frames of reference. We feel the issue is better served by our sketching our own perspective and the 'map' which emerges from it. We will, however, comment from time to time on contrasting perspectives which complement, or stand in stark contrast to, our position. It is because of the inherent reflexivity built into the problem of identity that it is necessary for us to combine at least *three different points of view*. We begin (1) in a phenomenological vein, to be followed by (2) a social structural analysis. These tacks are informed diffusely, on occasions specifically, by a framework of (3) cultural sociology.[4]

We thus begin with a treatment of 'identity and difference', centred upon logical and phenomenological reflections which we feel are necessary in order to establish a universal analytic frame. From there we turn to an analysis of social identity assessments in the context of social structure. This yields a conception of social identities as consequences of assessed performances and attributes within the framework of analytical spaces structured by the modes of social cognition and the dimensions of social valuation. The view of identity that emerges from this perspective is reminiscent of Durkheim's thought, in that it emphasizes the significance of external constraints and symbolic representations. In the next section we proceed to modify and elaborate this view by turning our attention to the dynamics of social constitutions, solidarities, and the structure of collective actors. These dynamics, which involve especially the forming of social boundaries and the structuring of actors, are in our view the major contexts for the determination and anchorage of symbolically defined models of identity. The dynamics in this domain are linked on one side to very large socio-cultural entities such as civilizations, and on the other to specific identification demands on the individual level.

Yet another shift of perspective is required to introduce briefly a sharper focus on individual identities and the experience of meaning. Finally, we attempt to link the different perspectives from which the problems of identity have been treated with authority—in terms of a typological delineation of collectivity/individual relationships. Our treatment of identity thus places the phenomenological perspective on meaningful experience into a dialectic interplay with the sociological insistence on social-structural contingency and cultural constraint. It is the apparent need for a variety of perspectives in the treatment of identity, together with the necessity to draw on a multiplicity of theoretical notions in sociology, which in our view gives the topic much of its significance and interest.

IDENTITY AND DIFFERENCE

In order to speak intelligibly about the historically and anthropologically manifold forms of personal and collective identity—which are subject to evolutionary change—it is necessary to have a conceptual framework which is, in principle, of universal applicability. We look for this in the phenomenology and logic of identity and difference, reducing in the beginning of our analysis the identity concept to its starkest simplicity.

We speak of something as having an 'identity' when it can be determined that it is the same with itself over time, or in a context of different relations. Heidegger (1969:23) expressed the matter as follows:

> The usual formulation of the principle of identity reads: A = A. The principle of identity is considered the highest principle of thought . . . [but] what does the formula A = A state which is customarily used to represent the principle of identity? The formula expresses the equality of A and A. An equation requires at least two elements. One A is equal to another. Is this what the principle of identity is supposed to mean? Obviously not . . . for something to be the same, one is always enough. Two are not needed, as they are in the case of equality.

> The formula A = A speaks of equality. It does not define A as the same. The common formulation of the principle of identity thus conceals precisely what the principle is trying to say: A *is* A, that is every A is itself the same . . . The more fitting formulation of the principle of identity 'A = A' would accordingly mean not only every A is itself the same; but rather that every A is itself the same with itself. Sameness implies the relation of 'with', that is a mediation, a connection, a synthesis: the unification into a unity. This is why throughout the history of Western thought identity appears as unity.

Heidegger continues in his argument to explore the inevitably existential grounding of the principle of identity in Being. It is not necessary, however, for our purposes to follow him far into his particular existential philosophy. We may take from these observations specific suggestions for the sociological treatment of identity.

The principle of identity, the 'sameness of every A with itself' requires assessments which can be said to be measurements. In order to establish what a social object is and whether or not it maintains some invariance and continuity over time and space, and difference in social relations, assessments in the manner of measurements are necessary. It is through such assessments that a social object becomes a determinate entity. Thus it follows that identity in this obvious and important sense is contingent upon measurement operations, and the at-least-implicit construction of an analytical space into which an object can be placed. By implication, identity determinations are discriminations, establishing differences in the measurement sense, and are thus even from this basic perspective related to social boundaries. However, as our reference to Heidegger suggests, the concept 'identity' refers to something deeper than the unmistakable location of an object in an analytical space so that it can be 'identified' in the sense of 'located' in a unique manner. Without such *locating* assessment there could be no conceptions of identity; but social objects are also subjects, conscious, and existential focal points of experience. While Heidegger would speak here of the 'grounding in Being' we will speak of the criterion of *authenticity* for social identities.

In a general sociological conception of identity two aspects must inevitably be considered: the object assessments in a field of social measurement, and the aspect of authenticity. The identity of actors has always, and inescapably, the two aspects of determinations of the actor's objective nature, and his subjective experience (Cf. Habermas 1972:140–60). This latter is sharpened in the notion of authenticity, by which we mean a wholeness or integration of identity experience. Identity in one regard may be considered to be an entirely private phenomenon. However, the degree to which there is a separation of private domains from public ones, and hence a differentiation between public authenticity performance and private authenticity experiences, is itself *variable*.

In every society actors are assessed in terms of their performances and attributes, and identified in the sense of 'located' in this respect.[5] In every society there is also some requirement for the assessment of authenticity, which in its form may vary. The assessments of an actor's 'nature' and the requirements for authenticity come together in the conception of trust in identities. In the trusting attitude actors take their situation and objects as reliable, and as presenting themselves authentically. Trust is an essential quality of social bonds and a constitutive element of society. Where conditions of trust must be explicitly established, as through measurements, the pressure towards the explicit and reflective construction of actor identities becomes great. The basis of trust will thus be related to the modes of identity assessments through social measurements and the social requirements for authenticity (Holzner 1973). For example, in jurisprudence the oath has played a very special role in transforming statements into assessed evidence. It can be shown that changes in the formal and substantive legal conception of the oath relate directly to emerging models of identity, especially in the notion of conscience.

We may then view the identity of actors as determined in relation to a grid of social measurements, as a consequence of assessed qualities and performances occurring in a social-force field. This emphasis upon location in social space in the construction of actor identities is quite close to Simmel's answer to the questions: how do individuals come to be observed? and how is the trait of individuality identified? Basically, Simmel answered these questions in terms of a figure-backdrop contrast with the supplementary proposition that the more numerous the intersecting axes of differentiation (the 'forces' in the field) the greater the cognitive pressure to see individuated objects (and, reflexively, subjects).

Identity requires difference at least in the sense that measurements can be performed which result in the location of a social object as identifiable with itself in analytic social space and time. In addition, the actor whose identity is to be ascertained is known to be an experiencing subject, and thus authenticity requirements are 'levied against him'. Both of these find their expression in the modalities and criteria of trusting. Identity construction thus is inevitably reflexive to some degree. Social actors are objects and subjects at the same time. The modality of assessment poses constraints with which the authenticity requirement in some fashion musɩ come to terms. 'Identity' in this view is not inherent in objects, but in their relational assessment and the validation of authenticity. In other words, it is an achievement in an interactional process in which identifying performances are assessed and their authors located in analytic space and time constituted by dimensions of valuation and measurements (Cf. Guiot 1977).[6]

Reflexivity occurs where an actor experiences resistance that requires determination of his boundaries and if the environment yields information about his assessments. It is indeed the symbolic transformation of resistance and constraint that leads to a differentiation of conceptions of self, even in the Meadian view. Reflexivity in the individual case implies consciousness of self; in the collective case consciousness of social boundaries and collective actors. It is for this reason that the assessment of differences at the point of constraining boundaries leads to the requirement to determine the 'sameness' of an actor over a period of time and in regard to different relations. Tests of social boundaries, and tests of loyalty within social boundaries, are in a sense collective parallels to the developmental schemata of self and personhood in the individual. Reflexivity in the establishment of social identities, therefore, will be a variable—depending on the nature of symbolism available for the establishment of social measurement and differences; the (partly consequent) perception of boundaries; and the multiplicity of boundaries to be considered. In modern society the degree of reflexivity inherent in questions of identity may be virtually infinite, raising the spectre of infinite regression. But while identification and authentication assessments are universal, reflexivity is a matter of variation. The crossing of boundaries and release from boundary constraints is, as we shall illustrate, related to issues of authority.

Our basically phenomenological consideration of universals concerning the problem of identity has led us to assert that identity assessments occur in terms of the symbolism available for social measurements; they are reflexive to some degree, and involve identifications ('locations') as well as authentications ('valid authorship'). The conditions of trust in social actors are a critical aspect of modalities of identity construction. These involve the formal qualities of the symbolism used in social assessments as well as the nature of social boundaries and structures. Such measuring devices and rationales for their use will vary in their inherent logic, explicit precision, value rationales, and the resultant categories. We would certainly expect that social assessments such as those that become possible through, *inter alia*, a money economy, systems of taxation, procedures for certification, and measurements of prestige and honour, will have deep consequences for the construction of actors, including the modality of their conceptions of authenticity.

The point is, of course, that these measurements are consequential in terms of actors' life chances and determine outcomes of vital interest. It is also important to note that the formal structures — so to speak, the implicit 'folk mathematics' of social measurement — vary in different cultural and civilizational contexts and in the evolutionary process; and that these have great consequences for the establishment of social identity and difference, and especially the degree of reflexivity.[7] What, however, is common to all circumstances is the situational coping with the need to put order into the social world in terms of dialectics of apposition and opposition — with, on the one hand, affinities and identities, and on the other, dissimilarities and boundaries.

SOCIAL MEASUREMENT, IDENTIFYING PERFORMANCES AND SOCIAL STRUCTURE

Our reflections have taken us from the logical and phenomenological domain of identity assessment into the sociological realm. Now we will turn to a further exploration of the relationship between social measurements, identity, and social structure. In a sense it can be said that this relationship is self-evident. Dimensions of cognition and valuation underlying the analytic spaces in terms of which social observers locate and thus identify social objects are indeed the dimensions of social structuring and *destructuring* processes (Cf. Turner 1969; Tiryakian 1970). When sociologists analyse social structure, they do so in terms of certain dimensions that permit the representation of a system of social relations. The analytical account constructed by the sociologist should reckon with the dimensions of structuration and destructuration implicit or sometimes explicit in the folk analytic spaces. These social processes are reflexive and sociological analysis itself is reflexive; a scientific, second-order variant upon social agent-observer reflexivity.

It is the reflexivity of actors and their observers that has made the discussion of social structure in the literature complex. Some — for example, Radcliffe-Brown and many contemporary sociologists, such as Blau — have taken social structure as a to-be-discovered order which empirically exists 'out there'. Blau holds that 'social structure refers to the differentiated interrelated parts in a collectivity, not to theories about them . . .' (Blau 1974:615; also Blau 1977). By contrast social structure can be thought of as constructed solely in the mind of the analyst. Probably the most well-known proponent of this view is Levi-Strauss (1963:279):

> Social relations consist of the raw material out of which the models making up the social structure are built, while social structure can, by no means, be reduced to the ensemble of the social relations to be described in society.

One thus may view the parameters and dimensions of social structure as inherent in social reality itself; or, in contrast, they may be conceived as analytical constructions of the sociologist. It is, however, important to point out that the parameters and dimensions of social structure *are* (almost invariably) analytical accounts of measurements made in 'everyday' social life. The latter are 'folk measurements' — identity assessments performed by and on actors and in terms of those dimensions which they conceive to be important for the making of distinctions. Almost inevitably, any sociological talk about parameters and dimensions of social structure is about both an analytical account given by the sociologist, *and* a summary of structuring judgements, that is social measurements, made by those whom the sociologist observes.

The sociological understanding of social structure thus is possible only in relation to some explication of the spaces in terms of which identifying performances and attributes are assessed by the members of a society. These spaces can be thought of as the dimensionality of the orientation systems of actors in terms of which they assess situations, individuals, and groups. Such orientation systems can be described both in terms of the social realities experienced through them, and in terms of the formal qualities of the symbolic apparatus by means of which they function.[8] The manner in which actors categorize themselves and each other through measurements depends directly on what dimensions of valuation they consider particularly important, and what symbolic resources are available for measuring them. Sociological reflection introduces a particular set of dimensions into this matter, derived from the theoretical purposes of sociological explanation (but still undoubtedly refracting wider societal and civilizational attributes). The sociologist is a specialized, but not necessarily a privileged, social observer.

However, the structuring and destructuring processes which result from the social assessments also lead to differential allocation of situations to actors. It is then possible to speak of social structure as a differential ecology of situations, as well as a differential distribution of orientations (Holzner 1972). This duality of the sociological perspective concerning the phenomenon of social structure appears to us to be inescapable. It is inherent in the reflexive nature of the structuring and destructuring processes themselves. The view presented here does not fundamentally alter many existing conceptions of social structure. Rather, it shifts the focus of attention to the reflexive interplays between orientation and situation, and their consequences; thus, in effect, *combining* the two extreme, modern sociological attitudes towards social structure. In other words, we maintain that the concept, 'social structure', must refer *both* to social relations *and* to models of those situations. (Moreover this same principle applies at *both* the folk and the analytic levels.)

Whilst we have connected the core of an understanding of social structure to structuring processes in relation to measurements performed on identifying performances and attributes, we are clearly not reducing the problem of social structure to symbolism as such. In other words, ours is neither a symbolist nor a symbolic interactionist perspective *per se*. In fact, from the perspective adopted here, the emphasis on classifying and measuring operations as major determinants of structure (see Nadel 1957); the view that we should seek the source of symbolization and classification in experiences within and with social structure (see Durkheim and Mauss 1963); and the tradition which stresses natural symbolic imagery, such as colour oppositions and appositions, and left hand/right hand relationships (see Needham 1974)—all appear to be reconcilable.

Emphasizing the centrality of identity construction in social structuring processes facilitates a view of the significance of the logic of social measurement and classification as a dynamic aspect of the process. Symbolic devices for social measurement and classification are, of course, not static givens. They must be seen as becoming differentiated and increasingly explicit in an evolutionary sense. The explicitness of social measurement itself becomes a major factor for social structure, as well as for the nature of identity. Conversely it can be argued that the experience actors have with social structure as an ecology of situations forms a matrix for the creation of specific symbolic 'tools' to account for and/or convey it.[9] In this respect, symbolism for the representation of structure is a cognitive and expressive transformation of social experience itself determined by the encounter with society as an ecology of situations (Holzner 1965).

We have shown that the assessments of actor identity and the dimensions of social structure and destructuring processes are closely, albeit complexly, interrelated. For our purposes it is important to emphasize that the sociologist should focus upon the manner in which folk actors construct the analytic space within which identity assessments are to be accomplished. Sociological accounts of social structure are, then, designed to explicate such analytic spaces in terms of larger and more differentiated sociological conceptions of them; that is, they accomplish the construction of a 'map' of a society in terms of theoretically relevant dimensions of sociological analysis. It further involves the understanding of identifying performances and their consequences in the structural context.

But, it should be emphasized, our argument does allow for there being a great deal of variation in the degree to which cultural patterns are independent of and in a sense prior to social structure. At the same time all social structuring and destructuring has a symbolic, cultural significance. The idiosyncratically extreme position of Leach (1965:1) highlights some aspects of our argument:

> As far as I am concerned, the cultural situation is a given factor, it is a product and an accident of history . . . the structure of the situation is largely independent of its cultural form. The same kind of structural relationship may exist in many different cultures and be symbolized in correspondingly different ways . . . one and the same element of social structure may appear in one cultural dress in locality A and in another cultural dress in locality B. But A and B may be adjacent places on the map. . . .

An illustration of the symbolic nature of measurement and structuring processes with difference in culture has also been offered by Leach (1965:17):

> In any geographic area which lacks fundamental natural frontiers, the human beings in adjacent areas of the map are likely to have relations with one another — at least to some extent — no matter what their cultural attributes may be. Insofar as these relations are ordered and not wholly haphazard there is implicit in them a social structure. But, it may be asked, if social structures are expressed in cultural symbols, how can the structural relation between groups of different cultures be expressed at all? My answer to this is that maintenance and insistence upon cultural difference can itself become ritual action expressive of social relations.

Surely, the symbolic core of structuring and destructuring processes is the identity assessment of actors — in Leach's case collective assessments — in terms of attributions of 'cultural difference'. The example points to the significance of boundaries (in this case cultural boundaries) for the assessment of different identities.

Identifying assessments of social actors will vary in their consequential weight depending on who performs them and how they are performed. Roughly, identity assessments and the demand for identifying performances will be of greater consequence the greater the authority ('authorship strength') of the agent (or agents) actively involved. We now can think of social structure as providing a grid of social measurements with differential consequences for individuals and groups depending on the authority and power of the assessing agent. The latter, too, has an identity which in varying degrees and modes comprises authorship identity. Despite this, the authorship of identification is not always authoritative in the usual sociological sense of 'legitimate authority'.

In this manner our view of social structure emerges as producing, in a dynamic process, identification demands of individuals and groups. These are demands for 'identifying performances'; that is, declarations—overt, tacit, or by default—of identity, as for example in the demand for a password that identifies friend or foe. Each individual person, and every group, can be conceived of as engaged in responding to such identification demands, and in the process constructing an identity.[10]

The conception of society as a grid of measurement demands goes far in the explication of processes of social identity formation. It is a conception that emphasizes the social production and differential distribution of constraints, in this case constraints resulting from identity assessments. Such assessments always require performances, whether the attributes to be assessed are 'ascribed' or 'achieved'; they are determinations of an actor's 'quality' in response to the manner in which the actor presents himself.

Obviously, the distribution of differentially empowered assessment 'agencies' is not a random one. Such agencies tend to be constructed in relation to matters of power, authority and hierarchy. We have in mind such consequential measurements as those performed by states in levying taxes, defining citizenship and participation in societal communities; by economic actors in judgements of credit; by moral communities in judgement of moral worth; by professional agents of control in the identification of deviants.[11] Studying identity formation in the context of a conception of social structure as a set of occasions for assessing identifying performances allows us to connect heretofore relatively discrete strands of sociological theorizing, while at the same time directing our attention to domains of empirical inquiry often neglected by sociologists.

One such relationship may be established with the body of work called status crystallization (or rank equilibrium) theory. One may think of the identity assessments we have discussed as status determinations, which may have quite disparate outcomes for an individual actor. We think, however, that the generalization of status crystallization theory beyond the context of specific societies is unlikely to be successful simply by comparing problems of status disparity which actors in different settings may encounter and the manner in which they may resolve them. Instead, we would recommend that the problem be considered from the points of view of, first, identity construction in the force-field of agencies empowered and significant others authorized to make assessments of actors; and, second, variations in the symbolism available. Such views will direct our attention to the nature of the symbolism and rationales involved and to measurements in legal, political, economic practice which pose certain substantive identification problems for actors. It might then be possible to incorporate the perspective of status crystallization theory in a general framework suitable for the study of phenomena in different civilizational contexts.[12]

Another theoretical relationship connects the matters discussed to the problems of resentment, transvaluation, and the genesis of value-oriented movements. Underprivileged groups, whose identity determinations in the context of the valuation dimensions of a social structure yield no grounds for positive identification or who are denied authority, often attempt to reshape the valuational context. Such phenomena are well known, as in the creation of identities in relation to a supernatural world, or the revaluation of the dimensions of social structure through revolutionary transformation. Clearly, the reflexivity principle becomes important again. Social structure through measurement of identifying performances creates constraints. In turn, the revaluation of fundamental structural dimensions may drastically alter the patterns of constraint.

Much of our emphasis upon folk measurement implies that a central sociological question in the study of identity is how do people 'do identity'? In that sense a central feature of any exploration of identity must surely run parallel to the neo-ethnomethodological mode of asking; a particular example being how people *do motives*? In their important essay on motives, McHugh *et al* (1974:21–46) place the study of motives within a definitely socio-cultural context. To that extent their argument is at odds with a long tradition of twentieth century social science, which has allocated the study of motives to the personality realm, either in a mechanistic sense of motives as *sociologically unstated premises*, or in Parsons' (1968:14) sense of *identity* being 'the core system *of meanings of an individual personality* in the mode of object in the interaction system of which he is a part'.

Parsons' discussions of identity and processes of identification are without doubt among the most rigorous of those which have been worked out in sensitivity to both considerations of personality *and* the requirements of social *and* cultural levels of analysis. However, the firm locating of identity within the personality system presents a number of problems, at which we have already hinted. That perspective eschews interest in the social-interactional and reflexive dynamics of identity construction. The personality system supplies identification *to* the social system as the 'presumptive basis of solidarity'; it supplies 'establishment of identity' *to* the cultural system. Aspects of identity are, of course, to be found elsewhere in Parsons' processual delineation of action systems: the social system provides 'rational ranking of claims to identification' to the behavioural organism, and 'identification in institutional order (solidarity)' to the cultural system (Parsons and Platt 1973:439). But the ideas that identity and processes of identification are distinctively in-teractional matters, and that there is a crucial *bricolage* character to the construction of identities are absent. As McHugh *et al* argue in respect of motives, it is here denied that identities can be helpfully characterized in sociological perspective as 'concrete, private and interior "mainsprings" that reside in people, rather than public and observable courses of action' (McHugh *et al* 1974:23).

In criticizing Parsons' approach to identity it must be closely understood that we do so in complete recognition of his attempts to draw a sharp distinction between biological organism (where much of the energy and intelligence of psychologists has been spent)[13] and personality systems — systems 'composed of "objects" which have been learned in the course of life experience, that experience having been "codified" in terms of culturally given codes, however important the individuals' idiosyncratic modifications of those codes and of the object meanings "formulated" in them' (Parsons 1968:15). Parsons' depiction of the personality is indeed much more 'public' and social than most of the conventional psychological wisdom makes it. Identity is in Parsons' words 'the point of coincidence of the "I" . . . and the "me" which is object both to self and to others' (Parsons 1968:19), and thus is the same as the psychoanalytic conception of the ego-ideal.

We have insisted all along that identification of social objects and the attendant matters of authentication and authorization are anthropo-logically ubiquitous. That is to say that identification is a necessary and contingent feature of all forms of social life (as is authorization and the attribution of authorship). The key notion of *boundary* which we have intermittently used is a major clue to variation in socio-cultural cir-cumstances. In many societies relatively clear-cut boundaries are drawn in *social-group* terms, with matters concerning synchronic and diachronic solidarity being closely bound-up with ritual — with praxial structures of consciousness (Nelson 1973). As Dumont argues in respect of the classic Indian case, that is a circumstance which denies in cultural principle and in social practice the identity of all men. Identity thus resides at the level of group or quasi-group membership, as in the Indian caste system (which for present purposes means to ignore the impact of Western ideas on social stratification in modern India). In contrast, Dumont notes the tendency in the Western world for us to believe in 'the basic identity of all men, because they are no longer taken as samples of a culture, a society or a social group' (Dumont 1970:304). That, as Durkheim emphasized, comes about through the process of individuation — an experience which makes men and women increasingly conscious of their *generic* characteristics as human beings to the degree to which they become aware of themselves as separate and distinct personalities. To that, in turn, we must add Simmel's cogent argument (with Durkheim seemingly agreeing) that it is nevertheless in group contexts that the *individuated* man or woman realizes his or her *individualism*.

Thus questions concerning *how* are 'I-ness', 'me-ness', 'you-ness' and 'it-ness' 'done' relate to the interstices of personality and social system. *One* major reason for arguing thus is that the *phenomenal* concept 'personal identity' is not a human universal. In other words, 'identity' and self-conscious talk of identity are not to be found at all times in all social places. Thus 'the problem of identity' arises only when there is a relatively high degree of differentiation of personality from the social system — when individuals are not taken to be 'walking pieces of social structure' — *or* when social boundaries are dislocated in relatively undifferentiated circumstances. The latter indicate situations of individuation-by-default and such situations are, undoubtedly, a matter of frequent occurrence. They include uncertainty about the status of the gentry in post-medieval Europe, the Samurai in Tokugawa Japan and numerous less-easily specifiable cases of status uncertainty in Africa resulting from colonial intrusion. These cases of individuation by default vary in the degree to which they lead to individualism in the Durkheimian sense. The 'cult of the individual' is possible only when there are *cultural models* of individualism available (as well, of course, as other conditions). That is the circumstance in which one can speak safely of codes of *personal* identity and identification of personal individuals.

We cannot do better at this point than to quote from Lofland's characterization of the identification process: 'The phenomenon of humans adopting a category as pivotal and scrutinizing all other categories in terms of their consistency with it, implies, in practice, that whatever is taken as pivotal *is* Actor — *is* his essential nature or core being' (Lofland 1969:127). When inconsistency is discerned then further efforts must be made to ascertain what kind of person he 'really' is. Some discrepancies may be then defined as 'excusable' or not 'really' important. If such strategies fail it will become necessary 'to assign Actor to a different pivotal

category with which his complement of categorical placements is more
practically, if not ideally, consistent (Lofland 1969:128). Each strategy
successively reaches towards the goal of discovering a person's *actual* or
special core. As Lofland notes, the quest to assign individuals to a 'true'
pivotal category is mounted on the same kind of principles in such apparently different cases as seeking out and identifying witches and, on the
other hand, submitting an individual to a battery of psychiatric tests. To
be sure, Lofland's particular interest is in the identification of *deviants*,
but that does not obviate the insightfulness and wider applicability of the
theme: [14]

> When a human's features 'map onto' — show a correspondence to — an
> operative pivotal category and its correlative features, the human so
> successfully assessed may be said to have been *socially identified*. That
> is, social identification has occurred in the sense that those making the
> assignment have at least tentatively concluded that this instant human is
> *an instance* of the more abstract model. Such placement is likely,
> however, to be more than a judgment that the instant body is similar to
> or practically equivalent to a model. As noted, it is likely to be a
> judgment that Actor *is* the pivotal category to which he has been
> assigned (Lofland 1969:128).

This, as we have said, is addressed particularly to the problem of
identifying deviants — the problem of identifying in broad anthropological
perspective evil and threat to the predictability of the social order. One
may in full recognition of the special circumstances of Lofland's analysis
propose that the perception of inconsistency in itself constrains the
identifiers to conduct a search for an underlying pivotal category which
will remove the object identified to the margins of society. Individuals
manifesting seemingly inconsistent social profiles are by phenomenal
definition 'unusual' and it is precisely the difficulty of locating them in
terms of readily available categories which leads to their being labelled
dangerous. The tendency for students of the phenomenon of witchcraft to
conclude that the diagnosis of witches occurs in situations of social uncertainty and unpredictability (in non-institutionalized social vacua)
supports this view — as do the examples of indigenes of primal societies
sometimes regarding those attempting to *establish authority* over them as
witches. The latter point seems to suggest that it is difficult to establish
authority over those who have no self-identificatory 'tools' — unless, of
course, the putative authorities supply those tools.

To summarize: folk analytic spaces for social identifications are the core of
the structuring and destructuring processes in society. Social structure is
not identical with these analytic spaces, but rather emerges as an

interactive and reflexive phenomenon from identifications and differentiations made in terms of them. The complexity of this matter resides in the fact that the understanding of any social measurement requires a reconstruction of the analytic space in terms of which it is performed, and of the frame of reference of the observer. In this regard, incidentally, social measurements are in principle not different from physical measurements which, too, are relational in character so that their understanding requires specification of the observer's frame of reference. The sociologist, then, is not different from other social observers except for his *specific* analytical reference frame. [15]

The social measurements discussed here are especially consequential when performed by or for powerful agencies. Measurements and identity assessments have consequences for the life chances of individuals in groups, that is for the allocation of situations to them or their 'ecological' placement. They thus become constraints with which actors must come to terms. The construction of social boundaries may be the critical expression of contests concerning constraints resulting from such social assessments. It is often in relation to such contested boundaries that categories of persons become constrained into reflexivity, that is they may become transformed into collective actors, through social organization and through the articulation of a collective identity. It is in this domain that one important interrelation exists between large-scale social-structuring processes and the differentiation of identities. The emphasis on social constraints, which is reminiscent of Durkheim, may easily lead to a misunderstanding that we advocate a static view of social identity. In fact, we are inclined to the opposite, and we see one major source of dynamics in social constitutions and the construction of collective actors. It is to this matter that we now turn.

SOCIAL CONSTITUTIONS: SOLIDARITIES, COLLECTIVE ACTORS
AND THE DIFFERENTIATION OF IDENTITY

Identity, we have pointed out above, is a relational construction and, as such, relative to situations and contexts which have both temporal and spatial dimensions. The broader context we see in social constitutions: those fundamental patterns that are formed as solidarities become organized collectivities for decision and action to varying degrees. These issues lead us into a consideration of the relation between individual and society, for which Parsons' (much criticized) formulation of the introjection theorem may serve as an heuristic point of departure.

Parsons said in *The Social System* (1951:42):

It is only by virtue of internalization of institutionalized values that a genuine motivational integration of behaviour in the social structure takes place, that the 'deeper' layers of motivation become harnessed to the fulfillment of role expectations. It is only when this has taken place to a high degree that it is possible to say that a social system is highly integrated and the interests of the collective and the private interests of its constituent members can be said to approach coincidence.

This integration of a set of common value patterns with the internalized need-dispositions structure of the constituent personalities is the core phenomenon of the dynamics of social systems. That the stability of any social system except the most evanescent interaction process is dependent on a degree of such integration may be said to be the fundamental dynamic theorem of sociology. It is the major point of reference for all analysis which may claim to be a dynamic analysis of social process.

This sharp formulation (which undoubtedly fails to capture important nuances of Parsons' more recent work) would lead one to think of identities as aspects or components of personality. However, the conception of social structure which we have sketched leads us to a view of much greater complexity (and fluidity) in the interrelations between individual and society.

The elegant simplicity of the introjection theorem appears to us to point to the limiting case in which there *is* a complete and unreflected fit between solidarities and member personalities; which was, we think, Parsons' actual intention. In addressing the specific issue of ethnic identity in modern societies Parsons (1975) presents a view which is more in line with our own analytical location of identity. In any case, wherever collective actors draw on mobilizations across several such relatively independent solidarities, mediating models of identity become necessary. In exploring this we now turn to a brief consideration of the construction of collective actors. We do this, it must be emphasized, in full recognition of the fact that Parsons' emphasis upon introjection and internalization is predicated on the type-case of the *society* as a social system. He acknowledges in his work that conformative membership in special-purpose organizations involves only *differentiated* forms of internalization of 'common value patterns'. The delineation is well exampled by his distinction between *diffuse* membership in a religious *sect* in comparison with *religious-role*, differentiated involvement in a *denomination*. [16]

When solidarities become organized for collective decision and action they can be said to be transformed from categories of persons to collective actors through organization and through articulations of identity. The central process in this respect is the assembling and maintenance of authority, which connects individual and collective identities, and the determination of the form(s) in which commitments from constituent members can be mobilized and brought to bear on behalf of the collectivity. Many such processes are highly contested, since the most fundamental determination of such a collective actor involves legitimation of its boundary, sometimes in terms of territorality, but certainly in terms of psychic, social and cultural domains over which allegiance is claimed. There is also a constraint to determine the placement of the collective actor in relation to its significant others, with respect to the most salient domain of values (Nettl and Robertson 1968:63–186). This, too, is frequently a contested process. The inequality and the distribution of values within and among collective actors makes coming to terms with stratified systems an inescapable aspect of identity formation. Boundary construction is not merely a process of the differentiation among social categories, but also a process of determination of durations of the actor in time, and of the terms of allegiance and mobilization of resources.

Reflexivity in social measurements then can be said to occur in relation to boundary setting and organizing activities of a collectivity. The single most important constraint faced by leaders and constituents of a collective actor in their mode of 'agents' (i.e., as 'acting on behalf of the collectivity') is to create and sustain the belief in the collective actor's existence. The paramount constraint on the feasibility of the reality construct of a collective actor is, thus, to demonstrate its identity, as a real object and as an acting subject. This in turn requires the adoption or construction of models of rationality and problem solving, and their linkage to the legitimacy base of the authority structure. Ultimately it is in this context that the symbolic articulation of collective identity becomes most significant. Symbolic articulations of past, present, and future, their relations to models of decision making, and their relation to patterns of mobilization can be seen as the central structure yielding interpretations of a collective fate and of desirable actions. It is in this sense that a symbolization of collective identity becomes an orientational pattern for the collectivity and its response to new situations. In this connection we must also point to the problem of the degree to which *other* collectivities are attributed with actorness and also the problem in certain cases of convincing other collectivities that the 'ego collectivity' has collective-actor capacities. Sometimes the latter is very difficult to accomplish — as in the case of political democracies dealing with authoritarian regimes. On the other hand, it is often in the interests of a collective actor to deny its actorness to other such actors — as a strategic bargaining point (Schelling 1963; Robertson 1968, 1976). Such complexities are focused sharply in the case of 'organized crime'. Criminal organizations have, ideal-typically, at one and the same time to convince members of their actorness, but many non-members of their lack of actorness — a situation which has posed intriguing problems of legal definitions of individual in relation to collective identity (Cressey 1972). [17]

We can draw upon the work of the classic sociologists to show how deeply embedded, historically and analytically, is the problem of collective actor formation in sociological theorizing. When Max Weber described the development of institutional patterns and conceptions of citizenship in occidental cities he highlighted a process, highly contested, through which a domain of social organization was established that was exempted from the rule of feudalism and dynastic legitimism surrounding it. The formal creation of *coniurationes* established a social boundary, and the terms of mobilization within the collectivity. The development of autonomy in the city had implications for military preparedness, taxation, and the maintenance of economic security. Construction of legal forms of the city as a collective actor required the specification of legal forms for its constituents, the citizens. In this context a legally formulated — authoritatively anchored and sanctioned — model of identity crystallized around the conception of citizenship (Weber 1968:1212–72).

A similar process of construction of collective and individual identities is more abstractly prescribed in Marx's theory of class consciousness (Lenin providing a more concrete image in his vanguard-of-the-proletariat policy). A class is transformed from a category of persons sharing similar positions through the recognition of common grievances and interests, and the establishment of communication and organizational patterns that sustain the capacity to make decisions, and to engage in a collective struggle as a politico-economic force. The transformation from a class *in* itself to a class *for* itself is the construction of a collective actor, which is described as a simultaneous transformation of individual allegiances and a transformation of collective consciousness. In spite of the many differences between Weber and Marx, and the empirical differences in their analyses, there are common emphases on the establishment of social boundaries, organizing capacities and rationales, and the emergence of a collective identity in concert with the collection of models for individual identity. [18]

Processes of collective and individual identity formation occur in contested arenas, but yet in the context of encompassing socio-cultural entities — that is in the context of civilizations and their encounters. Civilizational complexes include rationales for authority and decision that themselves derive from culture creation in strategically significant historic experience. There is, then, at any point in time, a finite supply of rationales and models both for collective and individual identity formation, which differ critically from culture to culture, and from one civilization to another. (At the same time, some aspects of the social dynamics in the construction of collective and individual identities are clearly trans-civilizational in nature.) That is not to say that each civilization provides a set of rationales and models which are available only to individuals, groups and societies operating historically within the confines of a simple set of civilizational parameters, nor that models adhered to are always already well-established in a cultural sense. On the latter point we have only to point to the shape which religious collective actors took from the seventeenth century onward in the Western world. Protestant collectivities drew in large part on available civilizational models in constructing collective actorness, and yet in some places the *contingent necessity to co-exist* in the context of a *number* of Protestant churches, denominations and sects, and with the Catholic church, led to an accentuation of the principle of voluntary individual membership and to redefinitions of the spheres of legitimate operations of collective actors. The ramifications of such changes were noted by Troeltsch in discussion of the Reformation and were clearly spelled out by Weber in his discussion of American religious collectivities. [19]

Weber (1948) argued that in early twentieth century America, membership of Protestant sects functioned as modes of trust and authenticity. Since it was widely believed that nearly all such sects maintained the membership only of individuals who had demonstrated their moral trustworthiness, proof of sect membership was used as a kind of 'credit-card', a demonstration of authenticity in public transactions. That, Weber argued, had an important function in the development of modern modes of economic intercourse. Weber was thus concerned with the generation and the generalization of an identity code: individuals were identified in terms of collectivities which had, so to speak, authenticated their identities. But, in a manner which converges with Durkheim, Weber also recognized that such was made possible largely by the coincidence of individual identity and collective-sectarian identity (Torrance 1974). In the immediate context we must point out that that form of identity code both had very significant civilizational origins and yet at the same time was in part a matter of structural contingency (namely the *modus vivendi* which had been established among the Protestant collectivities and which itself was accomplished with reference to much older ideas concerning freedom of conscience and the relationship between 'Church and State').

The development of national states, nationalism and of national ideologies provides particularly important sites for the analysis of the formation of collective actors and the relationship between individual and collective identities. [20] But in a sense the problem of the relationship between the individual and the state is peculiarly modern. For as Binder (1964:13) has put it:

> In medieval times, whether in Europe or in the Islamic East, the individual was properly a religious and not a political category of concern.

Subjective identity, too, was not political identity as nationalism holds that it must be. The unity of individual and communal political spheres was a characteristic of only the most perfect theocratic societies, the ancient Hebrew, the early Islamic, and perhaps the Greek city-state. The social and economic changes which led the rising bourgeoisie to demand the reaffirmation of the independent sphere of the individual also undermined the exclusive social basis of the state.

The remarkable change of modern times is that 'the state should represent the interests of anyone but itself'. Thus, when it comes to be acknowledged that the state apparatus does not 'belong' to a definite group, the issue which presents itself most saliently is that of the appropriate relationship between the individual and the collectivity.

The phenomenon of individual identity is clearly, then, a critical matter in our coming to terms with the development of national actors. That this is recognized in respect of the underprivileged societies of Africa and Asia is evinced by the vast amounts which have been written on the subject of political mobilization; while a rapidly growing recent literature is concerned with the issues of nation-building, citizenship inclusion and the origins and functions of the State in the older national societies.[21] In this connection we find it relatively easy to accept the idea that newly independent societies search for and adopt national identities from available ideological and structural models, or 'civilizational parameters'; and yet the idea that European states in the post-medieval period of what Wallerstein (1974) calls 'statism' adopted or rejected religions on a roughly similar basis is not so easily accepted. That a particular variety of Protestantism or Catholicism was adopted *merely* as a form of national identification—which Wallerstein comes very close to saying—is unconvincing, as the proposition denies *any* intimate functional link between internal social-structure and religious-cultural content (See Swanson 1967). The idea that those holding positions of political authority or seeking to legitimate power have frequently held the belief that the specific nature of the religious identities of the populace is of great political significance is well exampled by the vacillatory religious-political policies of English monarchs in the Reformation and post-Reformation period and of Cromwell in the English Interregnum. On the other hand, we should draw attention to the different conceptions of central political authority held among the main Protestant groups in the sixteenth and seventeenth centuries in terms of their connections with conceptions of religious identity.

Of course, it is rather conventional to argue that the long-term significance of the Reformation—some even arguing for the *universality* of 'The Reformation'—was to effect a differentiation of identity spheres to such an extent that democratic, citizenly modes of governance and participation became possible. And yet, as our quotations from Binder suggest, that has not settled the issue of identity in relation to authority and the maintenance of national collective actors. For, as students of the history of citizenship in the West have shown us, the old problem of identity spheres and the scope of identity in relation to central political authority have returned (Robertson 1977). In particular the growth of social welfarism has placed the old problems back on the agenda, in a new form. For the inclusion of a welfare component in Western conceptions of citizenship has inexorably led to the enlarging of the basis both of authority and identity and connecting them in complex forms. On a *functional* definition of religion it would not be at all far-fetched to suggest that national political centres have begun to focus on the 'religious welfare' of their constituents. The thrust of concern with the 'quality of life' is a good indicator. This we emphasize is a discernible trend in the Western democracies — quite apart from its facticity in the more embracive political systems in the Communist sector of the globe. [22]

This discussion of solidarities and the construction of collective actors makes it necessary to focus on basic 'constitutions' of societies. It is against this dynamic context that we take up the phenomenon of individual identity. This procedure avoids the pitfall of beginning the analysis with society as a given, but rather emphasizes the dynamics of collective and individual identity formation in a dialectic interplay.

We can now return to the point made earlier that relations with authority are an important dimension of personal identity formation. Each model of individual identity can be characterized by its relation to the salient conception of a collective identity and authority, be this relation positive or negative. Personal identity models thus are related to the drawing of social boundaries, but the individual model of identity will vary with regard to the degree to which it represents the collectivity in the agency mode. Further, since the model of identity involves qualitative symbolic articulation of what a person or an actor is and does, it must be articulated in terms of some standards of rationality (or, better, rationale provision) — which in turn will have some definable relation to the standards of rationality implicit in the salient authority structure. As identity models may arise from the demand for reducing the complexity inherent in a multiplicity of actors facing the identifying demands they must satisfy, they can also be imposed by authority with powerful enforcement.

These considerations relate the differentiation of individual identities and models for them to the force-fields of collective actors. Strategically important constraints of collective actors will often be translated into legal or quasi-legal requirements for individual conduct and identification. The nature and especially the mode of enactment of these identity models will vary, however, depending on the mode of collective mobilization. Collective actors which require total loyalty and complete definition of the modal individual in terms of his being always a diffuse *agent-for* the collectivity are not found with great frequency.[23] It is only this limiting case in which the introjection theorem formulated by Parsons would hold sway without modification. Larger collectivities face constraints for potential mobilization which may either take the form of contractual consideration among constituents or, on the other extreme, highly centralized imposition of uniformities. In the former case, pluralistic markets of identity models will prevail; in the latter case, publicly enforced identity models may create a uniformity of expectation and mobilizations in a public domain, while being compatible with differentiation of solidarities and widely divergent personality types.

The work of classifying and analysing collective actors with regard to the strategic constraints under which they are constructed, and their mode of mobilization, with regard to the formation of collective and individual identities remains to be done and we can only sketch it at this point.

AN INTERMEDIATE SUMMARY

To give brief review of our line of argument to this point: we began by considering the logic and phenomenology of identity, which led us to the recognition of the importance of measurements and assessments for identity, and the requirement of assessed authenticity. Proceeding from this most general framework to its sociological specification, we analysed social structure as a reflexive process of structuring and destructuring, emphasizing identifying performances, assessing agencies, and the analytic spaces into which actors are located, and the process of transvaluations. Instead of accepting these social grids for the assessment of identities as given structures, we turned to the exploration of some of the dynamics of collective-actor formation in the context of social boundaries and solidarities. The analysis of collective actors links this level of theory with the understanding of individual identity formation. However, the added emphasis on culturally articulated models of collective and personal identity brings into play rationales of a civilizational nature. This construction of identities we see as a contentious, often explicitly political process, with a tendency towards crystallization into legal forms. Indeed, a comprehensive sociological analysis of collective and individual identity would require us to draw upon the resources of moral philosophy and jurisprudence. In any case, the arguments we have produced so far show that a sociological theory of identity may well be possible from a systematic analysis of social constitutions, emphasizing the dynamics of collective actor construction; but it will have to come to terms eventually with a specific, historically differential sociological understanding of moral conceptions of virtue, ideas of freedom, loyalty, responsibility and trust.

INDIVIDUAL IDENTITY, MEANING, AND MODELS OF IDENTITY

Again we must turn to the problem of reflexivity because identity has both a self-reflexive and an interactional aspect. It must also be viewed from the perspective of the experiencing actor, who often faces the problem of integrating meanings, or a multiplicity of such across the several aspects of his identifying performances and their assessed results. The individual actor identifies himself in relation to others, resulting in assessments of quality. He or she also may identify others to others in the role of arbiter, engage in identifying others in relation to others for the purpose of constructing an intelligible map of his or her own location; identifies himself or herself in relation to others as in the forming of a stance toward the 'generalized other'; identifies the boundaries of collectivities; and identifies himself or herself as a member in relation to collectivities.

These multiple aspects of identity as achievement (our list not being exhaustive) each result in a possibly somewhat different determination of the actor as object and subject. The problem of meaningful integration thus does transcend the problem we encountered earlier when we discussed the actor's identity construction in the context of reconciling different assessments, as in the case of differential status allocations. The individual's problem of meaningful integration may well be a major source of deviance and innovation in identity construction in relation to the process as already discussed, as well as a major constraint on the possibilities for collective mobilization and identity formation through leadership. 'Authorities' must come to terms with the integration-of-meaning problem in some fashion.

One important possibility is that the problem of meaning can be resolved by resort to a transcendental idea as contrasted to more socially proximate actualities. The former tack would involve a self-consciously reflexive form of individual identity-formation, leading frequently to anchorage in ultimate values of a religious or political-ideological nature. Transcendent models of identity, anchored in ultimate values, may well be the results of identity innovations; but they also may become more standardized identity models for large scale mobilizations which, precisely because of their emphasis on ultimate values, permit considerable slippage and variation with regard to more proximate domains.

Identity formation strictly in terms of transcendent values is very rare, but where it occurs it may be of considerable import. That is a point stressed most strongly in the recent past by Wilson (1973) in his data-packed refutation of Wallace's theory of revitalization movements. Emphasizing the significance and recurrence of manipulationist and thaumaturgical responses to situational stress—responses which do *not* seek to institute new cultural models—Wilson argues that in the religious sphere only conversionist movements of the Wesleyan type approximate Wallace's idea of the allegedly ubiquitous reconstruction of individual and collective 'mazeways'. But even revivalist orientations do not seek deliberately to provide a new and more satisfying cultural source of identity formation, but rather to change the 'heart and mind of men who have claimed salvation by faith' (Wilson 1973:488). None of this denies that new cultural models of identity emerge *in the wake of* large-scale religious or ideological change.

Situations which can be defined very broadly as anomic ones of excessive uncertainty may be such that they lead to the destruction of existing identities and the search for substitutes. It is the stressful and contested nature of such situations that may account for the turn to 'ultimacy'. It is in this context that we should remind ourselves of the significance of charismatic innovations in identity models for which Weber's analyses have provided excellent examples. The charismatic figure can be seen as a virtuoso of identity construction, innovating models of identity in linkage with ultimate values. Weber's discussion remains, unfortunately, sketchy. Identity innovations of the charismatic nature may be either revitalizations or innovations of social commitment, or they may have a primary anchorage in existing cultural standards. This observation implies that there are varieties of impact and varieties of 'identity audience' for charisma. Virtuosos of identity become landmark figures not only for movement-formation, but also in providing models for atomized individual identity-alternatives. [24]

Models of identity can be viewed as cultural objects which have certain probable relations to the range of likely modes of experiencing on the parts of individuals. An important attribute of the personal identity model concerns the manner in which an individual may 'grow into it' or a conception of the process by which such an identity is acquired and fulfilled. This links the models of identity to the domain of personal experience. It has implications both for the modes of becoming socialized to the point of being able to enact the identity model and for the manner in which authenticity demands are both subjectively experienced and socially asssessed.

When we speak of personal experience, we mean in this connection the structure of potent aspirations and sanctions, which of course is socio-cultural in its origin. It can be said of every model for individual identity that it emphasizes certain rather definite virtues and separates them from particularly severe vices. Such a conception of virtue within the model of personal identity is an important link to the experience-structure of the individual himself. Where the conception of virtue is of the 'honour' variety, it is primarily related to collective loyalty and solidarity; its negative side is shame. Where the conception of virtue is in the neighbourhood of saintliness, its negative side would be sin or guilt; and where virtue is expressed in some claim to personal dignity, it is distinct from honour and its negative side may be expressed as resentment.[25] However these matters are sorted out, the conception of virtue in a model of identity relates to the quality of the cultural or social backing the identity enacted in its terms can receive, and it determines the mode in which authenticity is experienced by the individual as well as proved to others. Certainly, the code of honour of an officers' corps requires demonstrations of authenticity drastically different from the conceptions of romantic fulfilment of the authentic person in a youth movement.

Models of identity then can be seen as comprehensive prescriptions for conduct, but also as prescribing strategies of socialization and tests of authenticity. Adopting one of these models of identity thus does not by any means necessarily require a change of personality. It does require the successful managing of socialization, social-control and authenticity requirements, as components of the code of conduct demanded by the model. This may indeed be far short of the demands for total integration of the model's requirements with the personality structure. Often the acquisition of a new model of identity by an individual requires that there be a 'neutral space' within which ordinary sanctioning capacities are suspended and alternative ones are substituted. The neutral space itself can then work as a quasi-moratorium from normal constraints and restraints.

IDENTITY ACCEPTANCE AND ALIENATION AS STRATEGIES FOR AUTHENTICITY

We have seen the importance of models of identity in the context of collective mobilization and the construction of collective actors. We have further considered the differentiation of individual models of identity in relation to authority and their establishment as cultural objects. This has introduced considerable complexity into our understanding of the relation between individual and society. However, we must also argue that instead of innovating new models of identity, individuals or groups may pursue a quest for authenticity in relation to the present model of identity by adopting varying stances towards it. Unreflected acceptance of the model is embedded unproblematically in solidarities, or tightly-structured contexts and thus exists in the domain of the taken-for-granted. It may be, at the other extreme, in the domain of the highly reflexive total identity commitment as in the case of high drama. Here, reflexive authenticity draws on the merging between individual meanings and the identity model in the dramatic episode or performance. The relationship between this point and charismatic mobilization is apparent.

However, the enactment of an identity model in the alienated mode, creating multiple, non-synchronized identities in co-existence with each other, is a possibility as well. The strategy for authenticity here rests in the withdrawal from the identity model without, necessarily, leading to the innovation of a new identity. Acceptance of and alienation from identity models are, of course, processes that differ from the establishment of social identities through external constraints. These particular dynamics which so much complicate the picture only come into view when sociological analysis is enriched by the consideration of constraints on the individual following on from the integration-of-meaning-problem, as well as from the authenticity demands. It may well then be the case that modes of leadership can be distinguished not only in terms of the construction of collective and individual identity, but also in terms of the manner in which leadership relates to individual strategies for authentication. Such analysis of leadership and movements would be of very considerable complexity, as styles of authentication may not relate in a direct or simple manner to 'issues' or to explicit symbolic articulations of identity models themselves, but rather the stances towards them.

IDENTITY AND AUTHORITY: A CO-ORDINATION

As we announced at the outset, our discussion has focused more upon identity and processes of identification than upon authority and authorization. However, what we have stated thus far has implications for the relationship between identity and authority, most generally in our claim that conceptions of identity imply, in principle, congruent types of authority, and *vice versa* (Cf. Etzioni 1961). Some forms of identity construction are, in any case, developed on a singularly authoritative basis. That is clearly so in the construction of many forms of deviant identities — since the latter tend to have been developed by official agencies commanding authority in the making of laws and classifications of what is societally acceptable and what is not. But in a more general sense, notably in the case of categories of social stratification, identities are also constructed on an authoritative basis. In many circumstances components of systems of social stratification are fabricated by self-conscious decision —

that is they are officially authored and authorized. In many cases these have originated as a kind of book-keeping device, in order to monitor changes in occupational structures, income trends and the like. But the solidification of these category sets through bureaucratic routinization and publicization produces what amounts to an official system of stratification. (In modern times such tendencies have in effect been crystallized into official, authoritative attempts to implement one or another version of the functional theory of social stratification.)

None of this is to say that position in the occupational-income system of stratification is what constitutes in its entirety a total identity-model reservoir; but it is certainly a significant part of it, particularly in societies where social *class* is a pivotal feature of the culture of stratification. In any case, other aspects of identity are given the stamp of specifically political authority — most notably ethnic and racial categorizations. In societies undergoing rapid change in the wake of revolutions or decolonization comprehensive changes are often made in the reservoir of social identifications. Berger (1973:153), for example, draws attention to the identity ramifications of Chinese Communist reclassification of peasants: 'Not only is the world redefined, with others reclassified, but the individual literally no longer knows who he is.' Cases of detribalization and the attempt generally to destroy the primordial bases of identification in post-primal societies supply more examples.

Such examples, however, do not yet probe the relationship between identity and authority with sufficient analytic clarity. What is needed is a determinate array of variables which define codes for the production of identity models and conversely, for models of authority. We search for these in the domain of fundamental social constitutions, those basic patterns of relations that are structured around the problems of collective and individual commitment and decision, and that determine the terms under which commitments can be mobilized.

It is necessary to remind ourselves that such structures exist at varying levels of latency or articulate manifestation, ranging from the deep structure of constitutional styles to the overt formalism of a particular state constitution or other authority structure. Civilizational styles as codes for the production of identity models, such as the Chinese or 'Western', give rise to a great deal of further diversity and differentiation.

Is it not possible that there is a finite set of possibilities for such code formation at *all* these levels? The exigencies that have historically set civilizational codes were, by and large, those that arose in answer to great crises of power and meaning, being cast into key patterns of empire or state and religion. Such crucial events — for example, the setting of the terms of authority and belief for the Chinese empire, or the expansionist diversity of Europe — become relatively lasting constraints through institutional patterns, symbol availability and its opposite, symbol scarcity, limiting the creation of identity models in a certain direction. At the same time, they can be said to be resources for the solution of more specific identity-authority problems.

Great religious upheavals or revolutions may modify such patterns — as did the European Reformation. Yet, the constraints resulting from the underlying civilizational codes remain discernible. Witness the Russian fate of the Communist Revolution in the Soviet Union, versus the different Chinese pattern.

We seek, then, a set of basic variations of orientation that could be used to classify types of such constitutional codes for the production of identity models at all levels; our typology being applicable at both the civilizational level and at the differentiated levels within civilizational complexes, and descriptive of the basically available alternatives.

We emphasize further a certain important complexity in the conceptions of a *code*. A specific cultural model of identity, such as the conception of a late-medieval patrician burgher, can be said to be a code of conduct, in that it permits the generation of models and maxims of action, fitting a great diversity of situations and their identification demands. We are here speaking at a still higher level of abstraction (*and* in reference to an even *deeper* empirical level) namely of codes for the production of such identity models. These define the possible ranges of identity-authority relations and they pattern, with some stability, directions of change in the emergence of specific identity models.

Thus, our usage of the idea of 'codes' derives from our conception of basic social constitutions as setting terms for structuring and destructuring processes, accounting also for the possibility of very rapid social change.[26] For example, the recent redefinition of women's roles in America proceeded with surprising rapidity; it does not, however, signal a total alteration of the underlying identity code. Yet in their specificity such models of identity may, indeed, be novel.

In the search for the most strategically significant variables we note that at the heart of any discussion of identity in relation to authority there must lie a concern with different structures of orientation regulating the relationship between the constituent units of a collectivity and the collectivity itself. As Swanson has remarked on a number of occasions, there has been a long-standing tendency for 'Anglo-American' sociologists and analysts working within the Anglo-American orbit to see collectivities, in particular societies, as *associations*. 'An association is a relationship among its participants, each being tied to the other because dependent upon them for the satisfaction of his own needs' (Swanson 1968:31). This is an image of 'interdependencies and mutual influences', involving the idea that organizations, including societies, are 'social and patterned and bounded', but that they are also 'headless' (Swanson 1968:97). The effort, however, to maintain the collectivity involves energy, time, special procedures and proliferation of new roles and structures. In all organizations all participants, not merely those who are assigned the special task, must on occasion 'speak in the interests' of the latter and 'not simply in their own personal interests. In the degree to which people act as agents of the organization itself, the organization becomes a social system' (Swanson 1967:32). In a very general sense of the term Swanson identifies the social system with the political processes of a society or organization. 'To the extent a society has such a process it is a collective actor and can become a participant in primary relations' (Swanson 1968:100). Swanson summarizes his main theme by insisting that we must view society 'not *only* as a social system but as *also* a social system' (Swanson 1968:124).

From this basic distinction between associational and 'social-system' properties of organizations and societies Swanson develops the idea that whereas associations emphasize *social control*, 'social systems' emphasize *socialization* with respect to the problems of maintaining allegiance of participants. Societies emphasizing association have to assume that the participants have interests which are not perfectly transformable into the interests of the society as a whole; while in societies emphasizing social-systemness the view is taken that in principle all participants can come to internalize the normative guidelines of the society.

Extending his dichotomous reasoning even further Swanson proceeds to suggest that the two types—associational/social control and social-system/socialization—are associated with particular forms of political regime. The major type corresponding to the associational/social control emphasis is the *heterarchic* regime, which provides for legitimate participation only on the basis of a member's 'status in organizations that are not themselves agencies or creatures of the regime' (Swanson 1968:108). Corresponding to the social-system/socialization emphasis is the *commensual* regime which allows for legitimate participation only as members at large. These are the two most clear-cut forms of regime corresponding to the two images of collectivities which Swanson has used extensively in published empirical analyses. Two further types of regime, however, manifest respectively social-systemic and associational emphases: the *centralist* which stresses the former, and the *balanced* which stresses the. latter. Thus in addition to the variable which we will here label 'mode of authorization' there seems to be a need for another variable which will allow us to delineate clearly four types of regime. In fact since our purposes are much broader in scope than the typification of *regime types* we will form here on speak of types of *relationship between the individual and the collectivity* as our overall concern. Swanson's types of regime do not stipulate whether some members of a society or organization will or will not be objectively included in central decision-making. In other words, each of Swanson's regime types could be more or less democratic, more or less authoritarian in the conventional senses of those terms—even though one would surely think that, for example, centralist regimes would *tend* to be authoritarian. Thus any additional variable which is introduced in order to facilitate delineation of at least four types of relationship between the individual and the collectivity ought, we think, to relate quite closely to *social stratification*. We will label the additional variable 'mode of identification' and speak of two polar tendencies—namely, *vertical* modes of identification and *lateral* modes of identification.

Thus in terms inspired by Swanson's attempt to erect empirical types of organization and society we arrive at the following:

Mode of Collective Authorization	Mode of Unit Identification	Regime Type
Social-systemic	Lateral	Commensual
Social-systemic	Vertical	Centralist
Associational	Lateral	Heterarchic
Associational	Vertical	Balanced

Before abandoning any *specific* concern with types of regime we should point out that for Swanson a balanced regime is one in which some groups share power with government as representatives of independent powers in the collectivity; while centralist regimes involve a governor or small group acting on behalf of the collectivity.

Our purpose here is to address—*via* the basic ideas of the above typology—general issues of the relationship between units (in particular social individuals) and the wider collectivity of which they are, *as a matter of variation*, parts. Our two cross-cutting variables are most appropriately seen, as we indicated at the beginning of this phase of our discussion, as constituting a codal matrix. Specifically, that matrix consists in a *social-epistemological variable* and a *social-ontological variable*. When we speak of *modes of identification* we are referring to *the ways in which social objects are known and recognized*. When we speak of *modes of authorization* we are indicating codes *which govern conceptions of reality*. Briefly, identification has to do with epistemological issues because it deals with ways of knowing, whereas conceptions of collective authorization address the problem of what is most real in the collectivity (the collectivity itself or the units within it, and indeed the reality of sub-units).

These matters have an intimate connection with a major metatheoretical problem of sociology. The two variables which we employ here as features of phenomenal, folk reality have their 'correspondents' in the realm of a philosophy-of-science debate concerning analytic procedure. Generally that debate has been described in terms of a dispute between methodological individualists and methodological collectivists (O'Neill 1973). However, it has for quite a long time been recognized that there are at least three aspects to that debate: epistemological, ontological and methodological. We have cast our typology in terms of the first two, implying that the social-methodological aspect is a property of the relationship between those two (the epistemological and the ontological). These remarks are appropriate in the present context for two reasons. First, much of this paper is in the form of identification-as-folk-analysis-and-measurement. It is thus appropriate to point to general implications of that thrust. Second, we are convinced of the need to remain conscious — indeed *self*-conscious — of the close connection between analytic and phenomenal realities, not least because so much social-science has pitched its forms of analysis *against* 'its' out-there-reality. Until the subtleties of the analytic/phenomenal relationship are seen more thoroughly social science will be retarded. Many debates of an analytic nature ought on that view to be discussions of variations in *socio-cultural reality* (Robertson 1974).

This cannot be the place for full exploration of the implications of our typology and empirical enrichment. We will here elaborate only major theoretical points. While we would expect that the typology could be used fruitfully to characterize societies or indeed civilizations we will press the point only that the typology has to do with four codes for connecting individual and collectivity levels through the generation of identity models, which necessarily involve connections between individual identities and collective identities. The latter is the problem matrix from whence springs what is conventionally known as the issue of legitimate authority.

With respect to our two parametric variables we must emphasize in particular that the identification variable involves variation in the degree to which the force of constraint upon identifying — that is, assessing performances and attributes — is in terms both of hierarchy and of comparisons among peers and peer positions. It does *not* refer to the objective features of stratification; that is, whether a society or smaller collectivity is rigidly stratified or not in an objectivist sense. In civilizational perspective we can illustrate the difference by pointing to the accepted naturalness of hierarchy in the Indian case and the tendency in the Western world, notably during the last five hundred years or so, to think of hierarchy as *not* God-given or natural. The reference points are relative, however, in that we would want to apply the code differentially to clusters of societies or even to variations among clusters of collectivities within societies.

In view of our broad, general purposes, we will substitute the term 'holistic' for Swanson's more specific notion of social system emphasis.

Thus we obtain the following typology:

Types of Collectivism and Individualism

		Holistic Emphasis		Associational Emphasis
Vertical *Identification*	A.	Collectivism: *Imposition* Individualism: *Conformity*	C.	Collectivism: *Rank-ordering* Individualism: *Knowing one's* *place*
Lateral *Identification*	B.	Collectivism: *Composition* Individualism: *Manifestation* *of mode*	D.	Collectivism: *Aggregation* Individualism: *Demonstration* *of multiple affiliations*

Our intention in this typological display is to show how different com-
binations of conceptions of collectivities and of identification of individuals
yield differences in the ways in which collective-actor identities are
established and individual identities (both of alters and egos) are formed
and assessed. In this perspective, decisive differences exist between 'individualism' as well as 'collectivisms'. They result from the modality of
articulation between collective and individual identities, and thus
illustrate our claim that identity and authority stand in a relationship of
mutual dependency.

Type A codes involve holistic authorization from above in the name of
the system; and identification on the basis of reference to attributes of a
hierarchically arranged kind, and performances which serve the overall
state of the system. The sense of collectivism is achieved on an elitist basis,
the sense of individualism on an ingratiation basis. This means that both
individual and collective identities are created on a conform/deviate basis
with respect to overall system properties.

Type B codes involve holistic authorization, but in contrast with A
codes, this type involves groups in composing collectivity authorship from
among units within the system — that is, in 'playing a collective tune' on the
basis of available 'notes'. Identification concerns the spotting of those
attributes and performances which are most likely to, or actually do,
exhibit a modal form with respect to the 'collective tune'. This implies that
both individual and collective identities are constructed on a '*mana*-like'
basis of interactional assessment. There is an emphasis upon emergent
properties of the system and the potentiality of individuals to play a
positive role in the emergence process.

Type C codes involve authorization from above in the name of 'all', but
where there are *degrees* of membership in the category 'all'. Identification
is in this circumstance a matter of where an individual stands in a time-
honoured schema of nuanced categories of membership. On the other
hand, those at the centre and those at the periphery are thought to need

each other in the overall affairs of the collectivity. Thus the associationalism of this kind of code is basically of an hierarchical form (in contrast to the lateral form exhibited in type D codes). Individual and collective identities pivot upon the knowing of place in a hierarchical sense.

Type D codes involve authorization in terms of 'the greatest good of the greatest number', with particular institutional apparati being concerned with the specific purpose of aggregating in that manner and according to that principle. Identification is, as in Type B codes, performed on a 'constitutionalistic' basis — a weighing-up and inter-connecting of attributes and performances, but in the Type D case with a strong emphasis upon the *negotiation* of identities. It is in this type that we find the greatest applicability of the conception of identity negotiation as a *labelling* process.

These are, of course, only typological sketches. As we have already suggested, we see the range of beginning applications of the typology to extend in principle from variations among social individuals in small-group situations to inter-civilizational variations. For example, we might say in a civilizational perspective that Chinese civilization has operated in terms of a Type B code and that, in contrast, Western civilization has manifested Type D characteristics. And yet we might, in different vein, apply the whole typology only to Western civilization, in which case some Western societies would undoubtedly emerge as being of Type B. Naturally, the empirical indicators would have to be more finely grained for the second form of application. That reminder is particularly necessary in the present context because in much of our essay we have tended to wander in a fairly free-floating manner over large tracts of time and socio-cultural space. Our typological presentation is partly intended to correct that tendency — by showing how many of our observations and ratiocinations can be in the longer term co-ordinated into a more determinate theory-sketch. Not that we have here incorporated all of our reflections upon, for example, the construction of social structure in terms of identification and authentication; but we do believe that such *can* be accomplished.

Thus the typological sketches which we have presented should be taken as illustrative of the range of problems-to-be-addressed — they make no claim to analytic closure. However, we *do* feel we have made the point that the focus on identity and authority reveals multiple modalities in the articulation of individual and collective identities. By recognizing the signficance of social-epistemological and social-ontological variables in identity and collective actor construction it becomes possible to analyse the manifold but finite codes in their dynamic effect upon modalities of both authority and identity.

We conclude this problem analysis with the reminder that we felt it necessary to integrate phenomenological, social-structural and cultural-civilizational perspectives. On this basis we constructed a view of identities that emphasized external constraints, symbolic rationales of measurement, and representations. The dynamic forces in identity formation we found in the structuring of collective actors, social constitutions, and in the individual's integration of divergent domains of meanings.

The search for lawfulness in the domain of designs for authority and identity must continue. It will require the careful analysis of the manner in which collective actors are constructed, the codes and rationales operative within them, and the way in which actors 'do' identity. Some reorientation of the sociological enterprise for this end will be necessary—sociology continued *within* the conceptual and politico-cultural frame of the 'society' will not do, just as sociology would fail if it abstracted schemes from particular historical forms and treated them, mistakenly, as universal. A focus on identification as folk analysis and measurement, and a careful scrutiny of socio-epistemological and socio-ontological issues may be the source of useful directions.

2

Logics of Selfhood and Modes of Order: Civilizational Structures for Individual Identities

Vytautas Kavolis

Vytautas Kavolis has come to be widely known as a sociologist of art. The manifold forms of human intuition and creativity are the subject of his theoretical endeavour. He pursues such goals with a style of inquiry almost uniquely his since it requires an enormous range of erudition—historical, philosophical, artistic, sociological—as well as the ability to discover abstract objects, configurations, and symbolic designs, for sharp analysis. His work is speculative, of course, and 'intuitive' in a sense, but it is disciplined intuition and speculation, an exploration from the perspective of civilizational analysis.

In the preceding chapter we attempted to formulate analytic essentials for any discussion of the problems of identity and authority—the mode was necessarily a high level of abstraction. Kavolis, too, proceeds at a high level of abstract argument, scanning the range of man's diverse historical experience in different civilizational patterns (but not in the historical vein). Yet his focus is more specific: the symbolic resources civilizations provide for the comprehension and management of the 'self'. One might speak here of 'civilizational styles', but Kavolis identifies more definite objects: the cultural logics of selfhood, implicit ways of comprehending the meaning of human experience, which become resources, but also limitations for the concrete forms of selfhood and authority. Such cultural logics are symbolic in nature, but broader and less explicitly defined than (for example) the 'codes' Rainer Baum treats in the next essay.

The key to Kavolis' work, and to understanding its relations to the other papers, is the civilization-analytic perspective which defines his frame of reference. It is a mode of analysis which views the largest socio-cultural entities, civilizations, as contexts that encompass the most fundamental symbolic designs for action, indeed, the presuppositions for it. The very largest socio-cultural totalities are thus brought into relation to the very smallest: personal identities and meaningful action. A comparative perspective pervades this work, albeit in a special way: comparison serves the purpose of mapping the total range of alternative patterns, and as a corrective against premature analytic closure on the basis of only one civilizational context.

* The notion of identity, attached to an empirically concrete human being, seems to imply (1) the perception of an overall *coherence* —either 'substantive' or 'methodological' —within the experiences and expressions of an individual; (2) the memory in this individual and, normally, in at least some others of the *continuity* of the 'story' —or 'tale' —of his life; and (3) a conscious, but not wholly conscious, *commitment* to a particular manner of both comprehending and managing one's own self. [1]

The problem which a sociologist attuned to the civilization-analytic perspective (Nelson and Kavolis 1973) sets for himself is not how a particular individual arrives at a pattern of coherence or conscious commitment to a comprehension-management of his own self. Civilization analysis is a method for the systematic clarification of the structures of the presuppositions of action seen as differentiated symbolic designs within the largest socio-cultural totality to which they belong and compared with major alternative totalities of socio-cultural organization. In his approach to individual identities, the civilization analyst is therefore concerned, first of all, with the most general and historically durable symbolic structures from which individual identities acquire their presuppositions. Furthermore, he wants to see these symbolic structures placed, sooner or later, within the totality of the civilization to which they belong —that is, within the context of the largest identifiable organization of symbolic configurations attached to concrete socio-historical settings which over a period of time either sustain or undermine their credibility. And he wants to locate the phenomenon he is analysing within the full (cross-civilizational) range of major alternatives in the patterning of this type of phenomenon.

What are the intellectual structures provided by the symbolic organizations of diverse civilizations for the establishment of patterns of coherence within individual experiences? In what social contexts of plausibility and by what kinds of agents are these civilizational structures shaped and sustained, 'activated' and 'demobilized'?

* I am grateful to George Friedman, Burkart Holzner, Harry D. Krebs, Silvine S. Marbury, Roland Robertson, and Ralph L. Slotten for their reasonably generative criticism.

THE CULTURAL LOGICS OF SELFHOOD

The self has been conceived of in so many different ways and talked about in so many diverse languages (differences of language sometimes disguising similarities of the structure of experience, and vice versa), that it seems analytically essential to have some way of identifying the most fundamental alternatives for the comprehension of selfhood revealed, not in any one tradition of thought, but in the empirical experience of mankind as a whole. It is assumed that a 'universal language' for talking about selfhood would have to begin by being a 'formal' language, specifying the basic forms for comprehending selfhood, independently of the concrete ideological contents of particular systems of 'spiritual guidance' concerning selfhood. An analytical purpose can only be served within some such frame of universal categories by descriptions of the empirical variants in the particular rhetorics in which 'spiritual guidance' on selfhood has actually been dispensed in particular times and places.

In an effort to formulate a list of basic alternatives in orientation toward the self that could be used consistently (as initial approximations) in cross-civilizational comparisons, as well as for discriminating between types of theorizing about the self in a complex modernizing society, the concept of the cultural logics of selfhood is proposed.

A *cultural logic* can be defined as one of the major alternative ways for visualizing the meaning of a distinguishable focus of human experience and of conducting oneself in relation to it (Cf. Nelson 1965).[2] Cultural logics differ from 'codes' and 'rationales' in being, at least in part, necessarily implicit: psychologies of perception before they become, and after they have ceased to be, codes of conduct.

The cultural logics of selfhood are the most basic alternatives for discerning what the 'genuine self' consists of and how it is arrived at. They can be conceived of as explicit or implicit answers to the question: What is the 'true form' of the self against which 'false self-perceptions' can be identified? In what manner does the 'true self' become manifest in the experiences of the empirical individual? The notion of a logic of selfhood implies a goal or condition of 'genuineness' for the empirical individual and a standard by which the 'authenticity' of the actions of this individual can be judged.

In the historical record, at least four major types of logics of selfhood can be clearly distinguished.

(1) In the first type, at least one essential component of the true self is conceived as a *unique pattern of enduring internal coherence*, which the individual has either given to him by some version of 'fate' (as in Greek tragedy or twelfth-century Europe) or develops by his own initiative (as in the Renaissance and in the American notion of the 'self-made man'); and,

in either case, imposes as a meaningful performance on the universe in which he is placed.

This is the peculiarly — though not exclusively — Western conception of the self. Its strongest roots lie perhaps in the military-hero self of the Nordic peoples (Dumézil, 1970). But only the freely-formed band of warriors or the 'feudal' society based on contractually established loyalties, in the absence of control by a centralized state (as in Sparta and the agricultural empires of continental Asia) and of a hereditary tradition of obedience to a lord (as in the Japan of the Samurai ethic), can be expected to support the unique-pattern logic of selfhood. The presence of the warrior does not by itself give rise to confident self-assertions of the individual.[3] The emergence of an individualistically assertive hero from a warrior background probably requires not only a favourable social-structural situation (for example, the breakdown of tribal society and weakening of the kinship system), but also a specific 'sanctifying principle' in the cultural tradition capable of 'empowering' the individual to assert his uniqueness (Cf. Swanson 1973).

The mode of operation of the private-entrepreneurial capitalist system, especially before its extensive bureaucratization toward the end of the nineteenth century, permits individual assertiveness. But a rationalized capitalism is not likely to generate unique-pattern selves (Miller and Swanson 1958): the system either uniforms everything by its standardized rules, or it repels from all coherence. Within the capitalist system — or under socialism — it is mainly the traditions of aristocratic origin (the 'exalted idea of man') or those of mystical religiosity (the 'inner light') that provide the basis of justification for unique-pattern selves. In highly rationalized societies, the unique-pattern logic is also empirically nourished by vagabond-adventurer-pirate-pioneer elements (the 'frontier hypothesis').

The unique-pattern logic of selfhood may imply the absence of any meaningful relationship between the self and any larger universe. The self is *only* a unique pattern of its own coherence (which may incorporate elements of both order and disorder in a unique relationship to each other). More usually in Western traditions, the unique pattern of the self is asserted as a distinguishable moment of a larger universe retaining its irreplaceable value — its own 'character' or its 'soul' (or, in the last resort, 'free will') within (or against) the totality to which it ultimately belongs.[4]

The unique-pattern logic can be applied to relations with others in the mode of either 'control' or of 'receptiveness'. In the first case it tends to isolate individuals from each other. In the second it should facilitate the transformation of interpersonal attractions into enduring mutualities. If an attractive another is unique, one's relationship with him (or her) *must* be treasured, since he (or she) could not be replaced by anyone else; and if this uniqueness is durable, it is *possible* to make a long-term commitment to it, with reasonable confidence that neither 'I' nor the 'other' will evaporate as they approach each other.

This logic appears as an identifiable element in the Promethean myth, in Abelard's trust in his own reason and his own moral sensitivity, in St. Bernard's belief that his soul will retain its distinctiveness even when it comes to face God in Heaven,[5] in the Renaissance image of man as a masterful work of art (Burke 1972: 187–206), in the post-seventeenth century conception of conscience,[6] and in the modern Western idea of the person. Erikson's (1962) notion of 'personal identity' implies the unique pattern logic of selfhood: though it arises in interaction with collective identities, the individual is, nevertheless, a 'master-builder'. But it is by his 'internal pattern', rather than his objective achievements, that he is judged, and he remains as significant in his defeats as in his victories (if they can indeed, in his case, be separated).

This logic of selfhood tends to be upheld by a specific type of cultural interpreter: by organizationally independent — or 'personally inspired' — moralists, interpreters 'in one's own', autonomous, independently powerful voice of an inherited, supremely important and still viable tradition (for example, the tragic playwrights of classical Greece).

(2) The true self can be conceived of as *coincidence of the subjectively sensed core of experience of the empirically concrete individual with the essential structure, or fundamental quality, of the universe to which the concrete individual is oriented*. True selfhood of this type is manifested in the 'It is not I who exist, but God in me' experience, though with a wide range of possible substitutes for God in it. A self that is neither identified nor closely correlated with the 'supreme reality' is in a state of 'alienation' from the ground of its being (or, in the case of Buddhism, from the universal condition of nonbeing). A profound mutuality with another self is possible only when it is mediated through joint understanding of and devotion to the 'universal', as in medieval *Seelenfreundschaft*.

This type of logic, which may have originated in shamanism, governs the dominant Indian, Chinese, Stoic, 'mystical', and 'monastic' comprehensions of the self.[7] Pietist-Romantic notions relating the self to the 'inner fatherland' (Bruford 1975:85–6), and Jung's archetypal psychology, also belong here.

A major difference among coincidence logics of selfhood hinges on whether the universe with which the core of an individual's experience is to be aligned is conceived as a transcendent 'nothingness' detached from empirical reality, as in Buddhism; or as the 'mind of God' either radically separated from 'nature', as in Gnosticism, or as revealing some of itself in 'nature', as in the Judaeo-Christian tradition; or as a 'nature' opposed to 'artificial conventions', as in Taoism (and, in a very different way, in de

Sade); or as 'society' (either one's own concrete society, as in Durkheim's 'collective consciousness' and notions of 'ethnic identities', or as 'society in its historical development', as in Marxism); or, in the most comprehensive of all possible ways, as 'the accumulated experience of mankind', as in some contemporary versions of liberal education.

In Buddhism it is the awareness of the illusory character of all forms of being—and of linguistic categories—that aligns the individual with the 'generic form' (not distinguishable from 'formlessness') appropriate for him. The self is an illusion moving to attain harmony with the truth of non-existence (= absolute freedom) by abolishing itself.

In Taoism (Chuang-Tzu and Lao-Tzu), the individual seeks to experience such coincidence of the internal and external order that the two orders operate in the same manner. It therefore seems to have a logic of selfhood of the coincidence type. Unlike Buddhism, Taoists see nature as real, and it is with (metaphorically intuited) nature that the individual is taught to align himself. But it is a 'spontaneous' nature in which the self attains coincidence with universal order through reversals of 'conventional' structures.

This logic seems most likely to be explicitly formulated by a particular type of 'spiritual guides' or cultural interpreters: by expert spokesmen for a more or less organized, or organizable, community of faith (whether it be religious or secular). The initiators of such logics are the 'tradition founders' (in actuality or in aspiration).

(3) The third type of logic of selfhood conceives of the true self as a submerged luminosity (or a hidden savagery) that gives a hint of its presence only in moments of the most vivid, or purest *peak experiences* which are overwhelmingly complete in each case, but not necessarily consistent with each other over a period of time or with any order external to the individual (Cf. Maslow 1961; Otto 1965). 'Authenticity' is loyalty to these experiences, and to them alone, regardless of consequences. If justification is sought for the search for peak experiences, it is likely to be justified as a quest for unity with some darkly sensed, but still unknown universal structure or quality. But the search for this structure or quality turns out, in living experience, to be indistinguishable from an immersion in some bottomless abyss.

This logic is evident in Rousseau's *Confessions* and has attained perhaps the most extreme modern expression in Arthur Rimbaud's 'immense and calculated *disordering* of *all his senses*'.[8] It seems to have been, more than in other pre-modern civilizations, favoured in Japan (where it was, however, usually contained within the everyday obligations of a 'public personality'). It has erupted primordially in the mythological figure of the Trickster of the American Indians and other hunting peoples.[9] Romantic love traditions, both Western and Japanese, presuppose a cultivated form of peak-experience selfhood—and in general this logic does not exclude, and may even require, profound (but frequently either deadly or impermanent) mutuality. Mutuality, in this logic, signifies fidelity not to the totality of the individual, but to his or her peak experiences only (or, more precisely, to one's own peak experiences involving him or her). Peak experiences in responding to works of art are conceivable even within the Confucian persuasion, which in general avoids such experiences.[10]

The phenomenology of peak-experience selfhood includes a heightening of sensitivities, shifts in consciousness, higher (or perhaps merely novel) moral aspirations, 'exaggerated experimentation' with a diversity of 'cultural and ideological influences' (Lifton 1965:264); possibly a greater equality of the sexes—or a greater cruelty between them (Praz 1951:95–271); a preoccupation with the occult and with 'hidden truths' (and with languages of privileged insight), with the image of 'a reality moved by forces, by energies constantly in motion and in tension with one another' (Tiryakian 1972:499, 502); an increased, yet not necessarily a more humane, concern with suffering and death (and the symbols of redemption or immortality); a sense of distortion, and the absurd, the grotesque; the proliferation of masks and impersonations, the 'want of the faculty to express emotion in a simple and natural way', the 'unbridled exuberance of fancy' constantly endangered by its susceptibility to triviality (Huizinga 1954: 52, 80, 171). Enthusiasm intertwines with depression, enhanced emotional vitality with an internal freezing up (or burning out); the body becomes a prison for the soul, conscience an iron cage for the body.[11]   Strindberg, 'at once hypersensitive and crude, sensual and puritanical, harsh and sentimental, swinging between the poles of scepticism and faith, romanticism and realism, satanism and angelology', is a case in point (Sprigge 1949:226).

Peak-experience logics tend to appeal most strongly to the subjectively 'underprivileged' and 'emotionally deprived' (frequently including women), to people 'on the boundary' between two or more socio-cultural structures or statuses (for example, adolescents, half-assimilated minorities, individuals of ambiguous sexuality, displaced élites) or in times of *consciously experienced* 'civilizational crisis', when the social system and its cultural framework are subjected to rapid and psychologically threatening changes, resulting in a sense of a personally painful limitation or exhaustion, or moral or aesthetic discreditation, of a tradition previously held to be valid.

If one is already in a state of historical discontinuity, peak experiences represent the beginning of any kind of substantial selfhood, which, once sensed as a potent possibility, must either collapse or evolve toward either unique-pattern or coincidence types.[12] Peak experiences cannot be sustained over a length of time, and the inability to derive an evolutionary potential from them is subjectively experienced as a submergence into a 'deadness-in-life'.

To the extent that the peak-experience logic of selfhood can be institutionalized in a relatively stabilized literate society, it tends to be upheld by the 'men (and women) of sensibility' concerned with precisely grasping the extraordinary qualities of their own experience (and their experience of the extraordinary qualities of others), and not aligned with either a community of faith to be guided or a great tradition to be interpreted. In modern times 'artists' have held an exemplary position among them.

(4) The fourth type of logic of selfhood conceives of the true self as a process of *casual encounters* by an individual with external situations, entered into either passively or manipulatively.[13] Both of these versions of the casual-encounter self have been captured in Goffman's (1967:31) 'the self as an image pieced together from the expressive implications of the full flow of events in an undertaking; and the self as a kind of player in a ritual game who copes honourably or dishonourably, diplomatically or undiplomatically, with the judgemental contingencies of the situation'. Any more substantive conception of the self, any more specific symbolic content of it, is, in this perspective, only a deceptive 'performance' staged before an audience (or before an internalized audience), a mode of presentation of a temporary illusion making the claim of enduring validity (Goffman, 1959).

The 'casual-encounter' logic of selfhood is, of all logics of selfhood, least likely to allow of an experience of mutality. While the unique-pattern self may have a tendency toward rigidifying as a human steamroller, the casual-encounter self stands in danger of melting down into a messy pettiness: 'an inter-subjective atrocity, a mouth, a maw' perpetually ready for new experiences, never able to find a centre of gravity in any of them (Barthelme 1972:169).[14]

Casual-encounter logics of selfhood may perhaps be interpreted as expressions of 'apathy of self-satisfaction' or of 'apathy of despair' (N. Danilevsky, cited from Sorokin 1951: 65–6) and expected among those who have become resigned to a condition of existence which they perceive as neither intrinsically valid nor capable of being infused with significance. The prevalence of this logic would, in such cases, indicate a latent, *inertly experienced* 'civilizational crisis' — a process or state of dissolution of structures of meaning that transcend the current interests of the individual to which he seeks only pragmatically to adjust.

De Tocqueville's (1957 II:3–55) comparison of aristocratic and democratic cultures suggests an experience of the self in democracies — as a temporary moment of action, continuously (by 'a small, distressing motion') transforming itself — that should favour the acceptance of casual-encounter logics of selfhood. But this is likely to happen only when the symbolic foundations (the particular conception of the 'destiny of man' and the obligations imposed by it) on which democratic institutions are based have dissolved, and not the 'ethical' principles of the foundations, but the 'technical' modes of operation of the institutions shape the perceptions of selfhood. Emerson's self 'as an exemplary fluid consciousness' (McIntosh 1976) is also an expression of a democratic culture: it is casual in its perceptions, but with a 'selecting principle' determining what the individual will retain from his experiences and incorporate into his 'soul'.

Approximations to the casual-encounter logic may be seen in Montaigne, David Hume, *The Principles of Psychology* (though not *The Varieties of Religious Experience*) of William James, the other-directed of David Riesman. Individuals adhering to this logic of selfhood are likely to be 'game-players' or 'technicians' not committed to anything beyond the methodology (whether of action or of observation) of the enterprise in which they currently find themselves. The interpreters of this logic tend to be 'observers of techniques'.

I am hypothesizing that when—either in the life history of an individual or in the history of a civilization—a cultural logic of selfhood ceases to be dominant and is (partly) replaced by a radically different type, changes will take place in the following direction: casual-encounter logic (and an 'unfurnished', quality-less self) *to* peak-experience logic (and an intensely 'emotional' self) *to* coincidence logic (and the 'spiritual' self, in the sense of an individual's presuming to have a durable quality connected with some larger reality other than his or her spontaneous emotion and objective social role) *to* unique-pattern logic (and an 'heroic' self) *to* casual-encounter logic. This sequence presupposes that, once the possibilities of a particular type of experience of selfhood are realized and its limitations understood, the completed experience has left 'foundations' in the form of an ability or a need for moving towards another specific type of experience of selfhood and that a change can be effectively sustained only if such 'foundations' for it exist.

The four types of logics have been arrived at heuristically, to make sense of the available range of observations on the experiences of selfhood. But they can be accounted for analytically as points of intersection of two variables—stability *vs* instability and immanence *vs* transcendence. The unique-pattern and coincidence logics presume a self that has an enduring structure (or, in the coincidence logic of Buddhism, an enduring quality of nonbeing); the peak-experience and casual-encounter logics presume a self that has an unstable, processual structure. The peak-experience and coincidence selves are 'transcendent' in the sense that the true self is located outside the ordinary everyday activities of the individual (and is not fully, without residue, expressed in them); the casual-encounter and unique-pattern selves are 'immanently' located within the ordinary everyday activities of the individual (and are at least potentially capable of being fully expressed in them). But these are analytic types and it is possible for concrete individuals to contain elements of several of them in their experiences of their own selfhood.

It seems in principle likely that all the main types of logics of selfhood will be found to some degree at some point in the histories of all complex civilizations. But the degree to which any one of them is present varies a great deal, and the specific forms in which they appear may be so different as to reveal similarities of type only at the highest level of abstraction. Moreover, a particular historically concrete system of belief (such as Buddhism or Christianity) may incorporate elements of different types of logics of selfhood, putting primary stress on one or another element at different times or in different currents of thought within the 'system'.

MODES OF COHERENCE: ORDER AND DISORDER

What can be identified as the symbolic contents of the empirically concrete individual depends ultimately on the kinds of 'order' and 'disorder' within which such individuals are presumed to be located or which they find in themselves.[15] Comprehensions of order and disorder tend to be implicit and global and must be sought on a deeper and, in any case, intuited rather than consciously understood level of the symbolic organization of civilizations than the more explicit and differentiated cultural logics. While the 'self' may be more of a metaphor than a concept, comprehensions of order and disorder have even more of a metaphoric, and less of a conceptual, character than the logics of selfhood. 'Visual thinking' is even more important in identifying comprehensions of order and disorder than it is in distinguishing logics of selfhood.

Two comprehensions of disorder particularly relevant to the construction of symbolic designs for individual identities may be initially distinguished: (1) 'Meaningless chaos' — absence or disruption of pattern from which no valid innovation arises, and (2) 'Miraculous intrusion' (or 'extrusion') — disruption of routine through which something of enduring value is experienced or established.[16]

Whatever 'animates', either as a 'charismatic directive' or as a 'mystical illumination', that which is otherwise 'lifeless' or 'burnt out' is subjectively perceived as miraculous intrusion. But what is miraculous is 'beyond good and evil' or incorporates both or can be either. In Dionysian rituals as well as in ethical prophecy; in the mythologies of love; movements of liberation of nations, classes, and sexes; and even in the moments of aesthetic insight, the 'miraculous' contains, as its potentialities, both 'ecstasy' and 'destruction'. Any comprehension of order has to come to grips with these two varieties of symbolic comprehension of disorder when they intrude upon it.[17]

Four symbolic frameworks for comprehending the basic character of order have had particularly important implications for the organization of individual identities. They can be imagined as 'lawful nature', 'spontaneous nature', 'the factory', and 'work of art', — as metaphors of order somewhat comparable to the Greek categories of *logos, physis, nomos,* and *eros*.

THE TWO NATURES

'Nature' is a 'primordial' order which exists independently of human intentions and operates in a manner that men have not established (and, at best, can only partially understand). Natural orders, however, come in two versions. The 'lawful-action' version of nature—particularly prominent in traditions of Irano-Semitic origin (and in Hinduism)—insists: 'Everything is *obligated* to act (or, where conscious choice is possible, as with human beings, to seek to live) according to an identifiable set of specifications appropriate to its kind'. The 'spontaneous-action' version of nature— approximations to which can be found in dreaming, in contemporary sciences, in Buddhism and in Taoism—suggests: 'There are observable *dispositions* (or, in the case of nonconscious entities, probabilities) for particular kinds of behaviour, and action anywhere is the result of *inter- actions* of a variety of forces'.[18]

Lawful nature presupposes an eternal set of norms of ideal behaviour to which it is empirically possible—but not legitimate—not to conform. It therefore tends, in regard to the position of any given element in the total structure, either to *hierarchize* by the degree of conformity to the basic set of norms, or to *dichotomize* the empirically given into such categories as 'righteousness' and 'transgression', 'sanity' and 'madness', 'true con- sciousness' and 'illusion'. Hobbes, in reducing the imponderable diversity of feelings into the pleasure-pain dichotomy, employed the lawful-nature framework; Freud, in his mythologizing dialectic of Eros and Thanatos, made use of it.

Where either hierarchy or dichotomy is present, the possibility of *in- version*—turning the world (or the hierarchy of reason-passion) upside down, sanctification of transgression, the perception of 'madness' as superior 'health'—is always a live possibility, whether tempting or threatening. Inversion of structure is a symptom of crisis, but one that can occur only within lawful nature.[19]

With regard to change over a period of time, lawful nature incorporates an *obligatory direction*—either linear, as in theories of the golden age and of inevitable progress (or in Erikson's conception of the stages of psychosocial development), or cyclical, as in Hindu cosmic cycles of construction-destruction and in conceptions of history modelled on the movements of heavenly bodies or of clocks. Imposed on human experiences, both the directional and the cyclical conceptions of change, like the paradigm of lawful nature as a whole, have a 'mechanizing' effect.

In spontaneous nature, none of the structural principles that define lawful nature—hierarchy, dichotomy, inversion, obligatory direction—obtains. Spontaneous nature is conceived, like the universe of Japanese mythology or of the contemporary 'protean men', as consisting of events, encounters, collisions which are, in an ultimate metaphysical sense, 'accidental' occurrences (Pelzel 1970; Lifton 1970). In contrast, lawful nature—as exemplified by the late-medieval European conception of the universe—implies enduring categories, identities, and characters, all of which are 'essential' necessities that must be recognized (that is, respected as matters of utmost seriousness) by everyone, friend and foe alike, who acts within the framework of lawful nature.

If the lawful-nature paradigm prescribes unremovable obligations, it also, implicitly or explicitly, guarantees inalienable rights. *No one can be legitimately deprived of the right to perform his, or her, obligations.* This is the implicit meaning of 'natural right' where 'natural law' dominates over it, as in the classical world or in Confucian China (or in Russia). *No one has the right to interfere with the fulfilment of their 'natures'—which it is their obligation to fulfil—by individuals or by 'natural' groups, even when by asserting their own 'true natures' they transgress against the established order.* This is what 'natural right' explicitly means where 'natural right' dominates over 'natural law', as it has done, by and large, in the West since the seventeenth century (Strauss 1953).

Within the paradigm of a purely spontaneous nature, there are no inalienable rights which all, including the empirical powerless, can legitimately claim their own. The existence of a 'spontaneously natural' disposition does not imply any right to have it or the moral obligation of anyone else to respect it (though it may frequently be expedient, on utilitarian grounds, for others to do so). Nor is there, in spontaneous nature, any 'irrefragable rule of Reason' (Gierke 1934:39) by which existing social institutions or patterns of private behaviour must be measured. A 'spontaneous' reason can only understand empirical inter-relations, not criticize them by reference to a criterion of judgement.

But although there are no certifiable rights, obligations, or criteria of judgement in spontaneous nature, the quality of indifference is not uniformly attributed to it. Spontaneous nature can be perceived as moody or as coldly indifferent, but also as generally threatening or, as in Taoism (Chan 1969), as generally nurturant. (Spontaneous nature, as the image of

die gute Mutter Natur suggests, may have originated as a child's-eye view
of order). It is only official guarantees, not emotional qualities, that
spontaneous nature necessarily excludes.

The lawful nature metaphor seems to appeal most to 'organization' or
'movement' intellectuals — the 'clerics' — who judge themselves to be
responsible for maintaining conceptions of the universe in sound order, not
only for themselves, but also for their 'publics'. The plausibility of lawful-
nature paradigms tends to decline when cleric-intellectuals cease to be
acceptable as spiritual guides and as whatever has been respected as lawful
nature is approached as an object either of practical exploitation (by
economic or political entrepreneurs) or of contemplative or experimental
inquiry (by 'humanistic' scholars or 'naturalistic' scientists respectively).
For the entrepreneurs, lawful nature is apt to be replaced by the factory;
for scholars and scientists, by either the 'intuitive-synchronic' or the
mathematized-functional conception of spontaneous nature (Jung and
Pauli 1955; Dijksterjuis 1961). But both scholars and scientists construct
their *understandings* of what they observe or sense in spontaneous nature
as if they were building works of art; and indeed the work of art may, at its
purest, be conceived as a worked-out understanding of spontaneous
nature.

Spontaneous nature may have been the earliest comprehension of order
to emerge. Yet it is also the background for the most sophisticated
imaginations of it.

THE FACTORY

The symbolic framework of the 'factory' — which should appeal to the
urban middle classes in their assertive phase, but particularly to modern
economic or political organizers — implies that men (and, more recently,
women) may choose what kinds of structures to construct for the purpose
of transforming raw materials (including society and their own 'human
nature') according to their specifications, and that these structures need to
be constantly tested and can be endlessly improved in the course of trying
them out.

This orientation may be expressed 'occasionally', or 'systematized' into a
method encompassing all major areas of thought and conduct. It may be
operated in a 'dispersed' manner, by each individual separately, or in a
'centrally controlled' manner, by some managerial élite which imposes its
specifications on others. Perhaps the most pervasive form of the symbolic
framework of the factory is when it can be conceived of as operating
'automatically', with no one in charge, but everyone processing oneself and
everything else in accordance with one's current specifications.

The roots of the factory conception of order may be sought in magic, in primitive notions of contract,[20] in the military communities, in the sociological 'megamachines' of Lewis Mumford by which ancient Egypt and China accomplished the building of pyramids and irrigation works, in Chinese Legalism, Roman Law, and especially in the Western European God's assignment to men of the obligation to transform the face of the earth in accordance with divine specifications (White 1971). The secular individualistic democratization of this mission has made it possible for everyone to become a factory for processing everything (and even oneself) into its own current line of goods.

The idea of the continuous perfectibility of *man* has, since the abandonment of the notion of original sin — and outside the 'biology is destiny' tradition — tended toward partial convergence with the assumption, on which the factory operates, of the infinite malleability of *raw materials*.[21] The limitlessly perfectible human being is infinitely malleable raw material in the hands of a particular individual (his teacher or himself) or of a collectivity exercising the monopoly of effective will. In either case, he does not have a 'lawful nature' capable of resisting these manipulations (and in terms of whose rights and obligations these manipulations can be judged); and he never ceases to be 'raw material' subject to processing — that is, he is denied the dignity of *sufficient completion* (implicit in the notion of the work of art) to which the Renaissance man or a Chinese gentleman-scholar might feel entitled.

Within the fully developed factory framework of action, everything that human beings make — or even 'make exist' by perceiving them — is subservient to their current purposes and has no other justification for existence. Any construction by human beings (including the internal furniture of their own selves), that is less efficient for attaining their current purposes than a conceivable alternative to it might be, can and indeed must be thrown out, whereupon it is extinguished from memory. What has been an inerasable memory bank in lawful nature, in which everything is accounted for or properly placed, *to be preserved for ever*, as the Soviet stamp for files involving 'crimes against the state' religiously puts it, and what might have become, within the framework of order conceived as a work of art, a selective treasury (museum) for preserving what is judged to have attained uniquely adequate completion (and an amphitheatre for recalling the tragedy of its destruction), becomes, by the logic of the factory, a 'garbage heap of history' in which everything, sooner or later, must meaninglessly end.

But in a rigidly rationalized order — that is, an order which does not allow the incorporation of disorder into its structure — order itself, at some point, takes on the appearance of a disease. Order as a disease must then be combatted by a 'sacred disordering', which frequently assumes the form of a 'return of the repressed' (not necessarily sexual content, but whatever it is that a civilization, in a particular phase of its development, represses or 'treats as dirt'). The Dionysian mysteries of Greece and Tantrism in India can be interpreted, at least in part, as expressions of this kind of reaction to 'rationalization'.

THE WORK OF ART

As a symbolic framework for conceiving order, 'art' contains five defining elements: (1) it is *made* by human beings, an artifact, the result of labour — whether started with a practical intention or as a statement about an affecting or a perplexing quality of an experience; (2) it is *well*-made, a criterion that initially (or potentially) separates 'art' from the mass of 'artifacts'; (3) the goodness of its making *transcends* the functional utility (if any) of the object of performance, the purposes for which it was originally intended or subsequently used, and the aesthetic or ideological framework within which it has been conceived by its author or authors; (4) the quality of 'transcendence' originates in the *order* that has emerged only in the process of working it out and whose demands on its creator the latter has so adequately recognized, in concrete detail, that what he (or she) has produced compels admiration even by those to whom it remains alien; (5) the order of a work of art is such that only an adequate working out of it — the recognition and full acceptance of the discipline which it requires of its creator (the 'discipline of beauty', as the Japanese might call it) — gives sensuous *pleasure*.[22]

An essential characteristic of order comprehended as a work of art is that it can incorporate disruptions of order — both 'meaningless chaos' (accidents) and 'miraculous intrusion' (inspiration) — into its design. Within the symbolic order of the factory miraculous intrusions are identified with meaningless chaos and both equally treated as 'bugs in the system' (the factory version of 'impurity'), to be ironed out by better planning. Within lawful nature, both meaningless chaos ('evil', 'nothingness') and miraculous intrusions ('revelation', 'revolutionary spontaneity') have a lawfully predetermined place. In the process of creating works of art, they arise unexpectedly and are transformed into intrinsic constituents of meaningful order, as both challenges to it and sources of its vital energy. In a consistently conceptualized spontaneous nature, *experiences* of miraculous intrusion are possible (in the sense perhaps of a suddenly changed pattern of perception), but the *category* of 'miraculous intrusion' is incomprehensible and such experiences, therefore, intellectually unrecognizable.

While the order of the factory is orientated to the universal standard of efficiency of means and therefore specifically repudiates any local 'custom', 'tradition', or 'spirit of the laws' characteristic of a particular people, the order of the work of art is capable of incorporating, and usually does incorporate, a particular tradition or reminiscences or fragments thereof or constitutes, especially in recent Western art, a critical comment on a particular tradition. In this regard, the conception of law defined by Hobbes presupposes the factory comprehension of order, and the conception of law which Montesquieu initiated has something of the order of the work of art (as conceived by an aristocrat, not a plebeian craftsman) about it.[23] Particularities which are not given by nature (such as the sexual differentiation), but historically evolved (such as national differences or 'personal character'), can be truly respected only within an order conceived of, at least partly, as an assembly of works of art. Only the order of art generates the *right* for human works (or, at least, some of them) to be preserved, a purely secular basis for claiming that not 'Alles, was entsteht, ist wert, dass es zugrunde geht' (even if it in fact does).

The notion of order as a work of art has been forged in the practice of generations of more or less, or potentially, creative workers. It has been confirmed and sometimes ossified by exalted symbolic designs of aristocratic derivation: in Greece by the concept of the Craftsman God (of Plato), in the Renaissance by the 'man of genius'. This notion is now being undermined by the experience of the masses of industrial and bureaucratic workers. The experience of work in modern societies may well be increasing the 'objective' need for art as a countervailing principle to the mechanization of procedure and evanescence of the product (a logic applicable also to the production of 'selves'). But the contemporary organization of work does not provide, or even permit, enough perceptions and actions suggestive of the potency of artistic designs in human existence. Ordinary life — even the ordinary life of professional artists — refuses to contribute to the legitimation of the order of art.

A hypothesis concerning the logical relations among the four comprehensions of order may be permitted here. It is suggested that lawful nature and the factory constitute a modality which may be identified as 'ascetic' or 'managerial' (likely to employ the 'masculine' imagery of 'control'), and spontaneous nature and the work of art represent a modality that can be conceived of as 'mystical' or 'contemplative' (likely to employ the 'feminine' imagery of 'responsiveness') for comprehending order — both modalities being cross-civilizational universals.[24]

Within each modality of comprehending order, there is a type of order that is 'natural' (given to human beings independently of their action) and one that is 'cultural' (constructed by human beings themselves). Within the 'ascetic' mode of ordering, culture (conceived of in the image of the factory) is the result of the rationalization of lawful nature, a 'disenchantment of the world', retaining the obligatory structure of lawful nature without its 'spirit'. In the 'mystical' mode of ordering, culture (perceived in the image of a work of art) is the metaphorization of spontaneous nature, an 'enchantment of the world'.

If these processes of 'culturalization of nature' can be reversed, the 'naturalization of culture' would imply in the 'ascetic' mode of ordering the recovery of lawful nature, a firmly reassuring dogmatization of the world. In the 'mystical' mode of ordering, the naturalization of culture would be a dissolution of the metaphors basic to it, a 'disenchanting' loss of all durable meaning in a promiscuously spontaneous nature.[25]

In the comprehensions of disorder, it is frequently possible to distinguish between 'meaningless chaos', a mechanical kind of disorder, dry, clear, and abrasive, comparable to a heap of broken bottles, from which order cannot be generated except through a purging fire which melts everything down, and 'primeval slime', an organic kind of disorder, damp and dark, like mud or decaying life, in which nutrients for new types of order (whether healthy or diseased) accumulate.[26] I see 'meaningless chaos' (Calvin's 'formless chaos, full of desolation') as the ascetic modality of perceiving disorder, and 'primeval slime'—which comes close to the Taoist image of the primordial condition preceding the emergence of consciousness and order—as the mystical modality of perceiving disorder.[27] Primordial slime precedes the rise of spontaneous nature; meaningless chaos results from the breakdown of the factory. But 'mystics' tend to perceive all disorder as 'primordial slime', and 'ascetics' to see it as 'meaningless chaos'.

There seem to be some broadly specifiable relationships between the modes of order and the logics of selfhood discussed in the previous section. Lawful nature permits *only* that which ultimately submits to the coincidence logic of selfhood. But spontaneous nature can tolerate all logics of selfhood. Coincidence with universal order is, in this case, attained through a universal embrace—whether 'poetically' or 'matter-of-factly'—of casual encounters. Either unique pattern or peak experience can be seen as acceptable human responses to the processual structure of spontaneous nature. But, where the order that exists independently of human action is conceived as spontaneous nature, the superimposition of a unique-pattern self upon it must be regarded as a 'well-constructed dream'.[28] A peak experience, on the other hand, may signify either the discovery of the responsiveness of spontaneous nature—or the beginning of its 'transcendence' toward lawful nature.

Both the peak-experience and unique-pattern selves can acquire an enduring significance within the order of art—but the order itself is, 'sadly' (in traditional Japan) or 'tragically' (in the West), fragile. In the factory type of order, any notion of the 'true self' disappears among the unlimited possibilities of 'behavioural engineering'; there is therefore no cultural logic of selfhood, but only infinitely revisable sets of behavioural specifications.

The notion of 'miraculous intrusions' of disorder seems to be necessarily presupposed, or permitted, in the peak-experience logics of selfhood. But there could not be a logic of selfhood built within the symbolic framework of 'meaningless chaos' or 'primeval slime'. As in the factory framework of order, there cannot be any 'true selves' in meaningless chaos (and indeed, in both cases, any presumption that there is anything to be called a 'true self' must be treated as a deception).

A particular self — and perhaps not only in modern times — can be seen as composed from various kinds of orders and disorders, which are experienced on different levels of its organization, in different spheres of its activity, or at different times in its life history. The understanding of the symbolic structure of a self requires an explication of (1) the modes of order and disorder into which different areas of an individual's experience are arranged by his manner of comprehending them, (2) the 'occasions of contact', or lack thereof, through which he connects, or fails to connect, these modes to each other, and (3) the types of transactions that take place on these occasions of contact (for example, 'war', 'constructive co-operation', 'oscillating current', 'coincidence of opposites', 'mutual transformation', 'organic absorption'). The transactions between 'order' and 'disorder' are likely to be of particular importance both in the moral and in the psychiatric history of the individual (and on the occasions of contact between them).

The major alternative types of comprehension of order and disorder are presumed to be present, but to varying degrees, in all complex civilizations. But they are present as general architectonic principles, each with its own implications, several of which may be conjoined in the construction of a particular symbolic configuration. The critical issues are: (1) which 'empirical' contents are conceived under which mode of coherence and (2) how does one mode of coherence impose limits on another or — a more difficult issue — how does one modify the character of another or provide disguises for its perception.

In analysing particular symbolic configurations, the key issue is identifying the ways in which the *general* types of comprehension of order and disorder are related to each other in a *concrete* 'organic design'. In analysing civilizations as wholes, the basic problem for the theoretical analyst is tracing the trajectories over a period of time of each of the general elements — modes of comprehension of order and disorder — and identifying their historically most important points of mutual articulation.

ON THE AUTHORITY OF SYMBOLIC DESIGNS

I distinguish *political* authority or 'the power to command and the duty to obey' (Weber 1968:943), from *cultural* authority, the latter conceived of as a model for the conduct of human existence that, by its own qualities, claims and acquires a relatively enduring symbolic validity. The concept of cultural authority is already implicit in Durkheim's (1947:3) observation: 'Human passions stop only before a moral power they respect. If all authority of this kind is wanting, . . . the state of war is necessarily chronic'.

How do particular symbolic designs (such as specific conceptions of individual identity) acquire their authority (that is, come to be widely and continuously judged to be 'respect-worthy') and how do they become deauthoritized? The framework I propose for approaching this question contains two basic components: (1) 'psychocultural dispositions' — the socially shaped raw materials of experience (Kavolis 1970), and (2) the 'civilizational movements' which establish the basic categories and forms for giving coherence to assemblages of such experiences.

The *psychocultural dispositions* are the tendencies of perception shaped by the manner of operation of particular institutions, technologies, occupations, and socio-ecological settings. It is presumed that these 'socialization mechanisms' shape only the internally produced subjective raw materials of culture history ('experiences'), but not the symbolic designs ('interpretations') into which some of these materials become organized.

Civilizational movements are those 'revitalization', or 'cultural', or 'social' movements in which a new and relatively enduring symbolic design (whether 'conceptual' or 'perceptual') emerges and is popularized with such impact that the overall character and direction of development of a civilization is tangibly affected (Wallace 1956; Martindale 1962; Abrams 1971).

To appeal to large numbers of followers, and to acquire societal influence, a civilizational movement needs the background of both a widely prevalent sense of overall discreditation *or* situational insufficiency of existing symbolic designs and an accumulation of socially provided psychocultural dispositions potentially favourable to it. But the overall structure of the civilizing message that emerges from such movements is not predictable from the knowledge of such dispositions. Rather it constitutes a selection from the psychocultural dispositions *and* from the basic categories and perceptual forms provided by native or (in the case of conversions) originally alien traditions *and* from the impressions of significant current events (such as catastrophes or striking scientific discoveries). These selections from the 'raw materials of the imagination' must, furthermore, have been evolved into an 'organic form' within which even contradictory elements acquire a sense of belonging together.[29]

To be recognized as authoritative, the resulting symbolic design must constitute an interpretation of experience that is both intuitively credible over a *wide range* of changing specific situations and viable, or at least not obviously inadequate (in comparison with available alternatives), foundation for *practical action*. The intuitive credibility of a particular symbolic design is presumably grounded in both its concordance with a higher-order standard or principle by which its claims can be supported ('ideological validation' by established, or emerging, symbolic categories) and also its resonance to current emotional need and imagination ('existential substantiation' by present psychocultural dispositions and preoccupations). Dissolutions of the authority of symbolic designs should also be analysable in these terms.

A symbolic design must draw upon the socially available raw materials of the imagination to be established as a credible interpretation of the meaning of experience. But a particular symbolic design, the historically concrete 'text', presupposes some kind of a more *general* comprehension of the basic forms of order, of disorder, and of relations between them—a mode of coherence—within which this particular design is, consciously or unconsciously, presumed to be located. The intuitive comprehensions of the forms of order either precede the establishment of a particular symbolic design or are evolved in the course of working it out. But the basic forms which anything must have attributed to it if it is to be conceived as an order exist on a more 'fundamental', and in any case less consciously understood, level of organization than do the particular symbolic designs that exhibit the specific 'ideological' contents with which these general forms are filled out. The different comprehensions of the forms of order have varying implications for the perception of the authority of the symbolic designs conceived within such forms.

Where order is comprehended within the framework of spontaneous nature, authority of either the political or the cultural type cannot arise (as also notions of 'inalienable rights', 'compelling obligations', 'perfection', 'excellence' and so on). Within the factory comprehension of order, political authority can be produced but cultural authority hardly so since nothing located within the factory type of order is capable of generating a moral power worth being respected. If the notion of order as a machine for the production of results specified in advance possesses authority, it must have been provided with this authority by something that has originated outside the symbolic framework of the factory and normally within some sort of lawful nature. The factory must be comprehended as an externalization of God for it to constitute an 'authoritative' framing for the conduct of human existence.

Within an order comprehended as a work of art, authority is not binding on all, but only on those who participate in the creation or re-creation
of a particular work of art (that is, a particular project of producing order). Such authority is 'cultural' even when it masquerades as 'political'.
Durable political authority—a reliable complex of powers to command
and duties to obey—cannot be securely grounded within an order comprehended as a work of art. Within lawful nature, authority—both
cultural and political—is primordially given and obligatory to all (though
it may reveal itself more fully in time and though the specific form in
which it is obligatory may depend on one's position within the total
scheme, as, for example, within the Indian caste system).

Art is the only type of order that can be both authoritative and non-
authoritarian. A work of art establishes a meaningful (but possibly
temporary) order for the particular individual, or collectivity of individuals, who has worked it out. The general 'formal' adequacy of the
working out of this order may be, or become, universally recognizable. But
in its specific concreteness, in the multiple levels of meaning of its
reciprocally attuned disciplines and gratifications, the order one has
worked out for oneself remains, at best, an evocation of a significant
strangeness for those who do not participate in it.

The work of art as a metaphor of social action has one inescapable
limitation. It does not recognize ties of mutual commitment except among
those who co-operate in the production or reproduction of a work of art.
For the symbolic matrix of mutual obligation transcending a particular co-
operative relationship, some notion of *that which it is necessary to
defend*—of lawful nature—needs to be reconstituted.

CONCLUSION

Individual identity, as 'affirmed character' separable from functionally
specialized (familial, occupational, national, etc.) role-identities, is
authenticated by reference to the psychological qualities which constitute
its raw material. But a particular individual identity derives its claim to
validity (that is, its *authority* over the empirically concrete individual
whose identity it is, as well as possibly over others) from the basic cultural
categories by which these psychological qualities are judged by the 'self'
that perceives them as its own.

At any given time, one's identity is a stage in the process of judgement of
one's perceptions in the court, or sequence of courts, of one's categories of
consciousness. And these categories constitute one's selections from the
structure of one's civilization or civilizations.

3

Authority and Identity: The Case for Evolutionary Invariance*

Rainer C. Baum

There is a contrast between Rainer Baum's essay and that of Kavolis which precedes it. Kavolis sketched a picture of enormous scope, concentrating on symbolic designs ('cultural logics') in different civilizational contexts and thus reached well beyond the scope of most sociological analysis whereas Baum presents us with a study explicitly drawing on the debates and accomplishments in the mainstream of historical and political sociology.

Rainer Baum has devoted much work to the study of change of social systems in the perspective of action theory, grounded upon the work of Parsons. The frame of reference is clear, and so is the objective: to contribute to the understanding of continuity and change in macro-sociology. The matter is important in many different respects: there is the debate about the direction of modernization as to whether convergence must be expected; there is the question of the depth of recent revolutionary changes; there is the issue of the interplay between identity and authority which is the theme of this volume. Baum begins with the connection between identity and authority which seems to him inevitable and indissoluble, but also obvious. The central concern is with the persistence of variety among societies in the ethos of life, especially in the codes of authority (the rationales for obedience), and in the conceptions of individual autonomy.

Two codes are distinguished, the 'ex toto' and the 'ex parte' codes. In the 'ex parte' case, authority rests on the notion that it has been appropriately negotiated by all special and particularist interests in society; in this case

*Comments received from Victor Lidz, Roland Robertson, John Marx, Shmuel N. Eisenstadt and Wolfgang Schluchter are gratefully acknowledged. I am also indebted to participants in the Pittsburgh Conference on Authority and Identity, April, 1975. Reprinted by courtesy of Ferdinand Enke Verlag, Stuttgart, this essay was previously published in two parts in *Zeitschrift für Soziologie*, Vol. 6. Nos. 1 and 4, 1977 in a longer form.

*the 'true self' is seen as the emergent property of successive group af-
filiations. In the 'ex toto' case authority rests on the view that society is an
immanent reality from which all special entities are derived. The 'true self'
is seen as deriving its essence from permanent cultural imperatives. The
notion of 'codes' has been given precise and special analytical meanings in
Baum's work. He does advance analysis, even though the distinction itself
has antecedents. Indeed, the orientations of Tönnies, described as
'essential will' and 'arbitrary will', are closer to Baum's conceptions than
the so often misunderstood conceptions of* Gemeinschaft *and* Gesellschaft
would lead one to believe.

*Baum explores the facts leading to the observation that these codes have
been relatively stable in modern polities, and hence are invariant in an
evolutionary sense, and offers explanations for their formation and later
stability.*

*The conditions for the persistence of such codes in the polities to which
Baum refers, if viewed in the broader frames of Kavolis, may be a special
case. One might even say that the structure of Baum's argument has an
affinity with the structure of Kavolis' notion of relative stability in the
civilizational designs for identity which may well be thought of as having
crystallized in periods of ferment akin to the Reformation period in the
West. However, the foci of the two analyses are quite different: whereas
Baum deals specifically with political authority and its relation to personal
autonomy, behind Kavolis' thought there is a notion of 'cultural authority'
and personal authenticity.*

INTRODUCTION

In the sense of sameness the concept of identity is linked with the concept
of authority, a link that is inevitable, indissoluble, and, by now, obvious.
As Barnard (1938:163) recognized, the question whether or not an order
has authority is decided by the persons to whom it is addressed. Authority
exists only where those expected to obey meet four conditions: (1) understanding the order; (2) believing, *at the time the order is issued*, in its
compatibility with the purposes of the organization, as well as (3) its
compatibility with the personal interests of the recipients and (4) their
capacity to comply (Barnard 1938:165, emphasis in the original). Furthermore, change in motives and behaviour through a period of time is
always involved. 'Co-operation compels changes in the motives of individuals which otherwise would not take place' (Barnard 1938:41).
Obviously, too, having changed in order to attain a collective goal, participants must, at a later point in time, recognize themselves as *the same* as

those who started out to co-operate if any sense of goal-attainment is to be realized. Thus change over a period in some respects, and continuous identity over a period in others characterizes any co-operative system. This also pertains to society, for the power of a state 'is its capacity to achieve its goals by changing the interests of other collective actors', at home and/or abroad, *'without threatening its own interest in continued existence'* (Mayhew 1968:26, emphasis added). The problematical link between change and continuity in identity that co-operation produces becomes larger, the longer the time required in attaining the end in question and the larger the change in motives, interests, and behaviour involved for success. Modernization goals of societies require enormous change and frequently numerous generations for their realization, thus highlighting the problematical link between change and continuity in some identity — conferring symbolic structure.

I aim here at a modest contribution towards advancing our understanding of the problem of continuity and change in macro-sociology. Firstly, drawing on relatively 'hard' evidence, long-term continuity in the 'meaning codes of authority' in many societies will be demonstrated. This will involve a review of the relevant literature on political development in post-World War II social science. Secondly, and relying on 'soft', short-term, and scattered evidence, the plausibility of long-term continuity in culturally distinct conceptions of personal autonomy will be suggested. An attribute of personality structure, the autonomy at issue refers to 'culturally stereotyped' individualism (for definitions of which see below). Thirdly, continuity in these two objects will be explained in two ways. On the one hand, and complementing Durkheim's thesis concerning the concomitant growth of centralized state power and individual freedom. I shall argue that widespread, though not universal, empirical continuity in these respects is due to 'meaning congruence' between institutionalized and internalized conceptions of 'obligation to society' and 'obligation to self'. On the other hand, and following Hegel, I shall relate such persistence to a function. It is *one* among a potential variety of mechanisms productive of 'diachronic solidarity' which secure societal identity (definitions below).

Briefly put, complementing Durkheim here rests on an assumption, recorded facts, and a theoretical conclusion. It is assumed that Durkheim's *individuation* and Weber's *bureaucratization* are in fact cross-cultural evolutionary universals. They are also linked. Bureaucratization here refers primarily to a growth in 'societal power', the increased efficacy of society as a co-operative system (Parsons 1969:473–522; Baum 1972). This involves growth in the extent to which individuals are involved in authority relationships. Individuation refers to growth in the quest for a sense of personal autonomy. Though well-known the necessary link between these two is simply that no complex and functionally differentiated social system could conceivably rely primarily on coercion in mobilizing and steering motives for role performance. Even if coercive centre control were informationally possible, the administration of coercive compliance would require the allocation of socio-political resources to internal integration and control functions to such an extent that no upgrading in overall collective performance *vis à vis* environments would register at all.[1] This means that under conditions where 'obligation to society' and 'obligation to self' are meaningfully congruent neither increased engagement in authority relations nor growth in the quest for personal autonomy can destabilize each other. And complementing Hegel involves two things. Firstly, I stress compatibility between obedience to authority and personal autonomy more than a direct link between the two, whereby obedience amounts to self-realization and this has been the more usual Hegel interpretation in the English speaking world (Avineri 1972). Secondly, given compatibility of such obligations, this itself generates an extra force contributing to persistence in such patterns. In action-theoretic terms, such compatibility *produces* diachronic solidarity. This is an interchange product resulting from the exercise of authority in a given cultural key on the one hand, and on the other, the realization of personal autonomy in a 'matched' culture key on the part of those subject to authority. Diachronic solidarity secures societal identity over some time, maintaining it in the face of modernizing changes in *all* institutional subsectors of society.

Given a primary focus on personal identity, the relation with societal identity needs clarification. Relevant for this distinction are three versions of conceptualizing societal identity. They all focus on the *structure* of values but differ in the specific values they stress. Firstly, the most general formulation is illustrated in Max Weber's work on religion. What gives a socio-cultural system here identity is the organization of values in a meaningful symbolic whole and the values in question cover such diverse objects as religious symbols, images of the good society to have, the good personality to be or to become, relevant time-orientations, and the like. A classic of this genre but with an acute interest in the problem of societal identity over a period is Americo Castro's (1954) work on the *structure* of Spanish history.[2] Secondly, in Parsons' work there was first a perusal of the pattern variables as identity-conferring symbols for both social and personality systems (Parsons 1951a:180–200; 1951b:77–88); then, having tied the pattern variables in with the four-function paradigm for the first time, he proposed that it is a particular rank-order of importance that a given action system assigns to solving the four functions which gives it identity (Parsons 1959); and this was followed up with a stress on societal as contrasted with other kinds of values (Parsons 1968). But characteristically, identity foci declined in later work as concern with problems of evolutionary change became dominant. Thirdly, since action theory designates the integrative sub-system (societal community), as the very core of society (Parsons 1966:10, 16–18; 1971:12–26), the most theoretically cogent conceptualization of societal identity has been Eisenstadt's (1971a) designation of stratification codes as *the* identity-conferring symbolic structure for society. Among functional analysts he was also the first to formulate historical continuity in authority codes as a problem for system theory (Eisenstadt 1973). Very briefly and with respect to all institutionalized inequalities, stratification codes are value-standards that specify how much inequality there ought to be, the particular nature of status-crystallization that should prevail, how much crystallization there should be, the units in question, the units responsible for implementing these desiderata, and the reasons why. Being the best reformulation of Weber's notion of 'legitimate order', this multi-dimensional concept permits analysis of societal identity as a variable as well as the very processes of identity-formation in comparative historical perspective. Here I select one element from this complex bag: *viz* legitimacy conceptions of authority, specifying the reasons why one should obey. I shall endeavour to show that such conceptions crystallized during the late historical and early modern stages of social evolution[3] at a level of generality which proved sufficient for their persistence into modern society. That does not mean that these codes did not subsequently change at all. But postulating invariance in these codes means that subsequent change was confined to their legal elaboration and rationalization, thus firming up and securing the general principles involved against substantive change in their meaning as regards the relation between obligations to society and to self.

Here it should be said, I merely continue other recent work which aims at greater specificity in modernization theory and research in a direction beyond 'convergence', to include 'divergence' and 'invariance' as well. Convergence denotes reduction of cross-societal variance in social structure and process due to modernizing change. Starting out with differences, societies become more similar in some respect as they modernize. But in other respects there is also divergence, the opposite, denoting growth of cross-societal variance in structure and process due to modernization relative to an earlier given stage of social evolution. Invariance denotes continuity in identity-conferring symbolic structures as societies undergo modernizing change, that is, converging in some, and diverging in other, specific characteristics relative to each other. Heeding Bendix's (1967) clarion call that a sociologist's concern with modernization must focus on the way in which societies at different stages of evolution produce solidarity and the variety of distinct types of solidarities developed, as well as their organization into a system of solidarities, it has been suggested that convergence applies to instrumental, divergence to self-rewarding-expressive solidarities, and invariance to the symbolic identity structures of moral and political solidarities. Here I aim to specify those aspects of social structure and process where modernization amounts to convergence, divergence and invariance.

Further to the larger effort (Baum 1974, 1975),[4] the main point of this paper is that we now have facts available to the point where they constitute a critical mass for theoretical concerns with invariance in politics. The facts in question demonstrate that industrialization does not reduce cross-societal variety in political régimes or types of polity at the national level. What they suggest also is that it was already during the historical and early modern stages of socio-cultural evolution when political solidarities differentiated out from more functionally diffuse solidarities to a point where the accompanying conceptions of legitimate authority became encoded at a level of generality sufficient for subsequent development to the modern stage. This is due to the accomplishment of cultural élites during these stages which, having engaged in value-generalization, created ethical systems of obligations at a sufficient level of generality; and the political codes as well as those pertaining to a sense of personal autonomy, constituting a part of these ethical systems, are the foci here. But this paper offers no pertinent evidence in terms of the history of ideas. It relies instead on a kind of black box postdiction concerning such ideas, resting entirely on political development data, 'hard' and 'soft'. Another inference is that what subsequent rationalization of such codes probably amounted to was their more formal codification and more consistent implementation throughout society without substantive change in the culturally distinct meaning patterns already crystallized at these early stages. Subsequent rationalization firmed up and contributed to the completion of societal identity formation processes that started earlier, thus securing the base-parameters against fundamental change in subsequent stages. This is what is meant by invariant modernization: preservation of culturally distinct identities through religious, philosophical and legal rationalization.

Of the five phases of analysis, the first reviews the relevant literature. The second delineates the scope of invariance in evolutionary perspective. The third identifies the first objects of invariance which are meaning codes of legitimate authority and provides evidence concerning their invariance. The fourth identifies another object of invariance, *viz*, culturally distinct conceptions of 'individualism' or personal autonomy. Compatibility between authority and autonomy is shown to be a cause of their invariance. The final section presents a summary and concludes the argument by illustrating how modernization factors such as value generalization and law operate to elaborate and institutionally secure continuity in both authority and the quest for personal autonomy.

FACT AND FANCY IN THE ECONOMY-POLITY RELATION

A review of post-World War II research in the economy-polity relation relevant for the invariance problem shows broadly three phases of effort. The first was clearly directly influenced by World War II which seemed to have engendered an ambivalent cognitive response. Illustrated in Parsons' work, there was on the one hand a concern with sources of aggression associated with universal structures of modern society shot through as they are with arrangements, in both the familistic and the occupational realms, highly productive of anxiety related to channelled 'displaced' aggression; but on the other hand, some notions about socio-political 'under-development' among the enemies just vanquished were also present coupled with policy recommendations for 'development' even at a cost of commitment to private property (Parsons 1947; 1945).

But such cognitive hesitancy whereby the recent winners and losers shared centrally important properties did not persist for long. Instead a kind of 'main-line view' emerged which, in the hands of an influential compact majority, came to dominate the scene in the second phase. With theory and fact it argued cogently for a powerful, because very general, equation whereby political modernity was set equal to democracy. Various authoritarian forms of régime were relegated to 'tradition' in the 'tradition-modernity' contrast. Designating the 'democratic association' as an evolutionary universal, Parsons (1964:356) endorsed this equation explicitly and unambiguously slightly less than twenty years after the war and never rejected it. Sensitive to the possibility of falling prey to ethnocentrism, some tried valiantly to avoid the equation, but still draft a conceptual map of the shape of political modernity. On inspection their efforts to evade the equation failed (Pye 1966:31–88; Almond and Coleman 1960:4–64). Whatever the neutrality of terms such as 'interest articulation', 'communications', and 'interest aggregation', the speci-fications of political modernity could not avoid covering indeed classic features of democracy such as a free press, and electoral competition for the highest offices. These attempts foundered on the inability to come up with a credible non-democratic functional equivalent for that specific feature which marks democracy as a polity uniquely suited for any complex society, *viz* the fact that its very legitimacy principles enshrine the institutionalization of social conflict short of violence. Best illustrated in the work of Lipset (1960:45–96) this made the equation near unassailable.

Being at once historical, functional, and psychological, Lipset's theory that political modernity is democracy remains a complex one. But it can be boiled down to two essential elements. One is a dissonance-reduction thesis by which declining inequalities in wealth, education, and in-formation 'spill over' into declining political inequalities, hence a universal pressure for equality of chances for office holding and equality of the franchise (Baum 1968a). The other is a functionalist argument which asserts that any industrial society is also inevitably one with an hitherto unknown potential for social conflict. Consequently, industrial society demands a polity whose very construction of legitimate authority rests on institutionalized conflict; and of all the known forms of polities only democracy does that. This being quite cogent, the proof that political modernity does not equal democracy has come to rest on those who could come up with a non-democratic model equally well equipped in the management of conflict. Lipset's argument (1960:74; 42–96) was about the state of modernity, socio-economically (an industrialized economy, an educated population, and one exposed to mass media) and political!y, rather than one about correlated transition phenomena; indeed he denied the probability of democratization under third-world conditions of industrialization. But, and that is what counts here, the eventual victory of the fundamental equation was not doubted, and voices of doubt as well as expressions of scorn about the equation (de Schweinitz 1964; Moore 1966; Fischer 1968; Huntington 1968) found but a feeble echo, if the most prominent quantitative empirical work at the time is any indication.

For that research, once it had quantified degrees of democracy, used the 'cross-sectional correlational approximation' to the study of historical change with the advantage of many cases and many variables (Cutright 1963; Olsen 1968). The results tended to confirm the equation. This was partly due to concealing what qualitative research had already revealed, such as Huntington's law concerning 'political growth and political decay' (Huntington 1968:1–92), and partly due to quite prominent failures in the mensurational distinction between political modernity and democracy. For example, despite the fact that Olsen (1968:702) intended to improve on Cutright's work in this specific respect, he too failed in that eight of his fifteen indicators of political modernity on inspection turned out to be indicators of democracy.

It was only the construction of historical data archives and the very recent beginnings of their exploitation that inaugurated the third phase. This has already achieved a definite refutation of the 'dominant equation' of the sixties. For these data made possible the quantitative study of historical change through time. The new dynamic techniques eventuated in three studies which jointly achieved a volte face. First, with respect to Lipset's link between democracy and its ability to institutionalize conflict, a very relevant question is raised as to whether democracy does in fact institutionalize conflict short of violence? Using indicators of domestic violence, Flanigan and Fogelman's (1970) response to this question yielded but qualified support to the Lipset thesis. In general, democratic polities have less domestic violence than non-democratic ones, but the difference declines as one moves from 1800 to 1960. Also, poor countries attempting to democratize their polities need violence for success in that endeavour, while relatively rich countries need domestic peace if they are to democratize. The theoretical import of these findings is essentially two-fold. Firstly, they illuminate in new ways a venerated hypothesis about the 'birth' of democracy in the history of mankind which argued that inter-state conflict was necessary for the establishment of democracy in a context of 'limited' warfare among coreligionists (Hintze 1941). Secondly, they establish that accompanying violence prevents successful democratization in rich countries, presumably because men have too much to lose. There is here at least an implicit hypothesis: if a non-democratic régime succeeds in economic development, then it will stay non-democratic wherever democratization attempts cannot avoid domestic violence.

The next important study, modestly and somewhat misleadingly entitled *Origins of Democracy* (Pride 1970), on inspection turns out to be a test of a very general empirical modernization theory concerning the polity-economy relation. Its relevant findings are amazingly strong confirmations of six propositions: (1) where democratization precedes in time social mobilization, countries have stable democracy into the first half of the twentieth century; (2) where the relationship in the former variables is reversed, countries have stable non-democratic polities; (3) when democratization and social mobilization are associated with each other through time, that is with both expanding at similar rates, the outcome is mixed with some cases eventuating in democracy and others not. Essentially the same relations obtain between political mobilization and democratization, only clearer yet. Here again, (4) when the former out-strips the latter in time, non-democratic régimes are the result: when the relation is reversed, democracy results (5); but (6) in the joint movement from low levels of political mobilization and democratization to higher levels in each, there is a three-way outcome with some becoming stable democracies, others stable non-democracies, and a third group 'quasi-democracies'.

The theoretical import of this study becomes apparent when one applies the knowledge gained from the Cutright-Olsen correlational efforts of the previous phase. For then it becomes exceedingly likely that Pride's in-dicators of social mobilization (decline in agricultural employment, and urbanization) are at the same time indicators of economic development, and consequently of a country's wealth. So connected, Pride's findings constituted the first critical and confirmatory evidence for Eckstein's (1961) thesis concerning the positive relationship between a society's 'congruence in authority relations' and the stability of its political régime regardless of type, whether democratic or 'autocratic'. Pride's findings show no less than this tenable generalization: wherever a polity successfully weathers the storms of social mobilization which seem to be a near-universal accompaniment of industrialization without a change in the basic legitimacy of centre political authority, barring external interferences, that polity may well last into any foreseeable future. For it is very difficult to imagine domestic pressures for change subsequent to industrialization that could rival both the real need and the urgency to regulate conflicts which is everywhere the outstanding characteristic of the industrialization phase. Put otherwise, and more in line with the logic of Eckstein's thesis: if an authoritarian type of régime in a society relatively shot through with 'authoritarian' authority relations succeeds in the establishment of large-scale bureaucratic organization of economic life in factory and office, that success means the addition of an 'authoritarian' social structure into a society already thoroughly 'authoritarian' in its structure and therefore a further addition to the forces which make for régime stability. In this case, industrialization, instead of 'shaking up' authoritarian polities as the earlier 'equation' had it, might indeed aid in 'shoring up' and further secure authoritarian régimes afterwards. On the other hand, wherever democracy was established before economic modernization, successful industrialization eventuates in social forces outside the factory gate—such as increased participation in intermediary power structures—which shore up the stability of democratic régimes. In short, what are important are sequences in the development of different sub-systems of society, not straight correlations between the 'requisites' of sub-systems. For one can lift these findings to a yet more general formulation by using the language of functional system analysis.

From the perspective of diachronic functionalism in the systems analysis key (Parsons 1969a) Pride's findings suggest the following interpretation. Whichever of the four functional subsystems of society is subject to sub-system-formation with genuine boundary maintenance before any other, that one will control the development of these others; and this will be the more likely if the subsystem that develops prior to any given other one is also one higher in the cybernetic control hierarchy obtaining among all four.

While probably not verifiable yet,[5] other evidence exists which already shows that polity development prior to industrialization is related to persistence in régimes thereafter. Covering the period 1800–1971, ninety-one national states with the exception of the new states established since World War II, and distinguishing three types of regimes, *viz* democracy, autocracy, and anocracy Gurr (1974:1501) has just shown the following (1) there is in fact a 'decline of the "minimal state" which prevailed in the nineteenth century and the growth of the "activist" politics of *both autocratic and democratic form*' (emphasis supplied); (2) while there is a trend of greater prevalence in two 'democratic' indicators, *viz* openness of chief executive recruitment and constraints on their power, these are not centrally significant with respect to the Lipset-equation for (3) 'levels of political participation, that other bellwether of pluralist democracy, did not change significantly over a period of time. In short, the typical nineteenth century polity was an autocracy with minimal functions. The typical mid-twentieth century polity was either an activist plural democracy or, only slightly less likely, an active autocracy'. While there is a decline in the prevalence of anocracy, which may be in part due to its definition which includes minimal 'directiveness', for present purposes a further significant finding is that persistence and adaptability of régimes are not a function of their type, but rather of congruence in authority relations. In short, contrary to much theory before, democracy is not more persistent and adaptable than autocracy, and Eckstein's thesis seems sustained.

Thus the available evidence is pretty conclusive: industrialism is not associated with democracy. However 'systemic' modernizing change and its products may be (Black 1966; Cutright 1963; Olsen 1968), in other respects the universal transformation of an agrarian and/or commercial economy into an industrial one does not impact uniformly on politics. Autocracy as well as democracy are forms compatible with industrial society. These are the significant facts for a theoretical interest in evolutionary invariance.

From this survey of relevant facts one can glean that polity-forms known to man since ancient times have somehow survived to the present. This is especially poignant in view of the universal rise of the activist polity, whether demo- or autocratic in basic character. To be modern is to subject far greater ranges of social problems to governmental regulation than ever before. But as to basic and mutually distinct forms of legitimization which surely must be involved in political régimes so different, these data show no change.

Why no change? That is one question.

EVOLUTIONARY INVARIANCE: PROBLEMS OF SCOPE AND CAUSE

Arguing invariance demands meeting two scope restrictions. One question is: invariance in what, since when, or what stage of evolution, and why? Another pertains to socio-cultural geography: invariance where, everywhere, or in only specific civilizational areas?

As mentioned, above, the invariance problem as regards identity and authority was born during the historical and early modern stages of socio-cultural evolution. The historical stage gave rise to ideas which created a whole series of ethical paradoxes in the relations between obligation to society and to self. But at that stage the effects were largely confined to élites and inter-élite relations in society. The early modern stage, however, completed the development of invariance as a problem because it pushed the paradoxes involved 'down to the masses', converting them into problems that every man had to meet.

What were the heightened problematics in the relations of social and self obligations? Critical during the historical stage were the emergence of monotheism and, as an accompaniment, the birth of the idea of a 'responsible self, a core self or a true self, deeper than the flux of everyday experience, facing a reality over against itself, a reality which has a consistency belied by the fluctuations of mere sensory impressions' (Bellah 1964:367). Monotheism concentrated contingency on ultimate meaning into one source with, however variable, *one* will holding throughout time; and the recognition of the idea of a self as a willing, responsible agency also holding throughout time was the matching development in moral psychology of the period. Ethically this signals the break with 'casuistry' as a legitimate way to solve problems. Once an injunction achieves the status of a deistic command, particularly when there is but one god, it becomes unalterable, interpretable but not alterable in ethical substance. The ethics of faith call for a meaningful total relationship of the pattern of life with a religious goal patterned in the form of an abstract order. And such an order leads to situation-specifications of expected conduct according to general principles, hence to the emergence of a functionally differentiated normative order loaded with antithetical expectations in different situations (Weber 1922:207–9).

In society the roles of believer and secular political subject become differentiated, secular and sacred authority become distinct matters everywhere, and cultural legitimization of the social order in general and political obligations in particular become a far more acute problem than in earlier stages because the tension between religion and the world has been tremendously increased (Bellah 1964:367–8; Parsons 1964:345–6; Weber 1922:209).

For present purposes these tensions between religion and the world involved three paradoxes, one pertaining to interélite relations, another to centre-periphery relations, and a third to the relation between individuals and their groups. And maintaining rather than resolving the tensions in all three relations proved the evolutionary 'adequate' response. Removing the tension, as for example in caesaropapism or theocracy which really hierarchized the relation between secular and sacred élites to the point of domination where it occurred, constituted an evolutionarily regressive 'solution'. For built-in tension is an inevitable accompaniment of in-stitutionalized moral complexity which is the hallmark of social life since the historical stage.

As to secular and sacred élites, to be sure the extent of their organizational differentiation varied enormously in historic societies being most distinct only in the Feudal Occident (Hintze 1941), yet mutual contingency between them as regards the legitimacy of both characterized all of these societies. *Everywhere* 'political acts could be judged in terms of standards that the political authorities could not finally control' (Bellah 1964:368). The paradox here relates to the fact that while differentiation also brought forth élite specialization, the relations between them could not be 'definitively ordered' without destruction of their mutual contingency. There were cultural élites for religious solvency, political-secular élites for survival in this world, and legal élites for articulating and integrating the complex demands arising from these two concerns. But while such élite-specialization can be seen as *adaptive* for society in the long run, their relations in the short one had to remain conflict-ridden *because* they claimed autonomy *vis à vis* each other. Specialization implies relative autonomy, but the latter also makes for conflict. Ever since that stage, the legitimacy of the secular order has acquired impressive precariousness at any given moment in time while also, over the long term, becoming more securely established.

The second paradox pertains to centre-periphery relations. For since that stage, political centres must assume the right and obligation to co-ordinate the relations between constituent groups in society which are in principle accorded some degree of autonomy *vis à vis* the centre (Swanson 1967; Eisenstadt 1963). Consequently, there remained the normative complexity of articulating partial contrariness: the centre had to acknowledge the idea of 'self-government' among constituent groups, but also assume responsibility for the conduct of their interrelations.

Usually captured in the phrase 'obedience to Caesar and to God', the third paradox concerns the individual-group relation. The idea of a self that must assume responsibility for its action denotes the birth of culturally stereotyped 'individualism' which covers both: self-consciousness about self-responsibility in the inner life of persons *and* ability to communicate the sense of responsibility when it comes to managing role-conflict. This puts the individual into a genuine and finally irresolvable dilemma. His salvation chances are contingent on meeting the demands of the world, but while such demands are made in the name of collectivities with primarily long-run interests, his individual interest in salvation is relative to the time-span of all social organization always acutely short-run. Church, state, oikos, and army are regarded as practically 'eternal' beings that do not die; but the individual 'owing' valid obligations to the long-run interests of collectivities also 'validly' owes himself in his short-run. And no agency provides any final solutions to the individual's need to respond to expectations coded on contrary time horizons.

With the early modern or Reformation stage in religious evolution, these paradoxes which formerly affected only the upper status groups became part and parcel of mass culture. Mention of the label of this stage, postulated as a universal one (Bellah 1964), raises the second scope restriction specified at the beginning of this section. Since all my empirical material covers only the Christian world (East and West Rome), I offer it only as a work on the theme of Occidental rationalization. However, interest in general theory dictates using the early modern stage as a universal one, such that the Reformation in those of its products specified below, is treated as having already had, having now, or going to have a kind of Reformation fall-out for all societies.

This stage, then, 'completed' the paradoxes of the historical stage. As regards the brittleness of the legitimacy of the social order at any given moment in time, the Reformation fall-out hypothesis states two things. Firstly, a potential for counter-élites to establish political authority to mobilize mass fundamentalist resentment has been institutionalized in all societies ever since. Secondly, the idea of the state as a value-implementive agency charged with 'revising the social order', that is 'pressures to social change in the direction of greater realization of religious values' (Bellah 164:370), has become a cross-societal universal ever since, with the only qualification being that secular values in addition to, and often in competition with, religious values form the basis of fundamentalist pressures for such change. One universal consequence has been to transform the legitimization of centre authority into a near-continuous task, taking the form of competitive elections for office in only some polities at the highest levels, but not in others. Finally, the fact that individuals must now balance the time-contrary demands of self-realization and obligation to society, has since become the property of mass-man and élite member alike, though again self-consciousness about this paradox may empirically correlate positively with education, and thus retain a certain élitist character.

The problematical relation between obligation to society, particularly to authority, and to self was probably first formulated by Hegel, though his explicit concern was not with the problem of articulating the relatively *permanent* interests of one's membership identities in collectivities with the relatively *short-term* interests of one's time-bounded and historically restricted 'cultural self' at the level of the individual's inner life. Hegel hit upon this problem incidentally. He raised the question how one might explain the transformation of a classically 'congregational' and sect-type religious organization like early Christianity into a similarly classic 'church organization'? His answer was an early formulation of the 'ethical disenchantment of the world' under conditions of increased social differentiation. The Christian religionists became church members during the later Roman Imperial period with its bureaucracy (and hence a tendency to transform humans into cogs in a machine). In contrast with the earlier Republican period, this made participation in public affairs 'ethically empty'. No longer able to 'identify', in a deep sense of meaning, attachment with institutions of permanence into which part of oneself had been poured through participation 'the fear of death' was rising to levels where only a rigid church organization could supply answers with acceptable certainty (Avineri 1972: 14, 25–8). Whatever the indirectness, all four of the critical elements of the psychological aspect of producing diachronic solidarity were recognized by Hegel. Firstly, permanent collective interests far outlasting individual lives form a part of the individual's identity; secondly, consciousness of death and the associated and necessarily short-term interests of salvation form another part of individual identity. Institutionalized and internalized contingency of the interests of mortals in their ethical self-realization on the interests of collective 'immortals' and their long-run interests in ethical perfection constitutes the third element. The role of authority in articulating the two sets of interests and the placement of the burden of making sense out of inner and outer obedience on the individual through the Reformation is the last element. It is institutionalized in the conception of the citizen-role as the simultaneous creator and subject of authority. These four elements would seem to be the sociological core of Hegel's philosophy of history usually referred to as 'the struggle for freedom from meaningless nature through collective action' (Fetscher 1970:26–7).

Given the tremendous expansion of the problem of cultural legitimization of the social order, these two stages were also the birth-site of the invariance problem in societal identity. Distinctly different symbolic orders of human action now had to be articulated in order to maintain and perfect their contingencies. Weber's work suffices to establish the point, once two common and one cross-societally variant elements are singled out for attention. It should be re-emphasized, then, that monotheistic deities fashioned commands that could be interpreted, though not substantially altered. Also the state as value-implementation agency of ethical dictates became a universal. Jointly this meant for all subsequent historical effort that unalterable ethical precepts were to be subjected to implementation with growth in efficacy through political authority, among other means.[6] So much for the common elements. But maintenance of a distinct identity in society, hence cross-societal variety, also became *the* problem. For as Weber has shown, the world religions developed variant ethical systems by selecting from a common pool of archaic and primitive socio-morals variant elements. It was such variant elements as filial piety in China, truth in Zoroastrianism, and the idea of voluntary contractual ties, quite anti-kinship in spirit, which were subjected to the *same* amount of value-

generalization. Such variant elements thus came to serve as general blue-
prints for social organization at the *same* level of functional differentiation, but with contrary or at least radically different ethical
precepts, giving each civilization its distinctive ethos (Weber 1922:210). If
this is true for the historical stage, it follows that treatment of the early
modern stage as a universal one amounts to a serious theoretical commitment to the proposition of variant societal identities in all subsequent
evolution into the modern stage. It is unlikely that such identities showed
either convergence or divergence, and no change in cross-societal variety
remains the most likely prospectus for whatever form of post-modernity
one might envisage. As far as the ethos of everyday life is concerned the
image of universal modern man remains improbable.[7]

Invariance in societal identity is the logical implication of the theory of
functional differentiation. Culture and society were already differentiated
in historical societies to an extent where religious-ultimate and socio-moral
worldly meanings were coded on profoundly variant themes. In China 'this
world' was organized according to a highly generalized kinship blue-print
which ordered normative demands in economy, polity and family according to principles of filial piety. But the 'ruling religion' of Confucianism was practically devoid of kinship symbolization. In the medieval
Occident, Christianity cannot be thought about without the father-son
imagery, but social life in economics, politics, and even the family was
already coded according to the principle of voluntary contractual
association (Bellah 1960; Hintze 1941). Temporary episodes apart, it is
simply inconceivable that subsequent evolution should amount to
dedifferentiation, thus constraining the two realms more tightly than in
historical societies. Now equipped with a deity possessing through-time
stability in ethical demands as regards their substantive contents and
equipped with the state as a value-implementive agency, barring conquest
or merger by other means, there is simply no source left that could reduce
variety in the ethos of societies. And this is easy to see once one combines
use of the Reformation stage as a universal one with Hegel's lens on history.
This can be done *without* endorsing Hegel's idealist emanationism as
follows:

> According to his abstract definition [of the knowing subject that wills
> itself, individually and collectively — RCB] it may be said of Universal
> History [which only starts with the historical and the Reformation stages
> because earlier ones lacked both: a monotheistic source of ethics stable
> throughout time, and the state as implementive agency of values —
> RCB], that it is the exhibition of the Spirit in the process of working out
> the knowledge of that which it is potentially. And as the seed bears in
> itself the whole nature of the tree, and the taste and the form of its
> fruits, so do the first traces of Spirit virtually contain the whole of that

history [albeit in a particular form restricted to each culturally distinct ethos, and albeit having a chance for becoming manifest only through 'interests' operative in both the power and the realms of individual freedom — RCB] (Hegel 1837:360–1).

Fortunately for this Hegel resurrection, there is evidence that one can run an industrial society without anything like the profound elements of social utilitarianism found in the originators of 'capitalism'. Though we do not know, the Japanese too may well be incarnations of Inkeles-man (Inkeles and Smith 1974). But even if so, where the interest is with the problem of persistence of cross-societal variety in the ethos of life, particularly political life, it remains far more significant to stress what is already known: Japanese workers neither behave nor experience themselves like British ones, and those differences are even more true for the managers involved (Dore 1973).[8]

THE FIRST OBJECT OF INVARIANCE: AUTHORITY CODES

In varying degrees of explicitness as well as variable format a case for continuity in the conception of legitimate centre authority over long time periods has been made for France, The Netherlands, the German Democratic Republic, Russia, and the United States. These studies deserve brief review even though they do not permit more than preliminary identification of some sort of code as the object of invariance.

Crozier (1964) argues that neither the conception of the nature of authority nor that of authority relations have changed in France from the Ancien Régime to the present. And taking these as givens, he has been able to explain such contemporary French organizational behaviours as the absence of informal organization within bureaucracy, strata isolation, recurrent 'delinquent communalism', and extreme formalism which contrast so greatly with American organizational behaviours (Blau 1956, 1964; Whyte 1961). In Crozier's work these constants are two: what men perceive to be the intrinsic nature of authority, in this case involving such characteristics as 'a propensity towards omnipotence', and how men must regulate interpersonal dependence to make subjugation to authority tolerable, in this case 'a counterpropensity towards procedural formalism' that forever searches for a utopia: where no persons have power by reducing their discretionary powers to zero. In the Frenchman's passion for the rule of law no man should have power; procedure should govern all.

Another classic case is The Netherlands which served to develop the conception of consociational democracy. Here again it has been demonstrated that a code which developed in the seventeenth century

(Geyl 1964: 148–72) has persisted to the present (Lijphart 1968a). The central characteristics here are great deference to functional authority on the part of followers for leaders which secures unusual leadership autonomy, and, among élites, an explicit accommodative style of mutual tolerance concerning variant value-commitments. Legitimate authority at the centre here rests on acceptance of the veto from minorities.

In the German case there runs a line of continuity in corporatism which starts with the 'absolutist' strains of Prussia's estate society in the seventeenth and eighteenth centuries and continues in identifiable constitutional features of Imperial nineteenth century Germany, the Weimar Republic, National Socialism, and contemporary East Germany (GDR). To be sure, the corporatism at issue here which places the collective interest of all supraordinate to the interests of constituent groups was weakest in Prussia which still resembled for the most part the reverse principle. Nevertheless, the rationalization of law during the eighteenth century (*Allgemeines Landrecht*) in Prussia featured such characteristics as placing the legal burden of defence on the aristocratic estate which entailed classic characteristics of liturgical political resource mobilization (Weber 1968: 1006–69; Büsch 1962; Schoeps 1966:79–100; Dietrich 1966:99). According to Wolfe (1974:323–30) this mode of 'corporatism from above' found its continuation in recruitment to the senate (*Bundesrat*) by monarchical appointment to Imperial Germany (1871–1918), in the two legislatures of the Weimar Republic (1919–33) where the Economic Council of the *Reich* had separate legislative powers, the guild controls over the economy attempted by the National Socialist régime (1933–45), and the practice of *Blockpolitik* that characterized the German Democratic Republic beginning in 1949. The central feature of this system is that it 'is representative', of functional interests 'but not democratic, in that the choice of goals is dependent upon the outcome of a continuing struggle between private and functional interests' (Wolfe 1974:329–30). This struggle seems essentially devoid of procedural regulation at least when compared with the competitive electoral process in democracies.[9]

Writing directly about legitimacy codes of political authority, Eisenstadt (1973) has recently claimed their continuity in Russia from Tsarist days to the present. In this instance Bendix (1956) had been able much earlier to document continuity in a behavioural element, *viz* managerial ideologies. In Russia, and in contrast to the West, legitimatizing economic activity always involved the triangle state-entrepreneur-employee. One can even generalize this to state that legitimating social action in Russia always involved the articulation of an agency presumed to represent the interest *of* society and *therefore* 'to hover above' all special interest *in* society, on the one hand, and the rights and obligations of dependent strata on the other.

Finally, though exaggerated, Huntington's (1968:93–139) claim that political development in the United States essentially remained stuck at the level of the Tudor polity lends itself to an interpretation of stability in the legitimate conception of centre authority as resting on 'the divisions of power at the centre' principle which did not essentially change in the near-two-hundred year history of this nation.

So much for some pertinent qualitative data on the theme of historical-continuity in authority codes. But in stating a proposition of non-change in this area, the most important question is: which codes? It is a fair guess that history and sociology alike share Mannheim's dictum of 'fundamental democratization' as a piece of conventional wisdom. And it should be noted that of the five classic cases enumerated above it was only The Netherlands and the United States which had democracy at the time of the Reformation stage. The other three moved from the 'divine rights' principle of absolutist monarchy to the principle of 'sovereignty of the people'.[10]

The codes for which I argue 'invariance' are *not* the more conventional ones. They do *not* directly regulate who has the right of command; they do *not* directly specify the mode of participation in decision making at the national centre; and they do *not* immediately govern modes of succession to office. The codes at issue here are more abstract. They specify the meaning of authority relations by stating *only* the grounds on which an authoritative decision is binding on units of the collectivity in question. At the micro-level these codes constitute normative images about the in-dividual-group relationship. At the macro-level it is the 'society as a whole-constituent parts' relationship.

For illustration, three democratic cases are useful. Covering two con-temporary and one historical case, these are (1) the Anglo-Saxon com-petitive two-party democracy, (2) the consociational plural-party democracy as in The Netherlands and Switzerland, and (3) the Venetian Republic when it was a city state. Now being democracies, all three share the idea that votes 'legitimatize' authority. But other differences between the competitive and consociational types aside, these two democracies have a different meaning code of authority than had the democracy of Venice. There was no direct connection between the meaning code of authority and type of régime as conventionally understood already at the early-historical stage of evolution. One should not expect one at higher levels of differentiation either.

As is well known, while in Anglo-Saxon democracies the outcome of the electoral process determines who shall form the government and who the opposition, this is not the case in consociational democracies where that question is settled in a post-electoral process of negotiation among party leaders dealing with the problem of forming a coalition government. Clearly the idea that *neither* the popular *nor* the electoral-college vote *ought to* determine who becomes President of the United States would meet with fierce resentment in America. That illustrates the different legitimacies involved. In fact, Lijphart (1968a, 1968b, 1969) has demonstrated that consociational and competitive democracies use opposite legitimacy codes as regards the incumbency of executive office; the former use an 'anti-majoritarian conception of legitimacy' the latter a 'majoritarian' one. But behind this contrast stands a common element which asserts the need to let distinctive and different parts participate directly in the process of ultimately arriving at decisions which are to be binding on all. It reflects the conviction that the societal whole is never more and can be never more than a negotiated social order, a product of 'somehow' lesser reality which relies for its bindingness on negotiation among units with greater reality which are either voters directly, as in the competitive case, or representatives as agents of aggregate votes constituting real social groups with diverse purposes and interests, as in the consociational case.

Now, at that level of abstraction, the Venetian Republic was quite different as regards the conceptions of differing realities and the associated norms. Venice had a Grand Council to which all adult males belonged, 'regardless of creed, occupation, and education' as we might say today. That council elected an executive with very short terms of tenure (Swanson 1967:39–41). Specifically then, Grand Council membership was premised on what all had indisputably in common *as granted by nature*. For the Venetians this meant that a greater reality was attributed to what all had in common than to the diverse purposes of constituent groups. And it was to the common rather than the diverse parts that they assigned significant normative meaning as regards the legitimacy of authority.

Meaning codes of authority are at issue here. They specify the grounds on which obedience is owed. And it is these meaning codes rather than other rules regulating legitimate authority which should show evolutionary invariance, such invariance pertaining to the meaning principle involved, but *not* to its legal codification as regards all situations. The latter remains subject to continuous elaboration and refinement. For the sake of convenience in keeping them distinct, I should like to propose new labels for them. Thus where a notion prevails that society as a whole is merely a negotiated social order deriving from the direct interaction of its 'more real' constituent parts one can speak of an *ex parte* code of legitimate authority; and where the reverse is the case, as in the above example from Venice, one can speak of an *ext toto* code. These meaning codes of authority presuppose the separate existence of images of 'self' and 'collectivity' in the symbolic universe of a society. Given such separate images which state that 'self' and 'social system' are manipulable entities means that the capacity to solve 'the problem of co-operative organization' through ascriptive mechanisms has drastically declined. As a consequence, legitimatizing the 'individual-group', 'constituent parts-society' relations becomes more salient. For now the special nature of political relations comes into focus. These involve the articulation of the diverse and often conflicting interests and purposes of the constituent parts with those activities and mobilization as well as disposal of resources which must necessarily be expended to maintain the organization as a going concern. Since the two meaning codes of authority suggested here as invariants derive from the work of Swanson (1967) as does this formulation of the nature of political relations, a quotation is in order:

> All organizations are both associations and social systems . . . people form organizations, join them, and remain in them in part for what they individually get from them. If the organization no longer profits them, they will abandon it if they can . . . *An association is a relationship among its participants, each being tied to the other because dependent upon them for the satisfaction of his own needs.* It happens, however, that to get what they want from an association, its members must also make an effort to maintain it. *They must consider the special problems of keeping it in operation and must devote time, effort, and other resources to that end* . . . In large organizations some people come quickly to have special responsibility for these tasks of maintaining the organization. *They speak in the interests of those tasks and not simply in their own personal interests* . . . But in *any* organization all participants must on occasion do likewise. *In the degree to which,* . . . , *people act as agents of the organization itself, the organization becomes a social system* (Swanson 1967:31-2; emphases added).

Accordingly, the essence of political relations is to be found in the fact that they articulate the associational and social system aspects of collective life. Beginning with their differentiation and persistent since, every central government faces the task to co-ordinate the activities of groups in society which: (1) have a certain autonomy *vis à vis* central control behaviourally and/or normatively to varying degrees and (2) are characterized by diverse and frequently conflicting group interests. Consequently, ever since, the politics of centre-periphery relations has been saddled with a dilemma. Central government depends on the support of organized social interests with diverse purposes. But it also claims a monopoly over the legitimate use of force. Therefore, central government must assert the existence of one common interest transcending all particularist group interests. Since one can safely assume that some periphery groups are better organized than others which also means that they control more of a society's scarce and unequally distributed resources than others, it follows that at any given moment in time central government is more contingent on some groups for support than others. The dilemma of politics then is a product of a factually unequal contingency of central government on the periphery and the normative need to promulgate a universal overarching common interest as a source of contingency which is credibly devoid of group-discriminatory characteristics. That dilemma cannot be 'rationalized away' in the sense of making the contradiction disappear. Finding greater acceptance of the dilemma through legal codification aiming at reduction of arbitrariness and specification for different functional authority relations likely constitute the only 'rationalization' to be found.

In the Occident finding acceptance of the dilemma involved the development of meaning codes of legitimate authority which resulted from a correlated struggle about man's dependency on God *and* the social meanings of political interdependence. There was a relationship between the dilemma of politics of historical societies and the emergence of monotheism as well as between the struggles about the nature of the deity as regards the question of its immanence and the way the dilemma of legitimate authority was 'settled' (Swanson 1967:23, 42, 232). For purposes of generalization beyond the Western case and making the postulate of the Reformation fall-out hypothesis work, Swanson's analysis is very useful. Stripped of its content-particularities, this correlated religio-political conflict resulted in political legitimacy principles highly suggestive of the very nature of finding evolutionarily successful mechanisms to cope with such dilemmas.

The general formula seems to be this: at higher stages of evolution people typically face dilemmas irresolvable in principle, but needing resolution in practice. Coping with the dilemma in a fashion 'adequate' to the evolutionary normative complexity achieved amounts to development of some interpretive schema that (1) places the horns of the dilemma into a hierarchical relation to each other, but (2) recognizes normative contingency between the two thus avoiding domination of one over the other. Such hierarchization without domination implies that the interpretative schema *must* preserve the idea of a tension-laden contingency including relative autonomy between higher and lower components. In authority relations the components are 'the parts' of society and 'the whole' of society, or the 'associational' and 'social system' aspects of social organization.

Swanson's data show only two such interpretive schemas or ideal-typical 'solutions' to the politics dilemma. They are so general as to suggest application beyond the Occident. In one solution intrinsic primacy was assigned to the social system aspect of organization; in the other such primacy involving the symbolization of some 'greater reality' went to the associational aspect. In *both*, however, the element of lesser reality or importance was explicitly recognized. For in both cases a monotheistic deity symbolized men's experience with the purposes and activities of independent organizations by emphasizing the idea of 'an *overarching source of decision and purpose* (providing) unity among *groups diverse in purpose*' (Swanson 1967:23, emphasis added). Crucial to Swanson's analysis is men's experience with social interdependence and its authoritative regulation as well as their experience of interdependency with God. And with the roles of political subject and believer differentiated (Bellah 1964), this also involved men's 'social' and subjective religious identities.

For present purposes Swanson's findings are the significant facts. They tell us that a correlated struggle about the nature of God and the nature of meaningful authority[11] evolved solutions at the level of basic principles as regards man's contingency on man *and* the issue of 'individualism', that is, personal responsibility for articulating obligations to society and to self. These solutions were couched at a level of generality sufficient for all subsequent *inclusion* phenomena. The latter refer to the way in which industrialization, mass communication, mass education, mass conscription, and political mass mobilization — these belfries of modernization theory — included the mass of the population into the dilemma of politics in the broad sense of participation in co-operative systems.

What is asserted here is that the Reformation Settlement produced two *final* ideal-typical *solutions* to the authority-identity dilemma of politics *in one restricted sense*. The sense covers the principles on which obedience is owed. Under the *ex parte* code one must obey because diverse social identities have constructed a common purpose; under the *ex toto* code one must obey because commonalities have been mobilized to defeat diverse identities. Under the former, a common purpose is a negotiated social order, under the latter the common purpose is an immanent given that must be awakened. Only these solutions to the dilemma of politics are final. But elaboration in terms of spelling out their meaning and codification particularly as regards co-operative systems with different functional significance for society constitutes continuing evolutionary process. The significance of such 'spellings out' of meaning in industrial relations and the doctor-patient collectivity will be illustrated below.

The absence of a tight correlation between type of régime and authority code — as evident in the Venetian Republic, a democracy with an *ex toto* code — does not mean, however, complete independence between the two. It invites instead extension and application of Parsons' four-function paradigm in the following three tasks: (1) classifying régime types in industrial society, (2) locating the meaning codes 'hidden' beneath the surface differences of régime and thus showing one reason for their persistence through (3) demonstrating that such codes articulate antinomy functions (across the diagonals in the usual four-function-box) in Parsons' (1963a:259–60) media paradigm applicable to any differentiated polity.

Apart from the possibility that this treatment might render a sharper focus to genuine theoretical interests in the problem of 'partial modernization' (Gusfield 1967; Bendix 1964:177–213), elucidating the universal functions of such codes constitutes the most general explanation of their persistence or invariance.

LOCATING THE AUTHORITY CODES IN A FUNCTIONAL TYPOLOGY OF MODERN POLITIES

There seem to be four basic types of political régime extant in industrial societies: consultative authoritarianism, corporatism, competitive democracy, and consociational democracy.

Following Weber in the recognition that charisma purely exists only in *status nascendi* must rule out totalitarianism as a stable type. Furthermore, while the one case where it occurred in a society with a fully developed economy, Nazi-Germany, had little chance in developing routinization of charisma, the decline of Stalin's personality cult and the subsequent failure in the Soviet Union to develop another, points to the transformation of totalitarianism in the modern world into what is called here 'consultative authoritarianism'. Studies of conflict management and more general analyses (Ploss 1965; Koklowicz 1967; Stewart 1969; Meyer 1965; Fischer 1968; Hough 1969) seem to permit the following clues as regards the authority code at work. First, functional interests must be disrobed of their functional particularisms before they can legitimately float demands or the proferring of advice. This is related to the prominent role of AGITPROP efforts which wage a constant war against 'the disenchantment of the world' by offering meaningful interpretations of events under *one* umbrella of interpretations.[12] Such institutionalized ideological-moral inequality is not only presumed, but also organized, in a communications bureaucracy which functions in public life in ways analogously to and equally important as the institutionalized office charisma of the Roman Catholic Church. For the destruction of ascribed differential salvation chances, that the early modern stage produced, does not mean the end of institutionalized moral inequality (Parsons 1968). With the Kantian breakthrough it is not only possible to treat theology as a science (Bellah 1964:371); the same applies to secular moral philosophy, as for example the well known claim of Marxism-Leninism to scientific status. That status, combined with the monopoly position of the political centre as its sole interpreter, gives consultative authoritarianism a 'theocratic aspect': power and its most important legitimacy resources emanate from one source. In Russia, this represents a historical reversal of that other alternative to institutionalized hierocracy, the ceasaropapist solution. For Russian 'feudalism' during the historical period was closer to caesaropapism, in that power could be used to get other resources (including to a certain extent legitimation), but 'it was much more difficult to get power through such other resources' (Eisenstadt 1971a:96). Secondly, interest articulation requires the appearance of stalactite (from the top downwards) mobilization (Nettl 1967:271ff), while interest aggregation proceeds according to shifting alliances among functional interests in fact, though in theory according to superiority in divining the meaning of unchanging Marxist-Leninist principles under changing environmental conditions. Finally, whatever the reality in the balance of forces between bureaucratic vested interests and the interests of clients, the parallelism of 'technical' and 'leadership' hierarchies serves to symbolize the supremacy of party over all other interests. If Fischer's (1968) theory about the role of 'double-executives' is to be believed, then consultative authoritarianism might be a very adequate label for this type of polity if for no other reason than this: the capacity of leadership to draw on special expertise in policy making has certainly been institutionalized to the point where any obvious inferiority to the United States (Rose 1967) on this score is no longer discernible.

The classic case of corporatism can be found in the Iberian Peninsula and its Latin American off-shoots.[13] Already a 'centralized state' in the fifteenth century, rather than featuring the political policentrism characteristic of feudal hierocracy, the long-term military use of religious beliefs, and the very forging of Iberian consciousness out of the encounter of Christianity with Islam and Judaism, supplied historic and early modern Spain with a certain amount of theocratic tendencies, a 'theobiosis' (Castro 1954:17, 19, 132, 153). Towards modernity, and particularly overseas, this history worked itself out in a caesaropapist direction characterized by an uncanny mixture of obsessive idealism and slipshod ideological sloganeering with imported models of and for society, behind which seem to stand neither understanding nor genuine commitment as regards anything fundamental in the political structure of society (Castro 1954:127; Tannenbaum 1965:136-137; Linz 1964).[14] The caesaropapist tendencies are mild, occurring only if there is conflict at the same level which tends to be typically avoided so far as at all feasible. But in Latin America there is continuity in this tendency. For there the church became subordinate to secular authority as regards buildings, nomination of priests, collection of tithes, and even publication of papal bulls fairly early during the colonial period. Also during the wars for independence from Iberia the lower clergy had no role in this struggle while the higher clergy was allied with Spain (Tannenbaum 1965:60). And while Rome never came to acknowledge the state's right to meddle in church affairs, even today a Leftist parish priest can easily get into trouble with secular authority, though a bishop far more rarely, if at all.

The central distinctive character of contemporary corporatism is 'expressive' politics: the use of power in the service of a belief officially in theory and its expenditure in response to interests in practice; insecurity concerning feasibility and fulfilment of the promise of belief, and a near-selfconscious refusal to escape from the importance of believing towards a more pragmatic ordering of authority relations through reduction of diffuseness in obligations (Castro 1954:55). The retention of personalism has its root in the persistence of *images of the good personality to be*, described for the Spaniard as '*an impulse to express the consciousness of his existence in his world*. . . . The characteristically European activity of doing and reasoning, in which the agent or the thinker is unmindful of his empiric presence in his work, has as its counterpart in Iberia *a personalized activity which is not evaluated according to its useful results, but rather according to what the person involved is or wants to be*, . . .' (Castro 1954:4 emphasis added). The most important persistent trait of expressive politics has been an idealist 'halo' that pertains to all legitimate authority; 'for in the Latin American tradition, authority that is not moral is intolerable' (Tannenbaum 1965:68).

Though pertinent available research remains less clear than in any of the other types of régime (Stevens 1974; Malloy 1974; Schmitter 1971), the following aggregate picture may be offered.

The whole-parts dilemma in terms of a differing reality ascribed to society as a whole and its constituent parts remains compromised in the Hispanic authority code. Such compromise involves a conception that some greater and lesser forms of cultural traditions must interact if a common weal is to become manifest. Hierarchically organized functional interests of diverse kinds must engage in contest seeking to subordinate each other if the true interest of the whole is to become visible. This follows in part a historically conditioned instability in the corporate stratification typical in this case. For where 'belief rather than deed counted, . . . and the shining sword of the Apostle . . . made them all equal' (Castro 1954:157), respect for hierarchy was potentially challenged by appeal to ascriptive egalitarianism. Practically and in contemporary forms this means that inequalities among internally hierarchically organized corporate groups which form the relevant units of stratification in this case cannot be institutionalized in as stable a fashion as in the other régimes. Stratification in Iberian societies remains subject to continuous challenges and reassertions through the political process (Rogowski and Wasserspring 1971). Such struggles take the form of multiple parallel hierarchies attempting to construe an overall hierarchy on their relations. Whosoever gains supremacy, for however long, claims the role of promulgator of the interests of all. If this is not a fundamentally wrong interpretation of

Huntington's (1968:192–263) 'praetorian society' metaphor, it is essential to keep in mind that relative constancy in executive control of one institution, such as the military, does not at all amount to the dominance of one functional institution. For these systems are support-contingent, and policy outcomes are a function of changing institutional alliances on which executive incumbents depend. The other contrast feature to consultative authoritarianism rests with the compromise on interest articulation patterns typical for corporatism. Following the explicit recognition of the need to represent functional interests with genuine quasi-autonomous rights of their own, which seems to coexist with the notion of the absolute need to 'dictate obligations' from a supravening perspective, interest articulation takes a mixture of stalactite and stalagmite forms which tends to be positively correlated with the rank position of a given hierarchically organized functional interest in the pecking order of all such interests. Well organized blue collar unions and the 'professional' interests of the service bureaucracies seem to operate with stalactite techniques, the underorganized *campesino* strata more with stalagmite modes. This seems to be a function of command over more sophisticated political means as against sheer numbers, which in turn rests on the degree to which a given group has secured a form of liturgical entrenchment into the critical sectors of the economy. In sum, the most telling difference between consultative authoritarianism and corporatism is the presence of a systematically rationalized ideology in the former and its relative absence in the latter. This alone would seem to account for much in the 'mimicry', the inarticulateness, and the contrariness on which the corporatist compromised perception of ultimate societal reality rests.[15] At the same time, despite the compromises, the authority code displays more *ex toto* than *ex parte* features.

Following the work of Lijphart and Huntington already referred to, we can summarize the principle differences between the competitive and the consociational types of democracy as follows. They share a notion of the *constructed* collective interest assigning greater reality to constituent parts of society. But the pursuit of this construction by pure contest can be afforded only in those cases characterized by a relatively homogeneous political culture. In the consociational case where the latter is fragmented and historically based on ascriptive collectivities, which, furthermore, during the stage of nation-building when the state-church separation issue predominated gave rise to party-formation (Lipset and Rokkan 1967), such a path is precluded and all efforts are geared toward aggregating those interests compatible with a shared commitment to the maintenance of essentially segregated political subcultures. Consequently, stalagmite mobilization is quite legitimate in competitive, but factually 'broken' in consociational, democracy where the electoral process is completely divorced from interest aggregation and amounts to a legitimization ritual engaging parallel hierarchies of *zuilen* or *Lager* with stalactite mobilizations all orientated to fixed constituencies. As to administration in terms of the patterning of bureaucracy-client relations, democracies, regardless of type, seem to be characterized more by clients sharing responsibility with administrators for policy implementation on a near-egalitarian basis[16] than is the case in consultative authoritarianism and corporatism.

A more systematic account of the elements of authority codes used above will be rendered below. At this point one needs to emphasize that what has been outlined is in the nature of ideal-types. So conceived, it is possible to locate these types in a four-function classification.

Following Parsons (1959, 1951:180–200) any subsystem of action can be analysed from a perspective of having to solve four universal functional problems (adaptation, goal-attainment, integration, and pattern maintenance). Since no system can fully solve all four problems at the same time, one can classify them on the basis of which of the four problems is given primary emphasis. This applies to systems at any level of analysis and therefore to the polity. It too has to solve the four problems despite the fact that it has goal-attainment functional significance for society as a whole if one follows Durkheim's conception of the state as the value-implementive agency of society. The notion of one-function primacy as a classificatory device does not vitiate the need to solve all problems through phase-movements of a system (Parsons 1953a). All it says is that polities can be usefully classified according to which one of their four functions they seem to assign paramount importance. The focus of classification is a functional perspective on the polity-society relation. One can distinguish overall organization of political structure and process which (1) is geared toward maximizing adaptation to utilitarian interests (the *a*-primacy polity); (2) maximizes the provision of direction *for* all functional interests in society (the *g*-primacy case); (3) maximally serves the integration of functional interests *in* society (the *i*-primacy case); or (4) constitutes primarily an *expressive* arena *of* constituent parts (the *l*-primacy case).

In this light competitive democracy figures as an *a*-primacy case. Historically the United States is the classic example. Here modernization of society occurred through private economic and social forces, not through government, leaving the latter relatively retarded with federalism and political parties the only significant additions to the polity. Thus the polity mainly adapted to social and economic change (Huntington 1968:93–139, 130, 132) though more recently she may be in an integrative phase (Parsons 1969b:438). Lijphart's (1968) analysis of The Netherlands makes her the classic example of consociational democracy which has *i*-primacy. The Soviet Union ranks as the most important empirical example of consultative authoritarianism, a case of *g*-primacy, and the 'praetorianism' of many Latin American cases are the ones best approximating corporatism with *l*-primacy. Figure 1 locates these ideal types in the usual format of Parsonian functionalism.

Figure 1

The Modern Societal System and Its Polity Types*

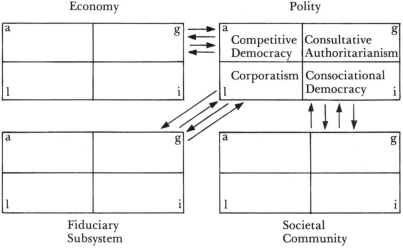

* Following Gould's (1976) revised interchange paradigm clarifies the polity types' one-function primacy through the lens of mediated interchanges.

If the most salient feature of feudal hierocracy was indeed the curious mixture of the contrary elements of 'personalized fealty' and yet a 'contractual stipulation of right and duties', of 'hereditary controls over land' and yet 'a depersonalized rent nexus' (Weber 1968:1074), then Figure 1 illuminates how the rudimentary parliamentarism of the waning Middle Ages in the Occident constitutes a precursor of the two modern democratic types. 'Personalized fealty' and 'hereditary controls over land' stress the famous integrative aspects of the medieval synthesis which found their extension in consociational democracy where fealty has been transformed into accommodative élite behaviours presupposing a shared primary commitment to work jointly against all divisive forces in society, and where the 'hereditary control over land' has been institutionalized into the ascriptive organization of political support. On the other hand, the 'contractual stipulations' and 'the depersonalized rent nexus' display the maximization of adaptive functions of the polity to society so characteristic of competitive democracy. As all summarizing devices carry the danger of oversimplification, it should be stressed that the 'bordering' of competitive democracy on the economy does not imply the predominance of unmitigated cash-nexus polities; but it does refer to the dominance of regulating autonomously adaptive groups of all types relative to other political objectives. Historically a parallel case holds for the two non-democratic modern polities. Both of these would seem to have retained important elements of liturgical political resource mobilization so prevalent in patrimonial bureaucratic empires. One, the corporatist form, constitutes an extension in decentralized form, the other, an extension in centralized form.

Turning to the most general explanation as to why there is invariance in authority codes, it is useful to re-emphasize two points. Following the logic of one-function primacy, it must be clear that all modern polities have their consultative authoritarian, their competitive, their consociational, and indeed their corporatist elements. As Rose's (1967) study makes clear with the case of medicine, there certainly is representation of functional interests in American political process. The same is true for Britain as well as the Soviet Union (Gilison 1972). Indeed functional interest representation is a moral duty of institutionalized expertise in modern society in general (Baum 1972). Though the modes vary profoundly in detail, professionalism means autonomy, hence a corporatist element is ineradicable from modern political process everywhere. Equally, executive functioning involves an element of authoritarianism, interest aggregation one of consociationalism, and the pursuit of office an element of competitiveness.

Next, the opposite function types of polities share one meaning code each. In the democratic case this is the *ex parte* code, in the non-democratic cases the *ex toto* code, a matter to which we shall return later. In the present perspective of the universal functional elements of any polity this means that *elements* of each code are also present. Displaying these features, as in Figure 2, shows that these contrary elements of codes regulate antinomious functions in the polity.

The *ex parte* elements regulate interchange across the double functional boundary between external-instrumental and internal-consummatory function; the *ex toto* elements perform this role for internal-instrumental and external-consummatory functions. It is important to notice that in each case the codes of the same societal media are involved, *viz* money and influence across the a-i axis and power and value-commitments across the l-g axis. This yields a proposition. Since one-function primacy in any system means relative under-servicing of the functionally opposite needs and interests, it is not only likely that primary phasing in political process involves oscillations back and forth across the diagonals in the functional

Figure 2

Universal Functional Aspects of the Modern Polity

Polity

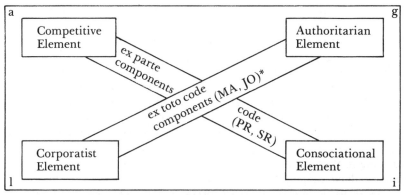

*where: MA = Moral Authority Code; JO = Jurisdiction of Office; PR = Property Law;
SR = Stratification Rules (Parsons 1963a, 1963b, 1968a)

table *because* the 'typically neglected' needs demand attention first when strain builds up, but it is also empirically probable by virtue that identical codes and media constitute the function of adequate medicine, as it were. Thus the hypothesis of invariance in the primacy of one type of meaning code as against another rests importantly on the recognition that such empirical oscillation across one or the other diagonal does indeed touch all functional bases, so meeting external and internal as well as instrumental and consummatory problems. This is the most general reason for in-variance.[17] Democracies oscillate between consociational and competitive stresses primarily, non-democracies do so primarily between corporatist and authoritarian emphases in political process. And because all func-tional aspects are touched through such oscillations, the basic codes at issue here need not change in their primacy at the symbolic legitimating level. Put differently, genuine one-function primacy constitutes too un-stable an arrangement to qualify as an evolutionary invariant since the historic stage. But oscillating 'double function' primacy, if it involves antinomious functions across the diagonals in the usual function diagram, does qualify. It is because the two authority codes under consideration regulate antinomy functions that placing one above the other can con-stitute a long term solution to the political paradox born during the historic stage. The solution is the hierarchization of horns of a dilemma which without would be on an equal plane.

FINAL SPECIFICATION: INVARIANT AUTHORITY CODES: 'PARTS AND WHOLES'

The codes at issue here constitute a normative rule which specifies the grounds on which a decision by central government ought to exact obedience by all units in society. Thus an *ex parte* code asserts that such a decision is binding on all units of society because special and particular interests *in* society have participated in its making their status as such special and particularist interests. This implies a theory about finding the common or general will. That theory states: the only way of finding the common unitary purpose of a society is to let the diverse and particularist purposes of constituent groups engage in direct negotiation, whatever its form; for it is constituent groups which make up a society, and only their direct encounter will render what all have in common. In contrast, an *ex toto* code asserts that a centre decision is binding because none of the many and diverse special particularist interests in society has participated in its making in their status as diverse particularist interests. This too implies a theory about finding the general will, and it proclaims: the only way to arrive at the common will is to let special roles designed for its discernment do their work undisturbed and unencumbered by divisive interests, because society in its essence is an immanent reality rather than a negotiated order and all its constituent particularist parts derive their legitimate status only from the function they perform for the whole.

These types of codes show impressive historical stability over long periods of time. Counting only polities which maintained their independence throughout the periods under review, and classified in this dichotomous fashion, Swanson's data reveal the following information: (1) over a 290 year period from 1490–1780, 20 of 26 polities maintained stability in these codes; (2) over about a century from the Reformation Settlement to 1780, 26 out of 27 maintained stability (Swanson 1967: 238–41). Furthermore, *before the French Revolution* there was no correlation between these codes and the types of régime normally classified as more or less democratic in nature. Brandenburg-Prussia, for example, showed continuity in an *ex parte* code. The Venetian Republic, on the other hand, showed continuity in an *ex toto* code, and it was a democracy by common sense standards. *After the French Revolution*, while further domestic legal development may tend toward bringing code and régime form in line, if that were the only factor, such development cannot be predicted because of outside factors in the international relations context. Here one need mention only dependencies and interdependencies involving concrete flows of resources as well as more symbolic matters, as for example the fact that fascist régimes today lack legitimacy in the international community simply because they are designated fascist, and quite apart from their performance.

The codes at issue here say nothing in themselves concerning who participates in centre decision making, but they say a lot about the symbolic legitimizations of such participation. One may safely assume that the adaptive function of any modern polity demands participation in centre policy making on the part of specialized expertise, or the non-political technical periphery of society as one may call it, as positive functions of the division of labour in society, the extent to which the polity is an 'activist' one, and the degree of contingency of intra-societal interest-realization on the relevant international environment. *Pari passu* modern societies need more participation by the non-political technical periphery than pre-industrial societies, and those who are geographically located within the centres of international power blocs need more than those sitting on the geographic periphery and enjoying benign neglect from major powers. Under the *ex toto* rule legitimate participation in goal-choice action at the political centre on the part of the technical periphery demands that such periphery symbolically divest itself of its periphery characteristics, while the *ex parte* rule insists on the opposite: symbolic retention of periphery characteristics.

One should note that the latter rule is more easily practised than the former. One can simply rely on the 'integrity' of 'societal nature', as it were, drawing on the relevant resources from the division of labour in the occupational complex. That rule indicates what the respective functional primacies of adaptation *to* and integration *of* societal forces imply, *viz* leaving the drive towards the implementation of societal values largely to non-political organizations while letting the polity concentrate on their facilitation and regulation, respectively.

But the task of politics is relatively more difficult under the *ex toto* rule. Here periphery participation at the centre's goal-setting and choice-making activities was to strip off particularisms of value differences inevitably associated with possession of special skills and knowledge. It must achieve the awakening of value commonalities, however, without significant costs in special knowledge and skill capacities. To illustrate, it is rather likely that an economist's image of society is largely composed of economic data. Indeed in his role as economist it is part of his special professional morality to see his society in terms of economic requisites. The psychiatrist's image of his society is probably a product of his mental health lenses and, once again, that is part of his professional obligation. Professions, so one is wont to assume, are granted monopoly rights over their affairs in modern society *not* because of economic welfare considerations coupled with the political centre's need for reliable resources and just sufficient support as in ancient modes of liturgical resource mobilization, *but rather* because only the members of a profession possess requisite technical knowledge to regulate their affairs. That means inevitably leaving various aspects of society's health in various hands. Yet when it comes to value choice, that is, the political centre's most salient political obligation which is to determine what men shall be made to care more about: economic growth *or* distributive justice, defence *or* mental health, then the *ex toto* code commands that no particularist lens be permitted a chance to pollute what men shall be so made to care, *by* the use of power, and hence *at* the recipients' risk of negative sanctions, whether situational such as jail or internal such as guilt (Parsons 1963a, 1963b, 1968a).

The moral use of power at the centre always involves a double dilemma. One is that it is the centre's obligation to make and enforce such choices and a kind of sin to evade, and sometimes even to delay, the need for choice. The other dilemma is that these are real choices in the short run, though not in the long one. They do involve differential resource allocation drawn from a symbolically equal, common pool of citizenship obligations despite progressive taxation ideals. Related to this double dilemma is another, to be considered further below, which is that the centre has to make such short-run choices in the long-run interest of an entity: society which, because of its presumed indefinite life-span, faces no such choice, but has to exact the sacrifice of choice from definitely short-run creatures as finite, mortal individuals.

Dilemmas of this kind permit of no 'final' solution. They cannot be rationalized in the sense of making the illogical logical after all, or making them significantly more easy to bear. Rationalization of dilemmas such as these is confined to legal codification in a direction of reducing ar-bitrariness in authority relations and incessantly further specification of the meaning of obedience in different types of authority settings such as the family, the factory, the doctor's surgery and the hospital, as well as obligations to the state. But as far as the raw and contrasting principles of legitimate authority are concerned, interpretable meaningful acceptance is all they permit. Both codes do this by constructing a kind of social reality of shared interests across the contrary time horizons involved. The *ex parte* code achieves that by postulating a greater reality of finite man than of indefinite society with the presumption of an eternal cycle by which there is and can never be more than the real interests of people, a version in which society and man become one by the reduction of the properties of the former to the latter. The *ex toto* code manages the problem in opposite fashion, reducing man in his social essence to society by postulating a greater reality of the latter and assigning ephemeralness to private selves. Both versions, therefore, must permit variant and compatible forms of 'individualism' if one subscribes to Durkheim's theory of the latter as a profoundly distinctive feature of modern society.

This, it must be emphasized, is a *general* reason concerning the invariance of authority codes. There are more specific reasons for such invariance which cannot, unfortunately — because of space limitations — be systematically presented in this context.

THE SECOND OBJECT OF INVARIANCE: TYPES OF INDIVIDUALISM

Given that the historical and early modern stages of evolution evolved a cultural imperative for individuals to articulate the contrary time perspectives of obligation to society and to self, it is since these stages that 'the conscious experience of time (has become) the staff that has helped modern man in his laborious march toward autonomous being' (Castro 1954:479). And, given two authority codes legitimatizing the attendant responsibilities in different ways, that march must have involved common as well as variant elements in the quest for personal autonomy or individualism.

Starting with the common elements, it is essential to stress that even 'primitive' and 'archaic' man was a Median actor capable of some reflection as regards 'self', 'other', and 'world' as separate objects with potentially problematic relations. In that sense individualism is treated in the social sciences as a transhistorical cross-cultural universal (Schlottmann 1968). However, given the low level of differentiation at these first two stages of evolution, a structured demand for such reflection hardly existed. Just such a demand arose, however, with the emergence of a sense of 'personal self' above and beyond all social identities and the idea of personal responsibility concerning all conduct *vis à vis* a monotheistically concentrated source of ultimate meaning during the historical and early modern stages (Bellah 1964: 366–70). The result was Durkheim's 'cult of the individual'. Minimally this covers three things. One is having a sense of identity, a cross-situationally and transtemporally stable sense of self beyond all role entanglements. A second element covers a sense of freedom of choice in investing that self more into one role or set of roles than into others coupled with the burden of personal responsibility for such choice. A third covers freedom of choice and personalized responsibility for a sequential order through the life-course as regards such 'personal investment of self' into various roles.

The individualism at issue may be described as an institutionalized and internalized capacity of the 'personal self' for partial self-direction in multiple environments. These involve the internal action environments of culture, society, and behavioural organism and the 'non-action environments' of nature, and 'the problem of ultimate meaning' (Parsons

1966:5–29; 1971: 4–28). This Parsonian interpretation of Durkheim's cult of the individual as an evolutionary universal needs amendment in but one respect, treated below, which calls for adding history as an important partial environment of action to the others just enumerated.

At this point the idea of *partial* self-direction needs emphasis. Modern action systems are so complex that they require a balance of inner and outer controls as regards individuals. Neither socialization, enculturation, nor direct social control could conceivably suffice for a social structure with built-in fluidity and change. To this point one can follow Schlottmann (1968). But his conceptualization of individualism as an additional mechanism of integration operative through 'personalization' and his insistence that it occurs only in cases where the value-system is distinctly 'individualist', stressing in fact a kind of individualist utilitarianism as a priority commitment (Schlottmann 1968:65, 110ff) remains inadequate in that it over-emphasizes the need for inner and under-emphasizes the need for outer controls (Miller and Swanson 1960). However limited the empirical base, problematical the analytical distinction (Wilson 1974:21–30), and improbable the finding of the centrality of 'shame' in high civilization cases (Eberhard 1967), the earlier literature on 'shame' and 'guilt cultures' was probably right as regards basic differences between primitive and archaic societies on the one hand and all more highly differentiated societies (Piers and Singer 1953). The individualism at issue here must involve both outer and inner controls and a balance between the two. Ever since historical and early modern times men need both; the only difference being in the number of men in society who have such need, which grows as one approaches modernity. A sensitive gyroscope to pick up orientating cues from a fluidly and complexly organized environment is needed just as much as a conscience structured with commitments to highly abstract evaluative standards. Neither the predominance of one nor of the other will do as some literature suggested (Riesman and Glazer 1952). The reason is simple. Modernity is organized complexity. Standards of evaluation must be abstract; they cannot involve detailed prescriptions of conduct in concrete situations. Persons must be committed to abstract standards such that detail specification of integrous situational meanings can be entrusted to them. But they must also be sensitive to the opinion of others such that personalized implementation remains sufficiently supplied with informational variety to constitute responsible implementation that can be justified *vis à vis* others in case of demand.

History must be added as a relevant partial environment to action since the time of the historical and early modern stages. This is so because developments during these stages incorporated historical consciousness, and with that history itself, into the organized complexity that systems of action have come to be since. Basically two reasons suggest this. Firstly, the development of religious symbolization in the historic stage characterized by the emergence of a monotheistically concentrated contingency focus on ultimate meaning also generalized societal values to the point where, as has been pointed out above, they came to constitute the identity of a society. Already at that stage the state became the value-implementive agency of society. Onto this background of a societal identity and an agency legitimatized for its preservation, the Reformation-stage added the imperative of action to revise society in line with cultural ideals. In principle this turned the state into an actor legitimatized in terms of contributing to the perfection of society. Ever since, demands for social change have had historical roots at least in part. Change in society follows patterns of perceived historical imperfections, and their correction legitimatizes mobilization for change no matter what other models for change may be involved. Secondly, this is so because no mobilization for change *in* society can entirely disregard the perennial problem of mobilization for defence *of* society which was another inevitable consequence of the attainment of societal identity. Thus, whether it is for internal development and change or for external defence, societies since these two crucial stages of evolution rely in their political process on as much uncontested history as they can in order to mobilize the largest possible quantum of political support for the realization of national goals. The term uncontested history also points out that history is but a partial environment to action. Being subject to revision regarding the meaning of facts, but protected from rampant revisionism through scientifically established facts, history constitutes but a partially manipulable resource for the steering of conduct in the present.

Next, given the institutionalization of a 'revisable self' in conjunction with that of a 'revisable society', increased historical consciousness can be postulated as operative in the private lives of individuals as well. A first consideration here is the ubiquitous fact of man's extreme infancy dependence on caretaker roles. No one can ever escape wholly from his social and biological parentage. One also tends to assume that membership in a family of procreation recapitulates, in however modified a form, key themes of childhood for their adult members. A second cause of increased historical consciousness on the personal plane—who one was, is, and will be—then results from simultaneous membership in the 'erotic association' that is the modern nuclear family on the one hand and that other differentiation-product of the household-economy, the bureaucratized occupational complex on the other (Smelser 1959; Parsons 1968b:16). For such simultaneous membership requires participation in normative systems antithetical in content as well as personal assumption of responsibility for the implementation of different norms, most notably those demanding action according to the different time-horizons involved. Thirdly and finally, whatever the range of variation among industrial societies in actual amounts and types of social mobility as well as normative orientations to it (Fox and Miller 1966), increased consciousness about social mobility also constitutes an evolutionary universal. This too emphasizes to each one's stratum origin as one moves through a life-course. These considerations should suffice to assert that the individualisms here at issue must cope with contingency on history both publicly and privately, collectively and individually.

The common elements of the individualisms in question must, then, manage contingency on several action environments as outlined. They must involve a balance of inner and outer controls. But the way in which such contingencies are managed differs. The differences with respect to culture and society are the main focus of interest here.

The first difference between the two forms of individualism derives directly from the 'deep contrast' in the image of society associated with the two authority codes discovered by Swanson. This contrast bears repetition. Under the *ex parte* code, society is never more than an order negotiated from its constituent parts which in turn have greater 'reality'. Where the *ex toto* code prevails, 'society as a whole' has deeper, because immanent, reality than its constituent parts, which in turn derive their 'lesser reality' in secondary fashion only by assuming a role in a functional division of labour. If one assumes that the question of immanence, in both its outcomes of affirmation and negation, applies to the image of society *and* that of personality, the first sense of individualism of interest here is supplied by Swanson himself. It is one compatible with the *ex toto* code of authority.

'Immanence of soul is most likely to appear . . . if a man's personality cannot be readily construed as acquired through his importation of the purposes, traditions, and attitudes of groups to which he belongs' (Swanson 1967:23). Therefore, in the opposite case, when the basic conception of personality is non-immanentalist, personal identity is seen as the product of a biography of group affiliation. One way to formulate this difference is that a sense of personal identity compatible with an *ex toto* code demands that one seek the source of one's uniqueness outside the members of one's immediate group affiliations and use these near-others as contrast-resources to separate constantly 'personal' and 'social' selves. Individualism under an *ex toto* code involves a more direct relation between the individual and cultural standards. That relation must of course be mediated, but one uses 'specialist' roles for that mediation rather than Mead's 'generalized other'. Since immanence connotes a *given essence*, the focal points of a sense of personal self are ideals rather than concrete others and their practice. Such ideals, furthermore, are not chosen as one chooses the parts of a menu but are, in however incoherent a form, givens to which one must yield. The sense of personal identity is realized in some kind of struggle over what one *must be* and *must do*, never just over what one wants. The *ex toto* individualist gets a sense of personal self through conforming to the demands of group affiliations to the hilt of his capacity, while at the same time upholding a near-ideological commitment to the idea of never becoming what he does as a mere social actor. In the extreme case, he knows that he is not just the sum total of his social identities because he can do perfectly—in terms of fulfilling his social obligations—what he himself does not want to do at all. While the ideal-typical opposite of a deceiving con-man, *ex toto* individualism succeeds by playing nothing but roles on quite a conscious fashion yet manages never to think of a personalized self as a role player at all. The best short formula to describe this type might be to say that *ex toto* individualism amounts to being a sociopath without being a deviant. As McClelland (1964:80) put it for his ideal-typical German: 'Paradoxically it is the very sacrifice of one's personal interests, feelings, and pleasures that one gets a sense of individuality . . .' After all, how can one have a sense of personal self if that, at any given moment in time, were no more than the internalization of one's concrete affiliational ties? How can there be a sense of personal self, so says the logic of *ex toto* individualism, if one is never more than a programme of societal identities?

But what the *ex toto* individualist abhors as slavish conformity at any given moment of time is precisely what the *ex parte* individualist uses to gain a sense of personalized self throughout all time. His mode of realizing a revisable self takes the form of a sequential movement through a series of group affiliations, each one of which he takes as sources of deep identification. His success as an individualist derives from his ability for deep yet temporary identification. Given the notion that 'no social order is possible except that based on the desires of its members' (McClelland 1964:73), what he wants becomes the focal point of the universe in which he seeks to gain a personal sense of self. Consequently, his is a kind of tenuous 'group-individualism' by which he genuinely feels, thinks, and acts in line with those of his associates without, however, this leading to a sense of permanent obligation to others. *Ex parte* individualism is also extremely voluntaristic. As McClelland put it for his ideal-typical American, he acts according to the formula 'I want to freely choose to do well what others expect me to do' (McClelland 1964:72). This type can really believe in the particularist group perspectives with which he is engaged, but then also leave them behind if an opportunity arises, join another group and take on another set of perspectives. Being convinced in his heart that organizations are at bottom never more than associations formed for the mutual advancement of individual goals, he can also believe that he can contribute to organizational advancement by his departure; and, in the reverse case, his involuntary dismissal can be justified as being 'better for him'. The best short formula to describe this type may be that *ex parte* individualism amounts to group-conformism without a belief in any *sui generis* reality of groups.

In sum, the types of identity at issue here involve a reversal between the patterning of symbols concerning the greater or lesser reality of the individual or his groups and the behavioural strategies adopted to generate a sense of individualism. *Ex parte* individualism assigns greater reality to individuals and relegates groups to a piece of negotiated social order. But when it comes to implementing that symbolic order, a sense of personal identity is achieved through temporary deep identifications with groups and voluntaristic change of group affiliations through the life-course. *Ex toto* individualism, assigns greater reality to the group and lesser to the individual. But here a sense of personal identity above all identities is realized through perfection of role-conformity without any deep identification of mere social demands except a very deep indentification with permanent cultural ideals. The *ex parte* path of individuation involves a change through time of being, successively, different kinds of 'average man'; the *ex toto* path rests on a self-conscious concerned avoidance of ever being average man by adherence to explicit cultural ideals serving as the central resource for generating a sense of unique self on the one hand, and on formalized role-conformity as an instrumental concession for the achievement of personal identity on the other.

How groups can come to constitute a greater and externally given reality confronting the 'weak' individual clearly shows up in comparing socialization practices in Russia, France, and the United States. Soviet children display less 'anti-social' behaviour in general than American children. Furthermore, among Russians, peer-control exerts as much 'sociality' as adult-control which it does not in America (Bronfenbrenner 1970:78). Thus, when it comes to behaviour, institutionalized collectivism in Russia is more continuous across the generational barrier. Also, Soviet children strike the American observer as so well-behaved and 'strongly motivated to learn' as to display a definite *idealistic attitude to life* (Bronfenbrenner 1970:77). But when one examines conformity to overt external behaviour demands as contrasted with internalization of *social* standards such as telling the truth, it turns out that Soviet children stress far more the former and significantly less the latter than do children from countries of classic democracy such as Switzerland, the United Kingdom, and the United States (Bronfenbrenner 1970:81). Thus, one can observe the essential bifurcation among *ex parte* and *ex toto* identity formation already among twelve-year olds. The former seeks consistency between outer constraint and inner reality and finds a secure sense of self in being an average child. The latter, however, can already conform without 'becoming' what he adheres to by balancing outer control and inner experience through identification with ideal standards and selective dependency on their bearers and representatives in society. The key element in this early bifurcation seems to be the profound difference between the conception concerning the very nature of personality and the socialization ideals and practices following from it.

It is a basic assumption of Soviet personality psychology to view man as developing 'in the collective, through the collective, for the collective' (Bronfenbrenner 1962:83). When it comes to socialization ideals and practices, the Russian approach hinges everything on the natural postulation of a supraordinate goal shared alike by both parties across the socializer-socializee gap. American practice far more resembles confrontation across this gap with different commonalities shared separately on each side which have to be laboriously articulated with each other. In the Soviet Union, family authority is one essentially delegated from the state to the parents, and parental duties constitute but an instance of the essentially similar obligation to society exacted from all throughout life (Bronfenbrenner 1962:72). Under this symbolic umbrella, man is and never can be more than a part of society. Where a postulated supraordinate goal asserts symbolic sameness between parent and child, resources for generating a distinct sense of self must necessarily be located outside the direct relationship itself. Where the American can choose a near-generalized other, *viz* an age cohort member, to find distinctiveness of the group-contrast variety *vis à vis* parents, no such opportunity exists for the child in Russia. But one has to add the extraordinary stress on self-discipline, and its apparent effectiveness in conformity to overt behaviour demands in Russia, to see that the search for a 'personal self outside society' is not only motivationally necessary, but also socially possible. Persons can become predictable social actors through a deep introjection of ideal standards coupled with a primarily cognitive and almost instrumental attention to the opinion of generalized others. Then the interests of society are satisfied and details concerning commitment to articles of faith remain a matter of relative indifference to the immediate social environment of persons.

If the essence of corporatist politics — the advancement of collective over individual benefits — rests squarely on the institutionalization of a person's social stratum membership as *the* effective *social* identity, as Rogowski and Wasserspring (1973) have persuasively argued, a classic cultural locus of *ex toto* individualism should be the caste order of India. Not surprisingly, one finds there that Hindu *dharma* constitutes a religiously sanctioned set of social imperatives to observe the rights and obligations of one's station, but not any pronounced concern with the social enforcement of the individual's commitment to doctrinal details of religious belief. So long as a person does not violate the social conventions of caste 'he may think as he pleases' (Parsons 1937:557). Indeed Weber (1916–17:184) stressed complete inner detachment from outer conformity as a central characteristic of personalized salvational striving in that case.

In comparative work a culture which for whatever reasons develops value stances to sheer excess can be truly revealing because the comparative perspective prevents one from taking evidence at face value. As regards *ex toto* individualism, Spanish personalism proves revealing. Here the deep identification with abstract ideals coupled with an automatized social-expectational conformity has been so individuated, hence personalized as regards inner introjects, that belief frequently fails to function as a guide to shared commitments and action altogether. Instead one encounters compulsive rebelliousness, a repugnance toward social discipline, and the idea that non-submission to law constitutes the ultimate and noble expression of man's freedom. Life is 'a shout' about the personally achieved integration of inner commitment and outer events. It is obedience to values believed to have been selected from alternatives by individual choice coupled with instrumental acceptance of constraints from others by sheer necessity, and is almost devoid of ethical significance (Castro 1954:281, 608, 619–28). Yet despite the inbuilt tendency to excess in this case, the deep bifurcation of inner experience and outer constraint has apparently made the Spaniard a natural sophisticate concerning self-consciousness about the inevitable selectivity attendant on any commitment to a given value-system as such. For it is said that 'contrary to primitive man, the Spaniard always realized the high price paid for being a Spaniard' (Castro 1954:614). Self-consciousness about the nature of one's commitment and how one must be separate and different from others constitutes a central distinguishing mark between *ex toto* and *ex parte* individualism.

Evidence concerning such differences is also contained in socialization data from France, Germany, and the United States. First, as in Russia and unlike the United States, one meets again the ability of *ex toto* individuals in France to conform outwardly without anything like the introjection of social standards necessary for the *ex parte* individual. At least differential parental behaviour reflects it as an operative assumption. As in Russia, where 'social control is focused *not* on sentiment but behaviour . . . so that (a person) would do what was expected of him *regardless* of his feelings' (Inkeles and Bauer 1959:282, emphases in original), the French father limits the exercise of his authority to the control of the children's behaviour, but refrains from extending it to their ideas and feelings (Wylie 1963). Again one encounters the *ex toto* paradigmatic theme of 'stressless compartmentalization' which contrasts so starkly with American adult organizational behaviour (Crozier 1964; Blau 1956, 1964) as a difference in relating obligation to self and to society already learned in childhood. The American middle-class father's attempts to be 'a pal', on the other hand, offer sharing mutuality of ideas and feelings through the joint negotiation of a shared order.

There is, furthermore, a special pathos to such attempts at being a pal in that both parties share an underlying sense of futility concerning the very goal at hand. For as members of a culture perceived to be in continuous transition, they share the notion that they can both be sure 'that their fathers' youth was substantially different from their own and that their children's youth will again be different'. Western liberal society with its stress on the greater reality of the individual over the group, and that of the constituent part of society over society itself 'creates a cherished distance between youth and adult, if a distressing one' (Naegele 1963:45, 54).

No comparable self-doubt and pathos characterizes the French father-son tie. Society there, regardless of the shape it may take, is and can never be anything but an external given reality to which man must adjust if he is to live at all. *Ex toto* individualism implies constraint of outer behaviour, freedom of inner experience; while *ex parte* individualism insists on consistency between outer and inner reality, but permits freedom of choice where and with whom to seek it. As Wylie (1963:246) put it:

> The French child learns that life has been compartmentalized by man and that the limits of each compartment must be recognized and respected. The American child learns that life is a boundless experience. The Frenchman recognizes that rules are a convenience, but that they are man-made and therefore artificial. The American believes he has discovered his rules for himself and that they reflect the essential structure of reality. For the Frenchman, reality is dual; there is the official reality of man-made rules, but it is only a facade concealing a deeper, more mysterious reality which may be felt by the individual in moments of introspection or revealed by art or religion. For the American, reality is a unity, and any apparent discrepancy between the ideal and the actuality is essentially immoral.

Not surprisingly, the contrast governs the experience of adolescence as well. For the French and the German, there is no need to discover that life is run according to a double-standard; that is already known. The problem is to find one's own position towards that inevitable natural fact. There is here a tendency to 'escape into oneself', dwell in one's private domain of thought, feeling, and 'meaning', even though one common emotion may be hatred for *les autres*, those others who, not *Menschen* but mere *Leute*, force one to conform. But so long as the adolescents' reaction is confined to emotions or verbal or artistic expression, the others do not care, 'society imposes no sanction'. But the American identity-diffusion stage faces a different dilemma. With a unitary reality conception, one must strive to

realize what one has been taught to believe one discovered for oneself. But
while everyone proclaims the existence of a real code, no one seems to
know exactly what it is, and the older generation places the onus of finding
a more acceptable gap between the ideal and the real on youth (Wylie
1963: 250–1).

Just as the American adult response to the anxiety of illness is to seek
security in 'average man', assuring oneself that one is like everyone else, for
'the *average* is normal, correct, accepted, safe, and secure' (Zborowski
1969:74), so the adolescent response is to 'extend' himself into others in the
same condition, his peers, and there find himself. Adolescence under the
ex toto code is a reaching out for explicit cultural orders that mere *Leute*
cannot grasp, with the gratifying consequence that their opinions become
irrelevant in so far as fashioning one's own stance is concerned. Furthermore, the matter does not stop with adolescence. Of the adult in Spain
it is reported that he lives 'fixedly oriented to church and state' but
remaining 'shut up in himself' in spite of living in the main 'to express
himself' (Castro 1954:126).

While German high school boys as another *ex toto* example show a
greater concern over obligations to 'an idealistic, explicit code of decency
and propriety', American high school boys display greater sensitivity to the
opinions of others without a corresponding expectation to be given reasons
concerning social expectations because they live more in accordance with
implicit rules (McClelland 1964:70–1). While 'obligation to society' in
Germany—as in Russia (Bronfenbrenner 1970:100; Bauer 1952:142–3),
and in France (Pitts 1961:704) where the stress on *mesure* is focussed on the
breach of public order 'more so than the motivational state of the actor'—
involves self-discipline, 'proudly controlling one's selfish interests to fulfil
one's explicit duties to the whole of society', Americans do that by
'achieving in conformity with group expectations'; and here the very idea
of a 'whole' recedes from the significant emotional horizon because here
'no social order is possible except that based on the desires of its members'
(McClelland 1964:72–3).

The contrast between a dual conception of reality and a unitary one is
also reflected in educational ideals and student behaviour, particularly at
the secondary level of schooling which demands more impersonal relations
than the primary school and the family. American educational philosophy
emphasizes the unitary concept of reality in its stress on the development of
all the individual's potentialities for action, which means for use in society.
German education 'tried to combine humanistic and technical interests
and so to reconcile the ideals of the cultivated man with the culturally
more transcendent and qualitatively emptier ideal of the competent
specialist' (Naegele 1963:51). Authority relations in French secondary
education also reflect the dual conception of reality typical in *ex toto*

individualism. They may serve as a final illustration.

In France, authority relations in the school are characterized by two syndromes. There is an 'authority syndrome' when youth is compliant, non-participative with, and acceptant of, the teacher's authority. Instruction is accepted 'indifferently'—with low cathectic involvement. But there is also the *chahute*, a pattern of rebellion and defiance directed at teachers who lack influence because they are either considered incompetent by students or teach what are regarded as unimportant subjects, or both (Schonfeld 1971). But the *chahute* has more apparent than real resemblance with the American peer-group and its anti-social characteristics as described by Bronfenbrenner (1970) because the French is a kind of 'instant' delinquent community, lacking in both stability of informal group structure and leadership. No doubt, the *chahute* is a powerful mechanism to vent aggression against social targets. It seems to operate as a learning mechanism on which the process of *ex toto* individuation relies in achieving its product: the ability to rely for one's sense of personal self on self-selected cultural ideals. That, after all, demands strength, living without the crutch of seeking assurance in others. Seen in the perspective of the 'double existence' of accepting authority without involvement from some and 'chahuting' against others, the pattern suggests a mode of acquiring ego strength of the kind where a person can do what 'reality' insists on without identifying himself with the exacted behaviour in any deep way. That way, one may become a 'social authoritarian' without becoming an 'authoritarian personality'. And this is indeed necessary if one is to behave successfully in French bureaucracy. For the authority relations of that context rely on alternation between long periods of 'rule by rigid procedure' which means never being 'a subject' of any person, and short periods of direct 'military-like' rule, obtaining when the rules of procedure demand re-writing in the service of the organization's adjustment to change in environments (Crozier 1964).

Fig. 3 (overleaf) summarizes the differences between *ex toto* and *ex parte* individualisms.

Since McClelland (1964) was so successful in describing the special strengths and weaknesses associated necessarily with the organization of any set of rules, it seems valid to close this section with a brief enumeration of the typical weaknesses associated with each form of individualism. Thus, driven to excess, taking responsibility *vis à vis* culture under the *ex toto* form, implies a compartmentalization of life where Bellah's (1967) civil religion could not operate at all. And there is empirical evidence. Spain's personalism is so extreme that a society-wide civil religion does not exist (Castro 1954:127). The same was true of Germany's excess under the Nazis (Schoenbaum 1966). Under such conditions the right of the individual to construct his own meaningful universe has been carried to a

Figure 3

Types of Personal Identity Compatible with Types of Authority Codes*

Obligation to:	EX TOTO Individualism	EX PARTE Individualism
CULTURE	Given the dual structure of reality with greater reality of 'whole' than 'parts', deep identification with abstract ideals constitutes the primary material of a sense of self, maintenance of commitment to culture-standards, the main mode of continuity in a sense of self.	Given the unitary nature of reality with the primacy of 'parts' over mere 'negotiated wholes', deep but temporary identifications with a changing set of generalized others constitutes the content of the self, maintenance of the ability to leave and rejoin others, the main mode of continuity in a sense of self.
SOCIETY	Loyalty to formalized, functionally differentiated, explicit codes of proper behaviour.	Fidelity to a negotiated order, its negotiability, and revisability through other-directedness.
BEH. ORGANISM	Individual self-direction, maintenance of self-discipline over impulses, and self-actualization through the exercise of will power that channels selected skills in a fixed direction.	Self-actualization of all potentials for action through serialization over the life-course, and letting utility to others be the criterion as to what has been realized.
HISTORY	Loyalty to one's culture of birth, its historical roots and present stage of development in its particularisms, that is commitment to historical responsibility where the present is a constraint of the past and a selected future.	Commitment to an open, more universalistic future of mankind constrained but by the most general features of the history of one's culture of birth.

* This is clearly an attempt to generalize from McClelland's (1964:78) comparative work on value formulas of two societies to types of individualisms characteristic of two types of industrial society.

point where society-wide appeals to public morals are outrightly rejected as stupid sentimentality. On the *ex parte* side the corresponding excess is the moralization of everything and therefore essentially of nothing. As to excess in obligations to society the *ex toto* formula tends to eventuate into Merton's ritualism, empty conformism with the detail demands of society in blithe disregard of larger aims involved. The corresponding *ex parte* excess involves distorting demand for reform into a spiral of 'change for the sake of change' which substitutes novelty *per se* for any genuine improvement. As regards the skill potential, and hence what has been called here the assumption of responsibility for the behavioural organism, *ex parte* excess amounts to beatnikism and rampant license while arrogance, pride, and personality rigidity characterize the *ex toto* case (McClelland 1964:78). Finally, with respect to history, excess under the *ex toto* category means particularist chauvinism whether on ethnic or national lines, while the *ex parte* variety, when driven to excess, displays a mixture of historylessness coupled with the most parochial and uninformed convictions concerning the alleged universal nature of man.

There remains the task of relating these descriptions of individualisms compatible with a complex modern society to analytical categories of personality psychology. The whole effort, after all, is designed to go beyond the single model of modern personality, *viz* Inkeles-man, even though, as a start, this attempt had to be confined entirely to the political aspect of individual lives. Anchorage of the descriptions in psychological concepts must necessarily remain tentative, but is possible. Towards this end, the following summarizes selectively the most essential features of the above.

Firstly, regardless of its type, modern individualism demands a balance of inner and outer controls of behaviour. It does not permit a relative primacy of one over the other. But secondly, achieving such a balance admits nevertheless of at least two profoundly different modes. These involve *type-specific* conceptions of the structure of reality as regards the individual-group contingencies and *type-specific* uses of time to achieve a sense of personal autonomy and freedom.

Ex toto individualism relies on a dual conception of the structure of reality characterized by stressless compartmentalization. There is deep identification with abstract cultural ideals and a primarily cognitive, instrumental, adjustive orientation to the constraints of social reality. A sense of uniqueness is achieved through expressive behaviour at any given moment in time, a sense of membership-identity is attained through expectational conformity over time. Inner experience and outer constraint are articulated by letting the latter serve as a security base for the courage required to live cost-consciously with a given set of value-commitments.

On the other hand, *ex parte* individualism relies on a unitary conception of the structure of reality in which all compartmentalization remains stressful being subject to reduction by effort. There is deep identification with the opinions of generalized others and their moral elaboration into a shared universe of commitments at any given moment in time. This is coupled with an extraordinary ability to move into new social situations, both laterally and horizontally as regards stratification, and find oneself deeply motivated to forge new bonds. A sense of membership-identity is achieved at any moment in time, while a sense of uniqueness is attained only over time. It results from the conviction of having exercised choice in the selection of changing affiliations where even nuances of differences in life-style, encountered and made real for oneself, attain significance for having achieved what one is. Less compartmentalized to begin with, inner experience and outer constraint are articulated over a whole life-course guided by a relatively cost-unconscious commitment to values.

Locating Individualisms in Personality Structure

This should make it apparent that balancing inner experience and outer constraint in the *ex toto* case involves a primary reliance on the ego-ideal and the ego. The former provides the pattern of what one must be and/or become; the latter supplies a reality check as well as protection against the potentially polluting impact from mere others on the self. But the conception of a unitary structure of reality between individual and group coupled with a moralization of identifications with shifting others distinctive of *ex parte* individualism points to the fact that this type of balancing inner experience and outer constraint relies particularly on the super-ego and id structures of personality. This is possible when the latter is conceived as a generalized energy reservoir, a differentiation-product of Freud's original id with its bipolar structure of libido and destrudo as in Hartmann's (1945–49) reformulation. Then it becomes at least probable that the *ex parte* individual's amazing capacity to be motivated to forge new affiliations again and again rests on a super-ego 'guided' mobilization of generalized cathexes in the libidinal key. For he who must rely on generalized other, when it comes to who he is, must also be capable to endow those others with special positive significance for his own security. 'Encoding' of generalized energy with libido through the super-ego probably constitutes the most significant 'enabling mechanism' in this form of self-realization.

This formulation uses Parsons' (1968b) four-function reconceptualization of Freud's original structural triad as filtered through Hartmann's (1945–49) genetic model. Accordingly, all four functional components are conceived as differentiation-products of an originally undifferentiated mental life. So differentiated, id specializes for adaptive functions, ego for goal-attainment functions, super-ego for integration, and ego-ideal for pattern-maintenance and tension-management functions. Whether that is a formulation consistent with critical clinical facts must remain an open question here. But connecting the types of individualisms with a differential reliance on either of the two functions placed diagonally in the usual four-function box does serve one useful purpose. It places the emphasis on tensions, thus making the formulation somewhat more consistent with Freud's persistent stress on ambivalence than Parsons' (1968b) own first outline managed to do. With the particular kind of id concept already mentioned, this calls for one clarifying comment on the super-ego. Freud conceived of it as 'peopled' with the lost objects of one's parents. But this is too restrictive. Life under the imperative of 'a revisable self' makes of personality growth too a life-long genetic process (Erikson 1963:247–74). Consequently, parents as lost objects could not conceivably exhaust the supply of relevant introjects of the super-ego (Parsons 1968b:19); instead, the super-ego must be in continuous receipt of relevant figures.

The possibility to identify types of individualism with a differential reliance on familiar psychic structures shows a gratifying parallel with the way it proved feasible to locate functionally the authority codes. Again the balancing of inner and outer imperatives is stressed. And again it must be stressed that all four functions need tending. So a primary reliance of two functions and a secondary exploitation of the remaining two is all that is claimed; it cannot be a question of exclusive reliance on any two. Once again as in the case of authority codes, the particular functional use that render distinctiveness to the two types of individualism involve anti-nomious functions. *Ex toto* individualism with its preferential reliance on ego-ideal and ego articulates internal-instrumental with external-consummatory functions. Thus oscillation across this diagonal assures tending to all four functional requisites. The same is true in the *ex parte* case with its differential reliance on id and super-ego which articulates external-instrumental with internal-consummatory needs. Oscillation across the diagonals assures stability in the preferential reliance on functions involved by virtue of the fact that all four requisites are being touched upon. These features are shown in Figure 4 which invites one to view the types of individualism distilled as compatible with the authority codes by virtue of parallel organization in psychic and socio-political structure.

Figure 4 suggests that what gives individualisms their culturally distinctive mark is the primary articulation of a given antinomy. *Ex parte* in-dividualism does this by a mode of self-actualization involving the fullest exploitation of skill potentials (id) controlled through a consecutive serialization of introjecting 'generalized others' throughout the life-course

Figure 4

Secondary Individualism and Its Placement in Personality

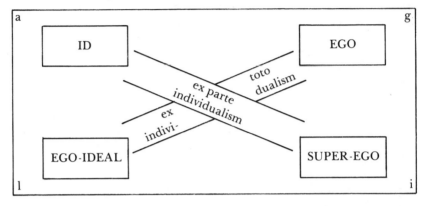

(super-ego). When it comes to paths of self-actualization, and only when it comes to that, ego-ideal and ego play a secondary if very significant role. In the *ex toto* case the reverse obtains. Self-actualization relies predominantly on a self-selected developmental ego-ideal taken from cultural ideals and this is controlled by ego-functions in which adjustment skills to societal demands substitute for the need to rely on generalized others as a guidance mechanism. And in this primary mode of self-actualization id and super-ego play a secondary though indispensable role.

ON COMPATIBILITY BETWEEN AUTHORITY CODES AND INDIVIDUALISMS AS A CAUSE FOR INVARIANCE

The question of the compatibility between authority codes and their respective forms of individualism involves three separate issues. The first concerns the nature of citizenship in modern society; a second has to address the problem of intra-national empirical variation in codes and individualisms; and a third concerns the invariance hypothesis in terms of the interaction of authority codes and individualisms.

Firstly, the formulations concerning individualism above have been premised on the universality of active citizenship in the modern world for all adults while it was for the most part confined to élites in pre-industrial societies of the early modern and historical varieties. This is a question of centre penetration of the periphery with political mobilization which has been gradually expanding towards the modern end of the evolutionary scale. Though there may well be profound variations along class, ethnic, and regional lines drawing some sectors of the population more into the political process than others as far as institutionalized empirical reality is concerned, the normative ideal of active citizenship for adults has become a fact in all industrial societies. In the Anglo-Saxon and other Western democracies this has taken, in the main, a stress on the individual's right to participate. In the Soviet Union one encounters formulations stressing a 'feeling of duty' as a result of social motives like love of the fatherland, devotion to the party, and the like. This doctrine is a rationale for subordinating individual interests to that of the state and for making man 'personally responsible for serving the interests of Soviet power' (Bauer 1952:141), so would say the foreign observer of Russian educational psychology. Whatever the empirical adequacy of formulating service to the collectivity just that sharply, for us the important reference is to personal responsibility. That is an institutionalized aspect of political modernity everywhere.

Secondly, since invariance in authority codes depends in large measure on the fact that society has also institutionalized the 'matching' form of individualism, change due to such events as conquest or peaceful cross-national merger aside, the empirical history of state and nation formation remains a critical factor as regards intra-national empirical variations in both objects of invariance. There may well be in any given empirical case considerable accumulations of opposing conceptions as regards the meaning of legitimate authority and the modes of achieving a sense of personal autonomy. While this matter cannot be examined here, one might leave the issue with venturing an analytically informed guess concerning such empirical variations. By and large the longer the time elapsed since state formation and nation-building, which in practically all non-colonial societies followed the former rather than coinciding with it in time, the more likely it is that the respective patterns among the state and nation-building élites gradually become the property of the mass of the population. Not the least important factor in this trickling down of the patterns that were crowned with success in fashioning the modern state is surely education, universally financed from public resources subject to political mobilization.[18] Such trickling down takes time. And there are known cases such as Spain, Germany before the break-up of the nation in the wake of World War II, and probably Italy characterized by a continuing failure to develop a politically effective civil religion.

While cases of conquest have been excluded from the invariance hypothesis several times above, one must acknowledge that temporary conquest has been more than once the recent historical experience of the majority of Central European countries. With the German armies sweeping towards East and West in both World Wars, the rise and demise of fascism, and the success of Communism in Eastern Europe, most of this part of the world has been subject to severe political instability. Quite apart from the question whether or not such instability was accompanied by changes in authority codes, there can be little doubt that the ideologies involved — particularly the Communist one — attacked the prevailing societal identities directly. For whatever the practice, Communist ideology proclaims no less than the abrogation of structured inequality in society, hence that set of rules which most clearly gives a society its identity. It is plausible then that such conditions of profound instability even if only visible in the more external signs make it very hard for individuals to identify personally with the state, as well as other central societal institutions such as the stratification system, the church, and even the family wherever political power was proclaimed to serve their fundamental change. In these cases producing diachronic solidarity, a sense of trust in the continuity of societal identity, through the channel of identification with centre institutions seems practically precluded. One principal alternative mode may be producing diachronic solidarity on the personal plane through an unusually highly developed state welfare system. The issue can only be mentioned here, it has been treated elsewhere (Baum and Baum 1975).

But thirdly, and the states of very recent independence aside, there are a large number of cases of either successful revolution or the avoidance of any. For these one may postulate continuity in authority codes and the 'matched' forms of individualism since the crucial stages of state and nation-formation. Such continuity is interpretable in basically two ways. One is a kind of Hegel function: it is not governmental relations *per se* but rather engagement with the political aspect of social structure in general that is the issue. Then it is possible to show that where authority code and individualism match, obedience to authority and the quest for personal autonomy can simultaneously function to supply society with the requisite conformity and personality with a sense of autonomy. The other interpretation, and probably the empirically more prevalent one, relies on compatibility between authority and personal identity which neutralizes their potential mutual interference.

'Whereas stability of liberal society is based on the loyalty of citizens, . . . the loyalty of the Soviet citizen has been based on the stability of the political system' (Inkeles and Bauer 1959:290). In Russia collective identification amounts to an institutionalized expectation, internalized in persons, hence also filling deeply felt and widespread personality need-dispositions. As always in the work of Alex Inkeles, this insight is not speculation, but based on impressive fact. There was not only an amazing level of system support and appreciation in this refugee sample, there were also genuine gems of Hegelianisms. A few may suffice for illustration. Respondents demand that government should look after cultural and even spiritual needs of citizens. In the words of one articulate respondent: 'It is not enough (for the government) merely to provide material security, it must secure the person. After all a person has a soul'. A strong central government is assumed to give the nation direction and purpose. It should be active, may be autocratic, but must not be arbitrary. And when these conditions are met, 'the state can do anything. Without a government you cannot exist. On the contrary when you love the government you will do as it wishes' (Inkeles and Bauer 1959:238, 250). In general, hostility goes to persons—incumbents of leadership positions—not the system. These facts invite generalization to the *ex toto* authority relations.

It has been stated that the authority codes are distinct by assigning greater and lesser reality to the system as a whole or its constituent parts. In addition, one may suggest without detail elaborations that it is in the nature of all activist social systems to institutionalize doubt regarding the adequacy of performance. And no doubt, such institutionalization of doubt must refer to a situation where members can continuously question some exigencies *because* they take others completely for granted. If it were not such a mixture of presumed certainty and the production of un-certainty in other respects, continuous questioning would spread to everything, eventuating in a near-anomic state. When it comes to political systems then, it seems likely that institutionalized doubt concerns the 'lesser realities'. Where the *ex toto* authority code prevails, this is the realm of the constituent parts, those collectivities which are assigned identity through the division of labour, and perhaps ultimately persons. Consequently, one might say that *ex toto* régimes institutionalize personal doubt. Where the *ex parte* code prevails, the 'lesser reality' is assigned to the 'whole' rather than the 'parts', that is the negotiated common order. Consequently, one might say that *ex parte* régimes institutionalize system doubt.

While the matter cannot be documented here, the following may suffice to make this assertion plausible. In Western democracies, particularly those with stable party systems (Rose and Urwin, 1970), the operation of a free and relatively competitive press in pursuit of relevant exciting news seems to be characterized by an inherent tendency to question whether the system really works. Electoral processes, blaming non-performance on problems of consensus construction, and investigative reporting are only a few of the sources making for system-doubt. Excepting *samizdat*, there are no analogues in consultative authoritarian régimes. These are charac-terized by a controlled press. But while a free press does characterize many corporatist régimes, where there is the inherent personalism of political leadership, and the very features of praetorian mobilization which leaves the political structure essentially unchanged, though it may eventuate in enormous change in the economy and the educational system, one finds conditions which make men count in fact while system concerns remain academic.

These different forms of institutionalizing doubt in authority relations systems show maximal adaptive fit with the respective personality needs for security prevalent in the two types of individualisms. In both cases the typical structural weakness associated with each type of individualism, visible especially when these forms are driven to excess, is one where tending it at the personality level can be done through rendering obedience.

With institutionalized personal doubt characteristic of *ex toto* authority relations, the identified structural deficit of the political system pertains to the ability of persons to forge effective affiliations. Relative to the other case, what this system needs is persons willing to co-operate. Now, as shown, *ex toto* individualism encounters rebelliousness and lack of social discipline as the typical structural weakness of personality. There is little doubt as to who one is and must be with respect to a sense of 'personal self'; the ego-ideal tends to be strong.[19] There is also little doubt as to what one can afford to be, given prevailing conditions; one also knows how much one can get away with and the ego tends to be strong. But there is often doubt as to one's social identities. The 'self loved by others' and the 'self that makes itself' through providing demanded contributions to society remain problematical; the super-ego and Hartmann's id constitute the structurally weak parts of personality. When doubt about the latter surpasses critical thresholds, obedience to authority aids in reducing it. This occurs through a transformation of the normally instrumental if not opportunistic adjustment to social constraints. In response to a need of certainty as regards one's social identities, the normally amoral sphere of adjusting to others becomes infused with moral significance. In this fashion, obedience to authority supplies society with expected effectiveness in co-operation and personality with reassurance in social identity. Thus the reason why system stability in the Soviet Union 'conditions' citizen loyalty becomes apparent. In a format of effective societal demand, the very capacity of a citizen to *be* really loyal, rather than just *feel* loyal, depends first and foremost on assurance and confidence as to who one is socially. Otherwise one cannot even know relevant performance expectations with sufficient certainty. And a stable political system, providing maximal legitimacy to political demands, then enables persons to use obedience to authority for attaining reassurance and confidence on just that aspect of personality structure typically under strain.

With institutionalized system-doubt typical of *ex parte* authority relations, the identified structural deficit in the polity is consensus construction rather than the capacity of persons to form effective groups. Interest aggregation is in deficit relative to interest articulation. The 'system as a whole' tends to need trust as regards its real existence in the minds of constituent parts, ultimately persons. Now, *ex parte* individualism is characterized by structural strength as regards social identities, but structural weakness as regards a secure sense of 'personal self'. This is necessarily so where one lives through deep identification with shifting group affiliates at any moment in time, but gains security of 'personal self' only retroactively over time through a sense of experienced control with respect to having selected significant others. Here Hartmann's id and the super-ego constitute the peculiar strengths of personality, ego-ideal and ego the weaker parts. While the former can be trusted, secured as they are through a constant supply of meaningful associations, the latter remain relatively problematical. In the ego-ideal sector this is particularly true concerning the required certainty as to who one *must be* and become when time-consciousness about mortality bears down on persons. In the ego sector there remains a nagging doubt as to who one *can be*, potentially. Given the ease of entry and departure in the area of significant affiliations, groups serve well to assure persons who they are socially at any given moment in time, but they do not constrain persons' fantasies with respect to potentials. Thus consensus construction; the need of the polity can feed on institutionalized and internalized personality needs to find assurance who one must be in the ego-ideal sector and who one can be in the light of death by reducing surfeit complexity in personal potential. Once again, obedience to authority can supply the political system with its need: commonalities, while simultaneously serving personality in search of acceptable limitations as regards an integrous 'personal self' realized through ego-controlled and interpreted contributions to the system as a whole.

But as to such maximal adaptive fit between socio-political and personality needs there remains one difference between the two cases discussed which makes such fit harder in the *ex parte* instance. Here adaptive fit has to operate primarily at the level of national political process engaging national citizenship roles. It may also operate at some lesser scales of inclusiveness such as region, province or state. But the smaller the grouping, the more one approaches that which is in relative surfeit and needs no shoring up: the constituent parts and their affiliational realm. This makes the effective adaptive fit in this case peculiarly contingent on the existence of a civil religion and its effective use in processes of national political mobilization. There is very little chance for an adaptive fit in democratic regimes which lack a civil religion.

Finally, one can also argue compatibility between types of individualism and authority codes. In contrast to adaptive fit, compatibility describes a situation where collective processes of social constraint leave the individual free to seek solutions for structural weakness at the personality level on his own, while such search, within limits, remains neutral in its effect on effective collaboration. This argument can be summarized as follows. Above it has been shown that the *ex toto* code demands symbolic divestment of social periphery characteristics among all those who can legitimately participate in centre goal setting. It should be obvious by now that this is something not only easily achieved among *ex toto* individuals whose particularist social identities normally remain somewhat attenuated, but it should be equally evident that for the same reason claims regarding symbolic divestment can be trusted by every man with relative ease. In such societies everyone knows, and indeed occasionally suffers from the fact, that social identities are but skin-deep. This is after all part of the experience of everyday life when one focuses on authority relations in general rather than merely governmental relations in particular and has available the type of individualism that matches authority. Meeting the requirement of symbolic divestment of particular constituent interests is easy and easily understood among men who have lived a life of concerned avoidance of ever becoming mere social actors.

Ex parte individualism matches up with the requirements of the *ex parte* authority code in a similar way. Since social identities, though changing, are the real and trusted ones for most humdrum everyday conduct, meeting the requirement of the retention of periphery particularist characteristics when it comes to legitimatizing centre goal setting activity in politics is practically guaranteed. For where man is fundamentally seen as a 'generalized other' at any given moment in time this other, its label not withstanding, must be a particular other: a family man, an occupational man, a party man, ethnic, class member, or whatever. This seems inevitable where men are seen to be what their group affiliations amount to. And under these conditions, even the adoption of an ideological stance to represent the haunted 'whole' can never ring so true as to effectively communicate the total divestment of the interest of groups to which such spokesmen belong. Thus, what is ultimately proscribed for legitimate authority, but demands some limited practice given that all polities need both authority codes, has little chance of being accepted as the way things really are. Meeting the legitimacy requirements of the retention of periphery characteristics is easy and easily understood by men accustomed to trusting their social identities.

In sum, whereas the interpretation of maximum adaptive fit involves mutual reinforcement between authority code and individualism, the compatibility argument describes mutual neutralization between the two. To the extent that the latter obtains, neither of the two pursuits — the quest for personal autonomy and the drive to establish more effective co-operative systems — can interact in a mutually destabilizing fashion. For a perspective that sees in growth of effective co-operation *and* personal freedom the hallmarks of modernization this indeed constitutes an important condition for continuity in both authority and culturally distinct patterns of individual autonomy.

SUMMARY AND CONCLUSION

The main features of the invariance argument can be summarized under five points to conclude the essay.

(1) Evolutionary invariance in codes of authority and conceptions in personal autonomy dates from the 'historical' and 'early modern' stages of evolution, because these stages identify societies with the following correlated features. Monotheistic religious symbols were involved in the development of culture-area-specific value-systems which raised *different* elements from a common pool of archaic and primitive value-commitments to the same level of generality. Conceptions of meaningful authority and a 'true self' capable of understanding and taking responsibility for obligations to God, society, and self were encoded in different ways. All, however, showed tensions in man's group affiliations and the development of a conscience that balanced inner and outer sources of control, though achieving that balance in different ways. A four-class stratification system prevailed, composed of social formations with varying degrees of autonomy from each other and centre élites. With secular and sacred authority differentiated, and hence in potential tension, exercising authority therefore faced the double problem of articulating the permanent interests of social systems with the transitory interest of mortal men and, given the division of labour achieved, of creating unity of purpose among groups and roles diverse in purpose.

(2) Resulting from a simultaneous struggle about the nature of God and the nature of man's contingency on man, the tensions between secular and sacred authority eventuated in basically two types of very general solutions as regards meaningful authority relations and conceptions of personal autonomy or individualism. In terms of the value-principles involved in these conceptions, though certainly *not* in terms of their institutionalization in human action, these solutions were so general as to become exempt from further evolutionary change. Such subsequent change was confined to codification and specification of the principles with respect to their meaning in different areas of society's division of labour.

(3) The solutions were as follows: (a) under the *ex toto* version, authority was premised on the inherent primacy of a societal unity that ultimately ranked above the apparent diversity of groups and their interests; the whole was assigned greater reality than the parts. Corresponding to this was a conception of personal autonomy or the 'true self' premised on an assignment of greater reality to permanent universal cultural imperatives and a lesser one to particular group attachments; (b) under the *ex parte* version the reverse relations obtained. Here authority stressed an *ex pluribus* notion resting on the premise of the greater reality of constituent groups which had to interact and negotiate a common

purpose. And corresponding to it there developed a conception of a 'true self' as an emergent property of a series of successive group affiliations.

(4) The most important reasons for continuity rather than change in these elements of the structure of human action are three. Where obligations to society and self are 'matched' there is maximum adaptive fit in the sense that obedience to authority supplied, at one and the same time, society and personality with precisely those elements in structural deficit in each. Where there is less than a perfect match, or other factors interfere with the individual's capacity to identify with the political regime of society, there is still compatibility such that neither increasing centralization of authority nor increasing individuation can interfere with each other. Third, and in both instances, matched conceptions of obligation to society and to self function in the maintenance and enhancement of societal identity over time.

(5) Nothing in the above asserts that these objects of invariance are secured against any kind of change from any kind of source. They may well change, but if they do, this will be essentially non-evolutionary change which may involve conquest or peaceful merger of nation states for example. The reason for stressing non-evolutionary change as the only likely one rests on the adequacy of these conceptions of authority and individualism for presently known forms of the complex organization of human action on the one hand, and their function in maintaining societal identity on the other.

4

Religion, Identity and Authority in the Secular Society

Richard K. Fenn

Fenn approaches the theme of this volume from the perspective of the sociology of religion and explores certain trends of major importance in American society. This focus, with a concern for a diagnosis of the relations between identity and authority in present-day America, is also the central topic of chapters five and six, by John Marx and Guy Swanson respectively. The theoretically abstract, comparative and historical themes of the preceding essays now give way to the sociological effort to discern meaningful patterns in the present.

It is apparent that Fenn approaches his task quite differently from either Marx or Swanson; while some concern with religion is inevitable for any study of identity, it is given most importance in this volume in Fenn's work. Indeed, he is concerned about the role of religion in the secular society. There appears to have developed a disjunction between the ideas and value commitments by which individuals identify themselves and the value themes by which collective actors, especially the state, legitimize their exercise of authority. It is a different disjunction from the one seen by Marx in the following chapter—he sees the disjunction between culture and a proliferation of models for identity on one side, and social structure, which he feels is increasingly rigid. Yet, some similarity of concern does exist here.

Fenn proposes a theoretical framework that allows us to grasp the ways in which religion may intervene in this process of differentiation between collective actors and individuals to limit relationships between authority and identity. His conclusions might well be interpreted to support the claim by Baum that identity codes, in the American as in other cases, are relatively invariant, except for their progressive elaboration. Fenn finds that the function of religion in America is now 'to establish the bona fide identity of the individual claiming exemption from compliance to a particular law'. Yet, he is most cautious and does not preclude the breakdown of such secular, individualistic codes in a possible 'wave of moral enthusiasm'.

An axiom of sociological theory states that a variety of changes in Western society have increasingly separated the self from the local, familial and religious groups in which it had been encapsulated. As the self emerges, the individual becomes more aware of his separate identity; he becomes more autonomous. But sociologists have been less certain whether the individual will also be more responsible to the authority of particular institutions or to society as a whole.

Durkheim's preoccupation with this question took the form of an inquiry into the social conditions which minimize the person's tendency to the unmitigated pursuit of his own continually expanding desires; there was little reassurance for Durkheim in the notion of a utilitarian society in which order emerges from such a pursuit (Cf. Poggi 1972:169 ff.).

On the other hand, post-war theorists, notably of the Frankfurt School, have focused on a different question of attitudes toward authority (Cf. Adorno *et al.*, 1950). Given the specialization of roles which divide a person's functions and relationships into many parts, and given the co-ordination of these roles into hierarchies of command and obedience, they have asked whether the individual will take responsibility for the consequences of his decisions, instead of sloughing off responsibility on authorities, the system, or 'others'. On a theoretical level, social theory has predicted that the shift from traditional to modern societies would result either in unbridled expression of individual demands for freedom and gratification or in an 'escape' from the responsibility of ethical decision-making in a bureaucratized society (Cf. Mitscherlich 1970).

In taking up the question of the relationship between authority and identity, therefore, the contemporary sociologist inherits a theoretical framework of relatively low density. He can deduce from this inherited framework propositions to the effect that rationalized authority-systems generated relatively unlimited demands by the individual for autonomy and gratification; or that the same type of authority-systems generate individuals who hide behind roles and subordinate their wills to their peers and superiors in order to avoid the responsibilities of freedom.

In an attempt to reduce the uncertainties which remain in such a broad theoretical framework, social theory must inevitably focus on cultural variations within and between societies. Culture, it is commonly assumed, 'transcends particular social and psychological systems' (Parsons and Platt 1973:13). In doing so it precedes and survives individuals and societies; it is this characteristic which enables culture to provide societies with a sense of continuity which extends beyond the life-span of particular individual and corporate actors; and from this continuity derives the 'transcendent' basis of the authority of institutions and nations. At the same time, however, culture provides some control over the development of characteristics which distinguish the individual from other individuals; it is this operant or patterning characteristic of culture which underlies the formation of discrete individual identities.

Every society, however, has the potentiality of developing differences between the symbols and ideas which, on the one hand support the authority of the society and its major institutions, and on the other provide a basis for individual identity. Under the impact of governmental patronage and the impact of charismatic personalities, there may be a temporary synthesis between the ideology of the state and the beliefs which organize and interpret social life for individuals, as Nash (1971:106 ff.) makes clear was the achievement of U Nu in Burma during the 1950s. But even this temporary synthesis was precarious and could not be sustained in the absence of a stratum of intellectuals devoted to the task of rationalizing Theravada Buddhism (Nash 1971:110). The possibility that two systems of action will develop — the one orientated to providing the individual with a stable and meaningful identity, the other orientated to legitimatizing the authority of the state is — of course, a potential factor in both pre-modern and advanced countries. Geertz (1973:142 ff.) notes that a contradiction of this sort produced extraordinary strains in the life of Javanese villagers; and, in speaking primarily of American society, Bell (1973) notes the development of an 'adversary culture' which provides a basis for individual identity and life-style quite apart from the systems of action (i.e. 'knowledge') which provide guidance to decision-making by government and its agencies.

As it was noted at the outset, sociological theory has been preoccupied with processes which foster the emergence of individual identity and their impact on traditional bases of social authority; and its exponents disagreed about whether this emergence posed a greater threat to social order than to individual freedoms. Sometimes the issues were sublimated into discussions of the ontological, causal, epistemological bases of sociological theory. But it is possible to detect in these discussions pre-theoretical commitments to order, justice, and freedom, with justice occupying a middle ground between the polar conceptions of freedom and order. In arguing, for instance, that what is 'really real' about societies are the processes by which individuals interact around their various values and goals, Weber was making a normative statement about corporate actors such as the state, *viz* that the state and other formal organizations ought to be responsive to the real needs and goals of real individuals. Weber's position was also programmatic in its implications for social action in that the sociologist as statesman should participate in the design of structures which are responsive to the intentions of persons and therefore protected from the tendency of the state and other bureaucracies to give priority to their own goals of control and expansion (Cf. Loewenstein 1966). It was significant, as well, for a sociology of *verstehen* by which the analytical rigour of the natural sciences could be applied to the explanation and interpretation of social behaviour. Durkheim, on the contrary, in giving ontological priority to society, was making a latent normative statement about the degree to which individuals' systems of action should converge with the collective; it was a programmatic statement with regard to the type of moral education with which the sociologist should be prepared to supply his society; and it was programmatic as well with regard to a methodology which focuses not on the individual and his subjectivity but on social facts (Cf. Lukes 1972; Bellah 1973).[1]

To summarize: every society is confronted with the problem of providing relatively consistent cultural bases for individual identity and societal authority. And every society contains the potential contradiction between the two systems of action, that is, between the ideas, values, and rules by which individuals identify themselves and act on their projects, and those by which the state legitimatizes the exercise of its authority. In exploring the possible consequences of advanced levels of differentiation between the two systems of action, two quite different outcomes have been predicted: rampant individualism and passive compliance with rules and orders issued by executives and leaders. Whereas the metaphysical and moral preoccupations of particular theorists help to account for why Weber and Durkheim came to such different predictions, they do not help to reduce the uncertainty in the theories themselves.

In this paper, therefore, I wish to elaborate a theoretical framework for analysing the conditions under which religion, as a primary carrier of metaphysical and moral interests for large numbers of personal and collective actors, intervenes to influence the impact of this process of differentiation on the relationship between identity and authority. When, for instance, does religion provide overlapping bases for personal identity and national authority? When does religion serve to retard or obscure the separation between the values and purposes of the state and those of the individual? Are there types of religious culture which neutralize the impact of differentiation, such that the separation of cultural bases for individual identity from the cultural basis of legitimate authority has relatively little impact on legitimacy? Under what conditions does the separation of the two systems of action on which authority and identity are respectively based have subversive or positive effects on the authority of the nation? Since, within the limits of this essay, answers to these questions can only be illustrated rather than tested in empirical detail, the attempt here will be simply to elaborate the terms of a theoretical framework within which to approach them.

Early sociological theory inevitably focused on religion as a source of variables which affect the impact of changes in the basis of authority in a society on the development of individual identity, and vice versa. To Weber it was clear that the individual's perceptions of social life were partly a result of a prior orientation to 'this-worldly' or 'other-worldly' realities: an orientation which results in selective attention to the empirical or non-empirical; to the cognitive or to the expressive and to the moral or to the aesthetic dimensions of society and culture. Weber was equally clear that religion affected the adoption of an attitude toward social life which could range from a desire for active mastery to passive accommodation; and he understood the capacity of religion to support the development of innovative roles and institutions. A this-worldly, active, and innovative religious orientation could have a negative impact on traditional authority and yet be quite congruent with the claims by new collectivities to social authority. Simmel (1971) understood also that religion is one of the factors available to a society in resolving the conflicting demands of the individual for both inclusion and autonomy: religious solutions to the demand for inclusion would affect the sources of identity, just as religious solutions to the demand for autonomy would affect the problem of authority. One key factor, then, would be the emergence of social institutions which provide particular models for the resolution of the conflict between autonomy and inclusion. A second factor relevant to the resolution of the problem of inclusion *vs.* autonomy is the degree to which particular types of religious culture reinforce knowledge of, and trust in individuals and corporate actors. Finally, in his study of religion in a primitive society, Durkheim focused on the impact of religious symbols and symbolic acts in expressing and developing the relationship between individual identity and the claims and goals of the larger society: on the contribution of religion to social cohesion.

In view, however, of the several processes normally lumped together under the heading of 'secularization', the reason is not obvious for including religion as a source of intervening variables in a consideration of *modern* societies. Weber felt that bureaucracies generally had succeeded in developing a sharp distinction between organizational and personal values and standards. Simmel felt that there was no technical reason why societies could not resolve the antinomy between individual demands for simultaneous inclusion and autonomy; and he certainly saw no reason to think that societies would require a specifically religious solution. Important as religion may be in some situations towards understanding the relationship between identity and authority, there are obviously many other situations in which religion has no impact on either compliance with or rejection of the authority of particular organizations or institutions. Finally, it is by no means clear whether, and for whom, religion continues to influence an individual's orientation to 'this-world' or his predisposition to develop an attitude of striving toward mastery and control of his environment rather than of accommodation and adjustment.

It may help, nevertheless, to recall that Durkheim, Weber, and Simmel do not speak with one voice on the subject of secularization. Durkheim is usually credited with arguing that social organization inevitably results in the expression of its underlying aspirations or ideal elements in religious symbols. He regarded society as a 'person' or 'being' (quoted in Bellah 1973:xxiii); it is ultimately real in a sense which leads Bellah to speak of Durkheim's 'piety toward the real' (Bellah, 1973:xxiii). Yet even Durkheim was apparently as convinced as Weber of modern society's disenchantment: the loss of its power to attract the loyalty and commitment of its members. A similar tension can be found in recent interpretations of Weber. His notion of rationalization, it is argued (Cf. Wilson 1973), indicates that secularization is the inevitable outcome of charismatic breakthroughs as individuals organize into groups and plan to realize their transcendental purposes in history; yet Weber saw the process of rationalization as resulting in a concern for the ultimate grounds of action and organization (Gerth and Mills, 1958). And Simmel argues that the perception of unity and coherence among actors, a perception to which religion has contributed significantly in the past, is imposed on the social object just as concepts are imposed on the raw sense data which we receive from objects in nature (for a concise summary on this point, Cf. Holzner 1972:72 ff.). The process of secularization would in that case have important epistemological consequences for the perception and analysis of society.

But to many historians and sociologists, America has seemed to be an exception to the European experience. Although the United States was the first nation to be created under the auspices of the Enlightenment (Ahlstrom 1972), American culture has presented a synthesis of the Enlightenment's values and norms with those stemming directly from the Judeo-Christian tradition (Lipset 1963; Marty 1969). American nationalism has depended heavily on the symbols of the Covenant; the colonies were an American Israel and the expanding state had an exemplary, perhaps even an emissary role to play in demonstrating the potentialities of democratic nationhood (Ahlstrom 1972; Marty 1969). America, in Bellah's (1967) phrase, has enjoyed a civil religion quite different from any European nationalism. It was a mixture of religious and secular symbols which sanctioned the sacrifices which the nation requires of its citizens (Cf. Warner 1953) and defined the common identity and purpose of a people with divergent and particular religious loyalties (Greeley 1972; Cf. Herberg 1955).

Recent historiography and sociological theory, however, suggest that the

United States has moved closer to a European type of secular society. Ahlstrom (1972:824) notes that Protestantism never recovered from the impact of millenarian and Pentecostal sectarianism of the late nineteenth century; after World War I its fissures opened again and continued to widen 'disastrously'. It is difficult to imagine so flawed a Protestantism as capable of providing the religious basis of national identity and purpose. And as Ahlstrom also points out, the Catholic religious community was divided over the extent to which Catholics should identify themselves as Americans in language, life style, and politics. Bell (1973) has described American society in terms which cast doubt on whether it is integrated or legitimatized around any coherent set of values at all, let alone those provided by the Judeo-Christian tradition. Noting that abstract values like 'fairness' fail to 'create any positive ideal of the kind of individual a society wishes to have' (1973:483), he faults American liberalism for failing to provide any set of positive values which could serve as a basis for national identity and purpose (1973:479). While American society is becoming increasingly interdependent, it lacks a 'communal ethos'; indeed, any such ethos may no longer be possible (1973:483). These are criticisms, it is worth noting, common to the criticism levied by religious intellectuals against modern society at other times and places, as indeed in the case of Eliot's (1940:51) celebrated question whether England was integrated around 'any beliefs more central than a belief in compound interest and the maintenance of dividends'. What makes the observation of particular importance is that it is now being made by Bell and other sociologists who have cast doubt on the symbolic integration of American society.

The primary question, however, is not whether American society lacks *any* set of common beliefs and values; it is whether religious culture provides the symbols around which the society, as a collective actor, legitimatizes its authority and defines its identity and purpose. Is Bellah's thesis of a civil religion still appropriate to contemporary American society, or has Bellah in fact identified a form of 'nationalism which professes a Christianity from which all Christian content has been evacuated' (Eliot 1940:62)? Although it is possible to phrase the question in sharp terms which present an 'either-or', we find it preferable to note with Parsons that modern societies may be primarily secular with religious aspects: the direct obverse of primitive societies. 'It is,' Parsons (1973:169) notes, 'a question of relative primacies, not of presence or absence' of religious culture in the collective identity of American society.

As a guide to the following discussion I offer these summary statements of the argument. Durkheim's model of mechanical and organic solidarity points to the separation of the solidary from the political systems of the society. The symbols by which individuals identify themselves with the nation as a whole are therefore not utilized by the polity to legitimatize the authority of the state. Durkheim also hypothesizes that under these conditions, the state acts as a corporate actor with specific interests relevant to the security of the nation as a whole but not on behalf of the nation as a moral community. There follows a shift in the codes by which the state legitimatizes its exercise of authority to resolve conflict between individual and corporate actors and the perceived interests of the state itself. In view of Coleman's (1974) recent essay on power in American society, it becomes possible to speak of a trend toward the development of two 'structures of relations' in the United States: one pertaining to individuals, the other to 'corporate actors'. Coleman's thesis is compared with, and assimilated to, related views of Weber, Durkheim, and Parsons. What Bellah (1975) has taken for a breaking of 'the covenant' or a violation of the civil religion is therefore simply a result of the separation between the symbols governing the authority of the state and those expressing national identity. Further, what Bellah construes as the saving grace of American society are simply groups who use traditional symbols to express personal identity and non-Western symbols to express the withdrawal of their identity from the dominant institutions and corporate actors of American society. (I consider the implications of Simmel's prediction that the boundary dividing the sacred from the secular will become increasingly indeterminate in modern societies.)

THE SEPARATION OF THE POLITY FROM THE SOCIETAL COMMUNITY

Terms on so abstract a level as polity or 'societal community' require careful definition; yet there will not be total agreement on the concrete objects to which the abstractions refer. The 'societal community' and the 'polity' represent what Parsons would consider 'analytical' definitions (Cf. 1966:29). The societal community assumes that any society depends on shared moral commitments to define membership and to support the political and economic activities which are essential to the maintenance of the society itself (Cf. Parsons 1966:18–19). The polity assumes that societies must organize collectively to achieve certain goals (1966:13). The notion of societal community therefore leads one to examine the organizations and ways by which societies achieve solidarity or a sense of membership in a moral community; whereas the polity refers to the organizations and ways by which a society chooses goals, assigns them priorities, and attains them (Parsons 1966:25). The more the 'polity' is separated from the 'societal community', the more there will develop a legal system which is regarded as binding on the members of a society regardless of their moral differences (Parsons 1966:25). Again, the more the 'polity' separates from the 'societal community', the more complicated will be the gradations of leadership, authority, and competence by which individuals and groups are permitted to take part in decision-making (Parsons 1966:13–14). And a particularly important issue in the development of these positions of leadership, authority, and competence, is the role of religious leaders (Parsons (1966:14).[2]

In understanding the separation of political from solidary aspects of modern societies, it is essential to recognize the central place which the 'cult of the individual' occupies in Durkheim's thinking. He is quite aware that the old prejudices and common faith that used to link individuals have perished; it no longer provides the basis for a single system of action in modern societies. And the new god of justice has been born, although perhaps by Caesarean techniques, in the French Revolution; its future remains uncertain although essential to the reintegration of advanced societies. In the meantime, as Poggi's useful summary puts it, values and standards are no longer 'widely shared', 'deeply held', 'diffuse', and 'sharply defined' (Cf. Poggi 1972). They tend to be abstract, limited in their social base and scope of application, and held with uncertain conviction. To the general trend of the weakening of religion, the only exception is an increasing regard for the worth and rights of the individual. But this 'cult' itself, however widely shared, confronts the State with a problem since the object of the cult is not social. The ends, that is, which appear to unite individuals in modern societies are precisely those which cannot serve to establish social goals (Cf. Bellah 1973:xxv–xxvi). Of course, it can be argued that the welfare of the individual is the very social goal to which the State addresses itself in protecting the individual from the excessive controls of occupational, kinship, and other institutions. But this argument overlooks precisely the role of the State as the executive and deliberative organ for the corporate actors of modern societies. The liberal ideology, in fact, masks this contradiction, although Durkheim is aware of it and begins to explore it (Cf. Bellah 1973).

Durkheim's exploration of the issue is more suggestive than complete. With the weakening of the 'collective conscience', laws do not have the same moral force behind them or the same repressive consequences. This is the price of the 'autonomy' of the legal system. More important for Durkheim's political sociology, however, is his further recognition that *the State therefore acts as one agency co-ordinating others rather than for the society as a whole* which includes individuals and organizations in a common system of ends and means. Lukes states it this way that 'Durkheim identified the area of civic ethics as that of "political society" which he defined as "a society formed by the union of a more or less considerable number of *secondary social groups*, subject to a single authority which is not itself under the jurisdiction of any other superior authority properly constituted",' (Lukes 1972:268, emphasis added).

The function of the state was the moral education and guidance of individuals in the process of bringing their several ends into congruence with social ends; at the same time the function of the state is to protect individuals from the pressures of 'the social machine' (Lukes 1972:272) so that they will not be weighed down by any of the institutions and organizations of the larger society. The state, then, intervenes between two 'structures of relations': the one pertaining to corporate actors, the other to individuals. The goal of that intervention is to ensure proximate justice: an adjudication between the values of the two systems and fairness in the rules. Durkheim does not go on to argue that the two systems of action have separate values; and he does not describe a lack of symmetry between the rules and sanctions governing corporations and those governing individuals, although it would have been an interesting and perhaps important contribution to the sociology of law had he investigated the extent to which the laws governing corporate actors are more likely to be less punitive than those governing natural persons. Recent criminal justice in the United States, for instance, provides ample illustration of individuals being sent to prison for burglary, but corporations pay fines and are required to allocate sums to ensure the future prevention of criminal activity.

Like Durkheim, Weber understood that, on the macro-social level, the shift to modern societies attenuated the relationship between the state and society. In terms of the shift from mechanical to organic bases of solidarity, in which values and attitudes become less widely shared and deeply held, the state can no longer claim to act on behalf of the entire society, although that remains its function. While Durkheim called for the moral education of the citizenry to raise their consciousness to the level of societal needs and purposes, Weber called for the development of structures which would generate authentic political leadership. Weber castigated the German politicians that made spurious appeals to national glory, while remaining fully convinced that appropriate statesmen could make rational appeals which would elicit a responsible commitment to the hard tasks facing the German nation (Cf. Jaspers 1964:218 ff). The leadership did not develop, however, and, in Jaspers' compelling phrase describing the situation in 1933, '. . . the "state" no longer held anything in tenure from the German nation,' (Jaspers 1964:228). It was a secular state appealing to a pagan past in the absence of an actual base in the values and attitudes of its citizens: a possibility to which critics on the other side of the English Channel pointed as one possible outcome of the collapse of the relationship between the state and national moral community (Eliot 1949).

Weber had noted, in connection with the rise of modern capitalism, that one aspect of the separation between personal and corporate systems of action was the development of a rational capitalism which pursued ends which were not precisely those of the entrepreneur himself, who perhaps 'furthers his interests but never really succeeds in enjoying his profits' because he has reinvested them according to the objectively determined needs of the enterprise (Jaspers 1964:233). The separation of personal from corporate values on this micro-social level is parallel to the separation of personal from rational loyalties characteristic of bureaucratization generally; and the same master-trend presents the conditions which Weber regarded as requiring an ethic of responsibility among statesmen who would not resort to inauthentic appeals to the personal loyalties of individuals based on a romanticized past. Weber had clearly identified the cultural developments which had permitted such an ethic of responsibility to sustain motivation under the conditions of modern capitalism, but his analyses revealed no comparable cultural resource to sustain the requisite motivation or to support political rationality *under the conditions in which the state itself is radically differentiated from the nation.*

Weber might have agreed with Brzezinski that 'A leader can then be a substitute for the integrative tasks of society, which are otherwise performed by a formal or an implicitly shared ideology. In the absence of social consensus society's emotional and rational needs may be fused — mass media make this easier to achieve — in the person of an individual who is seen as both preserving and making the necessary innovations in the social order' (1970:118). Advanced differentiation between the political and solidary aspects of a society therefore accentuates the need for leadership. Such leadership can arise, in Weber's view, either through charisma or through the democratic process. Germany lacked the latter, and charisma was generally lacking in a disenchanted universe.

There are alternatives capable of ameliorating the separation of the polity from the societal community. Brzezinski in the above quotation refers to a 'formal or implicitly shared ideology', and a number of theorists focus on the same possibility in terms of cultural integration. Parsons and Platt (1973:278), for instance, argue on the macro-social level that abstract religious values serve to define important aspects of national identity and purpose. In their view, that influence is both manifest in the civil religion and latent as a commitment in institutions concerned with other values. Parsons, in other words, defends a macro-social hypothesis by reference to data on the level of the individual which are both hypothetical and latent rather than manifest (for example 'commitment'). Bell refers to the neutralization of religious values in post-industrial societies. He notes the simultaneous development of high levels of political and economic interdependence (a communal society) without a corresponding integration of beliefs and values (the lack of a communal 'ethos') (Bell 1973:483). On the macro-social level, therefore, Bell does not see any manifest cultural integration; and he by inference excludes the possibility that a post-industrial society could be integrated by religious beliefs and values. Although values seem to Bell to be relatively unimportant to technical élites and to large-scale organizations, (Bell 1973: 481–2), they are of manifest relevance at the level of the personality and in the choice of life-styles (Bell 1973:481–2).

For Bell, it is this separation between the normative basis of individuals and large-scale organizations which typifies post-industrial societies (Bell 1973:475): an argument which anticipates Coleman's thesis on two parallel but separate systems of action in modern societies, and to which we now turn. It is important to note at this point, however, that Parsons sees religious culture as of manifest relevance to national identity and purpose, with religious values operating as *latent* commitments at the level of the individual, whereas Bell sees no manifest role for culture at the macro-social level, but he identifies values as of *manifest* importance to the normative structure of individual personality and life-style.

There is a further consequence of the separation between political and solidary aspects of modern societies: a shift in the codes by which the state itself exercises authority. In his study of the Protestant Reformation, Swanson (1967) alludes to two basic types of régime. In one, the exercise of distinctive governmental functions, for example setting and carrying out policies, was monopolized by a régime which stood for the interests of the society as a whole. In the other a number of special interests shared in the governmental process. The resultant policies therefore reflected a mixture of public and private interests. Up to this point, there is enough correspondence between Swanson's and Parsons' viewpoint to say that Swanson divides régimes into categories according to whether there is much or little separation between the government and the society as a whole (between the political and solidary aspects of a society). Régimes therefore vary in the extent to which 'the structure and acts of government embody not the personal traits of a single collective actor but the inter-relations among several actors' (Swanson 1967:39). In some régimes, individuals and groups participate not as agents of the régime *per se* but as representatives of special interests in the larger society. In this case the régime becomes permeated by the relationships among many several corporate actors. As an example of the former type of régime Swanson cites Venice, in which the government did not provide legitimate institutions or processes for special interests to participate in and influence its decisions; and Zurich is Swanson's example of a régime in which individuals participated not as individuals but as representatives of the guilds (Swanson 1967:40–1). As Swanson's examples suggest, during the Reformation a society in which a régime acted on behalf of the whole society tended to retain Catholicism whereas a society in which a régime produced decisions which reflected a compromise among the special interests of various corporate actors tended to shift to Protestantism. In the United States, as I will attempt to show through an analysis of certain Supreme Court decisions, there is a comparable distinction between decisions which are intended to reflect the 'general will' of American society (Swanson's Venice-type) and those which are clearly the outcome of negotiation among corporate actors and reflect a temporary compromise of interests.

There is one other aspect of Swanson's contribution which must be considered at this point: his concern with the notion of immanence. When applied to the relationship between a government and the larger society, immanence means that a government's decisions are embodied or present in the variety of agencies which comprise a régime; the more the government is permeated by other corporate actors, the less the government itself is embodied (immanent) in these agencies. A similar meaning is reflected in the use of immanence to apply to individuals. The more that individuals participate in organizations and delegate their interests to corporate actors, the less can their actions be said to express their own particular qualities; rather, they reflect the interests of other actors and agencies (Cf. Swanson 1967:22 ff.; 256 ff.) In a society in which the actions of an individual reflect the special interests which somehow stand behind him, as in the case of a noble acting simultaneously as a member of a régime and of a group of nobles, immanence is decreased. Briefly, the more that collective and individual actors pursue their goals in interdependence with one another, the less the purposes of a single corporate or individual actor can be perceived in concrete decisions and actions; and the less that concrete decisions and actions reflect the purposes of a single actor, the less immanence there is in that society.

Transcendence, however, is not the opposite of immanence: it is a second and parallel dimension which I shall here call 'the scope of interaction'. The two dimensions may vary independently, of course, but in the process which Swanson describes they tend to vary alongside each other: that is, the more interdependence there is (the less immanence), the wider the scope of interaction (the more transcendence). In common sense terms, as individuals and groups have to compromise their purposes in order to achieve their objectives, they also find themselves interacting with a wider range of individuals and groups. It is a process which has been described, without analogies to religious language, in studies of 'the logic of collective action' (Cf. Olson 1971) and in Coleman's recent study of power, which expands on Olson's logic and applies it to new contexts.

Given the difficulty of translating religious metaphors of transcendence and immanence and the sometimes obscure meaning which they have in Swanson's discussion, it is reasonable to ask why one should bother to make the translation at all. Like the term 'secularization', isn't it better simply to avoid such multi-dimensional notions as immanence and transcendence or at least to de-code them into sociological terms, such as interdependence and interaction?

The merit of Swanson's approach is that it forces attention on the relationship between religious change and secularization. The process of secularization, on the one hand, places the individual actor in a network of relationships with other actors who affect him and are in turn affected by him, and whose numbers increase as markets, political processes, and the media provide increased channels for interaction; on the other hand, secularization deprives the individual or corporate actor of a sense that social structure and process have an ontological basis or an historical *telos* (Cf. C. C. West 1966). Religious change expresses and legitimatizes this process by freeing the actor to participate, with high levels of commitment to a social process in which knowledge of other actors is limited and the outcome of the interaction is ambiguously related to specific individual or group purposes. Or religious change may insist on the legitimacy of more limited patterns of interaction in which corporate actors' purposes are less compromised and in which the scope of interaction is more limited. It was precisely these alternative responses to social change which were expressed in doctrinal controversies over the sacraments. Similar alternatives characterize fundamentalist *vs* reform movements in the history of American religious groups. But Swanson's approach has one serious limitation when applied to more modern societies. The individuals who participated in various régimes were generally governors who therefore were acting on behalf of some governmental agency (Swanson 1967:233 ff.). As the religious choices of individuals changed during the Reformation, therefore, the codes of corporate actors, such as groups of nobles or governmental bodies, also changed. Thus, there was a high degree of association between the symbols by which individuals coded and expressed their purposes or identities and the symbols generally used by corporate actors.

As societies have become more internally complex, the bases of personal identity have become more distinct from the symbolic bases of institutions. Organizations may use one set of values to express these identities and purposes, while individuals will use others. Not even churches can guarantee much overlap between the two (Cf. Bellah 1964). There is also apparent agreement among theorists of quite different perspectives that pluralism in religious culture and in social values and norms provides the conditions for personal types of religious culture to express the separateness of the individual from the larger society and also, under certain conditions, his hostility to social controls (Cf. Berger 1967; Platt and Weinstein 1969).

Despite these general theoretical reflections on the differentiation of social systems and religious culture, however, much American social theory has until recently taken a unitary view of American society as a more or less integrated system of action (Cf. Williams 1970). Nonetheless, a recent theoretical statement points to the necessity of considering a social system as consisting of at least two quite separate systems of action: one pertaining to individuals and one pertaining to social organizations.

I will discuss that statement briefly in this context, although its importance for the sociological theory of religion requires a separate and much more extended treatment than can be given here.

According to Coleman's (1974) recent analysis of the emergence of corporations as new persons in Western society, a major transformation has occurred over the past three centuries in the unprecedented level of differentiation between persons and social organization. Corporate actors are those forms of social organization in which the component parts are positions or roles rather than persons (Coleman 1974:36). Even individuals who are owners or agents of such corporations enjoy their powers only as owners or agents and not as natural persons and they are therefore replaceable. Individuals, regardless of their investment in or commitment to a corporation, are free to leave. There has therefore been a net increase in the freedom to move in and out of corporate positions on the part of individuals, but there has also been a net decrease in the amount of power which natural persons can exercise over the corporate actors which they have created (Coleman 1974:37). Although Coleman does not elaborate this point with regard to churches it is an argument without which one cannot understand the religious dilemmas of churches: one must assume with Coleman that individuals are becoming as mobile with regard to these institutions as with regard to others. The embeddedness of individuals within the family and the nation-state has been slower to yield to this transformation than the embeddedness of individuals in other corporations which stand between the nation and the individual, but Coleman (1974:29) is convinced that each generation in the West finds individuals increasingly mobile even with respect to the family and nation-state: a point quite opposite to Durkheim's conclusions, for instance, regarding the increase in social regulation regarding adoption.

When the basic unit in a society is therefore the position or role rather than the natural person, opportunities are increased for a radical separation between the symbolic system of corporate and individual actors. There emerge two parallel structures of relations coexisting in society — the structure of relations among natural persons, and the structure of relations among these corporate actors that employ the services or resources of persons (Coleman 1974:36). The key phrase in that quotation is 'structures of relations'. Each of these structures is clearly a social system with its own actors and set of interdependent relationships and each system may develop its own set of norms and values, expressive symbols and beliefs: its own system of action. I would add that it is also possible, although not necessary, for each system of action to develop its own religious culture: i.e., a set of symbols which relate the actors' identities and purposes to an ultimate ground for action.

It may be helpful at this point to identify precisely what distinguishes the notion that persons and corporate actors now operate increasingly within different 'systems of action' from other current applications of the concept of differentiation. Clearly more is involved in Coleman's formulation than the familiar notion that differentiation is occurring between 'culture', 'social structure', 'personality', and 'organism' (Cf. Parsons 1966). Both organizations and natural persons have access to elements in the culture of the larger society. But if they operate within different 'systems of action' their general ideas of what is right and valuable must increasingly diverge. Corporations may identify their ends with those of the nation, whereas individuals, including employees of those corporations, may derive their values from a consideration of what constitutes the potential of human nature, to take only the most commonplace example. It was precisely this possibility that perturbed Durkheim with regard to the 'cult of the individual' (Cf. Bellah 1973:xxvi); hence Durkheim relied heavily on professional associations to attach the loyalties of individuals to the needs of the larger society and to strengthen society through 'a consciousness of the whole'.

Coleman's thesis does not proceed to a consideration of values and general ideas, of course, concerned as he is to identify discrepancies in power between the two types of actors, for example the extent to which organizations have access to more information than individual actors and yet enjoy the same protections under the law (Coleman 1974:76–7). But if the 'structure of relations', as Coleman puts it, which characterizes corporate actors is distinct from that which unites individuals as persons in a system of action, it is logical to predict that the rules and values of the two systems, as well as their general ideas, if any, about social reality, will also diverge. Hence Durkheim understood the importance of justice itself to replace the common faith that had integrated primitive societies (Cf. Bellah 1973:xxv).

There are other elements of continuity as well as difference between Coleman and Parsons. If the two structures of relationship diverge markedly, we can infer that corporate actors will treat each other — corporations and individuals as well — in ways that can be clearly identified as 'neutral', 'specific', 'performance-' and even 'collectivity-orientated' (whether the collectivity in question is the organization or the nation as a whole), whereas individuals will increasingly be involved in the types of relationships which Parsons characterizes as 'affective', 'diffuse', and orientated to the self or to the qualities of the other. Strain may occur, of course, in the role of the helping professional. And in particular settings in which the two structures of relationships are only partially differentiated, overt conflict may occur, as in universities during the 1960s, in which the two types of actors disagreed over what norms should apply both to the relationships among faculty, administrators and students, and to relationships between the universities, persons, and corporate actors outside academia. As corporate actors, the universities tended to speak the language of formal organizations interested in rationality, efficiency, and service to the larger society, whereas individuals were more likely to speak the language of persons interested in the needs, aspirations, and identities of specific individuals and groups. The conflict between the two languages on occasion erupted into physical confrontations over whether universities, as corporate actors, should pursue goals which were antithetical to personal values. In this sense the 'cult of the individual' is in fact an ideology which obscures the extent to which organizations and individuals are constrained by different rules and have quite different opportunities for access to information and other resources.

The role of ideology in obscuring the separation of solidary from political, or personal from corporate relationships, can be illustrated in terms of what Bellah (1967) *inter alia* has identified in American society as a civil religion. Bellah's thesis suggests that the civil religion sustains individual motivations and contributes simultaneously to social solidarity. It also points to expressive symbolism in the national culture which indicates that the nation as a whole has figured in individual action as an end rather than as a means: as an object which is to be taken with the same seriousness as the sacred. The process of differentiation between corporate actors and natural persons, viewed somewhat speculatively, leads to quite opposite conclusions regarding the role of religion in American society: *viz* that religious culture serves to support individual identity and motivation without contributing to national solidarity; that it reduces the nation to the level of instrumental rather than ultimate concern; and that it is not in the present a constitutive aspect of the society, regardless of its relationship to the society in the past.

The possibility of this type of interpretation clearly exists within Bellah's essay on the civil religion, but it remains unexplored. Bellah starts out with Rousseau's notion of the civil religion: a theistic type of religious belief-system generally found among individuals, but he soon shifts to a type of religion which is an aspect of American national ideology. Having located the civil religion as an 'aspect' of national culture, Bellah, within the same paragraph, isolates it as a separate entity in itself: a civil *religion*. Bellah transforms in other words an analytically derived aspect of the national culture into a separate, empirical system of beliefs and symbols. But Bellah raises some hard questions concerning newer forms of religious culture in his most recent work on the civil religion. These he defines as expressing concerns which 'are *personal*, local, and universal but seldom national' (1975. 161 emphasis added); and in addition to being personal these newer forms of religious culture emphasize direct experience rather than a consummation postponed until some end-point; they are consummatory rather than utilitarian (Bellah 1975:156–7). While many of them take an ethical standpoint altogether outside American culture, some represent vestiges of the old civil religion in their ethical criticism, their emphasis on postponing gratification until a judgement day, and in their notions of themselves as a saving remnant in American society (Bellah 1975:168). The civil religion, then, is reduced to the ideology of a saving remnant where it returns to the level of individual rather than corporate ideas.

It is apparent that these varieties of religious culture in American society reflect more than the process of differentiation between two systems of action, the one pertaining to natural persons and the other pertaining to corporate actors. That type of differentiation, I am hypothesizing, accounts for the radical disjunction between personal and societal types of belief system, which in turn limits the degree to which the individual expresses his personal identity in symbols belonging to the larger society at the corporate level; for the personal type of civil religion is essentially timeless and unrelated to any particular national collectivity. Within this basic differentiation between personal and societal types of civil religion, however, there are clearly other sources of variation: for example between those which are conventional or non-conventional, and between those which do or do not express a type of protest against the larger society.

It would appear that when there is relatively little differentiation between the two (personal and corporate) systems of action, little differentiation in types of religious culture within the society, and high levels of inequality, religion with a potential to undermine legitimacy in the larger society combines the societal-personal types of civil religion, projects the symbols of an ideal social system into an eschatological future, and personifies leadership in the form of a collective person, such as a national messiah (Cf. Mowinckel 1955). On the other hand, when high degrees of inequality occur in a social system in which there is a high level of differentiation between personal and corporate systems of action and a high degree of variation in types of religious culture, it is more difficult to hypothesize what type of religion has the capacity to undermine the legitimacy of the larger society. Under these conditions the symbols by which individuals express their personal identities are more separate from those which express the authority of the larger society: a development which in the Protestant Reformation brought a serious challenge to secular and ecclesiastical authorities. When the two (personal and corporate) systems of action and their respective beliefs and values become *radically* separate, it is more likely that religious culture will have significance for individual identity without affecting corporate systems of action. A case can be made that over a relatively long timespan the varieties of religious culture available to individuals will provide symbols, perhaps utopian or millenarian, for the eventual cultural re-integration of the larger society but this seems likely to underestimate the extent to which religious pluralism prevents any large-scale movement from developing around a single cluster of religious beliefs and values.

INDEXES OF SECULARITY: AUTHORITY AT THE MACRO-SOCIAL LEVEL

The most important point to be made in this context about religious pluralism is that it makes it difficult but not impossible for the state to use religion to legitimatize its authority while claiming to act on behalf of the entire society. Pluralism makes it difficult, of course, for the state to use religious symbols in defending its decisions, but it can still argue that the nation as a whole is 'religious' if not 'Christian': that certain actions are therefore not compatible with the general respect which a free people accords divinity. The sheer fact of religious pluralism is still compatible with the existence of certain religious beliefs or standards that are so widely held or deeply shared as to make it possible for the state to reflect and enforce them. It is possible to have a neutral attitude toward religion in the public schools, for instance, despite the objection of certain segments of the population. But it is questionable whether an overtly atheistic programme could be supported against legal challenges.

Pluralism reinforces the separation of the state from the society as a moral community, but it does not prevent the state from claiming some religious legitimacy for its authority. So long as the state can articulate its purposes in terms of the religious beliefs and values of persons, the possibility remains that the state will appeal to some highly generalized set of religious beliefs and values. The following discussion of specific decisions by the Supreme Court illustrates this possibility. The illustrations point to a state whose basis of authority is only partially secularized: religious beliefs and values continue to play an important role despite the official separation of church and state.

In many areas of the state's authority, of course, the need for the use of religious symbols would not naturally arise, as in the control of major corporations, for instance, or in laws regulating the behaviour of political parties. There is one area, however, in which the explicit use of religious symbols to legitimatize the authority of the state has often been observed in American society: in the regulation of claims by individuals, groups, and institutions to various exemptions from obligation to the society on the grounds of religion. Over the past two centuries individuals and groups have petitioned the state for exemption from a variety of legal obligations: the obligation to pay taxes, serve in the armed forces, observe legal codes regulating the use of drugs, take oaths of loyalty to the state, and to provide education equivalent to that offered in the state schools, to name a few of the most important obligations from which exemptions have been claimed on the grounds of religion.

The official policy of the state toward the claims of religious groups, and particularly toward the claims of marginal or deviant groups, is thus a particularly important site for the observation of religious legitimizations for the authority of the state. There is little disagreement among observers of religion in America that the dominant beliefs and values of this society are explicitly Judeo-Christian, although, as I have argued, they are not necessarily held deeply enough, or defined sharply enough, or diffuse enough to affect law-making by the state. And there is little disagreement among observers of the Supreme Court, for instance, that the justices take into account the religious preferences and standards of the population as well as the formal limits imposed by the Constitution on governmental regulation of religious belief and practice (Cf. Pfeffer 1974; Burkholder 1974). To the extent, therefore, that popular religious preferences become criteria for the state's decision-making under the First Amendment, the authority of the state can be said to rely on religious legitimizations.

Two recent studies by Burkholder and Pfeffer provide a useful survey of major decisions, especially by the Supreme Court, regarding religion over the past two centuries. Four types of legitimization may be observed. The first makes explicit use of the Christian beliefs and values of the nation's population, as in the Supreme Court's opinion in 1931 that 'We are a Christian people according to one another the equal right of religious freedom, *and acknowledging with reverence the duty of obedience to the will of God*' (emphasis added), (from *US* vs. *Macintoch*, 1931; quoted in Pfeffer 1974:11). It is a judicial opinion with strong antecedents in the nineteenth century, in which the Court referred approvingly to a New York opinion upholding an individual's conviction for blasphemy on the grounds that it violated 'the morality of the country which is deeply ingrafted upon Christianity' (Burkholder 1974:11). In the late nineteenth century the Court enunciated a more general principle to the effect that any religious belief or practice is acceptable so long as it 'does not violate the laws of morality and principle'; general laws which presumably covered a wider variety of occasions than specific instances of blasphemy or Christian immorality (*Watson* vs. *Jones* 1872; quoted in Burkholder. 1974:11–12). The transition from the nineteenth century, in any case, has been to replace specific Christian standards with generalized religious beliefs as criteria for legitimatizing exemption from obligations to the larger society.

Since 1940, however, in a series of decisions which have enhanced the degrees of religious freedom on a variety of issues, the Supreme Court has arrived at a principle which nicely balances the rights of the individual with the requirements of the state to preserve peace and order. As Burkholder (1974:36) summarizes this principle, it appears to be an extension of the liberal formula which prevents the state from infringing upon First Amendment rights except when a 'clear and present' danger exists to the 'paramount interests' of the society as a whole. Under this principle not only the privately held beliefs of individuals but certain religious activities which conflict with informal or legal norms have been protected from regulation: the most notable of these activities being those pursued by Jehovah's Witnesses and the Seventh Day Adventists. Instead of appealing to specifically 'Christian' or to generally 'religious' principles, such as a belief in a Supreme Being or its ethical equivalent, this principle envisages a negotiated balance between the functional requirements of the state and the religiously motivated individual. *The notion of a religious or Christian people disappears from view; and in its place emerges a recognition of the social order as a structure undergoing a continual process of negotiation concerning the relative needs of the state as a corporate actor and religious individuals or groups.*

In his summary of judicial opinions affecting religious freedom, Burkholder (1974) observes a shift in the Court's reasoning on two major issues. The first is a shift away from the state's right to regulate matters defined as 'secular', such as the practice of polygamy, to a more narrow right to inhibit only those practices which are deemed to be a 'clear and present danger' to peace and order. The refusal of Jehovah's Witnesses to salute the flag *Virginia State Board of Education vs. Barnette*, 319 US 824, 1943) and the use of peyote by American Indians of the Native American Church (*People vs. Woody*, 0.2d 813, 1964) failed to provide such a threat. And the Court found that the state similarly lacked a 'compelling interest' in preventing a Seventh Day Adventist from being exempt from the provision that she work on Saturdays in order to qualify for unemployment compensation benefits (*Sherbet vs. Verner* 374 US 398, 1963). The other major principle was to make marginal religious definitions as legitimate as those of the majority: a principle implicit in the Court's recognition of the use of peyote by the Native American Church (Cf. Burkholder 1974:34–8).

Before comparing these decisions to the theory outlined above, it is worth noting that there is considerable ambiguity in using Supreme Court decisions to indicate developments in the relationship of the state to the larger society and to individuals. The Court is sometimes inconsistent, as in its ruling against released-time in Illinois but in favour of released-time in New York (*Illinois ex. rel. McClollum vs. Board of Education*, 333 US 203, 1948: *Zorach vs. Clauson*, 343 US 306, 1952). And sometimes a dissenting opinion must therefore be taken as seriously as an atypical majority opinion. The reference here is to Justice Black's insistence that 'Government should not be allowed, under cover of the soft euphemism of "co-operation", to steal into the sacred area of religious choice': a clear rejection of Justice Douglas's argument based on the assertion that 'We are a religious people whose institutions presuppose a Supreme Being'. Douglas's opinion may be seen either as a regression from, or a periodic episode in, the general trend toward increased State neutrality regarding not only one religious group or another but regarding religion, non-religion, or irreligion as well (Cf. Tussman 1962). Similarly, not all cases reach the Supreme Court which would provide adequate measures of tendencies in one direction or another. While the Court upheld the religious freedom of the Native American Church to use peyote, it did not rule on the claim by Timothy Leary that his freedom to use marijuana as a priest of the Brahma Krishna sect was infringed upon by his arrest and conviction for the possession of marijuana. So generalization will necessarily be limited and circumspect.

It is difficult to avoid seeing a clear progression, however, from the willingness of the Court to cite specific Christian standards to more generalized sensibilities of a religious people. If the polity is thoroughly differentiated from the society as a moral community, however, it will avoid making even these claims about the religious aspirations of the society as a whole. Its assessments will be restricted to determining whether the individual or group has a *bona fide* claim to religious freedom: not whether that religious expression is congruent with widely shared or deeply held beliefs and values in the nation as a whole. The willingness of the Court to exempt the Witnesses from a ceremony which they regarded as idolatrous while the nation as a whole considers it patriotic; the Court's affirmation that the Native American Church is engaged in *bona fide* religious ceremonies as it uses peyote; and the Court's agreement that certain regulations of unemployment benefits discriminated against the Seventh Day Adventists, all these indicate that the laws of the state are independent of the society considered as a moral community.

These data indicate that the state as a corporate actor is aware of the diverse religious beliefs and values of other corporate actors in the United States and therefore unable to determine what constitutes any generally acceptable religious norm. The Court, once sympathetic to the notion that a Christian nation could agree on the evils of blasphemy was by 1952 unable to assume that the nation could agree on a definition of sacrilege which would indicate whether or not Rossellini's film, 'The Miracle', was sacrilegious (*Burstyn vs. Wilson,* 343 US 495, 1952). In the words of Justice Frankfurter; 'But only the tyranny of absolutes would rely on such alternatives (as censorship) to meet the problems generated by the need to accommodate the diverse interests affected by the motion pictures in compact modern communities' (Tussman 1962:284). But if the Court cannot assume any standard for sacrilege in the nation as a whole, how can it define religion?

The question of defining religion goes to the heart of a matter too complex to be considered in detail here, except insofar as it points to the degree to which the state must function as one corporate actor among others and recognize in addition the difference between its own understandings of religion and those of concrete individuals who come before it. Timothy Leary, it will be remembered, was not considered a priest by a lower court, and the Supreme Court did not rule on that question. Muhammed Ali, on the other hand, was considered 'sincere' and his beliefs 'religiously based' (*Clay vs. United States,* 403 US 698, 1971; cited in Burkholder 1974:42–3). In its opinion on the Neo-American Church, which uses hallucinogens in a ritual context, the US District Court for the District of Columbia disputed the religious sincerity of its members (*United States vs. Kuch,* 288 F. Supp. 439, 1968), but two courts have upheld the claims of Scientologists to be members or ministers of a religious organization (Cf. Burkholder 1974:43–4). At times the criteria seem to be the existence of a corporate actor which is legally identified as a Church under the laws of incorporation of a particular state; at other times, however, it is the sincerity of the person which seems to be the issue, as in the case of both Timothy Leary and Ali. The Supreme Court on another occasion seems to have supported judicial inquiry into the sincerity of an individual's religious faith, a decision which provoked a dissenting opinion from Justice Jackson which states: 'Such inquiries may discomfort orthodox as well as unconventional religious teachers, for even the most regular of them are sometimes accused of taking their orthodoxy with a grain of salt.' (*United States vs. Ballard,* 322 US 78, 1944, in Tussman 1962:192).

It is clear that Justice Jackson's warnings have not prevented judicial inquiry into the sincerity of individual religious convictions; and it is difficult to see how the course of judicial inquiry could be otherwise. When the formal criteria for religiosity no longer provide clear and distinct ideas by which to include some forms of religious expression and exclude others, the authorities are left with the question of accepting or rejecting corporate and individual claims to religious status. Even the incorporation of the Neo-American Church did not prevent the court from questioning the sincerity of the practitioners who used hallucinogens. And the Court felt it necessary to consider the sincerity of Ali's convictions despite the presence of Black Muslims as a religious movement within the United States. The point is that the Court's inquiry into the sincerity of individuals is necessary when formal criteria of religious adherence are lacking; and when these criteria are lacking there is no single cultural system which can provide common meanings for both the state as a collective actor and the individuals whose cases come before it on issues of religious belief and behaviour. The data are not yet conclusive on this point, but they increasingly point to the separation described by Coleman and others between the two 'systems of action' governing individuals and corporate actors.

It is clear, following Baum's earlier discussion, that there are at least two types of code regulating the authority of the whole society in matters pertaining to religious freedom. One is the *ex toto* code; the other code is called *ex parte*. Social policy which claims that Americans are a religious people or that the United States is a Christian nation is based upon an *ex toto* code because it relies on a particular type of estimate of the 'general will' for the whole society. It is a will which transcends the particular values and interests of the society's several groups; and it cannot be arrived at through negotiation. Under *ex parte* codes, however, social policy estimates the requirements of the whole society through a process of negotiation among competing and particular interests. The opinions of the Court which balance either the state's need to provide peace and order or public opinion with the individual's or group's particular religious interests are clearly based on an *ex parte* code. A shift from the predominant use of an *ex toto* to an *ex parte* code is apparent from the two surveys of judicial opinion which have been summarized above (Pfeffer 1974; Burkholder 1974), although the process allows for periods in which both types of code are in use even for similar types of issues.

Among *ex toto* codes it is possible to distinguish codes which correspond to what Boguslaw (1965) terms formalist and heuristic types of design. The former specify norms for particular types of behaviour or social organization, as in the notion that blasphemy, for instance, offends the principles of a Christian nation (Pfeffer 1975: 10–11). Heuristic principles are more generalized and abstract, as in the notion of America as a 'religious' nation. These heuristic principles are more flexible than the formalistic, and legitimatize a wider variety of behaviour on the part of those claiming religious exemptions. Among *ex parte* codes, moreover, it is possible to distinguish two other types of system design: the *operating unit* and the *ad hoc* (Boguslaw 1965). *Operating unit* designs determine decisions on the basis of the functional requirements of particular units: the requirements of the individual or group for religious expression, for instance, as compared with the requirements of the society for peace and order. Finally, *ad hoc* designs take into account the actual preferences of individuals and groups; they rely, therefore, on public opinion and assessments of individual credibility.

It is possible on this basis to assess the extent to which, in an area as strategic to the requirements of personalities and social systems as is religious freedom, the society legitimatizes its decisions on religious grounds. Clearly decisions which appeal to formalistic or heuristic principles with specific religious symbolic contents are indicators that the codes regulating authority are themselves religious, as in the Court's references to the United States as a Christian or religious nation. There are other types of formalist or heuristic codes, of course, which refer to national qualities which are not specifically religious, as in the case of references to race, blood, and soil or to a national *volksgeist*: traditional rather than legal-rational bases of legitimization which are not specifically religious. If one arranges societies on a continuum, however, between religious and secular bases of legitimization for authority, societies with formalist and heuristic (*ex toto*) codes with traditional symbolic content are closer to a religious-basis of legitimization than societies using operating-unit or *ad hoc* types of legitimization.

It is difficult to make any final judgement regarding the degree of secularization of a nation's bases of legitimization. Although the Court has recently appeared to lack any explicit (formal or heuristic) religious principles, it has operated on the basis of criteria which are clearly consistent with a Protestant code. The Court's occasional concern with the sincerity of the religious deviant may reflect a Protestant concern with 'purity of heart' and religious conscience, while the Court's reluctance to legitimatize the use of drugs as an act of worship appears to be a residue of Protestant asceticism. Unless explicitly supported by references to the Judeo-Christian tradition, of course, these judicial references may indicate only a residual and autonomous core of values once encapsulated in a specific religious tradition. Their continued presence, however, in collective decision-making suggests that the decision-makers may rightly have estimated the wishes of a large proportion of the population. If the proportion is large enough, a political movement could mobilize a wave of moral enthusiasm with strong regressive or reactionary consequences for secularization at the national level.

Where the codes governing the authority of the state have been secularized, in other words, religious culture no longer functions in such a way as to support the decisions of the state. The function of religious culture is, however, to establish the *bona fide* identity of the individual claiming exemption from compliance to a particular law. Where there is no national consensus on the boundaries of religion, it is difficult for the Court to develop other criteria for accepting the religiously based claim for exemption than the sincerity of the individuals.

It would be premature, finally, to see in this development an unmitigated achievement of religious liberty. It is conditioned by the right of the state to circumscribe individual behaviour when it conflicts with the requirements of peace and order, and the inquiry into the sincerity of the individual is itself a potential source of more totalitarian controls. The tendency to expand such controls may be intensified by the proliferation of cults, each a 'collective expression' of the search for identity (Cf. Klapp 1969). If, following Klapp, we agree that a cult is religious the more it is the serious, ritualized attempt to develop and change identity in the light of esoteric knowledge or the 'mysteries' (Klapp 1969:147), the religious search for identity may increasingly come under the protection of the free-expression clause of the First Amendment. But where religious identities come into conflict with particular statutes or lead to the withdrawal of the individual from patriotic ceremonies or from service in the Armed Forces, the courts will increasingly be faced with the need to inquire into the seriousness of the individual's commitment. Where such an inquiry is not conducted within the limits of respect for privacy and conscience, totalitarian methods have been found useful by both Church, when it had the power to use them, and the state.

Certainly the cases which we have reviewed are a select sample of such possibilities, in which the devotees have in a sense selected themselves by virtue of their resistance to the authority of the state which resides in school boards and draft laws. We cannot easily generalize from them to the variety of religious expression in the larger society. But as indicators of the confrontation between secular authority and religiously based identity, they have serious implications, both positive and negative, for individual freedom and responsibility.

5

The Ideological Construction of Post-Modern Identity Models in Contemporary Cultural Movements*

John H. Marx

Marx embeds his diagnosis of the present in a bold interpretation of social and cultural change. He argues forcefully that American society has entered a new phase, in which culture and social structure diverge—increasingly rigid post-industrial structures and role relationships become frozen, but post-modern culture produces 'a surfeit of meanings, models and interpretations for action'. This novel state of social life also calls for a novel examination of our analytic tools, especially with regard to the identity models and patterns. Such an exploration is provided by Marx in this essay.

There is a sense of the novel, of discontinuity—a sense shared, of course, by many other social observers. Such terms as 'cybernetic', 'technotronic', 'post-industrial' and many others have been coined to describe the new social pattern. This sense of the new, of a major discontinuity (into which, to be sure, continuities persist) informs Marx's work. There is a hint of it also in other pieces he has written, for example in his several studies and essays on contemporary movements and their forms. Yet, for all the deliberate and thoughtful effort to construct tools of social understanding adequate to the task of analysing the unprecedented, there remains also a sense of having roots in the sociological tradition. The effort to construct new conceptual models and theories 'in order to begin to understand the fundamentally new identity structures formed by a new

* The ideas developed in this essay are a direct outgrowth of countless discussions with two very generous colleagues and friends, Rainer C. Baum and Burkart Holzner. The intellectual guidance they have consistently offered is reflected throughout this essay. I am also indebted to Martha Baum for her patient and quiet insistence that my 'mental experiments' bear some discernible relation to empirical reality. Finally, both the theoretical and expositional coherence of this formulation have been profoundly affected by the extensive written comments which Roland Robertson provided in response to an earlier formulation of the essay.

type of society' proceeds by drawing, as a scholar must, on ac-complishments in the field.

The concern with identity models in post-modern cultural movements is the central theme of the work. The question of how identity changes occur, and what role cultural free spaces and ideological primary groups play in them, is treated in depth. The essay does not limit itself to global, historical characterizations—they play more the role of allowing the 'placement' of the specific analyses—but also offers rather close-up, even 'microscopic' analyses of identity construction. The evidence that there are, indeed, new identity models is impressive.

It seems, then, that there is a conflict between the view of Baum (with his emphasis on invariance), also that of Kavolis with his portrayal of a finite set of 'logics' in mankind's civilizational experience on one side, and that of Marx on the other. Yet, one must be careful here. Kavolis spoke of cultural logics, Baum of codes—both refer to some pattern of deep structure, being the enabling ground and constraint, simultaneously, for the articulation of identities and authority. Marx is quite clear in his concern with specific identity models—symbolic structures, to be sure, and akin to 'codes', albeit at a much greater level of concreteness than Kavolis' logics, for example. Indeed, Marx deals with specific designs for concrete individuality, especially when he deals with the processes through which such 'models' may be acquired in, for example, ideological primary groups. Indeed, the question remains unanswered, as to whether the post-modern proliferation of identity models is likely in a society with anything other than an ex parte code.

INTRODUCTION: THE HEART OF THE ARTICHOKE

Although concern about the nature of identity has woven through reflections on the human condition and social life for millenia, there has unquestionably been a recent precipitous upsurge in both public and scientific preoccupation with questions of identity. People are worrying about it: popular tradebooks offer interpretations, classifications, and reassurances—as well as a vast panoply of treatments, techniques, and gimmicks for understanding, constructing, and/or transforming one's identity. 'Identity crises' are held responsible for almost every conceivable kind of dissatisfaction and disagreement—ranging from generational and marital discord to foreign policy and international relations (for example, Erikson 1963; Slater 1970). Moreover, for the first time in history people are expressing violent indignation that they lack a clear and satisfying sense of identity. People must, of course, have wondered who they were and whether their lives made sense since the dawn of consciousness and have pitied the person who could not seem to find his proper place and sense of self. But the growing idea that such a person is an undeserving victim of social injustice for which society is responsible and the idea that everyone is *entitled* to the sense of purpose and worth that derive from a clear and fulfilling identity, is a historically new theme. In the second half of the twentieth century, the urgent questions being asked by Western middle-class publics are not 'What can or should I do?' but rather 'Who can and should I be and how do I go about becoming that?' Popular concern with personal identity is beginning to define a new right: everyone must be entitled to be whoever he or she wants to be and must be permitted to 'find self' or change self so as to achieve a more satisfying identity.

The past two decades have also spawned a growing dissatisfaction among some behavioural scientists with prevailing psychodynamically-based identity paradigms and models. Both conceptual and empirical inconsistencies and 'anomalies' have been discovered in the course of researches based on the reigning identity paradigms. There are, it is true, numerous divergent formulations about identity, conceptions of its development and significance, and both professional and popular techniques for dealing with 'identity problems'. Most of these varying approaches, however, are derived from a hydraulic, phenotypic-genotypic psychoanalytically-based model of personality that assumes a set of genotypic psychological dispositions that endure even though their overt response forms may change. (This model is the one shared by traditional trait and dynamic dispositional psychological theories.) The only other conceptual apparatus bearing on identity that commands considerable respect and attention has grown out of the work of Piaget and his associates. Growth of interest in Piaget's formulations results from the fact that there is a great deal of evidence that our cognitive constructions about ourselves and the world — our personal theories about identity — often are relatively stable and resistant to change; this is especially true of the features of problem solving called 'cognitive styles' (Mischel 1968 and 1969; Kagan 1969). But when behavioural scientists have turned away from the cognitive and intellective dimensions to the domains of motivational dispositions, identity, and interpersonal behaviour, evidence for consistency and continuity is much harder to establish. (See Mischel 1969, for an outstanding discussion of 'Continuity and Change in Personality' that bears directly on the problems embedded within contemporary identity models.) Finally, the most recent challenger to the reigning hydraulic, phenotype-genotype, psychodynamic identity paradigm, namely existential psychology, has not proceeded much further than the assertion that to find out who and what I am, I need to know what I do — and that I can elect what I do.

One compelling indication of the pervasiveness and undisputed position of the reigning psychological paradigm that underlies most efforts to clarify or study identity is the fact that the socio-cultural bases and symbolic constituents of both personal and collective have been largely ignored until quite recent times. Moreover, the notion that qualitative structural and cultural transformations in countries like the United States create new kinds of identity models and manifestations that cannot be described or understood in terms of theories that may have been appropriate to societal conditions in the past has, so far, been treated either by aspiring social prophets and gurus of the youth culture that emerged during the 1960s (Roszak 1969; Slater 1970; and Reich 1970, for example,) or by global sociological theorists-cum-social philosophers (for example, Berger, Berger, and Kellner 1973; Bell 1976). The central objective of this essay is to direct systematic attention to societal changes which have generated new contexts and processes for identity construction and transformation with the result that qualitatively new kinds of identity structures and models are emerging.

Any systematic discussion of identity must at least acknowledge, if not clarify, several critical issues. Firstly, is a scientific sociological conception of 'identity' indispensible, necessary or at least unequivocally useful? One could argue that the concept should simply be dropped from scientific discourse altogether and left to its fate in popular best-sellers. The existence of cognate, superficially overlapping concepts like 'mazeway', 'self', 'personality', 'ego', and 'character' — to mention but a sample of possible replacements for 'identity' — could lend weight to this argument for discarding the concept entirely. Yet, none of these other concepts captures completely the myriad nuances of meaning that are associated with the idea of 'identity'. None of these potential rivals captures the subjectively-experienced consciousness of oneself which emerges from the interplay of organism, social structure, and cultural reality definitions and models that are a central feature of most conceptions of identity.

Secondly, assuming that the concept of identity serves a unique and irreplaceable scientific function, then it becomes necessary to grapple with a far more complex issue: do we really need new conceptual containers for the same familiar wine or are we dealing with a fundamentally different species of wine distilled from grapes grown under historically unprecedented conditions? That is, do we simply need modified, more adequate conceptual tools for dealing with a phenomenon which despite its enormous cultural/civilizational diversity is fundamentally unchanged, *or* have the structure, meaning, and contextual sources of the phenomenon itself changed so rapidly and fundamentally that it is necessary to develop new conceptual frameworks and images of identity before we can even begin to theoretically locate its sociologically significant types, correlates, and consequences? This question immediately suggests a matrix for very crudely locating various theoretical formulations and their authors:

Typology of Theoretical Perspective on Identity

	Substantially unchanged empirical models	Historically different empirical models
Existing conceptual perspectives suitable	1	2
New frameworks needed	3	4

MODELS OF IDENTITY

However great the temptation to classify various theorists who have given identity a central theoretical significance in their work, such an effort would both be presumptuous and tangential to the purpose of the matrix which is simply to indicate the assumptions and frame of reference from which this essay proceeds.[1] The arguments and discussion that follow therefore assume that new conceptual models and theories are necessary in order to begin to understand the fundamentally new identity structures formed by a new type of society that generates with remarkable fecundity new cultural models and symbolic templates of/for both personal and collective identity. The most powerful justification for assuming that new kinds of identity models and patterns are emerging is, in my opinion, to be found in what Daniel Bell calls 'the character of societies'. More specifically, the assumptions that support the arguments developed in this essay are rooted in the notion that a qualitatively different kind of society involves social structural and cultural alterations that profoundly alter sensibility, consciousness, reflectivity, and cosmology—in short, the nature of personal and collective identity. After all, identity is not some Baconian infusion of dry light; it is part of the socio-cultural context in which it is constructed, legitimatized, transmitted, and manifested in social action.

It seems advisable to take explicit note of some of the limitations in the scope and focus of the present essay as well as the absence of adequate empirical substantiation of a number of interpretations. It should be clear that the following analysis refers almost exclusively to the United States — although there is no reason, in principle, why it would not apply to other societies as they increasingly assume the structural features of 'post-industrial society' and the cultural characteristics of post-modern meaning systems. A different qualification concerns the focus on 'cultural' as opposed to 'social' movements. It would be absurd to suggest that all contemporary movements or all movements emerging in post-modern societal contexts are cultural movements which emphasize the ideological construction of new identity models and resocialize normal adults. Traditional social movements demanding structural changes in social institutions certainly continue to exist in post-industrial, post-modern America. Such movements necessarily focus strategically upon some aspect of the authority structure: they typically rely on the authoritative co-ordination of effort and establish an elaborate administrative apparatus with formal communication channels for this purpose. Various economic interest groups, some reform movements, including some that are part of the American labour scene, and some radical right-wing political movements, such as the John Birch Society, exemplify these traits and should legitimately be conceived of as social movements. But the more significant contemporary movements (Turner 1969:586) are less concerned with structural injustices than with personal identity, social consciousness, and cultural meanings and evaluations. More specifically, they are concerned with constructing new identity models orientated toward claims to 'authenticity' and 'self-actualization'. A similar qualification must be made with respect to the construction of new identity models by movement groups; obviously, this kind of activity is not unique to contemporary cultural movements. Traditional social movements clearly had a profound impact on the identities of their participants. However, such movements tended to cultivate identity models which emphasized collective honour, shared commitments, and the virtues of allegiance to movement goals and authority structures. In contrast, contemporary cultural movements give primacy to ideologically constructed identity models that aim at personal authenticity and self-actualization.

Some additional qualifications need explication at the outset. This essay represents an interpretation of historically-specific tendencies that emerged in a specific societal context; namely, American society after 1960. Although the structural and cultural conditions responsible for the kinds of ideological movements that focus on identity are becoming more pronounced, it is necessary to acknowledge the possibility that the concern with 'consciousness' in movements as well as the general public/popular preoccupation with personal and collective identity is ephemeral and not likely to persist very much longer. Thus, it is entirely possible that a continuation of the deterioration of the American economy will generate more traditional social movements demanding redress of structural in-justices and inequalities, and focusing on winning specific, concrete material benefits for their members. At a more general level, however, the structural and cultural conditions that are responsible for the change in the focus, functions, and organization of contemporary movements are likely to become even more pronounced in the last two decades of the twentieth century. If this is the case, then the types of movements described here are also likely to become more pronounced — although perhaps supplemented by new *social* movements focusing on economic changes and material benefits.

Finally, it seems particularly crucial to maintain a clear-cut distinction between analytic and empirical referents and generalizations, especially when these pertain to subjectively-experienced concepts like 'identity' which have a considerable realizing potency of their own. The attempt to maintain this distinction between analytic and empirical formulations is more successful in the early sections of the essay than in the last two sec-tions and it must be said that this is certainly *not* entirely or even largely due to limitations of the length of the essay; the more important limitations are conceptual. That is, the need to maintain clear-cut distinction between analytic and empirical analyses of identity cannot be consistently fulfilled without the kind of thorough-going transformation in the reigning psychological paradigm that has provided the basis for most sociological and anthropological images and assumptions concerning identity. Much of the murky and imprecise discussion that permeates the literature on identity stems from failure to separate abstract conceptual formulations about identity, symbolic identity models that emerge in the cultural domain, and the subjectively experienced sense of self-in-relation-to-reality that people are increasingly concerned about; namely, identity. This issue of the self-realizing potency or self-validating socializing effects of analytic, scientific formulations about identity is explicitly discussed in the last section of the essay, but infuses and permeates the entire analysis.

THE NEW SOCIETY: EMPIRICAL CHARACTERISTICS

There is no agreed name for the new type of societal order and historical era which the United States has already entered. The new social order has been referred to *inter alia* as 'cybernetic' (Bell 1967 and 1968), 'technotronic' (Brzezinski 1967), 'programmed' (Touraine 1972), 'post-industrial' (Touraine 1972; Bell 1973 and 1976), and 'post-modern'

(Kavolis 1970 and 1974; Bell 1976) by social theorists who have noted the emergence of a new historical phenomenon. But this profusion of different labels conceals a surprising degree of consensus about the substantive phenomenon to which they refer.[2] Thus, most of these social analysts emphasize the critical importance of technological applications of theoretical knowledge to the productive sector, the shift from a manufacturing economy to a service economy, and decreasing economic or class-based conflict between capital and labour (or bourgeoisie and proletariat). In general, these social analysts, interpreters, and/or prophets of the emerging new kind of society have focused more on structural and institutional developments or demographic and ecological changes than on cultural meaning systems — with the notable exceptions of Kavolis (1970 and 1974); Berger, Berger, and Kellner (1973); and, most importantly, Bell (1973 and 1976).

The central disagreement among analysts of the emerging society concerns whether major, traditional-structural divisions will remain and whether they will affect the focus of social conflict. Toffler (1970), Brzezinski (1967), Aron (1968), and Bell (1967, 1968 and 1973) believe that fundamental structural divisions and conflicts, based on class ownership and control of the means of production, are rapidly diminishing: regulated, organized competition softened by multiple memberships and affiliations with cross-cutting ties will soon be the only form of conflict in the emerging society. Most importantly, these interpreters assume increasing public acceptance of rational control by technically competent élites. In this scenario, the scientists, professionals, experts, and specialists who compose the ruling élites are increasingly able to chart a relatively harmonious course of socio-economic growth. Under such conditions, this perspective does not foresee much likelihood that pervasive dissent or dissatisfaction could generate popular ideologies capable of mobilizing large-scale loyalties to movements attempting to radically transform society.

Neo-Marxian analyses of contemporary trends (for example, Touraine 1972) acknowledge that traditional class conflicts between capital and labour, and traditional economic bases of domination are losing the central importance they had in an earlier era. However, these analyses see social conflicts and cleavages emerging between those who control the institutions of decision-making, societal integration and symbolic manipulation and those who have been reduced to a condition of dependence, alienation, and powerlessness. (Touraine 1972:9 suggests the term 'dependent participation' to refer to the alienated masses in contemporary society.) Like its anti-Marxian counterpart, this perspective conceives of a new dominant class or élite defined by technical competence and theoretical-scientific knowledge — although the socially defined motives and roles of the dominant technical élite are viewed very differently in the two perspectives. Neo-Marxian analyses typically anticipate that the new subordinated and alienated class will ultimately revolt against its dependence on a dominating technical élite and embark upon an autonomous course that will endow social existence with unprecedented meaning and fulfilment. This perspective is (understandably) ambiguous as to the social sources of this new, structurally-defined revolutionary group, functionally analogous to Marx's proletariat, which will provide the dynamic for the creation of a new social order. Conservative neo-Marxians generally reject the idea that the working class will be the agent of future socio-historical change. Thus, Touraine (1972:18) indicates that:

> . . . sensibility to the new themes of social conflict was not most pronounced in the most highly organized sectors of the working class . . . [rather] . . . the most radical and creative movements appeared in the economically advanced groups, the research agencies, the technicians with skills but no authority, and, of course, in the university community.

In spite of disagreement over the role and likelihood of social conflict and radical (revolutionary) movements, then, both perspectives concur about a vaguely and often imprecisely conceived set of changes that occur to transform an advanced industrial order into a qualitatively different type of society. But neither of these perspectives include specific, explicit criteria for analytically distinguishing between a 'mature' or 'late' industrial society, on the one hand, and a society that has already entered a new, subsequent phase, on the other. Both perspectives embrace extremely perceptive, incisive, and sensitive observations of recent and contemporary trends; both groups of social analysts support their interpretations and evaluations with an imposing (occasionally exhausting) array of empirical indicators and research findings; yet, their analyses of incipient or embryonic societal patterns remain unsatisfying and unconvincing. They suffer from empiric myopia and the absence of a conceptual framework which distinguishes analytically the structural and institutional aspects of society from the cultural-symbolic aspects.

CONTEMPORARY SOCIETY: ANALYTIC DIMENSIONS OF POST-INDUSTRIAL AND POST-MODERN REALITIES

This section proposes a very crude conceptual framework in order to underscore the historically-unique characteristics of contemporary (American) society that are largely responsible for the pervasiveness and significance of identity construction and experimentation in cultural movements after 1960. Thus, the proposed dimensions are intended less as constituents of a general paradigm or socio-historical model than as a tentative heuristic.

The model proposes that there are four analytic dimensions or levels of society; these dimensions or levels refer to analytically distinguishable domains or realms. Firstly, there is a substructural, *material-demographic-ecological level* which refers to the natural world, the environment and its resources, the size and structure of the population as well as population density and distribution. Secondly, there is a *social structural/institutional level* which refers to normative patterning of interpersonal behaviour and larger social organizations and associations. This level includes all institutionalized role-statuses and positions which provide the normative frameworks for meaningful action by defining appropriate behaviours and 'performances'. Thus, the social structural/institutional dimension refers to the realm of recurrent, unproblematic, unreflexive human behaviour and interaction which exists by virtue of the institutionalized normative templates that define socially legitimatized rules, roles, and responsibilities in relation to structural positions. This means that the structural/institutional realm includes such diverse constellations as class relations and the relations of production; political parties and their relation to both the *polity* and various publics and interest groups; the structure of institutionalized kinship, marriage, and family roles, relations and regulations; this domain also includes legal norms, economic norms, and the stratification system. The third and fourth analytic dimensions or levels of society refer to different components of culture: *cognitive culture* and *expressive culture*. The general concept of culture refers to '. . . transmitted and created content and patterns of values, ideas, and other symbolic-meaningful systems as factors in the shaping of human behaviour . . .' (Kroeber and Parsons 1958:583). This cognitively-orientated conception of 'culture' excludes the observable patterns of behaviour that are the result of the structure of situations or role-statuses and, in contrast, emphasizes ideas, beliefs, symbolic meanings, models, and interpretations. But within this broad cultural domain, it is possible to distinguish the realm of *cognitive culture* which includes philosophy, science, and technology from the realm of *expressive culture* that encompasses all the shared symbolic meanings, models, and interpretive classifications which together constitute an individual's subjectively-experienced psychological reality system. This subjectively-experienced '. . . psychological reality of an individual is the world as he perceives it and knows it, in his own terms; it is his world of meanings' (Wallace and Atkins 1960:75). Most of the shared symbolic constituents of the expressive culture created and transmitted in any society refer, directly or indirectly, to either personal or collective identity or to religious beliefs and practices. It is even possible to tentatively and very roughly define personal identity as an individual's subjectively-experienced psychological reality system of meanings and images of himself in relation to the relevant social and physical world around'him.[3] In brief, then, expressive culture consists of personal and collective identity models and meanings, symbolic templates for shared social consciousness, and religious interpretations, evaluations, and rituals.

The four analytically differentiated dimensions of society will now be considered in relation to two axes: the horizontal axis will refer to distinctive periods of historical time; the vertical axis refers to the rate of change and/or growth of each of the four dimensions. Thus, this schema considers, in crude and global fashion, the relative rates of change among these four domains during different historical time periods in the West.

One additional prefatory distinction is necessary to clarify some of the terminological chaos and ambiguity which mars much current discussion of 'post-industrialism' and 'post-modernity'. It seems appropriate to limit the terms 'pre-industrial', 'industrial', and 'post-industrial' to analytically-differentiated periods or trends (abstracted from empirical historical events) in the social structural/institutional dimension of normatively patterned role-statuses and positions. Similarly, it seems appropriate to restrict the terms 'pre-modern', 'modern', and 'post-modern' to analytically-distinguishable periods in the dimension of expressive culture. In doing this, we are following Bell's early (1968:158) formulation:

> The concept of a post-industrial society deals primarily with long-run structural changes in society. It is not, nor can it be, a comprehensive model of the complete society; it does not deal with basic changes in values (such as the hedonism which now legitimates the spending patterns of an affluent society; it can say little about the nature of-political crises . . . it cannot assess the quality of the national will . . . by positing certain fundamental shifts in the bases of class positions and modes of access to places in the society . . . Just as an individual society has been organized politically and culturally in diverse ways by the USSR, Germany, and Japan, so too the post-industrial society may have diverse political and cultural forms.

However, even in this initial conception, and quite explicitly in the subsequent book on *The Coming of Post-Industrial Society*, Bell (1973) pollutes his structural/institutional conception of post-industrialism with cognitive- cultural determinants and components. Thus, of the five dimensions of a post-industrial society 'The first is the centrality of theoretical knowledge as the source of innovation and policy analysis in the society' (Bell 1976:198). This treatment collapses scientific and technological cognitive culture into the realm of institutional structure which is conceptually unsatisfactory and analytically imprecise. In Bell's latest work, *The Cultural Contradictions of Capitalism* (1976), there is considerable ambiguity as to the conceptual distinction between post-industrial society and post-modern society. Here we are informed that . . . 'The post-industrial society centers on the technology, the kinds of work people do . . . and the organization of knowledge.' In contrast (?), the '. . . contradictions of capitalism of which I speak in these pages have to do with the disjunction between the kind of organization and the norms demanded in the economic realm and the norms of self-realization that are now central in the culture' (Bell 1976:15). In short, Bell seems to be suggesting that 'post-industrialism' is defined by certain relationships between scientific and technological knowledge and the economic system whereas 'post-modern society' is distinguished by relationships between cultural and economic principles. All that one can say for sure is that Bell clearly perceives a 'disjunction of realms' in contemporary society and wants to bear witness to the moral corruption of post-modern culture.[4]

Bell is hardly the only writer whose conceptual distinctions between culture and institutional structure, between 'modernization' and 'industrialization' leave much to be desired. For example, Berger, Berger, and Kellner (1973:9) '. . . discuss modernization as the institutional concomitants of technologically induced economic growth . . . Modernization, then, consists of the growth and diffusion of a set of institutions rooted in the transformation of the economy by means of technology.' But this makes 'modernization' synonymous with 'industrialization'. Yet, surely, 'industrialization' refers to the *structural consequences* of the industrial technology that resulted from the application of scientific knowledge to the economic system. Even Bell (1968:158) is unambiguous in his initial restriction of the concept of post-industrialism to 'long-run structural changes in society'. In short, to use the terms 'modernization' and 'industrialization' interchangeably is to overlook the fact that in the feudal era, culture and social structure were fused in a distinct unity that integrated institutions and identities. It was this fusion that was rent asunder by the industrialization of the structural/institutional domain which had resulted from the staggering take-off of scientific and technological (cognitive) culture after they parted company from expressive cultural concerns with religion and identity. In fact, I believe that the analytic meaning of the distinction between 'pre-modern' and 'modern' — the point at which 'modernization' analytically begins — should refer to the point at which cognitive and expressive culture become clearly differentiated and begin to develop extremely disparate rates of change. Analogously, the distinction between 'pre-industrial' and 'industrial' society refers to the massive structural differentiation and institutional transformation of Western societies that occurred as a *consequence* of the technological application of science to industry for economic purposes. In this sense, then, 'modernization' refers to developments in the cultural domain: the differentiation of cognitive and expressive aspects of culture. The rapid growth of scientific and technological knowledge that followed, and the utilization of this knowledge for economic purposes, produced the structural/institutional transformation known as the 'industrial revolution'. Thus, the industrial revolution refers to the impact of cognitive culture on the structural/institutional dimension of society. Moreover, this formulation argues that, from an analytic perspective, 'modernization' and the beginning of the 'modern era' preceded 'industrialization' and the rise of industrial economic institutions and roles. The term 'industrial' (alone or with a prefix or suffix) therefore will refer to social structure: the realm of institutional patterns, role-statuses, and positions. The term 'modern' (alone or with a prefix or suffix) will refer to developments in the cultural realm, that is, to developments in scientific-technological cognitive culture or to changes in the domain of expressive culture-developments in shared religious meanings and/or symbolic identity models which together form the bases of subjectively-experienced psychological reality systems.

In the early feudal era there was no institutionalized distinction between cognitive and expressive culture and the generalized cultural domain was fused with social structure and institutional patterns to produce a distinctively integrated civilizational complex. During this analytically distinguishable stage, therefore, there were only two conceptually-separable levels or dimensions of society: the material-demographic-ecological level and the undifferentiated culture-structures which defined coherent identities and actions for most of the population. This does not imply little or no change, but only that the rate of development in each of the two domains was relatively comparable. Cities emerged and grew during this period, largely as a result of improved agricultural methods, and the population grew from 133 million people at the rise of Christianity to 545 million people by 1650. At some point after the thirteenth century and before the sixteenth century the social structural/institutional realm became differentiated from the cultural system, although they retained close interdependence. More importantly, by the end of the seventeenth century the rise of science and secular philosophy began to draw cognitive culture away from expressive culture, slowly at first, but with accelerating speed. Thus, by the beginning of the eighteenth century societal complexity had proceeded to the point where all four analytically-distinguishable dimensions had emerged. And at that point the four rates of change began to diverge rapidly.

The beginning of the eighteenth century accelerated the rate of change in cognitive culture, due to the emergence of organized scientific activity, as well as in the material-demographic-ecological realm, due to European exploration and colonization of newly discovered lands. The population of the world increased from 545 million people in 1650 to 728 million in 1750 and significant urbanization began in England. The rates of change in these two domains far exceeded that in the structural/institutional domain. However, even there changes began to occur with increasing frequency — due largely to developments in the other two realms. Thus, the decades between roughly 1600 and 1770 generated prototypes for the contemporary nuclear family, child-centred private household; pre-industrial capitalism emerged; monarchical political systems began to be challenged by the outrageous idea of popular, liberal democratic régimes; and current sex-role differentiation began to take shape. In contrast, this period experienced relative stability in the domain of expressive culture — perhaps as a result of symbolic deficits and exhaustion of symbolic resources in European expressive culture following upon the enormous upheavals in meaning associated with the Protestant Reformation. The pre-modern/pre-industrial analytic period closed with increasing rates of change in scientific cognitive culture and in the material-demographic-ecological realm. These change rates were followed by lower rates of structural/institutional change; new developments in this level were less frequent and pervasive in societal impact. Finally, the identity models and religious meanings comprising the analytic domain of expressive culture were relatively stable, generating the smallest rate of change among the four conceptually differentiated societal domains — marking an end to the most active conflict between Catholic and Protestant religious models and meanings.

The nineteenth century spawned the 'industrial revolution' and the dominance of industrial institutions and economic structures. These developments reflected further dramatic increases in the cognitive cultural rate of change with the application of science to concrete industrial problems leading to the institutionalization of technology and the transformation of economic structures. Dramatic increases also occurred in the material-demographic-ecological realm: in 1800 world population had grown to 906 million people, but by 1900 it reached 1,610 million (Deevey Jr. 1960). This 'demographic transition' was due to a high and stable birth rate accompanied by a sharply declining death rate. Scientific and technological cognitive culture was largely responsible for the sharp drop in the death rate in the form of rudimentary public health and sanitation measures as well as the emergence of 'scientific' medical therapies and preventive techniques. Although not quite so rapidly, the rate of structural/institutional change accelerated considerably and far outstripped the rate of change in expressive culture during the early and middle industrial era of the nineteenth and early twentieth centuries. In short, the astonishing growth rates of scientific-technological cognitive culture and the material-demographic-ecological realm during the 140 years after 1800 profoundly affected social structure, institutional patterns and the organization of role-statuses. The label 'industrial era' underscores the impact of cognitive cultural and material-demographic-ecological factors on bourgeois society through the use of economic technology; the major transformations that occurred in that era were permanent alterations in the basic structure of institutions. This means that the rates of change in the structural/ institutional and expressive cultural dimensions of society began to diverge markedly during the industrial era. Specifically, the rate of structural differentiation, institutional integration and interdependence generated by the application of the newly-developed industrial technology to a vastly broader material-demographic domain far exceeded the growth rate of expressive cultural changes until towards the end of the industrial era.

As the focus of attention moves closer to the present time, a number of changes begin to take place in the four analytically-differentiated dimensions of society. The rates of material, demographic, and ecological growth begin to decelerate in the most advanced societies. This reflects societal objectives concerning restricting population growth and anxieties about over-crowding. Zero population growth and population stability become important goals. Ecological concern over excess population concentration and density due to urbanization and then metropolitanization generates interest in population redistribution and decentralization. This ecological concern spills over into concern about the pollution and deterioration of the natural environment — and the demonstrable impact this has on health and 'quality of life'. In addition, natural material resources, generally considered inexhaustible during the industrial era, suddenly prove to be finite; some of them even start to be in short supply. Thus, towards the end of the modern/industrial era, the rate of growth of the analytically-differentiated material-demographic-ecological dimension of society begins to slow appreciably. Societies become aware of the 'limits of growth' and assumptions of scarcity replace former assumptions of limitless abundance in the material-demographic-ecological realm.

By the end of the modern/industrial era the institutionalization of science and technology increases the growth rate of the analytically-differentiated cognitive cultural dimension of society to unequalled heights: there is no doubt but that the number of both scientific and technological developments has increased with accelerating speed over the course of the twentieth century to date — and will continue to multiply in the immediate future. But there are also suggestions that the rate of cognitive cultural growth will begin to slow in the near future, if it has not already begun to decelerate in the most advanced societies, and that this will begin to approximate a stable or declining rate of change. In one sense some such outcome is a statistical necessity since the base number of extant scientific and technological innovations, against which the number or frequency of new scientific and technological developments in any given year would have to be compared in order to calculate the 'rate of change' in cognitive culture, is already staggeringly large. But it is also likely that the deceleration in the growth rate of the material-demographic-ecological realm will act as a braking influence on the rate of change in cognitive culture due to shortages in the supply of traditional natural resources and social restrictions on the technological destruction of the environment.

There is another property of science and technology which guarantees a tapering off of the unprecedented rate of growth in the cognitive cultural dimension of society; namely, its 'immediacy'. Derek J. De Solla Price (1963) suggests that science and technology are far more 'immediate' than other societal domains. That is, using a loose definition of what constitutes 'scientists and technologists'—so that even social scientists and engineers are counted—then the doubling time is every ten years for the past 300 years. In short, the number of scientists and technologists has been increasing at a constant exponential rate for three centuries. Assume that on average a scientist or technologist has a working lifetime of 45 years: that is, he begins 'doing' science or technology while still a student and continues until the age of 65. Under these assumptions 96 per cent of all scientists and technologists have been alive during a normal 45-year working lifetime of any given scientist or technologist during the past 300 years. Hence, the 'coefficient of immediacy' for scientists and technologists for the last three centuries is an almost unbelievable 96 per cent: 96 out of every 100 scientists who have ever lived have been alive during the normal working lifetime of any given worker in the cognitive cultural domain. Obviously, the population of scientists and technologists has been increasing much more rapidly than other parts of the population. For example, during the last three centuries the work force has doubled about every 50 years, which gives a coefficient of immediacy of about 46 per cent. Omar K. Moore (1974) estimates that it will not be until the year 2,000 that the coefficient of immediacy for the world's labour force will reach 50 per cent—meaning that half the workers who have ever lived will be alive and half will be dead. As Moore (1974:5) observes:

> The freshness of science, the sense of everything happening now, is not a new phenomenon. It was as true in the 17th Century as it was in the 18th, and it remained true in the 19th as it continues to be true in the 20th Century. However, exponential growth cannot go on. If we continue to breed scientists (and technologists) as we have for the past 300 years, then, we will reach the point that there are more scientists than there are people—and this is an obvious impossibility.

There are already clear indications that advanced societies are finding it increasingly difficult to continue doubling scientists and technologists every ten years. Thus, both changes in the nature of basic and applied research mean that the cost of research is rising disproportionately. Moreover, part of the reason for the high coefficient of immediacy for science and technology lies in the recency of science and technology compared to labour of all kinds—which has been around since the dawn of civilization. But that does not explain the consistency of the exponential growth pattern in the rate of cognitive cultural change. How has the domain of cognitive culture been so remarkably successful in maintaining its constant exponential growth pattern in all kinds of socio-political circumstances and international holocausts—and even avoided being seduced into increasing its recruitment in order to increase its rate of growth? This is a critical issue to which we will return after sketching the remaining outlines of contemporary society by considering the two remaining analytic dimensions.

At the structural/institutional analytic level the rate of change decelerates during the end of the modern/industrial era and stabilizes or begins to decline as attention shifts closer to the present time. This simply means that the institutional structure of social organizations and role-statuses becomes increasingly resilient, inflexible, and difficult to change. The structural interdependence and institutional complexity resulting from extreme differentiation in advanced societies 'fixes' the basic institutional patterns and role-relations within which social interaction can occur. In brief, contemporary structures have become more rigid and the rate of change in the institutional dimension of society stabilizes or begins to decline gradually.

Shortly after the structural/institutional change rate stabilizes or begins to decline, the rate of change in the domain of expressive culture begins to increase, slowly at first, but then with increasing momentum. It is always hazardous to attach specific dates to basic changes in societal domains—and almost equally irresistible. I would locate the most significant alterations in the rate of structural/institutional change as occurring shortly after World War II; the 1950s consolidates the stable and then declining change rate in American institutional structure and patterns. Analogously, I believe that the most significant accelerations in the rate of change in the expressive cultural domain began in the early 1960s. Insofar as these qualitative changes in the rates of change that characterize the two domains have, in fact, occurred, it is possible to analytically define and distinguish 'post-industrialism' and 'post-modernity'. Specifically, the significant decline in the rate of structural/institutional change analytically marks the end of the industrial era and the emergence of post-industrialism; the point at which the rate of expressive cultural change sharply accelerates analytically indicates the emergence of post-modernity. More importantly, the point at which the stable or gradually declining rate of institutional change at the structural level of society is crossed by the steeply rising rate of change in expressive cultural models and meanings analytically defines the emergence of a new kind of society and the opening of the post-industrial/post-modern era. Thus, the most salient and significant socio-cultural developments of the modern/industrial period involved institutional differentiation and development due to the application of industrial technology to economic structures; changes in expressive culture during that period were relatively modest in comparison to these structural transformations of industrial society. In contrast the most salient and significant socio-cultural developments in the post-industrial/post-modern era that is beginning will involve the domain of expressive culture. The most distinctive characteristics of post-industrial/post-modern society will be the bewilderingly rapid rates of change in the symbolic meanings, models, and interpretations that constitute the domain of expressive culture; the other defining attribute of this type of society is the stability, rigidity, and resilience to change of its basic institutional designs, structural patterns, and role-status relations. From this perspective contemporary post-industrial/post-modern society is not so much a further continuation or extension of the modern industrialized society that preceded it as its direct antithesis.

To illustrate the applicability of this analytic formulation, consider some of the more salient features of American society since 1960. The electronic mass media overwhelm all other channels of mass communication in the volume and variety of symbolic meanings and messages they transmit, yet the institutional structures and organizational frameworks within which these revolutionary, expressive culture transforming capacities are located are quite traditional. More specifically, the symbolic meanings and interpretations of political phenomena transmitted via the electronic media during the 1960s transformed conventional meanings and modes of operation in the American political arena. Traditional institutions, time-hallowed customs, and core national symbols were transformed and lost public legitimacy with bewildering frequency: flags were torn down and torn up, draft cards were burned or discarded, official pronouncements lost credibility, elected officials were convicted of corruption and jailed, and the absence of visible political alternatives was bemoaned or condemned. Yet, for all the profound expressive cultural changes in the symbolic meanings and interpretations attached to core political institutions and role-statuses, neither the underlying political structure nor its institutional mechanisms and party organizations changed appreciably. Similar changes occurred in the area of marriage and the family. Many came to view marriage as a prison that limited personal growth and freedom and to view fidelity as outmoded: tradebook best-sellers appeared bearing titles like *Open Marriage* and *Creative Divorce*. Marital roles blurred, marital stability declined, and the divorce rate hit new highs; 'alternative' marital and familial arrangements (experiments) were considered, if not actually tried out among significant (generally young, college-educated, upper middle class) groups in the population. Yet, for all the changing marital, sexual, and familial meanings and models generated by the expressive culture among youth on campuses and educated white suburbanites, the basic structure of marital and familial institutions and role relationships has not altered appreciably. Despite the sharp decline in the legitimacy of traditional marital and familial roles, despite the rising divorce rate, a larger proportion of the American population is married today than ever before, and the brief renaissance of interest in communalism and group marriage appears to have waned already. In short, the expressive cultural symbols, models, meanings, and interpretations as well as the general legitimacy of marriage and family institutions and role-statuses have turned over several times in the past decade or so, but the basic structures remain intact and substantially unchanged.

The formulation developed above suggested using the term 'post-industrial' to refer to contemporary structural/institutional forms and the term 'post-modern' to designate the contemporary domain of expressive culture. The rigid inflexibility and immobility of post-industrial social structures and institutions means that behaviour and relationships become increasingly routinized and predictable. In contrast, post-modern expressive culture creates a situation in which core symbolic meanings, models, and evaluations attached to institutional structures and role-statuses as well as one's own identity and relationships are in a state of constant and increasingly accelerating change. In this sense the number of disparate meanings, interpretations, and evaluations in the expressive culture that can be attached to anything and anyone is constantly expanding. The terminological distinction proposed here makes it possible to conceive of societies which possess the structural characteristics of post-industrial institutions, but which lack the symbolic fluidity and fecundity of the corresponding post-modern expressive culture and vice versa. In the historical sequence of analytically-distinguished periods modernization preceded industrialization — because the latter was a consequence of the science and technology that comprise cognitive culture — but post-industrial institutional structures preceded post-modern expressive culture, although only by one or two decades. For purposes of the remainder of the present essay, we will assume that the United States became both post-industrial and post-modern after 1960.

IMPLICATIONS FOR CONTEMPORARY IDENTITY MODELS

The proposed formulation stands in direct opposition to Bellah's (1964) description of the modern stage of socio-cultural evolution. Bellah (1964:370) argues that an increasingly flexible 'self-revising social order expressed in a voluntaristic and democratic society' is associated with a type of culture and identity that 'have come to be viewed as endlessly revisible' (Bellah 1964:373). Such liberal optimism seems analytically naive; social life requires order and predictability. In contrast to Bellah's interpretation, the present formulation suggests that expressive cultural religious meanings and personal identity models can be permitted to be 'endlessly revisible' *only* if structural stability, institutional inflexibility, and continuity in the performance of role-statuses guarantees routinized, predictable behaviour for which specific persons can be held accountable. In other words, the meaning and legitimacy of various behaviours and relationships can be treated as unimportant or irrelevant only insofar as the performance of the behaviours themselves are unproblematic. The performance of specific behaviours is guaranteed and unproblematic only when it is structurally determined to the point that a high degree of predictability is possible.

The proposed formulation also suggests that post-modern expressive culture leads to a 'psychological utopianism' (Manuel 1965) which emphasizes existential questions of meaning that are addressed with concepts like 'authenticity' and 'self-actualization', and which leads contemporary cultural movements to represent attempts to hold society responsible for unclear or unsatisfying personal and/or collective identity (Turner 1969). That is, the intrinsic dignity of all people, whatever their different structural position and role-statuses, is no longer a central issue: that issue emerged in the previous era when structural/institutional change was so rapid that highly mobile populations needed some stable foundation in which to anchor their identities. Contemporary post-industrial structures provide sufficiently stable and enduring institutional anchorages for behaviour that identity models can be 'subjectivized' and 'particularized' without disrupting social stability. One can experiment with new identity models; one can strive for 'self-actualization' and 'authenticity'; one can search for new religious meanings and rituals or new secular interpretations for conventional institutionally structured behaviours and relationships without posing any threat to social order. In contrast to the pre-industrial situation, the emerging post-industrial structural stability, immobility, and rigidity does not mean that identity is linked to institutional role-statuses and positions. Instead it means that identity as well as the rest of expressive culture is so thoroughly detached and segregated from institutional structures that it becomes a self-consciously constructed model of/for subjectively experiencing private meanings, meanings which have no (public) significance for (changing) the world out there. As Kavolis (1970:437) so perceptively observed,

> The detachment of culture from social structure results in the liberation of the creative imagination and, on the other hand, in an increasing irrelevance of culture to social life. The irrelevance of culture to society is then likely to be subjectively perceived as the 'meaninglessness' or 'absurdity' of . . . existence itself.

In a brilliant analysis of 'The theme of contemporary social movements', Turner (1969) distinguishes three significant themes or conceptions of injustice for which society as a whole is held responsible. The first was a 'humanitarian' political theme that arose around the time of the French and American Revolutions demanding participation (or more equitable participation) in the political arena — particularly for the economically increasingly powerful middle classes. The second 'socialist' theme that dominated most significant social movements after 1848 focused on concrete, material necessities in the economic arena — particularly for the increasing, impoverished urban proletariat. Whereas the philosophical basis for the first theme was Enlightenment rationalism, the philosophical grounding of the second was squarely lodged in materialism. Turner (1969) then argues that a new theme or conception of fundamental injustice has begun to emerge; this theme is partly psychological and psychotherapeutic in that it involves shared demands for existential and psycho-social meaning and identity, if not 'self-actualization' and 'authenticity'. This theme is prevalent among the new kind of constituency of movements; namely, youth or generational groups. The philosophical basis for this new theme of post-modern expressive movements is existentialism and the injustice for which society is held responsible is 'alienation' — in the psychological, rather than the socio-economic, sense of self-estrangement and identity diffusion.

All social or cultural movements have elements of utopianism in their ideological formulations; hence, it is instructive to scrutinize utopian thought to see if it bears any relation to the 'movement themes' that Turner (1969) suggested. Manuel (1965) divides utopian thought into three periods characterized by markedly different emphases. The first period involves utopian images of the political arena characterized by what Manuel (1965:294) refers to as 'calm felicity' and extends historically from Thomas More to the age of the French Revolution. The second period comprises the dynamic socialist and other historically determinist utopias which spanned the greater part of the nineteenth century. Then there is a hiatus in utopian thought due to the implications of Darwin's evolutionary theory of natural selection and Freud's discovery of the sexual basis of personality development. This absence of utopian thought as a significant intellectual-ideological ground for meaning permeated the twentieth century until after World War II when various philosophical anthropologists and existential psychologists began to construct a new basis for utopianism; Manuel (1965) uses Maslow's term 'eupsychia' to refer to these twentieth century 'psychological utopias'. And Manuel (1965:397) provides an incisive description of the 'psychological utopianism' that permeates post-modern expressive cultural models and meanings in the following analysis of Maslow as the principle architect of contemporary utopian identity models:

> Maslow is a psychological utopian not in the sense that he is blind to the economic and social miseries that inspired most past utopias, but with a utopian's license he moves up to another plane, where, beyond basic needs, he posits requirements for a psychic utopia that are more or less autonomous of any existing political order: the fulfillment of 'idiosyncratic potentials, of expression of the self, and of the tendency of the person to grow in his own style and at his own pace' . . . (Maslow is joining) . . . those philosophers of history who foresee a new spiritualization of mankind and an end to the sensate culture of our times.

The correspondence in the periodization used by Turner (1969) and Manuel (1965) is startling, given that the former is discussing the 'theme' or central conception of injustice that dominated movements in a certain era whereas the latter is discussing the emphases that permeated utopian thought in various periods. Both theorists agree that a political emphasis dominated around the time of the French Revolution, followed by a socialist focus on the economy that dominated the nineteenth century. But the correspondence between the two analyses grows even more astonishing in their discussions of the themes or emphases which dominate the contemporary era: both view what we are referring to as post-modern expressive culture as the dominant arena for utopianism and social movements and, within that societal domain, both discern a pervasive concern with identity models, problems of meaning, and 'authenticity' and 'self-actualization'. In fact, the two analyses are so compatible that both of them devote explicit attention to Maslow's writings, which they suggest are the most influential body of ideas in contemporary post-modern expressive culture. This is an evaluation with which the author must, most unhappily, agree.

At this point it is appropriate to integrate the Turner-Manuel theses with the formulation proposed in this essay. It has been suggested that there are analytic reasons for treating the period between 1800 and 1940 as the modern industrial era in which the social structural/institutional level of society experienced a rapid rate of change and dominated, if not determined, other socio-cultural phenomena. Conversely, this period was described as an era of relative stability in the rate of change of expressive culture. Insofar as the structural/institutional dimension of society represents the dominant or focal domain, it makes sense that both the utopian dreams and the significant attempts to bring about change in society focus on the critical (economic) institutional arena on this analytically-differentiated structural level. Both Turner and Manuel agree that socialist dreams and themes focusing on material well-being in the economic realm dominated nineteenth century industrial society. The movements and images of change in the industrial era focused appropriately on transforming institutional structures, with the underlying presumption that structural change in institutionalized inequalities would lead ineluctibly to a transformation in 'consciousness' or personal and collective identity. The discussion of contemporary society suggested that the change rate of post-modern expressive culture far exceeds that of post-industrial structure/institutions. Expressive culture is the realm of identity models, problems of 'religious' meaning, symbolic rituals and ideology. The declining change rate in the contemporary post-industrial structural/institutional realm would make it inappropriate for either utopian visions or movements for change to focus on the structural transformation of institutions. On the contrary, it makes far more sense for contemporary movements to focus on transformations in 'consciousness' and identities, since the latter are core constituents of the analytic dimension of post-modern society that is currently most salient and significant; namely, expressive culture. Hence, the 'psychological utopianism' and concern for identity and meaning in contemporary expressive cultural movements as well as the strategy of focusing on transformations in consciousness with the underlying presumption that a 'revolution in consciousness' will, ultimately, transform the structural/institutional bases for post-industrialism.

The 1960s made it clear that American movements have changed. No longer do they 'typically' involve the co-ordinated movement of discontented masses demanding specific changes in the institutional structure or the entire society (Gusfield 1968). No longer do shared perceptions of the need for fundamental change generate monolithic, centralized organizational structures (Turner 1969). Technologically based affluence (at least for some sectors of society), demographic changes in the age structure and composition of the population, and the exploding influence of the electronic mass media, especially television, have altered the nature, structure, and functions of contemporary movements in very fundamental ways, leading them to focus more on cultural claims to personal dignity, 'authenticity', and identity than public authority.

Traditional conceptions of social movements as one type of collective behaviour prompted an image of masses of people disorganizedly gathering in a particular place to forcefully, if not violently, express and dramatize their shared indignation and demands for structural change (Strauss 1947; Blumer 1957). In this perspective, the outcome of any particular movement demands depended on the number of people forcefully articulating the demands, their support-resource bases, the discipline and organization with which the demands were expressed, and the effectiveness of the agents of social control.

Cultural movements emphasizing identity models are not entirely new in social history. Youth movements, feminist movements, communal movements, and other kinds of cultural 'revitalization' phenomena have occurred in the past. However, the emergence of the self-conscious 'knowledge based society' (Holzner 1972:167) with its increasing supply of and demand for new expressive cultural models and meanings as well as the growth of the electronic mass media lend unprecedented impact and significance to such movements in the post-modern world. It is in this sense that analysis shifts from 'social' to 'cultural' movements which lack significant centralized organizational structures for co-ordinating and representing either the membership or ideology of the movement. Such post-modern expressive movements have as their central concern — at least from the perspective of their participants — the construction, interpretation, dissemination, and internalization of new ideological models of and for authentic personal identity and meaningful social consciousness.

The 'culturological' emphasis proposed above suggests that contemporary movements are most significant as settings for the collective construction of new expressive symbolic configurations or 'cultural *Gestalts*' (Wallace 1956) which provide more satisfying interpretations of social reality and more gratifying identity models. More specifically, post-modern expressive cultural movements are intentional, loosely organized and decentralized, socially shared sets of explicit and self-conscious indictments of some cluster of symbolic meanings and interpretations that is seen as arbitrary or unjust. Such indictments are accompanied by a set of prescribed solutions to the injustices which involve new or modified ideological models of and for personal and collective identity. The central objectives of movement participation and/or membership involve intentionally, self-consciously constructing a more satisfying expressive culture that is congruent with desired identity models and, therefore, less stressful. These 'mazeway reformulations' (Wallace 1956) prescribe and specify individual stress reduction mechanisms as well as processes and models for the production of new social strains and collective grievances. That is, what movement participants ultimately learn to experience as individual psychological stress and shared strain is actually the result of a socially constructed, subjectively experienced interpretative system that symbolically defines problematic or dissatisfying experiences and feelings as structurally determined injustices, rather than as unique, personal 'misfortunes' (Turner 1969).

This perspective also emphasizes the role of expressive cultural movements as 'media': that is, as alternative contexts, channels, and mechanisms for the ideological construction, legitimization, and distribution of new symbolic models of and for personal and collective identities, on the one hand, and post-modern socio-political realities, on the other. The electronic mass media continuously construct, organize, and transmit symbolic maps of and for personal and social 'reality' to vast audiences by communicating information that has been consensually legitimatized as reliable. It is in this sense that post-modern movements are alternative media that generate and mobilize commitment to certain expressive cultural models of and for action with respect to personal identities and shared socio-cultural realities.

Recent (post-modern) American cultural movements tend to be composed of innumerable diverse, largely (organizationally) unconnected and unco-ordinated small groups which form along the lines of friendship networks. Furthermore, these groups are ideologically quite heterogeneous. Rather than accepting and adopting some established, shared, and authoritatively legitimatized ideology as their own, the intensive groups so characteristic of today's movements deliberately and self-consciously construct their own, often quite unique, ideology and collective identity. And as the analytic formulation suggested, these ideologies and collective identities deal less with strategies and tactical proposals for changing institutional structures than with cultural models of and for personal identity, social con-sciousness, and collective meaning.

The critical social unit that sets contemporary movements apart from their historical predecessors represents a synthesis of attributes derived from previously distinct, if not incompatible, types of groups, group 'styles', and group techniques. Specifically, post-modern movement groups reflect the influence of traditional ideological informal groups, artificially-constructed primary groups, and the intensive (sensitivity training and encounter) group techniques which have emerged out of existential, humanistic psychology.

In an early attempt to describe 'ideological groups' among the small revolutionary circles that emerged in Russia during the late nineteenth century, Nahirny (1963:404) argued that:

Ideological formal groups do not admit . . . either the separation of public and private spheres of life, or the clear-cut segregation of the individual's roles. Their members do not participate in them merely in the capacity of one narrowly defined and functionally specific role of 'official'. They continue to demand, like ideological informal groups, a total commitment to the cause which is now authoritatively defined and institutionalized. It is here that they differ strikingly from ideological informal groups . . . Members of ideological informal groups . . . conform primarily to organizational principles.

It is these ideological informal groups, which recruit on the basis of individual contacts and mutual confidence, which are held together by 'inner convictions' and 'immediate rapport', that are such a prominent feature of post-modern American cultural movements. But the ideological informal groups in contemporary movements differ markedly from those which Nahirny studied.

Specifically, contemporary groups focus on personal qualities and experiences; they attempt to transform subjectively experienced individual dilemmas and psychological problems into 'consciousness' of shared cultural constraints and meaning problems through the ideological construction of new identity models. In doing this they all focus upon claims to and conceptions of personal authenticity and the 'actualization' of psychological potentialities. In fact, it is precisely on the basis of claims to psychological authenticity and personal identity made on behalf of a particular social category, often defined in terms of shared ascribed characteristics, that the reconstruction of expressive symbols and cultural meanings is being attempted. And the uniquely post-modern cultural content and identity focus on contemporary ideological informal groups derives from the popularity, pervasiveness, effectiveness, and appropriateness of sensitivity training-encounter group techniques and processes.

Regardless of its therapeutic and/or educational benefits or liabilities, and dangers; regardless of its scientific, religious, professional or recreational status; regardless of the soundness of its conceptual, methodological or technical armamentarium; intensive (sensitivity training-encounter) group techniques and procedures have become a regular feature of the post-modern American scene.[5] More importantly, intensive group *techniques* and *procedures* have been adopted by quite diverse contemporary movement groups, although they are most obvious and pervasive in the Feminist Movement (Mitchell 1970; Freeman 1972 and 1973; Cherniss 1972; Tanner 1970; Allen 1970; and Dreifus 1973); the Communal Movement (Kanter 1968 and 1970; Jacobs 1971; Bart 1971; and Marx and Seldin 1973a and 1973b); and the 'Jesus' Movement (Mauss and Peterson 1973; and Harder, Richardson and Simmonds 1972). These techniques and procedures were given substantive content through the

Maslowian 'humanistic psychology' that celebrated the fusion of Rogerian 'non-directive', 'client-centred' counselling with existential psychothera-peutic concern in the late 1950s (Marx and Seldin 1973a).

It may seem implausible to link the characteristics of ideological in-formal groups with those 'plastic' primary groups that advertise sexual and spiritual salvation through 'instant intimacy'. After all, these informal groups may rest on personal contacts and rely on mutual confidence in-volving shared 'inner convictions' that generate 'immediate rapport', but they are still *ideological* groups; they still '. . . require that their members orient themselves to one another primarily in terms of some central symbols and ideas . . .' (Nahirny 1963:397). And although sensitivity training-encounter groups adopt or create various expressive symbols and beliefs, these involve *personal* objectives—such as 'personal growth', 'self-actualization', 'authentic interpersonal relationships', 'enhanced personal and social awareness'—rather than ideologically defined, shared goals centred upon cultural reconstruction and change. Yet many of the techniques, processes, and assumptions associated with intensive groups were first linked with a humanistic psychology ethos which emphasized 'authentic identity' and the 'self-actualizing personality', and then fused with a substantive orientation to shared expressive symbols, cultural meanings, and identity models characteristic of ideological informal groups. The offspring of this somewhat surprising synthesis is the distinctively post-modern unit that permeates contemporary American movements which we refer to as the ideological primary group. What follows is a description of certain typical characteristics and processes that have been observed in those groups to which we were able to gain access.

ON IDEOLOGICAL PRIMARY GROUPS

Ideological primary groups are informal, unstructured collectivities that are sufficiently small for members to have direct, face-to-face relations and opportunities to participate at every meeting. They typically consist of from five to about ten people who meet frequently, if not regularly, to discuss, and analyse common personal problems, feelings, and experiences in a voluntary, supportive, permissive, non-professional context. Con-temporary ideological primary groups tend to be homogeneous with respect to some ascribed characteristic—such as age, sex, or race—and relatively uniform in terms of achieved attributes as well. However, it is the experiences and feelings associated with or derived from the ascribed characteristic which generally focuses the discussion. That is, the purpose of the group is to explore, understand, and consciously construct strategies for dealing with problems and issues that are common to the members by virtue of their primarily ascribed (or at least perceived as ascribed) characteristic(s). This homogeneity with respect to some salient and significant characteristic means that there is no 'objective', 'impartial' group leader or therapist: all present are directly involved.

This is, then, a setting in which a small number of socially similar people have repeated interaction in a context which encourages them to share and exchange intimacies about themselves, their lives, feelings and, most importantly, their experiences. Initially, this generates positive sentiments toward other participants, and group solidarity emerges. With the development of primary relations, interpretations of recurrent distressing events and experiences are exchanged. Usually, these interpretations involve psychological explanations which imply personal responsibility, inadequacy or failure ('It was really all my fault; sometimes I'm really dumb and paranoid!') or explanations which attribute the recurrent misfortunes to the incalculable random operation of chance occurrences (for example, 'consistently rotten luck', 'unforeseen accidents' or 'fate'). But repeated sharing and reinterpreting of intimate details of past and recent common experiences leads to the recognition of an underlying patterning to certain types of recurrent misfortunes. And this recognition, in turn, is the initial step toward the construction of an interpretation that points to some common, underlying, systemic source of recurrent un-pleasant experiences that were previously seen as unique and unrelated individual misfortunes (Turner 1969). There is the beginning of a vague, incohate sense that these experiences and others like them are likely to befall most, if not all, people like them—those sharing their particular ascribed characteristic(s). In Turner's (1969) terminology, there is the tentative, initial formulation of a shared symbolic interpretation of various independent, but similar, individually experienced *misfortunes* as *injustices* for which specific groups or the entire society are held responsible. This begins the collective construction of a shared ideology and, subsequently, group identity.

Ideological primary groups differ from other primary or intensive groups in that they concentrate group energy and member attention on the task of constructing, evaluating, and legitimatizing (through consensual validation) an expressive symbolic apparatus, an ideology, that publicly interprets dissatisfying or incomprehensible aspects of reality in a new way and invents (defines into existence) appropriate motivational patterns— stress, anger, indignation, grievance, outrage—for experiencing and modifying that reality. Thus, the purpose of these groups is the collective construction of a shared ideological interpretation of present reality and cultural models of/for a more satisfying state of affairs. These groups bear striking similarity to Nahirny's (1963) 'ideological informal groups' and differ considerably from intensive groups that have as their goals 'personal growth', 'self-actualization', 'authentic relationships', and 'self-exploration' and which are so popular among a bored, affluent, psychologically-sophisticated middle-class. Yet ideological primary groups share important characteristics with other primary groups and with intensive groups.

Like primary groups, intensive groups involve recurrent, direct, face-to-face relations that generate powerful interpersonal bonds and emotions that are consummatory and expressive. The result of encounter group techniques may be an *ersatz* 'instant intimacy' that is superficial, but it is nevertheless intimacy. From this perspective, intensive groups may be viewed as artificial or socially-constructed primary groups; they consist of voluntary primary relations among peers in an unstructured, permissive, supportive setting and usually have a finite, somewhat short, life-span. Although the group may discuss and even agree on common objectives, the goals of the members and their rationale for participation remain individual. The guiding ethos of these groups is humanistic psychology (Rogerian-Maslowian) which oscillates between therapeutic and educational emphases — with occasional recreational sorties into the religious realm. But for the purposes at hand, the most significant feature of intensive groups is that they are composed of self-consciously and explicitly artificial, socially constructed primary relations.

Ideological primary groups, then, represent one particular type of socially constructed primary group that uses intensive group dynamics and techniques to self-consciously formulate collective goals (mutual identity transformation and shared 'consciousness') through the ideological reinterpretation of present personal experience and past biography.

> In the typical consciousness-raising group, women discuss each other's personal experiences and problems in a usually supportive atmosphere; and in this sense, the consciousness-raising group is not unlike a therapy group. However, here the similarity ends, for the women in the group typically respond to a woman's problem or concern by encouraging her to view it from a . . . *social* rather than a personal perspective. . . . The women interviewed used this new ideological perspective to reshape and redefine their perceptions of key figures in their development . . . (Cherniss 1972:118).

Berger and Luckmann (1967:160) have described the general formula that characterizes this process of reinterpreting biography:

> 'Then I *thought* . . . now I *know*.' Frequently this includes the retrojection into the past of present interpretive schemas (the formula for this being, 'I already knew then, though in an unclear manner . . .') and motives that were not subjectively present in the past but are now necessary for the re-interpretation of what took place then (the formula

being, 'I *really* did this because . . .'). . . . In addition to this re-interpretation *en toto* there must be particular re-interpretations of past events and persons with past significance.

This collective re-interpretation of both personal-individual and common-shared biographies is critical for two subsequent developments. *First*, the process generates, organizes, and channels subjectively-experienced psychological stress and tension into the form of collectively-shared anger and indignation. This mobilizes both individual and collective energy in behalf of common movement purposes.

> Anger becomes for many of the women one of the cardinal emotional characteristics of the entire movement experience . . . . The ideology and rhetoric of Women's Liberation to some extent help the women to focus the anger and provide an intellectualized, social-political rationale for it, and the social support of the other women also helps. (Cherniss 1972:121–122)

In other words, this re-interpretation generates both the social 'dynamic' or energy source for subsequent collective action and organizes appropriate psychological motivations for unqualified individual commitment to group activities. *Secondly*, the collective re-interpretation of individual and shared biographical experiences represents a necessary prerequisite for the social construction and legitimization of new personal as well as collective identities. In the process of adult identity transformation, de-socialization is necessary before re-socialization can take place.[6] All of these processes are firmly grounded (and continue to remain anchored) in specific socially-constructed expressive symbols 'models of'/'models for' (Geertz 1966) personal and collective identity that are embedded in an ideologically-formulated, shared interpretation of reality. The terminal development in the process we are describing involves the fusion of expressive symbolic models of/for personal and collective identity with the collectively-organized but subjectively experienced energy (specifically, anger) which is then available for whatever objectives the movement emphasizes. The point at which this socially generated collective motivational energy becomes socially-available marks the ideological primary group's fully-fledged participation in a post-modern movement.

To summarize: ideological primary groups are contexts which encourage integrating collective examination of prior personal experiences and biography with more general socio-cultural analysis; the result of this is the construction of an ideological interpretation of reality containing new, more satisfying personal and collective identity models. One source of these contemporary groups comes from traditional 'ideological informal groups'. This source is responsible for the *ideological character or content* of today's movement groups. The other influence on ideological primary groups has been techniques, procedures, and psychological assumptions associated with sensitivity training-encounter group approaches. This influence is largely responsible for the general *structure*, procedures, and psychological point-of-departure in contemporary movement groups. Both these sources involve artificial, intentionally-constructed groups. However, the emphasis on personal intimacy and primary relations that is distinctive in today's groups derives from the sensitivity training-encounter ethos which merged with (Maslowian) humanistic psychology. The integration of these disparate influences in the context of post-modern culture has generated movement groups which use a collectively constructed ideology to interpret current individual dissatisfactions and biographical frustrations as symptoms of moral injustice and cultural decay, rather than personal psychopathology.[7] Thus, these groups use the psycho-social consequences of personal experience to illuminate and analyse larger public, cultural frameworks, whereas traditional groups within social movements viewed social structural (political and economic) changes as necessary prerequisites for personal, psychological changes. *Finally*, contemporary movement groups construct not only personal identity models which emphasize innovative claims to authenticity and fulfilment of psychological potentialities, but also culturally articulated models of the procedures and process through which the group itself is to create the proper state of 'consciousness'. The contemporary revolution is in and by 'consciousness'. And this means nothing less than that post-modern revolutions focus on expressive culture and aim at transforming personal and collective identities. Thus, Cherniss (1972:123) notes that,

> . . . participation seemed to follow from a crisis of personal identity. The conventional models of feminine development and identity provided by their culture only exacerbated the crisis for these women, who felt themselves to be different from stereotyped images of femininity. From this perspective, a 'pursuit of meaning' could be seen as a strong motive for involvement in the movement. Participation then in some ways resolves this quest, by providing a framework through which the women can more explicitly define who they are and how they came to be that way. The movement also provides social reinforcement for a new model of personal identity; this new conception of femininity is shared by others and expressed by them, and the group sanctions such as identity and defines it as socially and personally better than the conventional model.

ON ADULT MORATORIA AND FREE SPACES IN POST-MODERN EXPRESSIVE CULTURE

Ideological primary groups permeate contemporary American movements because of their appropriateness for post-modern expressive culture; they provide a social moratorium and a cultural free-space for adult identity, transformation and the resocialization of 'normal', conventional people. This argument involves several assumptions about post-modern identities and identity models.

Contemporary identity-orientated expressive cultural movements characteristically appeal to post-adolescent young adults and adults on the exuberant side of forty. This means that members have passed through — if not entirely resolved — the 'identity crisis' that is characteristically experienced *initially* during the adolescent 'psycho-social moratorium' (Erikson 1963:262–3). Most movement participants and/or supporters managed to psychologically force some kind of initial, temporary ego identity in the adolescent crucible of conventional society. In later years they may become 'alienated', dissatisfied, disenchanted, and frustrated by or with this identity framework, but they are not (clinically) mentally ill, 'sick' or psychopathological. In this sense, it is assumed that they are psycho-sexually and probably even psycho-socially 'mature' or 'typical' conventional young adults.

The second assumption concerns what might be termed 'structural adulthood' or 'sociological maturity'; that is, integration into the dominant institutions and role-statuses that define full privileges, responsibilities, and participation in post-industrial societal structures. Specifically, it is assumed that contemporary movement participants either have not yet attained structural adulthood, are systematically prevented from attaining it or, most frequently, having attained a sociologically mature identity find it either unsatisfying or undesirable. In short, these psycho-sexually and psycho-socially mature people (from an Eriksonian 'developmental' point of view) find that their repertoire of interpersonal styles, self-concepts, and meaning systems is profoundly unsatisfying and/or frustrating. In consequence, they sense, however vaguely and imprecisely, a need for change, and that their own situation is somehow tied to the situation of others like them.

The third assumption is simply that personal satisfaction and social integration require appropriate expressive cultural models of/for personal and collective identity. The appropriateness of such post-modern cultural identity models is a function of their cohesiveness, legitimacy, stability and, most importantly, detachment from the behavioural prescriptions and proscriptions of prevailing institutional structure. Furthermore, it seems safe to assume that long-dominant, highly-valued, and formerly widely-shared expressive cultural models of/for behaviour, identity, and consciousness are currently in a state of extreme disarray and instability.[8] (Despite the fact that such assertions have been incessantly reiterated and trivialized in 'pop' sociology, it is nevertheless true that dominant cultural frameworks and 'mazeways' are in the process of reorganization and transformation.) More specifically, 'needs' are culturally-patterned and organized subjective experiences of an inner state of affairs that are learned in the course of socialization. We need what we have learned to need . . . and contemporary post-modern Americans have learned that everyone needs to have their own unique identity: that is, a single, continuous sense or experience of self, of sameness over a period of time. (To subjectively-experience and express a sense of more than one self or a series of discontinuous selves over some time is considered schizophrenic — among an important, educated middle-class segment of the population.) And yet this expressive cultural model of and for psycho-social development, identity, and consciousness has begun to erode in the post-modern period after 1960. And the same is true for long-standing expressive cultural models of and for citizenship, morality, and sexuality. This generates a need for new, more appropriate expressive symbolic models of and for personal and collective identity, and social consciousness that are capable of producing more satisfying patterns of personal cultural integration.

The last assumption concerns adult identity formation and transformation. It is assumed that both personal and collective identity can, and increasingly does, undergo complete transformations after an initial psycho-sexual and psycho-social identity has been established in adolescence — and that this is symptomatic not of psychopathology but specifically of post-modern expressive culture. This assumption is the antithesis of the Eriksonian interpretation of Freudian psychoanalytic psychology that permeates contemporary sociological thought, Dennis Wrong's 'Over-Socialized Conception of Man' notwithstanding. (See Blum and McHugh 1971 for an imaginatively different set of assumptions.) For example, Erikson (1963:306) notes: 'Adolescence is the age of the final establishment of a dominant positive ego identity. It is then that a future within reach becomes part of the conscious life plan'. And in one of the few essays explicitly devoted to 'Socialization After Childhood', (Brim 1966) takes the position that the 'secondary socialization' of normal adults basically involves nothing more than the acquisition of additional skills and knowledge or techniques and behaviours, but certainly not motivations and values — which Brim considers far more basic, powerful, and enduring. In a similar vein, Berger and Luckmann (1966) treat 'alternation' — or adult identity transformation that is subjectively apprehended as total — as a rare, if not somewhat peculiar, occurrence. Thus, Berger and Luckmann (1966:158) note that 'The historical prototype of alternation is religious conversion', but suggest that the best contemporary examples of total identity transformations occur in the areas of political indoctrination and psychotherapy. In other words, Berger and Luckmann indicate that current total adult identity transformations occur only in the extreme situations (in, for example, political indoctrination) or in treating deviants (for example, in psychotherapy).

In contrast, we assume that 'typical', 'normal', psychologically 'stable' and sociologically integrated, non-deviant adults frequently undergo, and even intentionally bring about transformations in their (personal as well as collective) identities by constructing or borrowing expressive symbolic models of and for identity that are different from those used in the past. Put differently, one of the central, defining characteristics of 'post-modern' culture is that people increasingly take themselves, their lives and especially their identities, as objects that can and should be modified, manipulated, and transformed at will. (See Marin 1975 on 'The New Narcissism As A State of Grace'.) Increasingly, dissatisfaction with one's identities as well as the meaningfulness of one's life generates the 'quest for identity' (Wheelis 1953) and 'quest for community' (Nisbet 1952) that are, we argue, largely responsible for the popularity and significance of ideological primary groups in contemporary post-modern cultural movements.

Taken together, these assumptions suggest a scenario in which many psycho-sexually and psycho-socially 'normal' post-modern young adults are frustrated or dissatisfied with their current or available self-images, meaning systems, and identities and find traditional cultural models of/for personal identity and collective meaning equally unsatisfying and/or inappropriate. Casting about for other ways of satisfying their quest for (personal) identity and for 'community' (collective) meaning, they are likely to encounter other similar and similarly-situated peers. If strong interpersonal ties result, there is at least the potentiality for ideological primary group formation and wider movement participation. But more immediately, this group can then become a context for powerful adult resocialization processes which result in the transformation of personal and collective identity models and meaning systems.

For transformations in post-modern adult identity models and meaning systems to occur, new expressive symbolic formulations must be socially constructed or borrowed, and then legitimatized and internalized. Moreover, the validity, plausibility, and appropriateness of these new models will initially require relatively frequent reaffirmation and legitimization through positive reinforcement. The appropriateness of post-modern ideological primary groups in contemporary cultural movements for adult identity resocialization processes stems from a unique configuration of characteristics. Firstly, like adolescent peer groups which play so formative a role during an individual's initial identity crystallization, contemporary movement groups are *primary groups*, however artificial or superficial they may appear to an outsider, in which homogeneity rests more on ascription than on achievement. In other words, new symbolic identity models and cultural meanings can only be socially constructed, resurrected, or borrowed, then consensually-validated and legitimatized, and finally internalized in the context of powerful primary group relations among peers who possess socially-similar background characteristics that are seen as ascribed and immutable.[9] Social homogeneity based on ascription in the context of powerful primary relationships among peers is a prerequisite for the ideological construction of new expressive symbolic models of/for identity and cultural meaning.

Secondly, ideological primary groups provide a *social moratorium* analogous in some important respects to the adolescent moratorium in which 'ego identity' initially congeals. That is, adolescence provides a psycho-social moratorium for normal adult role-status relationships, obligations, and responsibilities that enables the psycho-sexually mature teenager to experiment with alternative sets of interpersonal role skills, styles, and partners in order to establish an initial, temporarily stable sense of ego identity. It is in this sense that identity construction and internalization involves the need for a socially accepted and personally subjectively experienced structural freedom or release from normal adult structural constraints and institutional responsibilities in order to experiment with and try out new role-sets, new role-conceptions, and new role-partners.

In short, then, the ideological construction and resocialization of new adult identity models and culture meaning patterns requires a structural moratorium from conventional institutional role-statuses, role-relationships, and role-responsibilities.

Finally, ideological primary groups provide a cultural 'free space' and freedom for expressive experimentation and cognitive inquiry that is necessary for the symbolic reformulation of personal identity models and collective meanings. Cultural free spaces are socially clearly defined and circumscribed cultural domains and arenas of inquiry as well as situational contexts in which individuals are both free and encouraged to borrow and adapt, invent and consciously construct, or experiment with new symbolic models of and for personal identity, cultural meaning, and collective consciousness. They are contexts or domains in which conventional cultural constraints on symbolic innovation are removed—provided the symbolic experimentation remains within certain culturally delineated boundaries that define the free-space.

It is the combination of (1) powerful primary relations among homogeneous peers that are based on ascribed characteristics with (2) a structural moratorium on normal adult institutional constraints and role demands, in the context of (3) a cultural free-space, which encourages collective experimentation and innovation with symbolic models and cultural meanings that make contemporary ideological primary groups in post-modern movements such a strategic site for adult identity construction and expressive cultural transformation processes — or for 'normal adult re-socialization'.

Identity and the Ideological Construction of 'Stress-Strain' in Contemporary Movement Groups

Many of the explanations social scientists have offered to account for the sources or determinants of both movements and ideologies involve a set of paradigmatic assumptions which we will refer to as the 'stress-strain model'. The literature contains an impressive array of synonymous terms for 'stress' and 'strain'. Among the concepts that have been used to describe and account for either movements or ideologies (or both), some of the more familiar are: 'malintegration', 'disequilibrium', 'pressure', 'disintegration', 'imbalance', 'friction', 'disorganization', 'inconsistency', 'conflict', 'deprivation', 'discrepancy', and 'discontinuity', to name but a few of the terminological and/or conceptual equivalents for 'stress' and 'strain' (Cf. Lindesmith and Strauss 1957:615–27; Sherif 1953:219–29; and Smelser 1963:47–8 for synonyms in the collective behaviour literature on social movements; Cf. Geertz 1964:54 for synonyms in the literature on ideologies). And scholars as different in intellectual orientation as Geertz (1964), Wallace (1956), and Smelser (1963) agree about the crucial paradigmatic significance of 'stress' or 'strain' — or some conceptually analogous term — in social-scientific assumptions about movements and ideologies.

The basic 'stress-strain' model underlying these analyses of movements and ideologies involves the following assumptions and images (Cf. Geertz 1964 for a brilliant critique of 'strain theory' approaches to ideologies). Structural strain (or 'disequilibrium', 'malintegration', 'friction', 'inconsistency', etc.) at the societal or institutional-structural level is chronic, pervasive, continuous, inevitable, and irremediable. The interpenetration of social structure and institutions with personality systems means that these 'strains' are subjectively experienced by individuals as psychological or emotional 'stresses' (or 'tensions', *'malaise'*, 'disorders', 'symptoms', etc.). Thus, the emotional-psychological 'stresses' resulting from larger structural inconsistencies or institutional 'strains' will be associated with a particular social class, category, stratum or collectivity. When the structural-institutional 'strain' increases to the point where the resulting emotional-psychological 'stresses' that are subjectively experienced by individuals exceed some (presumably shared and relatively constant) threshold of tolerable discomfort, a patterned collective response (or 'reaction', 'outburst', 'action', etc.) occurs. This patterned collective response serves (or 'functions', either manifestly or latently) to reduce the level of psychological 'stress' or personal emotional discomfort that individuals in the relevant social category are experiencing — either by removing the structural conditions ('strains') that produced the psychological 'stress' or, more frequently, by generating psychological defence mechanisms that enable the individual to cope with or adapt to the 'stress' more successfully. The symbolic expression of this patterned collective response is an ideology; the behavioural expression of this patterned collective response is a social movement.

There are innumerable problems surrounding the conceptual underpinnings of the 'stress-strain' model: the integration of basically incompatible biological, mechanical, and medical imagery; the failure to distinguish macro- and micro-levels of analysis and types of phenomena; the causal over-emphasis and the lack of attention to consequences; and most importantly, the threshold assumptions concerning tolerable levels of psychological 'stress' that can be sustained. These assumptions have been challenged elsewhere (Marx and Holzner 1973); the following discussion describes 'stress-strain' as ideologically-constructed, symbolically-formulated motivational patterns produced in ideological primary groups in order to define, guide and interpret behaviour in problematic, incomprehensible, and distressing situations. Put differently, the ideologically-constructed identity models generated in contemporary movement groups mobilize the necessary personal as well as collective 'stress-strain' to serve movement objectives while simultaneously ameliorating individually-experienced 'stress' and discomfort by rendering heretofore ambiguous and threatening situations and events comprehensible. By doing this, the ideological formulations 'model' (in both the 'model of' and the 'model for' sense) basic motivational dispositions and emotional patterns that are part of personal identity.

It is ironic that the ideological models prevalent in contemporary expressive cultural movements both reduce subjectively-experienced individual stresses and result in the social construction of collectively shared strains and anger through the production of shared grievances and indignation. It is as if the group member heaves a sigh of relief at having finally understood that he or she was fundamentally dissatisfied all along — without having realized or experienced it as such before now. This sigh of relief is all the greater and more satisfying because the person believes that he finally understands the ('real') cause of that only-now-realized-and-experienced dissatisfaction. Moreover, the person now has a set of collectively-constructed and legitimatized (ideological) explanations and unambiguous answers for a wide range of situations and experiences. These ideologically-formulated explanations acquit the individual of any personal responsibility for the (frequently negative) outcome of these situations and experiences. In addition to the decisive reduction of ambiguity and uncertainty which the shared ideological formulation provides, then, the abrogation of personal responsibility and causal efficacy as well as the denial of personal inadequacy serve as supplementary stress-reduction mechanisms of considerable import.

At the same time, however, one is now angry, indignant, outraged: situations and events that had previously left one mildly perplexed and/or frustrated now provoke indignant feelings of intense anger. Funnelled through the collectively-constructed symbolic apparatus of the shared ideological interpretation, the same circumstances or experiences now generate intense effect. And the ideology further serves to organize and mobilize this intense effect around particular expressive symbols in such a manner that the individual experiences considerable personal stress. It is in this sense that collectively-defined and constructed, yet subjectively-experienced individual stress and anger is closely tied to the ideological patterning and mobilization of motivational energy through personal participation in and commitment to the groups' ideological interpretations of movement goals and activities. It is in this sense that it is appropriate to speak of the ideological construction of models of and models for both personal identity, including motivational patterns, and collective consciousness or group identity. Cherniss' (1972:121–2) description of the process of 'finding' one's anger in Feminist ideological primary groups illustrates the ideological patterning of individual motivational patterns and the ideological 'modelling' of personal identities.

It is important to give some consideration to the nature and production of models of and for grievances as well as to the relation between grievances and personal as well as collective identity models. We have suggested that some expressive symbolic formulation or ideological interpretation must be shared by members of an ideological primary group before frustrating or unpleasant experiences are taken as the basis for a grievance and reacted to with anger and outraged indignation. Prior to the construction or adoption of an ideological formulation, group members perceive, define, and react to the experiences as involving individual misfortunes for which they can only 'petition' for charitable assistance or sympathy (Turner 1969). It is the emergence of an ideological interpretation of that class of events as involving '. . . deep injustice which provokes a sense of outrage against a system productive of such misfortunes . . .' (Turner 1969:391) that generates the production of grievances. More precisely, the ideological formulation contains a symbolic code for the subsequent development of clear-cut criteria for discerning and/or defining grievances. This symbolic code is closely associated with the particular 'stress-strains' that are constructed and experienced by the ideological primary group and, hence, with the ideologically-formulated symbolic codes that 'model' which the emerging personal identity structures members are acquiring. Cherniss (1972:124) notes in this respect that:

> . . . the direction for the perceptual organization that occurred for the women in consciousness-raising seemed to be derived from the ideology of the movement. The ideology is conveyed through a stylistically compelling political rhetoric, and the woman is encouraged to apply this ideology to her own personal experiences both within the group and *in vivo* outside the group.

In short, grievance models serve as a symbolic short-hand or relief-map which delineates the salient features of an event or situation that can indicate whether outraged indignation and/or opposition is the attitude or response that is ideologically appropriate in terms of the group's collectively-constructed interpretation of reality. Thus, these models include sets of symbolic criteria or 'tests' which can be applied to common empirical situations to assess the appropriateness of certain kinds of feelings, such as anger or scorn. But this is merely another way of saying that these grievance models symbolically specify the conditions under which group members are to personally-experience collectively-constructed, ideologically-defined 'stress-strain' when they encounter new or ambiguous situations. As Geertz (1964:63) so eloquently observes, 'It is in country unfamiliar emotionally or topographically that one needs poems and road maps.' And it is precisely in strange surroundings that ideological models of and models for the production of aggrieved anger, psychological 'stress', and both personal and collective identity provide new, collectively-legitimatized symbolic frames against which to match the myriad 'unfamiliar somethings' in order to determine appropriate motivational and evaluative orientations and behavioural responses. The ideological patterning of both the motivational components and the symbolic codes underlying the adult personal identity models and the shared social consciousness that constitutes the group's collective identity suggests that an intimate relationship between ideology and adult identity development and/or transformation may well be a characteristic or typical feature of post-modern culture.

IMPLICATIONS AND CONCLUDING REMARKS

IDEOLOGICAL RESOCIALIZATION IN CULTURAL MOVEMENTS: 'POST-
MODERN MAN' IN THE 'KNOWLEDGE BASED SOCIETY'

This essay has attempted to call attention to the nature, functions, and
sociological significance of ideological primary groups in contemporary,
post-modern cultural movements and to emphasize their importance as
legitimate contexts for intentional, self-conscious adult resocialization—or
identity transformation and reconstruction among (non-deviant) 'nor-
mals'. Most analyses of adult resocialization either focus on clinical
psychopathology and psychotherapeutic processes (for example Parsons
1950; Parsons and Fox 1952) or on correctional processes and institutions
for sociological deviants, such as prisons and mental hospitals (Wheeler
1966). Moreover, the guiding assumption that permeates discussions of
normal adult socialization is that it modifies role skills and/or knowledge
only insofar as it is compatible with more basic motivations and values,
established during primary socialization in childhood, that constitute the
core of a person's identity (Brim 1966). In short, the presence of adult
resocialization and identity transformation is assumed to reflect a failure of
primary socialization and child-rearing processes which needs to be rec-
tified; and normal adult socialization merely gives content and specificity
to the basic identity structure and pattern that are the permanent residue
of early childhood socialization. Underlying all this is an image of basic
stability and continuity in core identity structure after childhood—or at
most after the adolescent 'identity crisis' is resolved—in the case of 'normal'
individuals.

Perhaps stability and continuity in personal identity was true in the
past—although that seems highly unlikely—but it is clearly increasingly
difficult, if not impossible, to achieve in the rapidly changing contemporary world. A stable, continuous personal identity over the entire
life-cycle seems not merely atypical, but socially pathological and retarded
in a post-industrial, post-modern society. 'Post-modern man' (Kavolis
1970) lives in 'the knowledge based society' (Holzner 1972:167) which is
'. . . necessarily reflective, i.e., it is self-conscious and views itself not only
as a given matrix of living but also as an object capable of deliberate
modification'. And perhaps the principle characteristic that distinguishes
post-modern, knowledge-based social life is that more and more (increasingly well-educated) people become reflective, take themselves and
their identity 'as an object capable of deliberate modification', and begin
to self-consciously and deliberately attempt to psychologically transform
and socially re-construct themselves. This essay has argued that the
construction, legitimization, and internalization of new cultural models of

and for adult identity and social consciousness require a homogeneous primary group context containing intimate peer relations which provides a structurally legitimatized moratorium on normal institutional role performances and responsibilities as well as a cultural free space which encourages experimentation and innovation with prevailing symbolic codes. These conditions permit and facilitate an ideological re-interpretation of both personal-private and collective-public reality which leads to the construction of ideologically-appropriate identity models and symbolic codes for social consciousness. The essay also suggested that these are the principle conditions that distinguish ideological primary groups in today's cultural movements from earlier movement groups. It seems appropriate to suggest that these ideological primary groups represent the most, if not the only, socially available and acceptable contexts which offer these characteristics in contemporary society. In other words, ideological primary groups in cultural movements are currently the principle resocialization context for the construction, legitimization, and internalization of new adult identity models — for the transformation of personal and collective consciousness. But even more importantly, these group experiences transform psychologically-sophisticated 'moderns' appropriate to industrialized institutional structure into sociologically-sophisticated 'post-moderns' suited to the rigidity of post-industrialized institutional structures by virtue of becoming — in a non-technical way to be sure — aware of the socially-constructed nature of reality.

Pre-industrial, pre-modern society reflected an underlying conviction that individual well-being, fulfilment, meaning, and identity depends upon full, participant membership in 'positive communities' which '. . . offer a type of collective salvation . . . which transforms all personal relations by subordinating them to agreed communal purposes . . .' (Rieff 1966:73). This conviction assumes a '. . . relation between the sense of well-being which defines the health of the individual and his membership in the community . . .' (Rieff 1966:66–7) in which the former is considered dependent on the latter. In this situation, 'ultimately, it is the community that cures' (Rieff 1966:68). The industrialization of institutional structure and the modernization of culture produced an emphasis on individualism, competition, mobility, and achievement that sharply reduced the salience and significance of 'positive communities' as anchorage-points for personal meaning, fulfilment, and identity. But these changes did generate new, psychological and psychotherapeutic '. . . doctrines intended to manage the strains of living as a communally detached individual' (Rieff 1966:74). Specifically, industrialized institutional structures and cultural modernization produced self-consciously psychologically orientated 'moderns' whose central source of stability and continuity in an individualistic and mobile society derived from a sense of immutable personal identity. The psychological image of man appropriate to modern industrial society received significant conceptual legitimacy from attempts to ameliorate individuals who were troubled or troublesome. Again, Rieff (1966:73–4) notes that:

> . . . analytic therapy developed precisely in response to the need of the Western individual, in the Tocquevillian definition, for a therapy that would not depend for its effects on a symbolic return to a positive community; at best, analytic therapy creates negative communities . . . (Such 'negative communities' create) . . . a more purely therapeutic type, complete with doctrines intended to manage the strains of living as a communally detached individual.

But all of this changed as post-industrial institutional structures and post-modern expressive models and cultural meanings generated a new 'knowledge based social order'. This development rendered 'psychological man' and the conception of a unitary, continuous, stable adult identity less plausible and less satisfying, and socio-cultural images of man began to gain currency. In the knowledge-based society that emerged from post-industrial institutional structure and post-modern culture: '. . . sociology, of course, occupies a very strategic place . . . in that its very existence increases reflexivity and the range of conscious choices for alternatives' (Holzner 1972:167). This is particularly true with respect to sociological sophistication concerning identity. That is, the process of self-consciously constructing new personal identity models and codes by ideologically connecting private, subjective feelings and personal circumstances with larger public issues, collective concerns and cultural codes both required and increased sociological sophistication, reflexivity, and consciousness. The ideological primary group processes that lead to adult identity transformation necessarily generate an awareness, however rudimentary, of 'the social construction of reality'. In this sense, post-modern cultural movement participants start to become non-technical 'reality constructionists'.

The suggestion that contemporary ideological primary group members become lay reality constructionists rests on the following argument: ideological primary group processes make members aware that formerly imposing edifices of institutional and role constraints are not 'givens' which inhere in 'the nature of things'. Rather they are socially constructed structures which can be dismantled as easily as they were built, merely by withdrawing commitment and legitimacy from them. In addition, movement participants come to appreciate the 'relativity' of all perspectives and viewpoints. These insights, in turn, are responsible for the 'psychological utopianism' (Manuel 1965) so characteristic in contemporary cultural movements; the view that the only absolutes, the only objectives worth striving for and possible of attainment are within oneself. Perfection is a realistic objective insofar as it means fully realizing all one's potentialities! Everything external and structurally imposed is transient, artificial, unreliable, and oppressive! But this awareness leads to the kind of cultural dead-end which has already begun to emerge in the contemporary feminist movement. That is, if all external structural constraints and institutional roles as well as all symbolic personal and collective identity models are *merely* socially-constructed cultural codes which can be dismantled as easily as they were constructed, what impetus is there to formulate new symbolic meanings, models, and interpretations? The utopian strain in all movements until now has always rested on an assumption that the present was an evil to be overcome in order to construct a more, if not completely perfect future. But psychological utopianism combined with an awareness of the socially constructed nature of present role and institutional constraints vitiates confidence that the future is worth constructing. In this sense, we may well be witnessing not the 'end of ideology', but the ideological end of utopianism.

'. . . THE HOBGOBLIN OF SMALL MINDS': ON PREDICTABILITY IN POST-MODERN SOCIETY

From one perspective, the crucial function of social life is to ensure a certain minimal level of predictability in behaviour, so that one can make certain, taken-for-granted assumptions about the behaviour of others. However, it is possible to suggest that the sources and bases of predictability are linked to the nature of society; specifically, predictability is related to the relative strength and bindingness of cultural meanings and structural constraints. Pre-industrial/pre-modern social predictability rested on a fusion of cultural meanings and structural constraints. An internalized cultural model of identity was intimately linked to positional constraints embedded in the social structure, guaranteeing maximum behavioural predictability. Industrialized/modern society engendered by the technological expansion of the material realm produced a structural fluidity that rendered positional constraints less effective as guarantees of behavioural predictability. Yet cultural meanings, by themselves are relatively ineffective as sources of constraint and predictability; on the other hand, cultural meanings could provide the necessary consistency to ensure predictable behaviour, since they were the most stable and continuous aspect of societies over the course of the industrial/modern period. It was this situation which made the modern (industrial era) *psychological* concept of 'identity'—a conception not linked to institutional-structural position—the principle basis of and for predictability, stability, and continuity in behaviour until the beginning of the post-industrial/post-modern period. That is, the modern psychological conception of identity emerged during a period of rapid structural transformation and differentiation, but relative cultural stability in symbolic codes and models. This conception of identity represented a cultural model which, when internalized in the course of the socialization of children, could serve as an alternative to earlier structural constraints in its ability to provide a minimum level of predictability and continuity in behaviour. The manner in which this cultural identity model performed this function is related to the assumptions it carried. Specifically, the cultural model underlying the modern (industrial era) psychological conception of personal identity assumed (1) that every individual develops an identity; (2) starting in early childhood; (3) which becomes relatively crystallized and permanent during adolesence — at the latest (although childhood remains the key phase of human biography); (4) that this unitary, coherent personal identity is not completely present to consciousness and the unconscious is the matrix of decisive mental processes, mechanisms and motor forces, but (5) that behaviour and social action reflect this identity in ways that the conscious self does not understand; therefore, (6) predictable and consistent individual and social behaviour are characteristic of socialized individuals as a consequence of an unconscious but integrated, coherent, unitary, and continuous identity that determines behaviour from the end of childhood (or adolescence) until death. Thus, not only can one expect other 'socialized' individuals to act in a predictable fashion from one occasion, situation, and relationship to another; one also expects (demands) that one's own behaviour be predictable in that it is consistent across different situations and relationships, regardless of the changing structures and contexts in which these behaviours occur. To alter one's behaviour as a function of structural-situational or relational factors so that it is not predictable and consistent with one's 'true inner self' or identity is to be dishonest. In short, to lack honour in the pre-industrial/pre-modern period meant to divorce identity and behaviour from social structure and situational constraints; to lack honour in the industrial/modern period meant to modify behaviour as a function of structural and situational contingencies and, hence, to link identity to social structure and situations rather than make it autonomous and 'private'. This reversal rests on the crucial distinction that emerged during the industrial/modern period between 'public and private institutional spheres' (Berger 1965:36); the point is simply that the same identity structure was supposed to represent the fundamental principle ordering behaviour and rendering it consistent in both domains.

   We have suggested that post-industrial/post-modern society is characterized by increasingly rigid social structure and increasingly immobile institutional patterns and, simultaneously, by an increasingly fluid symbolic surplus of cultural meanings, models, codes, and interpretations. Insofar as this is the case, cultural models (of identity or anything else) can no longer serve as a reliable basis for predictability and consistency in behaviour, even if internalized during childhood socialization. However, it is also unnecessary to rely on internalized cultural constraints — such as a stable cultural identity model which emphasizes behavioural consistency and continuity — in a situation characterized by stable, rigid structural constraints which can guarantee predictable, consistent behaviour in socially significant institutional roles. To reverse the argument, it is possible to have extreme cultural fluidity, transience, and turn-over in symbolic models and codes for identity, consciousness, and meaning only if structural patterns and institutional constraints are sufficiently stable, binding, rigid, and specific to ensure behavioural predictability and consistency in functionally important social domains and arenas. Or to put the matter still differently, only when structural constraints and institutional norms alone are sufficient to guarantee behavioural predictability and consistency is it possible for members of a society to begin to experiment with cultural codes involving multiple-identities and/or symbolic models of and for situationally and relationally-defined identities.

6

A Basis of Authority and Identity in Post-Industrial Society

Guy E. Swanson

There is a contrast in mood between this essay and the preceding two, even though their themes overlap. Swanson begins with the theme of the crisis in authority and identity; but he rapidly moves beyond it through the confident reliance on sociological, theoretical knowledge. His sharp formulations are helpful: 'Authority and identity grow up together and pervasive difficulties in one imply pervasive difficulties in the other'. And: 'There is no authority except in the context of identity: power is not legitimate unless people find it meaningful and good; unless it is a source of their own empowerment, a resource for their pursuit of their own purposes, and a conserver of a social order within which they can act today and anticipate acting in the days ahead. Likewise identity is impossible without authority. Without authority there is no source of personal empowerment and no stable, meaningful order within which purposes can be pursued and a coherent life career formulated.'

Swanson describes new bases for authority and identity, especially for the sense of 'empowerment'. He derives these from the organization of work, emphasizing 'management by objective' and 'human relations' on the job. In fact, he asserts that a new stage of societal evolution has emerged, in which there also is a 'major reformulation of religious understanding'. There is now differentiation, within value, between purpose and norm. Optimistically Swanson discovers a sense of ultimate purpose in the emerging social order; it is in such purpose that authority is to be vested. Indeed, the transformation is seen to derive from the core of American society and culture: the new patterns emerged within the universities, churches, and business firms and agencies of government well before their antinomian dramatization by the counter-culture. There are also important continuities; but the sense of the novel prevails (as in the essay by Marx).

One of the things that 'everyone knows' is that there is a crisis of authority and of personal identity in all of the world's most modernized societies. What 'everyone knows' seems also to be true. If the word 'crisis' is too strong, we can say at least that these societies have serious problems in mobilizing consent and commitment around official actions, that many of their citizens feel personally adrift, and that these two sets of facts seem to be connected.

But how are they connected? What lies behind them? What will be the consequences? There is no lack of answers. There is a lack of answers that seem reasonably consistent with the available evidence.

Authority and identity grow up together and pervasive difficulties in one imply pervasive problems in the other. Authority is legitimate power. Identity is a sense of personal continuity, of personal resources, of engrossing purposes, and of one's being authorized to follow where these purposes may lead (Swanson 1973). It is also the faith that the course of one's life is meaningful. There is no authority except in the context of identity: power is not legitimate unless people find it meaningful and good: unless it is a source of their own empowerment, a resource for their pursuit of their own purposes, and a conserver of a social order within which they can act today and can anticipate acting in the days ahead. Likewise identity is impossible without authority.[1] Without authority there is no source of personal empowerment and no stable, meaningful order within which purposes can be pursued and a coherent life career formulated.

How have authority and identity fared in recent years? The answer is Daniel Bell's (1973, 1976) as presented in his book on *The Coming of Post-Industrial Society*. There is, Bell claims, an opposition between the way in which post-industrial societies are organized and the culture of gratification that has formed within them. The marks of post-industrial organization are the change from a goods-producing to a service economy, the pre-eminence of a professional and technical class, the 'centrality of theoretical knowledge as the source of innovation and of policy formulation for the society' (p. 14), the planning of technology and the control of technological growth, and the use of a new intellectual technology which is epitomized in systems analysis and is designed 'to define rational action and to identify the means of achieving it' (p. 30). Singly and together, these developments require that people be rational and efficient and that they exercise a technical mastery. Bell thinks that these requirements are generally met, but met without enthusiasm. More and more people, he says, find meaning not in their work and the style of life that it implies but in hedonism and ecstasy, in the exploration of fantasy and the acting-out of impulse, in altered states of consciousness and an insistence upon personal freedom: more generally, in the enhancement of the 'imperial self' (p. 478).

Is this culture of gratification primarily a protest against a dehumanizing rationality? Is it the latest in that series of protests against modernization (Eisenstadt 1966) that includes the machine-wreckers of the 1700s and the romantics of all centuries? Bell thinks that it is not. The earlier protests occurred on the fringes of economic and social modernization. The new culture is a part of the main stream. In the nineteenth century, as today, there was an 'anti-institutional and antinomian' impulse which

> found its cultural expression in such anti-bourgeois attitudes as romanticism, 'dandyism,' 'estheticism,' and other modes that counterposed the 'natural man' to society, or the 'self' against society. The theme . . . is that of the 'authentic' self, free to explore all dimensions of human experience and to follow those impulses regardless of convention and law. (p. 478)

But, what in the nineteenth century

> was private and hermetic has become, in the twentieth-century effulgence of modernism, public and ideological . . . Few writers 'defend' society or institutions against the 'imperial self' . . . (p. 478)

What is more, the new culture is only indirectly a culture of protest. Rather it is an affirmation of the fruits of capitalist civilization.

> Through mass production and mass consumption [capitalism] destroyed the Protestant ethic by zealously promoting a hedonistic way of life. By the middle of the twentieth century capitalism sought to justify itself not by work or property, but by the status badges of material possessions and by the promotion of pleasure. The rising standard of living and the relaxation of morals became ends in themselves as the definition of personal freedom. (p. 477)

And, again,

> This is the cultural dilemma of capitalist society: it must now acknowledge the triumph (albeit tempered) of an adversary 'ideology,' the emergence of a new class [of intellectuals] which sustains this ideology, and the collapse of the older value system . . . The inimical ideology is not the secular socialism of the working class—if anything, the working class covets ever-expanding goods and production—but the cultural chic of 'modernism'. . . . This new class, which dominates the media and the culture, thinks of itself less as radical than 'liberal' . . .

Bell himself believes that this situation is unstable, but not because there is an incompatibility between society's organization and its culture. He points, instead, to the meaninglessness of impersonal enterprise, of hedonism, and of unbridled freedom:

The traditional legitimacies of property and work become subordinated to bureaucratic enterprises that can justify privilege because they can turn out material goods more efficiently than other modes of production. But a technocratic society is not ennobling. Material goods provide only transient satisfaction or an invidious superiority over those with less. Yet one of the deepest human impulses is to *sanctify* their institutions and beliefs in order to find a meaningful purpose in their lives and to deny the meaninglessness of death. A post-industrial society cannot provide a transcendent ethic — except for the few who devote themselves to the temple of science. And the antinomian attitude plunges one into a radical autism which, in the end, dirempts the cords of community and the sharing with others. The lack of a rooted moral belief system is the cultural contradiction of the society, the deepest challenge to its survival. (p. 480)

Here, then, is a standard account of authority and identity in our time. In this account, authority and identity are dying of malnutrition: starved by a society that is impersonal and exploitative, that is destructive of community and that has spun beyond the control of significant human purpose, a society that weakens corrective protests with a mixture of affluence, drugs, and repression.

There are, to be sure, some empirical observations behind this account and some of these are sound. But too much is omitted. The fact is that many of the themes and practices which, in a context of protest, are taken to be counter-cultural or to be efforts at demodernizing (Berger, Berger, and Kellner 1973) have in the last fifteen or twenty years been institutionalized in the day-to-day operations of most types of complex organizations in the United States, institutionalized not as part of the underlife in those organizations but as essential features of management and operations. They have been defined not as concessions to human frailties or appetites but as keys to a more embracive rationality in human affairs. In this latter context, they are neither anti-institutional nor antinomian. Rather they feed institutions and they renew normative order. These changes in mainstream organizations are the ones that I wish to examine. I hope to point to their sources and their role. I hope also to show that these developments lead to a different understanding than is common of the problems of authority and of personal identity under post-industrial conditions.

ORGANIZING UNDER POST-INDUSTRIAL CONDITIONS

Post-industrial organizations are a response to world conditions that had begun to appear by 1900 and that became predominant following World

War II (Wilensky and Lebeaux 1965). These led to the growth of great and complex organizations, to the rise of professional and technical cadres who man, manage, and monitor those organizations, and to the spread of a technology of analytic tools and of computers to rationalize their operations.

What were the underlying conditions? There was, first of all, the expansion of markets and trade, within and between the modernized societies, this leading to the incorporation of local and regional economies into national and international economies. (And there were expanding populations in which to sell and to serve.) There was, secondly, a general and persisting prosperity which served as both the fuel and the outcome of economic expansion. There was, thirdly, the need, in this expansion, to develop a larger pool of capital, of raw materials, and of skilled labour and to compete successfully for access to it.

The sheer scope of these developments required new methods of management and production. It became necessary for firms to plan as never before. And the pressures for new styles of management and rational procedures were not confined to commercial and industrial enterprises. The whole of the organizational and institutional system of these societies was undergoing expansion and differentiation. Educational systems, religious bodies, welfare organizations, the media of communication, scientific societies, labour unions, professional associations, agencies of government, and countless voluntary associations experienced the same processes of growth in size and complexity and in the rationalization of their operations.

One outcome of these developments is the belief that change is a permanent feature of human life. More exactly, the idea is widely accepted that organizations cannot thrive and survive unless they are able to anticipate change through the explicit use of styles of management and planning that keep them in touch with changing opportunities and dangers (Galbraith 1971: 166–178; Swanson 1971b: 137–170).

A second outcome, and a third, are products of these new complexities when taken together with the need to recruit and to motivate skilled personnel. These two outcomes are (1) management by objectives and (2) attention to what have been called the 'human relations' on the job (Perrow 1972: 97–143). Both have an intimate relation to new forms of authority and identity.

MANAGEMENT BY OBJECTIVES

If post-industrial societies and organizations are to be managed at all, it must be by objectives. There is no other way to bring order to the vastly increased complexity of their internal structures and external relations (Drucker 1954; Ordione 1969). It is a shibboleth that dividing the work can bring both greater efficiency and a higher quality of performance to all aspects of a task and that organizations which have a complex division of labour can be controlled and co-ordinated only if administrators keep clearly in view the general objectives to which each specialized sector of the organization contributes and then monitor the contributions and costs that each sector entails.

Size, complexity, and competitive pressures favour not only management by objectives but management solely for the sake of objectives. Everything is considered of value only for its contribution to the attaining of objectives. Everything is subject to being discarded or changed in the interest of attaining objectives. This includes the way in which an organization is arranged to conduct its work, the kind of personnel it hires and retains, the sort of skills and personalities it finds appropriate, the criteria for judging a performance to be good, and all other aspects of its activities. When this approach is rigorously pursued, people tend to take nothing but a handful of objectives as ultimately given and even these objectives are constantly re-examined in a search for their essence.

This is a radical change from practices of the past. Managers have always been guided by goals and have always reshaped organizations the better to reach their objectives, but objectives tended to be defined in a way that assumed the employment of many traditional arrangements in attaining them (for example, the retention of long-service employees, the continuance of the organization in its present location, an enduring focus on the production of certain types of goods or services for a particular clientele, the continued usefulness of the general and technical knowledge of the staff, and the persisting effectiveness of present systems of authority).

Once it is established, management by objectives makes it possible to question almost every rule and procedure by which an organization operates. This includes all rules for the translation of objectives into policy and of policy into implementation. There is a heightened awareness that it is especially these higher-level rules and practices that may be confounded with the objectives themselves; that they may come to be taken for granted when they should be examined.

One way to make objectives paramount is routinely to abandon routine procedures and expectations. Methods for doing just that are regularly employed. For example, consultants are brought in whose views diverge from those of the staff of the organization and everyone engages in a re-examination of the staff's assumptions — and the consultant's. Regular occasions are made for looking at existing priorities and for challenging all of them. Meetings devoted to mundane business may be opened with the taking of half an hour for thought about greater objectives: after a brief period for reflection, participants may be asked to write down the two or three things they would like most to see accomplished or attempted in the next six months the better to fulfil the unit's mission. Or each person may be asked to suggest how that mission could be better accomplished — if it could — by a given increase in budget. When the group returns to its regular agenda, it does so with fresh awareness of the relevance of routine items for larger matters.

Another way to make objectives stand out is to employ methods of evaluation that show the impact, direct and indirect, of each of the organization's activities upon the attainment of objectives. This is the aim of the several computer-assisted procedures developed in recent years — of cost-benefit analyses, for example, or of systems analysis or of other formal procedures for rational problem-solving (Howard 1971; Mosher 1971; Newell and Simon 1972).

A third procedure for highlighting objectives is to recognize and create those changes in the status of participants that work from objectives implies. As Simmel (1890) observed, when people are under an ideal — responsible for it and responsive to it — they are to that extent equal. This is recognized in modern organizations in the conduct of meetings, or of those portions of them that focus on the relevance of procedures for objectives. Differences in authority among participants are put to one side and everyone is encouraged to say what he really thinks and feels about the organization's situation and prospects: to sketch the opportunities and difficulties that he sees and the courses of action that he would like to see develop. The effort is to obtain from people their vision of what it is that objectives require: the assumptions about the nature of the enterprise that give meaning to its specific activities (Selznick 1957:33–64). The more that a decision involves an interpretation of objectives and a specification of methods for implementing them, the more it is likely that these measures will be employed.

DEALING WITH SPECIALIZED PERSONNEL

There are other things to note about management by objectives, but we need first to bring into our analysis one of the conditions from which this practice springs and which moderates its use. It is the employment in complex organizations, especially in key positions, of people who are specialists. Galbraith (1971:70–1) refers to them as collectively the 'brain' of a modern organization.

> Management . . . is a collective and imperfectly defined entity; in the large corporation it embraces chairman, president, those vice presidents

with important staff or departmental responsibility, occupants of other major staff positions, and, perhaps, division or department heads not included above. It includes, however, only a small proportion of those who, as participants, contribute information to group decisions. This latter group is very large; it extends from the most senior officials of the corporation to where it meets, at the outer perimeter, the white- and blue-collar workers whose function is to conform more or less mechanically to instruction or routine. It embraces all who bring specialized knowledge, talent or experience to group decision-making. This, not the management, is the guiding intelligence — the brain — of the enterprise. There is no name for all who participate in group decision-making or the organization which they form. I propose to call this organization the Technostructure.

For our purpose, the crucial fact about specialists is that they are hard to supervise. They have special knowledge, special skill, or some experience with a special sector of the organization's work. Their special expertness in skill or outlook needs to be brought to bear in forwarding the organization's programmes. Whether this expertise is in fact available depends in part upon the specialist's motivation. To the degree that a worker is specialized, he is in a position to exercise discretion. The organization's problem is then to ensure that he exercises this discretion on relevant occasions and in the service of organizational objectives.[2] For this reason, among others, attention to 'human relations' on the job becomes imperative for an organization's effectiveness.

A sequence of managerial catchwords enables us to trace the emergence and meaning of this new type of worker (Miller and Form 1964; Perrow 1972). At the turn of the century when the bulk of the labour force, even in large organizations, consisted of unskilled and unorganized workers and when there was a surplus of labour, the phrase was 'Labour discipline'. It implied that men and women could be directed and even coerced into whatever behaviour was desired. Around World War I, in a period of growing skills, of unionization, and of a labour shortage, the catchwords were 'scientific management' or 'fitting the man to the job'. Here the image, and the reality, was one of jobs which were to be clearly defined and of people who were to be chosen or trained to meet their requirements. By the 1940s, with still higher levels of skill being required and still more unionization, it was 'personnel management' and 'fitting the job to the man'. The worker was seen as being needed and as having certain characteristics to which work must frequently be accommodated. Then came the 'human relations' movement, emphasizing not only the fitting of work to workers but the importance for their performance on the job of the employees' lives away from work: their personal crises, their difficulties at home, their need for a measure of respect and consultation on the job commensurate with their status in the larger society. The answer, it was said, was a style of supervision on the job that emphasized colleagueship over status relations, that focused on the facilitating of a common effort rather than on rigid observance of lines of authority. In addition there should be available at work counsellors who were paid by the company but who had a relation of confidentiality with any worker who cared to bring them his problems. This approach came to the fore just after World War II. It quickly broadened into a movement having many names but which frequently, in its early phases, was termed 'applied group dynamics'. I shall follow a common practice and call it 'participative management'. In this new movement, and in its many descendants, explicit attention was given to the nature of modern organizations. They were said to consist of specialized parts and to be manned by people with specialized skills. To make these organizations work, objectives and sub-objectives had to be identified and employees had to be given a significant role in deciding how best to apply their own expertise in attaining those of the organization's objectives for which they had special responsibility. Employees were also seen as needing to understand how sub-objectives fitted into larger goals, this in order to facilitate the work of the whole enterprise. They needed time to meet and plan. They needed consultants and facilitators and they needed training if they were to use the help that these could afford them. They needed a setting in which they could freely express their reservations and their hopes and in which they could work jointly with others so that the final plan would take the whole array of expertness into account and so have a better chance of success. Employees needed to have a part in the setting of at least sub-objectives if they were to give to these the commitment required for doing their best.[3]

Participative management thus moves an organization toward management by objectives and makes such management ever more imperative. But participative management moderates some of the impact of management by objectives. Not only objectives, but the development of loyalty, enthusiasm, and steady commitment to the organization by its skilled participants must be taken as fixed terms in any course of action that it undertakes.

FROM POST-INDUSTRIAL ORGANIZATIONS TO POST-INDUSTRIAL SOCIETY

As I see it, these developments in the size of organizations, in the division of labour within and between them, and in methods of operation have affected all institutional sectors of modernized societies. The lives of most of the people in these societies are changed because they must be lived within these new organizations and through them. Much of the labour force is employed by large organizations that are built along these newer lines. Most people get their formal education, their medical and spiritual care, and their share of community and other governmental services through such organizations. Labour unions, professional associations, and political parties are coming increasingly to have the organizational characteristics that I have described. In each of the most modernized countries, the political and governmental structures of the society at large, and not just those of particular organizations within the society, are coming progressively to be organized along those same lines.

This is not to say that these societies or organizations are constructed simply as complex and unified corporate bodies. Each contains interest groups grounded in the concerns distinctive to particular occupations or sectors of the economy or regions or generations or racial, religious, or ethnic situations, and these groups struggle to shape and control the society as a whole and the organizations within it (Gamson 1975). My focus, however, is not on the conflicts among interest groups — they appear in all societies, including the simplest. My concern is rather with the trends that are novel and distinctive in the most complex societies and within the cast they give to authority and identity.

Because these trends are novel and central and pervasive, they define much that is problematic in these societies. It follows that the media treat them as centres and models of what is to come; that political divisions and social movements are emerging around the special problems and the fresh opportunities that they create; that families and schools are socializing children to operate within them, and that religious bodies are focusing on those means by which people can attain transcendence in the kind of social order that is now emerging.

Social changes rarely have the same impact on all areas in a society or on all of its people. It seems that the developments that I describe had their fullest impact on people in the larger communities whose jobs required the highest levels of skill and who were employed by large organizations. By now they have ramified widely if unevenly across the structure of modernized societies: across the spectrum of their institutions and voluntary associations and out to the farthest reaches of their occupational and political hierarchies.

AUTHORITY

This introduction to management by objectives and to participative management enables us to see something essential about a post-industrial society. It is that organizations, and the society as a whole, are providing a

new basis for authority and are thereby recasting the conditions for forming a personal identity. We can see both of these developments as we
sample from contemporary movements and themes.

Among contemporary movements there are some that are self-described
as counter-cultural. It seems to me that many of these movements are
occasioned by exactly the developments that I have described. Their
participants want to gain control of the new bureaucratic structures, to
escape their reach, or to make certain that a society that is organized along
the newer lines is also fit for human beings. They challenge the objectives
that are set by the new structures and the right of the officials, members,
or employees of those structures to set objectives having so great a social
consequence. As we shall see, these movements address many of the same
problems of authority and identity that have been identified by people
exposed to the newer styles of organization and they propose solutions that
have a striking resemblance to the ones already being institutionalized in
operating the internal affairs of large organizations and in the governmental processes of the whole society. Among the themes that touch on the
grounding of authority and that are common to 'establishment' culture
and counter-culture we find the new concern for participatory democracy
and due process, the value given to a 'situation ethic', and the importance
attached to an organization of social relations that gives freedom to human
potentialities.

The words 'participatory democracy' were a battle cry of student leftists
in the 1960s (Swanson 1971b: 137–170). They constituted a demand that
everyone who was in any way involved in an organization have an equal
voice in its operations. They were a call for equality and community, a
denunciation of formal procedures, of secrecy, and of hierarchy (whether
it was a hierarchy of authority, privilege, or merit), and a plea for spontaneity. In the early years, meetings of New Left groups had a free-form
quality. Anyone who defined himself as interested and sympathetic might
come. Everyone had equal access to the floor. There were no continuing
officers, no fixed division of labour, no agendas that took precedence over
whatever the current participants might bring to the sessions. Everyone
was urged to be authentic: to say and do what he thought and felt; to 'let it
all hang out'. Collective choices occurred as clusters of people formed
around one or another line of action. There was no requirement that
anyone be committed to any policies other than the ones that he freely
chose.

This kind of group seems removed from the operations of modern
complex organizations and yet there are important resemblances. In both
cases, authority is ultimately lodged not in persons or offices or in standing
orders of procedure but in objectives—objectives already present or in the
process of being discovered. In both cases, occasions are made on which

the people who must implement policy are involved in identifying policy. This means that they come together to let collective purposes emerge. Differences in status and education and experience have no official standing on these occasions. What counts is vision: people's sense of interdependence, of common fate, and of the power of collective goals to order their lives together and to give force and meaning to their undertakings. Specific procedures for organizing people and for implementing goals are taken to be finally validated only if the group prevails in its efforts, but a first evidence that given procedures have the power to liberate collective action is found in their ability to translate diverse hopes and perspectives into a plan that is responsive to common objectives and to the immediate situation, a plan that wins commitment from the people who must serve it. What seems, in both participatory democracy and complex organizations, a procedure that is free of form is in fact a form of procedure designed to attain this specific and authenticated vision.

We can also find in both systems of organization a realization that a focus on objectives makes it possible for an organization to be responsive to the immediate requirements of a changing environment. The literature of modern organizations is at one with advocates of participatory democracy in urging that organizations succeed in coping with change by acting, not formalistically, but in terms of the relevance for one another of the immediate situation and of objectives (Lundborg 1974; Nonet 1974; Selznick 1974).

There are, of course, opportunities in participative management, and in participatory democracy, for the manipulation of people contrary to their interests. There will in either system be participants who have reservations about what finally is done. But it would be a mistake to think that such qualifications destroy what is accomplished. In both systems, action is legitimatized by showing that it makes a direct connection between the immediate situation and ultimate objectives.

It is also true that no organization can function solely by these means. Its daily operations must be routinized. Indeed, it is my impression that organizations, insofar as they employ participatory procedures, come under greater pressures to attain routinization in their autonomic functions: in clerical services, accounting, recruitment and promotion, production; in whatever is required for day to day viability and in whatever is relatively removed from major objectives. The result is a growing hiatus in these organizations between the nature of most people's participation in relation to ultimate concerns and their relations with one another in implementing common plans. In the first, they are equal, open, sharing. In the second, they are directed through a hierarchy of offices, through routinized procedures, and through a system of accountability.

The growing emphasis upon rules of due process may represent a mechanism to mediate these oppositions (Scott 1969). One way to ensure that a variety of points of view will be viewed and heard is to raise barriers against arbitrary decisions. For example, criteria for promotions and other rewards can be objectified and anyone who meets them — however unsettling his views — can be assured of being rewarded. It can be required that people be consulted before decisions are taken and implemented and, should a decision go against their preferences, that they be given a chance to express their feelings once more before the decision is put into effect. These measures for due process go beyond negotiation and co-optation. They embody respect and consideration. They symbolize the requirement for openness and the fact of interdependence among people who must support one another in their exercise of personal discretion and judgement in the service of a common undertaking.

A special danger in the new conditions of management is found in an institutionalized antinomianism. If it is only the master objectives that ultimately count, then the truth that no implementing routines are sacred may be taken to mean that no routines are necessary or useful. This leads to novel problems in obtaining a disciplined performance of work: to the appearance of executives, as well as of clerks and production workers, who feel that routines or standards of technical excellence are suspect, even idolatrous; to a principled exhaltation of 'good interpersonal relations' over productivity.

One finds a more generalized version of this antinomianism in the new 'situation ethics'. This ethic is consistent with the stress in post-industrial organizations and society upon people's doing whatever will free them to define and attain their major objectives — whatever they find that 'gives them life', personally and collectively (Cunningham 1970). A situation ethic advises that we treat all means as relative; that we base our choices upon a close assessment of values — of goals. It urges that ethically principled behaviour is not a matter of fulfilling obligations but of actualizing warranted values.

Anyone who has read this far, and who knows enough about the American scene, will appreciate that the human potentials movement is both a training ground for the kind of organizational life I am describing and a means for people's coming to terms with themselves as they participate in it. It had its origins in the training of executives. It has become a vehicle for 'self-discovery', 'self-actualization', and therapy.

Kurt Back (1972) puts the main themes and stages into the record. The movement began just after World War II with efforts by the Research Center for Group Dynamics at the Massachusetts Institute of Technology. Some members of the Center's staff brought together community leaders, some executives from social agencies, schools, and churches, and a number of social scientists to talk about problems of intergroup (that is, minority-majority) relations. The Center's staff believed that such problems went unsolved for lack of communication, for lack of appreciation of common objectives, and for lack of people's support and commitment to one another in their carrying out of the things that they might agree were desirable to do. The staff hoped that the leaders who attended their meetings would come to form groups that would develop and carry out plans in their community. They also hoped that individuals, as they became committed to a joint undertaking, would be more likely to follow through on their own. There were modest results of just this sort (Lippitt 1949), but a larger consequence was unanticipated.

The participants began spontaneously to meet each evening to talk about discussions they had had during the day. They tried to conceptualize what was going on. The setting was relaxed. People were open and spontaneous. Suddenly they realized that these evening sessions were the most significant events of their time together. They felt that they were learning things of great value: things about 'group relations as such'; about 'member relations, group procedures, and the influence of the group; in general, those features that could produce a change in the participants . . . that would make them better group members and leaders' (Back 1972: 12).

The staff then proceeded to design a workshop for another group of leaders, this time to have no objective but the imparting of just such information and skill. The workshop was to institutionalize those features of the original workshop that seemed so potent for this kind of learning: involvement in leaderless groups, a norm of openness to one another's ideas and feelings, frequent periods for everyone's open reflection upon what he was seeing, feeling, and learning (so-called 'feedback' sessions), and the creation of the role of the group observer, a role to be taken by participants in rotation with responsibility for noting, and later reporting on, the collective processes and interpersonal relations that the observer saw — this with a view toward uncovering problems and facilitating the group's processes. This workshop was held at Gould Academy in Bethel, Maine in the summer of 1947. As Back says (p. 12):

The decision to continue the workshops and to focus on group development started a trend affecting many fields of applied social research and social sciences, and many professions. Less than twenty-five years later, the types of workshops have proliferated; schools, industries, and government agencies use them in several guises. Thousands of participants go each month to some center to experience group methods. The many centers themselves have become a multi-million-dollar business, and almost every month mass media describe some of the more sensational aspects.

As 'applied group dynamics', this movement became a principal source of theory and training for leaders in government, business, unions, social agencies, churches, and countless voluntary organizations. It passed into the standard curricula of professional schools, preparing people for participation and leadership in all of these areas. It was, from the beginning, especially suited to the needs of people who found that they had to work closely and interdependently within and between complex organizations: who were themselves specialists and who were involved with other specialists in planning, in implementing, and in doing their best. It was already in operation when the new imperatives that led to participative management and management by objectives made their appearance, ready to be used and generalized in coping with these new conditions. And it was also the source of that family of movements, epitomized by encounter groups and the Esalen Institute, that are concerned with the problems of personal coherence and personal identity as these have emerged under post-industrial conditions.

IDENTITY

The new styles of organization root authority ultimately in objectives, especially in the power of objectives to formulate collective action and to liberate it for effective work. They give to each participant the right and the responsibility to judge the relevance that these objectives have for someone in his position, for someone having his specialized skills. But they also make him anxious about himself. He has discretionary powers, but he is also responsible if he errs. If he is encouraged to be his whole self in its relevance for the common enterprise, he also exposes his whole self and is likely to show himself to be irrational, fallible, disloyal, tired, over-zealous, misinformed, or otherwise unacceptable. The focus on objectives is releasing and empowering. So is the focus on the likelihood of change. Both of these make central the opportunities that may be seized, the important needs that might otherwise have been overlooked. They place the highest value on whatever it is that will generate plans and commitment, whatever will enable participants as they actually are to cope with the situation as it actually is and is becoming. The whole process is judgemental — an evaluation of people and practices and results — but in a way that promotes their life together. Rather than underscoring what is wrong, it orientates them to what can be done to reach their goals. But it affords traumas as well. People working in this way cannot help but realize that their skills, and even their personalities, could become irrelevant — or at least in need of change. Since no one is infinitely changeable or creative, and no one is able always to be clear-eyed about the action that the objectives now require him to take, he will find himself objectively condemned by the very standards and authority that he espouses. He will constantly encounter and evaluate himself, be asked repeatedly to express his thoughts and feelings and to make choices on his own behalf and on behalf of the organization, be expected constantly to uphold whatever will promote the collective task, but be constantly aware that he is inadequate or irrelevant or that, with the next turn of change, he may become so. In sum, what modern organizations and societies in principle eschew is a steady definition of the relevance—the meaning—of any of their participants: of their skills, their personalities, and, certainly, of their life careers.

They also employ measures to counteract this assault on personal identity. Those measures can be seen in the practice of participative management and in the human potentials groups that are developed within complex organizations, or outside them, and that are designed to help people to come to terms with themselves.

As we have seen, a first rule in participative management and in human potentials groups is that participants are dependent on each other and that their dependence is of such a nature that they must relate both as special persons and as whole persons: they must count upon one another to give freely of whatever from his talents is needed. Each participant has the option of doing less—a large measure of discretion. Each is uniquely the judge of what is his best contribution. He is free, and the others are free, but no one of them can do his share unless each is able to depend on contributions from each of the others that are given in freedom.

A second principle is that everyone is accepted as a person. Each is understood to be needed and deeply so. Each is therefore authorized and encouraged to 'do his thing' if it is for others. There is something special, irreplaceable about what each person does—special talents or the special possibility of doing something at a time or place that no one else can cover as well. What each person does will count for others and, since he depends on them, for himself as well.

In these circumstances, each person can do what is wanted only if he is free to exercise the discretion he has. His feelings enter into this, not just his judgement; his whole experience and concern, not just his experience in this particular organization. So he must be encouraged to express and test the whole of his outlook and his fellow participants must accept whatever this reveals: accept his deviance and disruptiveness as a part of the reality with which they live, value him for his being willing to share it with them and for letting them help him to transcend it and to free and shape the contribution he can give.

But all of this implies a third principle. To help others, and so himself, a person must be aware of the personal and collective needs and activities of others. These are diverse (specialized) and changeful (because they and the environment are constantly changing). Therefore each person must be open and flexible and must be responsive and responsible to whatever in the situation is new. He must be ready to change even himself if that is required. He must not, however, be required to destroy his freedom as a person. To do that would be to undermine a power on which he, and everyone else, depends. The third principle requires therefore that each person be open and ready to change and that all participants must be ready to support each other in dealing with the anxieties that this both engenders and requires. There must be adequate time and facilities to help people work through their difficulties and to develop the new skills and outlook that the situation indicates. Counselling, support for continuing education, and the provision of time to study, reflect, plan and consult have become standard appurtenances of jobs in modern complex organizations. So have occasions on which participants can together become a sharing community, meeting, as persons rather than employees, to know and accept one another.

Although there are no studies that encompass the whole of the situation of participants in modern organizations, there are several that focus on one or another aspect of that situation. Inkeles and Smith (1974) show in six developing countries that a person's being employed in a large, complex organization, whether as a white-collar or a blue collar worker, is associated with his feeling that he can, either alone or in concert with others, take actions that can affect the course of his own life and his community. It is also associated with his active efforts to improve his own condition, with his rejection of passivity, resignation, and fatalism, with his openness to change and innovation, and with his desire and ability to exercise choice and to encourage others to do likewise. And these associations persist when a person's age, education, marital status, and urban experience are controlled.

Kohn (1971) finds that, in the United States, employment in a larger, more complex organization is associated with a man's valuing of self-direction (the exercise of discretion, the formation of independent judgements), with openness to innovation and change, with a moral outlook based upon the spirit rather than the letter of moral rules, and with a preference for intellectually demanding forms of leisure. In Kohn's study, these relations hold up when the man's education is controlled. (Kohn also finds that several features associated with this type of employment — job security, substantive complexity of work, and size of income — are independently related to this roster of orientations.) Kohn also found in an earlier study (1969) that, among Americans, 'men's opportunities for self-direction in their work: freedom from close supervision, substantively complex work, and a varied array of activities' (1971:472) were similarly related to their outlook and conduct.

We have seen, however, that the same complexity of organizations and of the society at large that presses people to be open, changeful, concerned with objectives and self-directing also requires that they be responsible, that they find their own purposes in collective purposes, and that they submit in many things to hierarchical authority. In short, these complexities put people under incompatible pressures that bear upon their personal identity.

Ralph Turner (1969) thinks that just this combination of pressures is the source of features that most distinguish contemporary social movements:

> Today, for the first time in history, it is common to see violent indignation expressed over the fact that people lack a sense of personal worth — that they lack an inner peace of mind which comes from a sense of personal dignity or a clear sense of identity. It is not, of course, a new thing that people have wondered who they are, nor that people have wondered whether man and man's life are worthwhile. . . . The idea that a man who does not feel worthy and who cannot find his proper place in life is to be pitied is an old one. The notion that he is indeed a victim of injustice is the new idea. The urgent demand that the institutions of our society be reformed, not primarily to grant man freedom of speech and thought, and not primarily to ensure his essential comforts, but to guarantee him a sense of personal worth is the new and recurrent theme in contemporary society. (p. 395)

It is, he says, the combination of an encouragement of individuation and of independence of choice with the ordering of life through large, impersonal organizations that brings this form of protest into focus. I differ from his diagnosis only in proposing that contemporary complex organizations and societies are the source of both sets of pressures. On their positive side these organizations and societies provide a greater degree of psychological security and collective support, a greater measure of confidence and competence and of freedom for personal expression and impulsivity than was true of most large organizations in the past (Miller and Swanson 1958:206–12; 1960:182–3, 242–3, 264–5, 353–4, 390–1). On their negative side, they generate a sense of living in repressive, self-degrading, and identity-threatening conditions.

One might expect that it would be adolescents and young adults who would be hypersensitive to these cross-pressures. (They are at a point of identity reformulation. They are able to anticipate the lives they will lead in modern society and organizations but have not as yet encountered the stronger mediating and supporting features of such societies and organizations.)

Turner agrees that the young are most affected. He says that the distinctively contemporary movements are unlike most of the others that one finds in industrial societies in being based upon age rather than upon social class. He writes:

> The problem of alienation and the sense of worth is most poignantly the problem of a youthful generation with unparalleled freedom and capability but without an institutional structure in which this capability can be appropriately realised. . . . (p. 399)

Are the adolescents and young people who are most likely to be exposed to the sort of cross-pressures that Turner describes also the ones most likely to exhibit problems of identity? We do not know, but there is a suggestion of such an association in some new data. These are data from the archives of the Institute of Human Development of the University of California at Berkeley. They consist of interviews that were conducted in 1968-72 with the members aged 10 to 18 in two well-known samples of families: those in the Oakland Growth Study (OGS) and the Berkeley Guidance Study (BGS). These samples are described elsewhere in detail (Swanson 1974). They consist of families that have been followed from about 1930 when the parents themselves were children. As of 1968-72, these parents range in socio-economic status from lower-working through upper-class. They are, on the average, well above the national means on income, education, and scores on tested intelligence. They are almost exclusively Caucasian and are, for the most part, native-born of northern and western European antecedents and of Christian religious affiliation.

In 1968-72, 38 children aged 10 to 18 were interviewed from 28 OGS families. So were 146 children from 89 BGS families. These interviews were coded for ego functions by clinical psychologists who followed the system developed by Haan (1969). The code of special interest for our purpose is that for 'ego fragmentation'. Haan sometimes calls this a code for 'ego failure' and she takes it to mean that the person is not able to work directly on problems with an eye to solving them (is not able, that is, to 'cope') and is not able to ward off the anxieties that an encounter with problems may arouse (is not able to employ psychological defences). Rather he is 'no longer performing—or is losing . . . efficiency in performing—some . . . main functions of (self) management' (p. 30). He shows signs of panic, of 'various kinds of unmodulated affects—fear, fury and crude sexuality', of being torn by internal or external stresses and of being unable to get on with reformulating his behaviour. In Haan's interpretation, ego fragmentation is an at least momentary failure of personal identity: of a sense of personal continuity, and empowerment, and meaningfulness.

I have proposed, as has Turner, that modern societies and organizations put the personal identities of many of their participants under severe cross-pressures by requiring, on the one hand, that they have and exercise independent orientations and judgement and, on the other, that they be open to their fellows and adopt as their own the changing goals of the collective enterprise. We can identify families in the OGS and BGS in which the breadwinner works for such an organization (Elder 1966:6–7): those families in which the breadwinner (1) works under the supervision of a superior or a committee, (2) works in an organization that has three or more levels of supervision, (3) does not have responsibility for 'making the business' (that is, he is not the top executive and is not in charge of some activity, such as sales, that is especially responsible for the organization's reaching the ends that it is designed to attain). Families in which the breadwinner has such a job are designed in Table 1 as having 'bureaucratic employment'.

TABLE 1

Bureaucratic Employment of the Breadwinner, Types of Family Decision-making, and the Ego Fragmentation of Children in Two Samples
(Tabulated by Sibship)

Bureaucratic Employment?	Individuated Family?	Evidence of Ego Fragmentation?					
		Oakland Sample			Berkeley Sample		
		No	Yes	% Yes	No	Yes	% Yes
Yes	Yes	5	5	50	22	9	29
	No	0	1	*	10	1	9
No	Yes	6	1	14	13	2	13
	No	7	1	13	9	2	18
	Total	18	8	31	54	14	21

*N = 1.

We might assume that adolescents reared in such families would be more likely than others to be trained to anticipate the problems in the world of work that are characteristic of employees of modern organizations (Crowne 1966). But some of these families may come closer than others to putting their children into the kind of cross-pressures that make for identity confusions: for ego fragmentation. This should be more likely in families that stress, as do modern organizations, both the independence and the interdependence of their members. For example, there are families designated in Table 1 as 'individuated'. (Elsewhere, I have called them 'heterarchic' or 'balanced':Swanson 1971.) In these families, the pattern of decision-making is one in which the family as a whole is seen as having interests separate from those of its several members. Decisions are made in a relatively egalitarian fashion but they are binding on all members. At the same time, each member is assumed to have interests, tastes, and skills that are distinctively his and he is encouraged to pursue these both within the family and outside it and to contribute what he distinctively can to the family's common life.

Table 1 contains findings from families (26 from OGS and 68 from BGS) for which adequate data on the breadwinner's job and for family decision-making were available. It shows that the sibships of children aged 10–18 that are more likely to have a double exposure to the order of cross-pressures found in modern societies and organizations — those sibships of children that are reared in bureaucratic families which are also in-dividuated — are more likely than others to display ego fragmentation. (These trends are not affected by the application of controls for age, sex, birth order, social class (using Hollingshead's criteria), I.Q., or scores on the ability to cope or to employ psychological defences.) The numbers in this table refer to sibships, not to individual children. A sibship is said to display ego fragmentation if any child in the family is coded as fragmented. For the two samples combined, the difference in ego fragmentation between the sibships from bureaucratic, individuated families and the sum of the others is significant at the .05 level of probability (chi-square = 4.64, df = 1).

Taken by itself, ego fragmentation is not a sign of psychopathology. It is an inescapable part of every normal 'identity crisis' and, in that context, an aspect of personal maturation. What these data may imply is that ex-posure to a bureaucratized and individuated family is especially likely to generate a crisis of identity; that the successful resolution of such a crisis is necessary for the development of the more broadly adaptive personality required by life in the newer styles of organization and in the more modernized societies. Unfortunately, little is known about the conditions that lead to a person's transcending such a crisis of identity instead of being blocked by it or overwhelmed (Block and Haan 1971).

SOCIAL EVOLUTION

I have been describing the methods of organization that are characteristic of a post-industrial society and of its component organizations. I want now to focus on the society itself and through it, on recent changes in the widest formulations of authority and identity, those found in religious systems.

In a post-industrial society, and not merely in the organizations within it, there is a new basis for authority in human relations and this affects the formation of a personal identity. Because this new basis for authority rests on a new and more general principle of societal integration, it constitutes a new stage of societal evolution. The appearance of any such stage entails a major reformulation of religious understanding.

As commonly conceived, societal evolution means differentiation and then integration: the rise of new, specialized institutions and then the development of some more generalized principles and organizations that are suited to co-ordinate and give direction to these newly-separated, but thoroughly interdependent, parts of the whole (Parsons 1964). These co-ordinating, direction-giving principles and organizations are said to exercise cybernetic control: control by means of information: by means, that is, of superordinate standards, of objectives, plans, and the like. Post-industrial conditions, require a new and more generalized basis for cybernetic control.

It is customary to identify the steps or stages in evolution by the new basis for cybernetic control that they entail. In the evolution of whole societies, these can be seen especially in developments in religious conceptions and organizations. It is these that embody a concern with the ultimately integrating considerations in social life.

Bellah (1964) provides us with a description of major evolutionary developments in religion from the past and thereby brings us to problems of the present. To get some perspective on what is now occurring, we can join Bellah, not at the earliest stages in the series that he presents but at the rise of the world religions and, subsequently, of Protestantism.

The world religions, Christianity in particular, make normative a sharp distinction between man and God and between religious institutions and others. They also give to religious institutions a position above all others in the hierarchy of value: above kinship, above work, above the state. Reformation Protestantism involves a further differentiation, specifically a separation, within religious institutions, between values and the organizations that bear, promulgate, and conserve them: between God's Word and the structure and practice of the visible church. In Protestantism, God's Word is placed over the church.

As Bellah (1964) suggests, each of these developments gives a new place to ultimate value, hence to authority. With the world religions, the final normative test of policies and programmes is their religious legitimization: 'both the supernatural and earthly worlds are . . . organized in terms of a religiously legitimated hierarchy' (p. 366); the world religions 'implied that political acts could be judged in terms of standards that the political authorities could not finally control' (p. 368). With Protestantism, the final root of authority is Scripture and divine inspiration: there is a 'direct relation between the individual and transcendent reality' (p. 369); 'both church and state had their delimited spheres of authority, but . . . neither had a right to dominate each other or the whole of society' (p. 370).

And each development contains distinctive conditions within which identity has to be sought.

The criterion that distinguishes the historic [i.e., world] religions from
the archaic is that the historic religions are all in some sense transcendental. . . . [A]n entirely different realm of universal reality, having for
religious man the highest value, is proclaimed. The discovery of an
entirely different realm of religious reality seems to imply a derogation
of the value of the . . . empirical cosmos: at any rate . . . world rejection . . . is, in this stage for the first time, a general characteristic of the
religious system.
    . . . For the masses, at least, the new dualism is above all expressed in
the difference between this world and the life after death. . . . the
religious goal of salvation . . . is for the first time the central religious
preoccupation. (p. 366)

More specifically:

The identity diffusion characteristic of both primitive and archaic
religions is radically challenged by the historic religious symbolization,
which leads for the first time to a clearly structured conception of the
self. Devaluation of the empirical world and the empirical self highlights
the conception of a responsible self, a core self or a true self, deeper than
the flux of everyday experience, facing a reality over against itself, a
reality which has a consistency belied by the fluctuations of mere sensory
impressions.
    . . . the ideal of the religious life in the historic religions tends to be one
of separation from the world. . . . the devout are . . . set apart from
ordinary worldlings by the massive collections of rules and obligations to
which they must adhere. The . . . notion of a special state of religious
perfection idealized religious withdrawal from the world. In fact the
standard for lay piety tended to be closeness of approximation to the life
of the religious. (p. 367)

With Protestantism, however, 'salvation is not to be found in any kind of
withdrawal from the world but in the midst of wordly activities' (p. 368).

religious symbolism concentrates on the direct relation between the
individual and transcendent reality. . . .
    Religious action was now conceived to be identical with the whole of
life. Special ascetic and devotional practices were dropped . . . and
instead the service of God became a total demand in every walk of life.
The stress was on faith, an internal quality of the person, rather than on
particular acts clearly marked 'religious'. In this respect the process
of identity unification . . . advanced still further. The complex
requirements for the attainment of salvation in the historic religions . . . could themselves become a new form of identity diffusion. . . . Assertion of the capacity for faith as an already received gift
made it possible to undercut that difficulty. It also made it necessary to

accept the ambiguity of human ethical life and the fact that salvation comes in spite of sin, not in its absolute absence. . . . (p. 369)

This Protestant formulation has undergone elaborations and modifications for more than 400 years (Bell 1976:146–71). Under post-industrial conditions these take a new form. Once again the grounds for authority and identity are changed. Another evolutionary stage seems to be emerging.

The chief reason for thinking that we are again at an evolutionary transition, and not at some other great point of change, is to be found in the nature of current dissatisfactions with our understanding of ultimate value. The protests that are distinctive of our time, and of which Turner writes, have focused on the sectors of society that are most concerned with the definition and presentation of ultimate values: on the foundations of legal order (Selznick 1974), on the universities, and on religious bodies. The institutions in these sectors are charged with being unfaithful to their basic responsibilities. Their unfaithfulness resides in their confusion of traditional forms and standards with ultimate purpose. This, it seems to me, is a development within the society as a whole of the imperatives we have seen in considering the effort to integrate the organizations within post-industrial societies by means of management by objectives.

If we follow from the steps that Bellah outlines, we can say that just as the Reformation centred on a differentiation between the values with which religion deals and the organizations that bear them, placing the former above the latter, so we now are seeing a differentiation, within value, between purpose and norms. (By 'norms' I mean rules or principles that say how purpose is to be approached or implemented.) This differentiation and a new integration is formulated in current emphases in theology. God Himself is eternal purpose. The rules for a 'sober and godly life' are norms that tell us how we should come to God and how we should act in the world as a result of our relations with Him. Norms, we are told, are not God. God is not to be found especially in the following of this rule or that but in accepting Him for who He is and accepting His acceptance of us for who we are and who, through living together with Him, we can haltingly become.

This is a distinction that the Reformers did not clearly appreciate. As they saw matters, God is a person and comes to us in our status as persons. And we to Him. But we, at least, have to observe the proprieties. The Reformers thought that they knew what those proprieties were. They thought, for example, that we can come as fuedal servitors to their Lord, as corrupt but helpless children to their holy father, as broken sinners to their judge, as circumspect stewards careful of the talents given to their trust (but secretly aware that the trust is too great), and so on. The new theologies say that we *can* come in these ways, and, on occasion, that we must, will, and should. But, they emphasize, God reaches to us past these proprieties and all others. We are beloved sons and daughters and inheritors and friends — these first of all and beyond all formalities. If we stand on ceremony, it is our misunderstanding or comfort that introduces it, not God.

There is a second important feature of the new theologies. They are no longer fixed on sin and salvation. Neither of these is repealed, but both are placed in a larger context. The understanding of that context is a chief point of current theological struggles.

In this new, more immediate, and, in a sense, more equal relationship with God, certain guidelines are emerging. Here are some of those that seem most frequently advanced. I have phrased them as doctrinal statements in a 'popular' Christian theology.[4]

(1) God accepts you as worthy of His love. He accepts you just as you are and your big problem is to accept this acceptance and to let it work in your life to change and fulfil it. The Second Commandment means that one must love God, one's neighbour, *and oneself.*

(2) God is constantly active and at work in others and yourself. He is always opening a new path and you should be alert to see what it is and to act accordingly. You will be fulfilled if you are open to the new and to all the diversity of experience that exists around you and that should have a part in your life.

(3) The church is Christ's body, and all of its parts are necessary, inter-dependent, and must, necessarily, be open to one another to be in good health. Each member should be tolerant and supportive of each of the others as a whole person, with all his failings and divergences. Each is obligated to be at least tolerant and supportive of all who open themselves to him.

(4) No norm or motive is good in itself. The right ones are those that enable deep, sustaining purposes to be actualized in the situation at hand; that open up the consummation of those purposes within that situation.

(5) Like it or not, each person's whole self, even his body, is on the line. To be fulfilled one must be fully who one is and be open to becoming who, with God, he can.

(6) No one can tell you what to do. You have the right to choose, to be consulted, to use your influence, to express any and all of your needs and feelings, to control the conditions that influence your life. You are obligated to accord these same rights to others.

(7) Evil? Always present and always possible. You can and will do things that preclude your finding what is ultimately of value or that prevent the opening of your life to it. But guilt should not be the centre of your actions. You are needed and wanted for what you freely are. You are justified —

authorized and empowered—to do the thing you can. It is in doing it, not in pointless guilt or regret, that you and others are fulfilled. The focus in worship should be on celebration rather than on confession or forgiveness or even on submission or adoration.

I think that we have in these emphases much the same array of themes considered throughout this paper as features of participative management and management by objectives. Here, of course, they are raised to their meaning for ontological discourse; offered as new appreciations of the ground of man's being.

There is, simultaneously, a new devaluation of organized religion. Just as the Reformation defined values, not the church, as ultimate, so this new reformation introduces new reservations about the role and nature of a church. The Reformers saw the church as God's gift to man, necessary not for his salvation but for confirming and supporting him in that style of living appropriate to his life with God. When purposes are separated from norms, then this style of living, and hence a rationale for an organized church, is down-graded. Each person's direct experience of God provides him with a continuous revelation and it does so in all areas of his life. The people he meets in each area may participate with him in formulating the relevance of that revelation for his action. As Bellah (1964: 372) suggests,

> it is precisely the characteristic of the new situation that the great problem of religion . . . the symbolization of man's relation to the ultimate conditions of his existence, is no longer the monopoly of any groups explicitly labelled religions. . . .

And it is the case that:

> Now less than ever can man's search for meaning be confined to the church. . . . religious action in the world becomes more demanding than ever. The search for adequate standards of action, which is at the same time a search for personal maturity and social relevance, is in itself the heart of the modern quest for salvation. . . . Such diverse movements as the liturgical revival, pastoral psychology and renewed emphasis on social actions are all efforts to meet the present need. . . . (p. 373)

And so, perhaps, is the new stress on 'innovative' worship in the sense of orders of worship that provide an authentic sense of a relation to God in one's immediate situation. And so, perhaps, in the new mysticism, or, more exactly the new effort to find those direct and personal relations with God of which mystical disciplines such as yoga or transcendental meditation or chanting or marathon prayer are but examples (Hoge 1974; Wuthnow 1975). And so, in a secular context, may be some uses of drugs and sex: a part of a quest for an immediate relationship with what is ultimately real.

CODA

I have been presenting several trends in a post-industrial culture, calling attention to similarities among them, and suggesting conditions from which they spring. There are many questions here for research (Wilensky 1964). I may be wrong in thinking that these trends are associated with one another or that they share at least some of their more important sources. That needs investigation. So does my characterization of the nature of those sources. There are, after all, competing explanations, among them the one provided by Bell (1973). I will close by indicating why these alternatives seem to me less plausible than the proposals I have offered.

Bell sees what is new in culture as antinomian and anti-institutional and he believes that these themes are directed toward the support of a new hedonism. He says that this hedonism is a product of affluence and of a commercially-fostered ethic of consumption.

I think that Bell's interpretation overlooks too much. Antinomian movements seem of two sorts. When they accompany the break-up of a social order, they are individualistic and they approve an immediate impulsiveness and gratification as all that remains to a people who live in the void (Rieff 1966, 1973). When they accompany the rise of more general bases of social integration, they denigrate lesser regulations as idolatrous and they rally people to the new standard and to the responsibilities of acting upon personal insights (Huehns 1951). The common thesis of most contemporary 'counter-culture' movements, of situation ethics, of new styles of management, and of recent trends in theology seems closer to the second of these possibilities than to the first. It is not an individual hedonism that is promulgated but a stress on simplicity and community and upon a community that is shaped by personal freedom, that requires it, and that supports it.

It might be argued, however, that the sequence is other than the one I have suggested, that criticisms of the culture and the development of counter-cultural movements came first and that they were followed by accommodations to them in the universities and churches and in business firms and agencies of government. That seems not to be the case. The new theories of management were articulated and discussed from the early 1950s as were the new theologies. Together with the counter-culture, they came to prominence in the middle of the 1960s.

It could also be suggested that some of the trends and themes I note — the human potentials movements, perhaps, or the emphasis in religion upon self-acceptance — are only latter day versions of the American effort at self-improvement. There may be important elements of that effort within these trends and themes, but surely that is not all that they represent. They break with the past in their stress on community; in their assurance that impulsivity can be expressed because, under the new conditions, the social order can accept it, respond to it, and be strengthened rather than overwhelmed by it.

Whatever one's interpretations, they make a difference. If mine are in the right direction, they call us to a search for more adequate means to vest authority in ultimate purposes; means by which to gain the freedom that this investiture promises while avoiding the dehumanization of personal life that it can entail. They also call us to a search for new institutional means by which people can find and maintain their own relevance for ultimate purposes; the means by which they can be called, empowered, and fulfilled.

7

Aspects of Identity and Authority in Sociological Theory

Roland Robertson

This last chapter was written by Robertson after virtually all of our editorial tasks had been completed. It is thus based upon the efforts in this volume while yet pointing to a broad context in linking its theme to the sociological tradition. Indeed, from the vantage point of the perspective which is forming here—even though it contains fairly divergent views— there emerges an image of the sociological past in many points quite different from the representations with which contemporary sociology is familiar. This, of course, is always so when a new theoretical departure becomes the platform from which to survey the intellectual work out of which it arose. Even the present effort, which can only claim to have seriously urged the fruitfulness of a central concern with the com- plementarities of authority and identity, leads to such a reappraisal.

Robertson's piece then places the theme of this book into the context of central sociological themes in the classical period and since then. He makes no effort to be exhaustive—the chapter is no history of sociological theory—but he does revisit and provocatively reinterpret familiar land- marks in the field. It is remarkable how Georg Simmel emerges in this piece in much sharper profile than in most analyses of the substantive legacy of classical sociological theory.

In placing the volume into this broader context, Robertson's paper also goes well beyond its sociological confines by showing the interpenetration of philosophical and sociological themes. The challenge of seeing identity and authority not only in their purely social dimensions, but in ways that point beyond that domain to the sources of truth and freedom will, we hope, be further pursued.

B.H.

In this chapter we attempt to distill major aspects of sociological theory since the 1890s with particular reference to the *general analytical* context in which the themes of identity and authority are locatable. That context has primarily to do with problems centred upon the relationships between individual and society and subjectivity and objectivity. It must be emphasized that we do not attempt here to delve into the long-established philosophical discussion of personal identity in the Anglo-American orbit. Nor do we venture far into distinctively psychological work on that theme. Roughly the same applies to the focus in respect of authority, which has also been subjected to philosophical and psychological treatment in the relevant domains of literature.

Another preliminary point of some importance needs to be emphasized. This has to do with the use of the term 'identity' to refer to the equation of subjectivity and objectivity. In one very significant sense any sociological talk about identity addresses, if only implicitly, the synchronization, or the overcoming of the separation, of subjectivity and objectivity. However, in the tradition of 'Hegelianized Marxism', talk of identity, or of 'the identity principle', has involved specific reference to 'the equation of active individual subjectivity in history and objective historical and social conditions . . .' (O'Brien 1976:125).

In spite of its specificity—which has often involved a focus on the relationship between the work of Marx and that of Freud—that view is, as has been intimated, very clearly connected to the general themes raised by *any* discussion of identity. Those general themes pivot upon the issue of the nature and locus of human 'power'. The 'Hegelianized Marxist' approach to identity employs the latter term as a method of dialectically linking what other schools of thought have often regarded as rival sources of 'power' in human society. It attempts to knit together—or at least provide both an epistemological and a political programme for synthesizing—individual, subjective and objective structural components of the (Western) human circumstance. It seeks to *make identical* what other schools of thought have regarded as conflicting dimensions of the human experience (with particular reference to capitalist societies), dimensions which revolve around the relationship between individual autonomy, on the one hand, and material and/or socio-cultural constraint, on the other. In some offshoots of that approach personal identity is in effect made contingent upon collective identity. (Or rather, the epistemological and political programme is predicated on the assumption of the umbilical connection between the two.)

Thus, although the links are clear, we have to be mindful at the outset of the differences between the use of identity to refer to personal, individual identity, its employment in reference to collective identity and the use of identity in 'Hegelianized Marxism' to bridge the gap between subjectivity and objectivity. In effect the latter thrust attempts to define identity as the overcoming of that gap. More micro-sociological approaches to personal identity—such as those to be found among symbolic interactionists—tend to talk in terms of the manner in which the subjective component is given objective status, thus neglecting what more macro-sociological approaches regard as *'real'* objective factors.

In any case the immediate point is that even though we are not *directly* concerned here with identity in the sense of the 'equation' of the subjective and the 'really objective' the general issues which that sense raises are definitely relevant to the present discussion. This is so primarily because the closely related issues of the relationship between individual and society, and the relationship between the subjective and the objective have, we contend, been at the heart of the crystallization of sociology as a discipline (Cf Eisenstadt and Curelaru 1976:347–76; Bourdieu 1977; Robertson 1977, 1978). The ground for the development of sociology from the early nineteenth century had been largely exposed in reference to the philosophical (and in the German context the theological) 'gift' of autonomy to what Weber came to call 'the intra-mundane' realm, relative to the heteronomic control of the social by the supra-mundane (or its priestly representatives). The problem *within* a nascent sociology *then* became the status of *intra-mundane institutionality and culturality relative to individuals*. In other words the degree to which sociology itself— or more generally social science—posited a heteronomic condition for individuals (perhaps even more determinative than supra-mundane-centred heteronomy) became a central motif of sociology, as it developed directly as self-conscious Sociology or indirectly in the tradition of Hegel and Marx (Cf Dumont 1977; Sahlins 1976; Robertson 1980).

In recent years, with the revival of intellectual and academic Marxism, such matters have become central controversies in the disciplinary catch-ment area of sociology. In the orbit of Marxian and neo-Marxian social science the debate which relates directly to the issues of the present discussion is, of course, that between those adhering to the so-called humanist interpretation of Marx, on the one hand, and those who maintain that Marx achieved (after an early concern with the prospects for the elimination of that which lay externally beyond and thus diminished the individual) a rupture in relation to thinking in terms of the subject-object and individual-society antinomies, on the other hand. In various forms the latter attitude has resulted in processual-productional—in the *broadest* French sense, *structuralist*—views of society, views which insofar as they attend at all to subjectivity-objectivity and individual-society distinctions see them largely as contingent aspects of an encompassing process. The various 'Hegelianized Marxisms' lie between these two views, in the sense that they tend to focus on the *concrete, historical* cir-cumstances of the degree of cleavage between and fusion of subjectivity and objectivity and between individual and society, with particular attention to the forms of *mediation* of the individual-society relationship (Cf Colletti 1972, 1973, 1975).

The issue of *authority* can be located in this context primarily with reference to the problem, as perceived in some Marxian schools, of the degree of heteronomic control of individuals attributed to what in Durkheim's early work is called social fact. In the Marxian context the parallel concept is, of course, that of reified elements of the social structure. The basic point is that in both Marxian and non-Marxian sociologies the problem of the phenomenal status of the social realm in relation to the realm of individual subjectivity has been a central concern. In an important respect the issue of the autonomous lawfulness of the extra-individual social realm and its relationship to the individual 'level' has been a main focus of the question of authority and associated questions of legitimacy in the history of sociology (Habermas 1975). The rejection of both religious and purely political interpretations of the lawfulness of collective societal life were essential steps in the development of sociology. There then arose from quite early in the nineteenth century the question of *the manner in which* the social realm operated autonomously.

We may identify four ideal-typical responses to that question in pre-classical sociology. Firstly, there was the view which argued directly that the social realm did indeed operate autonomously, thus either constraining the individual by its sheer facticity or by 'casting' the individual as an abstraction. Secondly, there was the view which is usually called the idealist position — involving a stress upon culture (which in some cases veered strongly towards a religious conception). In that perspective culture tended to be used as a conceptual binding or a synthesizing of the subjective and the objective and of the individual and the societal at a level 'higher' than the purely social. Thirdly, there was the perspective which sought an infrastructural sub-realm within a wider socio-cultural realm, the infrastructure being the seat, as it were, of the lawfulness of the socio-cultural realm as a whole. Fourthly, there was the attitude which tended to see the apparent autonomy of the societal domain as really the outcome of the interplay of individual actions. Thus, sociology was in effect the study of processes in terms of which the pursuit of individual interest yielded a relatively stable, societal domain. [1]

The first of these positions in effect saw society, the social realm, as in itself 'authoritative'. Or, from a different angle, it *eliminated* the issue of authority by making the individual level simply subordinate to the societal level — it imposed upon the collective, human realm an external, analytic supposition that the society dominates the individual. The second position explicitly *posed* the problematic of authority by seeking to discover a 'vehicle' which synthesized individual subjectivity and societal objectivity. The third approach tended to render authority contingently — that is, as an *in situ* set of 'excuses' or rationalized justifications for the operation of the social realm at any given point in time prior to the phenomenal recognition of the true seat of societal lawfulness (which would eliminate the individual/society cleavage). The fourth approach *minimized* the issue of authority by recognizing only the need for central monitoring or shaping of the pursuit of individual interest.

This depiction does not differ radically from the situation which Parsons described in *The Structure of Social Action* (Parsons 1937) as obtaining on the eve of what we now call classical sociology. The major difference is that whereas Parsons read the pre-history and early history of sociology *as if* it had been centred on the Hobbesian problem of order (starting, in other words, with the problematic of the war-of-all-against-all analytic circumstance), the present depiction attempts to show that contained within different intellectual traditions there were ideas about the *ideal* form of individual-society relationships. Parsons himself was in effect to develop much of his sociological theorizing in terms of an analytic search for just such an idea. However, *Parsons'* search — at least in its earliest phase — was largely dictated by the problematic of *one* tradition, namely the utilitarian. This *working away* from one tradition (a tendency perhaps, as some have argued, consolidated by Parsons' own societal background) diverted attention from aspects of the pre-history and early history of sociology which explicitly or implicitly denied the appropriateness of the utilitarian problematic. Thus more emphasis is placed here on the claim in some traditions that the historical emergence of individualism and 'societalism' was one involving *concomitant processes*, while for the sociologistic tradition the *individual* rather than society was problematic (Robertson 1978a:149–81).

These are, it must be repeated, differences of emphasis. Their importance lies above all in the sensitivity of the present delineation to *presuppositions* within intellectual traditions concerning the 'coding' of the individual-society relationship. In this connection it should be noted that Parsons claimed in his first major work that his was in a sense an Husserlian endeavour. In the present context the significance of that claim lies in the suggestion that Parsons sought to transcend the presuppositions of intellectual traditions. His was partly an exercise in the phenomenology of theorizing (from a pure utilitarian problem-base). The major concern here, however, is to remain sensitive to the presuppositions of intellectual traditions rather than to provide a transcendent Archimedian point.

The contention that the problem of order is the pivotal problem of sociology has been subjected to a stream of criticism. Such negativism in relation to the problem of order is particularly ironic at the present time when so much is being written about such themes as forms of life; ground rules of social interaction; deep structures; cultural models, templates and codes; paradigms; modes of legitimization; modes of discourse; systems of historical action; civil religions; provinces of meaning; extra-societal warrants; and so on. If the central motifs of modern theoretical sociology and anthropology are anything to go by one might be justified in claiming that the one element common to the various competing 'paradigms' of modern social science is the problem of order. Indeed the concern with analytic paradigmicity is *itself* indicative of a tacit convergence on the problem of order in modern science. The thematic foci which have just been listed each centre — with different nuances and from different standpoints — on the problem of the terms in which social entities (most usually societies) operate. One of the more remarkable features of modern sociology is in fact its convergence — however latent a convergence — on the problems of what makes society in general — or more usually, particular types of society — *possible*. Moreover, although there is less agreement on this point, there is a strong thrust in the direction of rejecting accounts of modes of societal operation which emphasize the centrality of the purely utilitarian, the purely practical, the purely empirical or the purely instrumental. The 'culturization' and 'de-economization' of Marxian theory within pro- and neo-Marxian contexts constitute particularly good examples of this phenomenon.

The manner in which Parsons has extended and redefined 'the problem of order' since *The Structure of Social Action* has received little attention. The main focus of critique has been that of Parsons' initial problem of the relationship between individual interests and the 'interests' of society (Cf Giddens 1976). This is a central problem of the present essay, although not in precisely the same form as Parsons perceived it. But it must be mentioned here that in Parsonian theory there is no longer a one-dimensional problem of order, for now Parsonian theory focuses, *inter alia*, on such problems of order as individual order, social order, cultural order, action-system order and so on (Parsons and Platt 1973; Parsons 1978a; Robertson 1978b; Baum 1977). The problem of social order in the face of the problems of randomness of individual ends and the potentiality of the war-of-all-against-all *may* still be regarded as the in-principle departure point of Parsonian theory — but it is certainly not an ongoing 'fixation' of that mode of analysis. This is a particularly important point, since in his early work Parsons was severely critical of the utilitarian tendency to define the individual in such a concrete manner as to make genuinely sociological analysis of the social level impossible. In other words a dichotomy between individual and society was built into utilitarian theories (or variants thereof). Parsons' 'voluntaristic', analytic conception of the individual made the latter more social than did utilitarian theories precisely in order to render analysis of society possible. It is only in work after the early 1950s that Parsons has paid much attention to the question of the relationship between *the concrete individual* and other aspects of the human circumstance. This has been undertaken with reference to the idea of the *differentiation* of action systems. We can note only that there is a significant difference, though not an incompatibility, between the early emphasis upon the general analytic contours of the relationship between individual and collective-societal aspects of action and the later concern with the differentiation of those aspects from each other.

That aspect of Parsons' approach which emphasized the severe inadequacy of accounting for social order in reference to either the (positivistic) facticity of institutional patterning or (utilitarian) instrumental rationality has been echoed, it would seem, in a variety of ostensibly rival schools of modern sociology.[2] That aspect of Parsons' perspective which issued from Durkheim's emphasis upon the moral authority of society (an emphasis supplemented by Parsons' interpretation of Weber's ideas concerning charisma, value rationality and legitimization) has not, on the other hand, been anywhere near so widely accepted. In particular it is Parsons' ideas concerning internalization and institutionalization of orientational patterns from a cultural system (which, so to speak, stands over the social system and personality system) that has met with great resistance. And yet the question of what we have called, in as neutral a concept as possible, *the terms* in which particular societies operate, has become a central issue of modern sociological theory. Two quite closely related problems appear to be involved in that issue. Firstly, there is dispute about the extent to which 'the terms' of societal operation are explicitly available as a form of 'extra-societal warrant' (Touraine 1977); or whether, on the other hand, 'the terms' consist of a kind of 'deep-structure' or what Weber called 'irrational presuppositions' (there being other possibilities).[3] Secondly, there is variation in the degree to which, on the one hand, societies are seen as the ongoing product of the creative actions and interactions of individuals relative to external constraints and groups or, on the other hand, whether societies are regarded as 'systems of production'.[4]

Underlying such differences there has nevertheless been a discernible trend in modern sociology toward recognition that there is cross-societal (not to mention cross-civilizational) variation, as well as variation over a period of time, in the terms under which societies operate and their members participate. In other words, the debate about the terms of societal operation is really being conducted on at least two levels. At the most general level there is debate about the rival merits of such approaches as those symbolized by terms like modes of discourse; systems of historical action; societal codes; forms of life; societal presuppositions; and so on. At a more specific level there is the question of *the nature* of these modes of discourse, societal codes, etc. Thus there may be sharp disagreement, for example, about the degree to which societies operate in terms of an extra-societal warrant (as in the notion of the over-arching cultural system); but, on the other hand, there seems greater agreement—however tacit—that within these 'terms' societies will perhaps vary over their own histories, as well as vary among themselves. Moreover they will diverge across their own histories and among themselves to the degree that there is conflict or strain with respect to the appropriateness and institutionalization of the prevailing terms (Cf Touraine 1977 and Eisenstadt 1978). What, however, needs much more attention is the issue of comparability and translatability of *the theoretical perspectives* which are brought to bear on these matters (the perspectives themselves being embedded in—in varying degrees—the very circumstances which the sociologist is trying to analyse). Baum and Kavolis have addressed aspects of the societal and civilizational problem area in previous chapters. The present chapter is as much concerned with the question of *theoretical approaches* to the problem area.

DURKHEIM, WEBER AND SIMMEL ON SOCIETALITY

Sociology arose largely in response to a particularly crucial phase in the development of the centuries-old debate about the foundations and limits of authority. We refer to the Enlightenment preoccupation with the relationship between, on the one hand, authoritative tradition and, on the other, reason and rationality—in a catch-phrase, the tension between revelation and reason. The most explicit working-out of the relationship *on a sociological basis* was to occur during the period 1890–1920. Durkheim attempted to ground reason and rationality in society such that tradition and reason were to be seen as compatible, since they sprang from the same source. Modes of thought were inherently societal. Thus the self-conscious sociological study of society was at the same time the promotion of rationality. The more that society was understood, then—concomitantly—the more that rationality was in our grasp. The crucial innovation for which Durkheim reached—building, of course, on the work of previous thinkers—was agreement on the proposal that rational thought and the study of the development of human society were interdependent and mutually amplifying projects. The application of reason to society had to rest upon acceptance of the proposition that the former issued from the latter and that the study of the latter could only be accomplished adequately by acknowledging that theorem. With the benefit of hindsight it is now relatively easy to see the significance of Durkheim in effecting a transition—most particularly within twentieth century French sociology—from concern, on the one hand, with authority and the relationship between society and individual to the theme, on the other, of *societal production and reproduction.* In the sociological programme of 'the productionists' the individual *as such* plays no part while the theme of legitimate authority is, as it were, replaced by the idea of dominant, class-based modes of knowledge. Durkheim's emphases upon the societality of the individual and the societality of knowledge surely provided the most fundamental indigenous basis for the modern French intellectual emphasis on society as an autonomous, reproductive vehicle; even though there was a strong tendency in French thought along such lines before Durkheim, *and* in spite of the fact that the later Marx has been used more often than Durkheim as the major 'legitimatizing' reference point for the productionist conception of society.

Durkheim's attempt to bring reason and societal reality into alignment contrasts in many respects with the sociology and more tacitly conveyed philosophy of Max Weber. Weber inherited a set of intellectual problems centred upon the relationship between received cultural tradition and individual freedom. Since Kant a major stream of German intellectual thought had been preoccupied with the question of the manner in which *the individual* could assume for himself or herself the 'authority' which had previously been thought to reside 'above' the individual in doctrine and heteronomous ideas.[5] Thus although there were considerable overlaps with the work of Durkheim (since the *general* problem was to a large extent shared), Weber was influenced to take particular interest in the nature of individual autonomy and freedom *relative to* the problem of external constraints. He was also constrained for similar reasons—probably under the immediate influence of Tönnies and Simmel—to pay attention to the problem of *inter*action between individuals. The interest in interaction which Tönnies, Weber and, above all, Simmel exhibited may best be regarded as a corollary to the previous steps taken by, *inter alia*, Kant, Kierkegaard, Marx and Nietzsche away from a picture of the individual as necessarily heteronomously controlled by ideas.

In the classical period of German sociology so sharply was drawn the image of the putatively autonomous individual on the one hand, and the State-centred society on the other, that the development of sociology as a discipline was clearly carved out in reference to the resulting interstices. In other words, the German interest in 'the succession of freedom froms'—from God, from nature, from history, from culture, from society (even from life)—left, as it were, the problem of the relation *between* individuals very sharply exposed. That in itself was an important basis for the creation of an interest in identity among German philosophers, and less explicitly among German sociologists, from the early nineteenth century onward.[6] In Weber's work as well as in Simmel's a major preoccupation thus developed concerning the connection between individual freedom and the structuration of *relationships between individuals.* This in fact constitutes the nub of the 'tragic vision' which has often been attributed to the writings of Weber and some of his contemporaries. For it appeared to both Weber and Simmel that the very attainment of individual freedom from control by various facets of the human condition had then resulted in 'control' by the contingencies of interaction between individuals. Simmel's interest in social forms of interaction and Weber's interest in rules and regulations were undoubtedly conditioned by such an idea. In particular, Weber's *Protestant Ethic* thesis clearly centres on the notion of individuation giving rise to *procedures* which then assume the character of 'an iron cage'. In contrast, Durkheim's interest in interaction was more oblique. For in the French tradition the 'procedures' of interaction were regarded as *societally provided* — not as deriving from inter-individual contingency. Thus Durkheim placed considerable emphasis upon the division of labour providing the terms in which interaction was pursued and in effect the manner in which identities were formed. [7]

Although some Durkheimians of today would dispute the proposition, the main consequence of Durkheim's fusion of rationality and societal tradition was to divert attention from what in the German tradition became a preoccupation with problems of *authority and legitimacy*. Whereas some of the more conspicuous of modern French sociologists have tended to see societies in holistic structural terms, with their principles of operation embedded in them — operating that is on the basis of an *immanent rationale* — much of modern German social philosophy and sociology has tended to preoccupy itself with what Touraine calls the question of the *extra-societal warrant* (Touraine 1977). In other words, whereas the German sociological interest has been primarily in the question of the *explicit* basis upon which a society, or segments thereof, functions, the way in which what occurs in it is or is not legitimatized and phenomenally understood, the French interest has predominantly been in understanding not what provides a warrant for functioning but rather the structural principles of the 'movement' of society. Whereas the first has sought to understand the manner in which society operates in relation to explicit, *in situ* principles, the second has striven for a transparency with respect to the objective principles of operation. Without wishing to exaggerate the differences, we would argue that in the German case analytic attention has, relatively speaking, been more focused on the issue of *meaningful* relationships between society and individual considered as independent 'entities'.

Weber fits into this sketch primarily since he took an historical approach to the relationship between the authority of tradition and rationality. In the face of much controversy about Weber's work, we attempt to summarize his stance. Although Weber established a typology of legitimate authority (which, as has quite frequently been noted, was expressed sometimes simply as *domination*, or *lordship*) consisting of traditional, charismatic and rational-legal forms, these forms were not precisely on the same level. Whereas traditional and charismatic authority have much to do with substantive rationality, with 'ultimate values', the third, rational-legal authority, has to do with instrumental and practical aspects of rationality. In establishing the modern primacy of the latter and at the same time proclaiming that the scientist (including of course the sociologist) should not as a scientist enter the domain of substantive rationality, Weber left a sociological legacy of an ambiguous nature.

Specifically, Weber's image of the modern world, the world of the so-called 'iron cage', is one in which authority in the more classic sense (Friedrich 1972), namely, traditional authority (involving the use of a tradition to provide a rationale for present and potential actions), is no longer viable. Weber adjudged substantive rationality to have lost most of its power, mainly through processes of rationalization which, so he claimed, increasingly transformed substantive rationality into the realm of 'irrational', subjective values. In the course of Western history, particularly since the Reformation, the world had become progressively disenchanted. The modern, iron-cage circumstance was indicated by Weber as one in which individuals had become bound in terms of manipulability, calculability, measurability and so on, to a wordly domain which was characterized precisely by belief in its susceptibility to such operations. In other words, the two major (mutually amplifying) features of the iron-cage were, on the one hand, subscription to norms of instrumental rationality and, on the other, crystallization of orientations to worldly 'objects' which were treatable in such terms. Quite closely related to this major aspect of the iron-cage was Weber's *Realpolitik* view of the State. The triumph of 'the world' was thus to be seen in the two major dimensions of bureaucracy and secular politics. In that scenario, the orderliness of modern societies would depend largely upon ethics of responsibility *vis à vis* the domain of *Realpolitik* and the predictability of and adherence to principles of instrumental rationality and legality, in the face of a 'polytheism' of value systems rooted at the subjective level. Weber's advocacy in the German case (an advocacy partly based on trends he discerned in other parliamentary contexts, such as the English) of a charismatically flavoured plebiscitarian form of democratic leadership placed over the 'wheeling-and-dealing' domain of politics has remained a particularly controversial element of this scenario (Stammler 1971: Mommsen 1974).

What has led to Weber being such a focus of interest in the modern period with respect to the issue of authority and adjacent themes is undoubtedly his unwillingness to offer definitive *solutions* to the problems which he isolated. Therein for some lies Weber's strength as a sociologist —

namely, that he courageously laid out the contours of a highly problematic world, suggesting a number of ways of coping with the problematic circumstance but also warning of the dangers and difficulties ahead. Nelson has aptly praised Weber in this regard for his adherence to 'the social reality principle' (1971). On the other hand, it is precisely that adherence which has led others — perhaps most notably Horkheimer — to see Weber as the harbinger of an oppressive and meaningless societal situation. The major contrasts with Durkheim lie in the latter's eventual commitment to the idea that society itself was a moral entity — that is, for Durkheim what Weber called substantive rationality issued from society *itself*. Society became, for Durkheim, a moral-authoritative entity, and thus to him it was not so much authority *per se* which was of interest but rather adequate organization of society in such a way that its moral basis could be made manifest, an organization to be promoted in terms of the advance of the science of society which would, for example, explicate the moral-social relevance of education. Central to Durkheim's ideas was the problem of the relationship between individual and society, an aspect of his work which has been as controversial as has Weber on authority, domination and instrumental rationality. It is Durkheim who more usually bears the brunt of having diminished the individual than Weber, in spite of the fact that Weber's image of the iron-cage of instrumental rationality is *on the face of it* no less an image of individual subjection and alienation than that of Durkheim. The reason for Durkheim being blamed more than Weber for this is undoubtedly because Durkheim in his most program-matic, methodological statement (*The Rules of the Sociological Method*) spoke very explicitly of the primacy of society over the individual and of the autonomy of 'social facts'. And yet Durkheim subsequently developed the theme of *social* individual*ism* and the *increasing* significance of processes of individuation and individualization. In contrast, although less ex-plicitly, Weber committed himself *methodologically* to the primacy of the individual and yet in his analysis of modern societies sketched a gloomy prospect for individualism. It could be sensibly maintained that Durkheim's empirical prognosis was more favourable to the individual than Weber's. But we must not overlook the rather well-established facts that while Durkheim developed his *particular* conception of the individual in the course of his work *so as* not to make the individual a threat to society, Weber characterized — possibly caricatured — the iron-cageness of modern society in a manner such as *to draw* attention to the threat to individualism.

Such differences are not of course merely attributable to variation in intellectual conviction. They have, as we have indicated, much to do with different conceptions of individualism and its relationship to 'societalism'. Clearly, for example, Weber — like most German intellectuals before him and during his own time—*valued* autonomous individualism *as such* more than did Durkheim. The latter was more concerned to cultivate a distinctively *social* conception of individualism in a society where 'individualism' had an antisocial connotation. Weber worked in an intellectual milieu which had almost continuously vacillated between the competing claims of individual *wholeness*—cultivation of self *in relation to* society—and societal wholeness (Robertson 1978; Lukes, 1973). That both were deeply concerned analytically and normatively with the individual-society connection should not lead us to ignore crucial conceptual and normative differences.

Thus Durkheim was a crucial figure in effecting a transition from concern with authority and with issues of the extra-societal warrant to the modern conception of the self-production or re-production of society. (And in that connection due acknowledgement must again be given to the retroactive 'legitimization' of that transition in recent years to the work of Marx.) In Weber's case we have spoken of a transition within the German tradition (already prepared, *inter alia*, by Kant, hermeneuticians, philosophers of life, and the early participants in the *Methodenstreit*) from concern with (traditional) authority to the issue of the subjective-cultural bases of society. Weber's great importance in this respect was in dramatically *exposing* problems of legitimate authority, while Durkheim's significance was in shutting them off. Weber diminished the societal significance of subjectivity, by pushing it to the 'private margins' of public societality. Durkheim, on the other hand, incorporated the individual and (substantive) rationality *into* the 'total social fact'.

In terms of our present project the Durkheimian transition had the effect of a sociologistic cloaking of the identity/authority problem, while the Weberian transition disrobed it. But the differences between Durkheim and Weber were far more complex than that. Quite early in his work (in *The Protestant Ethic and the Spirit of Capitalism*) Weber announced his concern to comprehend what he called the irrational presuppositions of rational-material orientations which sustained a view of the modern world as sublimated in terms of its own laws. We would argue that much of Weber's work thereafter was indeed concerned with the explication of the internal presuppositions of the modern iron-cage circumstance and, moreover, that so-called rational-legal 'authority' was really more to do with the crystallization of a set of presuppositions about 'the world' than with questions of legitimate authority *per se*. In other words, the modern world was, in Weber's view, one which rested more upon ('irrational') presuppositions about its facticity, calculability and lawfulness than upon authoritativeness. The other side of the coin of such a world was that of great variation in individual subjective values. Indeed the latter helped to promote the iron-cage circumstance, while the iron-

cage circumstance amplified the phenomenal concern with 'deep subjectivity'. Weber was, of course, deeply concerned — particularly in his
later years — with the normative formulation of the bridge between the
two, in terms of the concept of vocation. Indeed Weber's focus on the
vocational structures of involvement in science and politics may appropriately be regarded as involving a set of prescriptions for a kind of
society based more on presuppositions about its functionality than upon
the reference of its functioning to a legitimatizing 'extra-societal' reference
point.

In contrast Durkheim sought, in roughly the second half of his writing
career, to discover the *a priori*s of *all* societies (or of society in general).
These *a priori*s were not, of course, *a priori*s in the Kantian sense. They
were, *produced by* society *via* its social-structural contours — contours
which were reproduced as a system of categories. There is no need to
rehearse here the weaknesses of Durkheim's argument in this respect
(which hinge on the problem of the contours being known without *prior*
categorial equipment). More to the point, Durkheim in effect claimed that
society epistemologically produced itself *for and in* the minds of its own
members — a process which involved not only the impact of social structuration but also of society *qua* society. In the latter respect much of
Durkheim's argument seemed to rest on the contrasting experiences of
individuals — the contrast between (profane) individual experience and
sacred immersion in society (Poggi 1972:245). The sacred experience
constituted a higher, moral-spiritual aspect of human life. Hence the *a
priori* status of society as morally authoritative.

Comparison with Simmel's posing of the question 'How is Society
Possible?' is virtually demanded by the character of this exposition of a
central theme of Durkheim's later sociology. Simmel, like Durkheim after
him, started with the problem of the applicability of Kant's *a priori* (which
made *nature* 'possible') to society. Simmel argued, as Durkheim was to do,
that the *a priori*s of society were produced, as far as the analytic observer
was concerned, 'out-there', in the 'object' of study. Society was made
possible by the experiences of individuals on the basis of their *partial*
inclusion in society. Each of the three *a priori*s of society which Simmel
pinpointed had to do with the contrast between experience of self in
relation to experience of the contingencies of interaction. Superficially
similar to — and indeed overlapping with Durkheim's position — Simmel's
conception of the *a priori*s which made society possible nevertheless differed in significant respects. Firstly, Simmel's view of the individual self
was less social than that of Durkheim. Unlike Durkheim, Simmel did not
believe that the individual was the more 'spiritual' the more he or she was
'societalized'. Rather, in Simmel's view the individual was shaped *in
reference* to the clarification of societality (and *vice versa*). It was their

'autonomy-in-interdependence' which interested Simmel. Secondly, the equivalent of Durkheim's categories was, in Simmel's work, that of social forms. The major difference—in spite of overlap—was that for Simmel social forms were modes of giving form to *interactional* contingency, whereas in Durkheim's work the categories were modes of classification. In sum, whereas Simmel's conception of society (*itself* a form) focused on its relationality—compared to the entitivity of the individual *per se*— Durkheim's conception of society focused on its 'hyperentitivity' relative to the lack of constraint in the case of the isolated individual.

Comparison with Kant highlights these problems. As has on occasion been noted, in his quest for the modality of societal functioning Durkheim 'societalized' Kant's transcendental ego, the latter appearing in the Durkheimian schema as the *conscience collective*—as a superego. Society was given its own *built-in ego*. Society had in that sense authority *and* identity—both in the sense of particular societies and society-in general. (Individuals acquired 'shares' of that societal identity in the form of individual identities.) On the Kantian basis, society thus fulfilled identity functions—*society* showing in effect, as has been put in reference to the *individual*, 'the unity of the judging mind as a synthetic *a priori* truth in the ordering of experience' (Hollis 1977:92). That this 'identity' subsequently became differentiated in the course of Durkheim's work, with his increasing interest in individualism, makes no significant difference to our interpretation, for the individualism of which Durkheim spoke amounted to no more (and no less) than the individuated *distribution* of the *conscience collective*, with *the State* remaining as the fulcrum of *superegoness* in the societal fabric (in effect the locus of what *in Weber's terms* was legitimate authority). On the other hand, in Weber's case the quest for the terms or modalities of societal functioning (which includes both synchronic and diachronic, including historical, dimensions) is much more complex. We are, however, of the following persuasion. Having early in the most intellectually productive phase of his life (namely, the last twenty or so years) crystallized his conception of modern life as an iron cage, Weber then set about discovering the historical origins of that condition. In the course of that long intellectual voyage Weber became increasingly attracted to the view that in different civilizations different 'forms of life' operated (a term which is used here advisedly). These 'forms of life' could be analysed in terms of their evolution over long periods of time. There were very basic, fundamental and very long-lasting forms of life which might operate as basic codes of individual and collective existence for many centuries. In Weber's later work the typology of other-wordly mysticism, other-worldly asceticism, inner-wordly mysticism and inner-wordly asceticism probably constituted the most fundamental, the most deep-rooted of these forms or codes.[8] Other forms, such as those of action and domination were, while universal, given particular imprints by virtue of their location within the more fundamental forms. (Weber's particular historical interest was of course in discovering the dynamics of change within these configurations, with an eye to coming to terms with the character of the modern world.)

This reading of Weber suggests more than passing sympathy for the argument that in Weber's later work he, by design or not, was in part addressing issues arising from *Simmel's* programme for a sociology of forms (Cf Rex 1971, 1974). The argument is bolstered further by noting that what Weber saw as the two most perfectly rationalized, in the sense of the most *consistently* patterned, forms of life were on the one hand—in the (ascetic) inner-worldly orbit—the Calvinist theodicy and, on the other hand—in the (mystical) other-wordly orbit—the theodicy of the classical Indian intelligentsia. Both of these were characterized by a remarkable synchronization of the individual and wider societal circumstance. They were, as Weber dealt with them, characterized by the compatibility of images of individual and society, although in very different respects. In the Calvinist case the pursuit of individual salvation was at the same time a contribution to the 'welfare' of the socio-cultural whole. Many of Weber's comments on the *modern* world show that he was at pains to demonstrate the lack of such synchrony—but sought it nonetheless in prescriptive terms. It is important to repeat that this question of the 'perfect' relationship between individual and society had been central to Simmel's sociology. In his philosophical introduction to his main work on sociology Simmel in fact argued that the very *possibility* of society *in its 'perfected' form* described a situation of complete consistency between society and individual (Simmel 1971:6–22).

In Simmel's work the Kantian ego, in contrast to Durkheim's position, appears as the ego *in its concreteness*. The equivalents of Kantian categories in relation to nature are complemented in Simmel's sociology by the *forms* of social interaction, forms which are subject to change over a period of time, but which at any point constitute the categorial modalities (or the frames) in terms of which interaction occurs. Without exaggerating the link with Weber, it is—in view of Weber's adamance *vis à vis* his own individualism—tempting to argue that Weber himself thought that the synchronization of individual life and the operation of society reduced the appropriateness of legitimatizing processes. Weber's interest in individual modes of existence, expressed *via* such motifs as that of vocation and types of salvational orientation, can be interpreted as constituting an attempt (in some sense parallel to Durkheim's efforts) to pinpoint what Habermas has recently and pejoratively called a new mode of socialization. In the latter prospect ascetic attachment to society is *combined with* mystical attachment to self.[9]

DURKHEIM, SIMMEL AND WEBER ON INDIVIDUAL AND SOCIETY

There is an important respect, often overlooked, in which the views of
Durkheim and Weber on problems of authority and individuality tan-
talizingly moved towards an area of potential agreement. This area has to
do with their conceptions of the extension of rationality in the modern
world, at the centre of which lies the emphasis upon impersonality. That
perspective is perhaps most explicitly thematized in Weber's work. Weber
suggested that modern modes of 'authority' were characterized by their
being pivoted upon subscription to rational-legal norms — norms which in
particular emphasized the impersonal application of laws, rules and
regulations. In that mode of authority *control* was exercised in terms which
forcefully precluded the relevance of what we might now call individual
identities (although clearly the stipulation of this type of authority *implies*
that there has to be a form of identification *of* both self and 'authoritative
other'). On the other hand, the preclusion of individual particularism
(personal identity) from the domains of impersonal rationality was
matched by subjective particularism in the more informal domains. In
turning to Durkheim we see a not dissimilar emphasis upon rationality as
involving what Durkheim called the rooting-out of subjective factors. In a
rather complex argument Durkheim argued that the process of individuation (the increasing sense of individual entitivity) and the increase
in the 'cult of individuality' (the moral emphasis upon the significance of
individuals *qua* individuals) involved ideal-typically the embedding of
society in individuals. The degrees of individuation and of individualism
had been much less in the past and thus individuals were much less clearly
defined and to that extent more — so to speak — at the mercy of society. In
the modern world, however, the complexity of society was made manifest
in the heterogeneity of individualism. It was individuals who were in that
sense increasingly the bearers of, both in particular and generic senses,
society. Absolutely central to this Durkheimian scenario was that this
individualism had therefore a *social* nature.

Durkheim had of course begun the mature phase of his writing career,
in *The Division of Labour in Society*, with a harsh critique of the utilitarian
conception of the individual, emphasizing that one could not conceive of
society as an amalgam of individual egos entering into contractual
relationships. Thus for Durkheim, in the now very famous phrase, contracts between individuals and groups must rest upon pre-contractual
elements. There must in other words be something in the nature of society
which in itself made contracts possible and effective. Durkheim was led
increasingly to emphasize the moral nature of society. In relation to individualism this moral element appears in two major and linked respects.
On one side, individualism was essentially a social category and the

relationship between individual and society was basically one of moral obligation of the former to the latter. On the other, Durkheim in even more specific vein, argued that the mutuality of what we might call 'societalism' and individualism could be accounted for with reference to the link between the State and the individual. The State, as what in modern terms might be called the steering centre of societies, granted (and continues to grant) rights and duties to the individual — to define social individualism — while the individual, in order to enhance his sense of entitivity and freedom, made demands on that aspect of society which is responsible in the last analysis for the operation of particular societies, namely the State. It is in this way, according to Durkheim, that the moral connection between individual and society is cemented.

Certain comments have to be added to this sketch of Durkheim's position. Firstly, Durkheim held to the view that without the impress of society the individual was but a bundle of undisciplined wants and desires. Thus the individual needed society, while society had to resist this inner core of the human individual. Society was a moral fact by virtue of its control of impulse. Secondly, it was characteristic of Durkheim to mix tough-minded analysis with idealistic prognosis, such that much of what he wrote was a concatenation of theory-informed observation and prescription *vis à vis* the preservation of societality. For example in his discussion of the amplificatory relationship between individual and State Durkheim took pains to state *a condition* for the efficacy of that relationship, namely that mediating institutions should link State to individual and perform the function of inhibiting particularistic, what we might now call 'sub-societal' loyalties, such as those to religious collectivities and to the immediacies of family life. The mediating institutions of which Durkheim spoke seem to stand more in a 'stalactital' relationship to the State than in a 'stalagmital' relationship to the individual. In other words they appear as a guarantee more of the State than of the individual (Cf Poggi 1972). Finally, but very importantly, it seems by now clear that Durkheim attached increasing importance during his writing life to the authoritative power of symbolic representations, which functioned as a focal point, as an evocation, of attachment to societal collectivities.

Thus Durkheim's model is cast very much in terms of an idealistic sociologism which although at many points — as in *Suicide* — acknowledging tensions and problems of modern societies, tends to the conclusion that modern societies are not *drastically* prone to problems of, what in the language of the present essay, we would call authority and identity. Probably the most problematic aspect of Weber's work, as far as present interests are concerned, is that while on the one hand Weber attributed tremendous historical significance to *Wertrationalität* — that is substantive or value rationality — his image of the modern condition is, as we and many others before have pointed out, pivoted upon the salience of *Zweckrationalität* (instrumental rationality). The tantalizing overlap with Durkheim's work in this respect requires explication.

Durkheim and Weber both stressed the great historical-sociological significance of the late-eighteenth century emphasis—made most manifest in the American and French Revolutions—on the Rights of Men. For Durkheim it is clear that that is the crucial, relatively-modern, crystallization of the cult of the individual; while Weber spoke of that period as being the final development in the 'fateful history' of charisma, culminating in the glorification of Reason. Freedom of conscience led, said Weber, swiftly to 'a general regard for a succession of inalienable individual rights' (Weber 1968:1209). Durkheim's way of putting an essentially similar point was to speak of individuals in the modern world having attained 'something of the divine'. Thus, he maintained, 'the members of a social group will no longer have anything in common other than their humanity' (Durkheim 1973:52). The rendezvous for these two approaches is, then, that of the impersonality of rationality in modern societies. By impersonality is meant the use of judgement without regard for the particularity—for the *identity*—of those involved in and affected by such judgement. On the other hand, that same impersonality, as Weber and Simmel (and, perhaps, Durkheim) well knew, was an enabling ground for individual particularity. The important difference between the two views is that whereas in Weber's perspective what he called rational-legality is basically a rationality which is bereft of the intrusion of ultimate *values* in the form of *Wertrationalität*, in Durkheim's conception such an exercise of rationality is imbued with morality, precisely *because* it transcends, is partly wrought in response to, individual particularity. I should quickly emphasize that the difference is not mere disagreement about the implications of the impersonal application of rules. The difference resides in the respective views about the origin of social norms. Weber's account of the rise of instrumental rationality—whose character he almost certainly ideal-typified *in order* to display its encroachment on individuality (Mommsen 1974)—is based upon the cognitive rationalization of basic value orientations in relation to social-structural contingency in the Western world. On the other hand, Durkheim's account rests largely upon the increase in the division of labour, relative to the *conscience collective*. Difficulties of interpretation of the latter notwithstanding, Durkheim's basic point was that society itself was moral. As that moral entity became more differentiated its moral constraints were, so to speak, distributed *via* the division of labour. The individuation produced by the latter gave rise to the circumstance under which *social* individualism arose. Durkheim's 'genuine' individualism is thus basically a manifestation of sociality. That conception of Durkheim's differs from the implicit conception of individualism in Weber's work, cast as it was with reference to the idea of personal salvation (relative to, rather than within, 'society').

There is, then, in Weber's work a concern with modes of existence *in relation to* society — a theme which had become increasingly a preoccupation of German social and political philosophy and, later, sociology, through the nineteenth century. That *motif* was, however, much more explicit in the work of Weber's friend Simmel than in Weber's own published work. The critical linkage to Simmel's long concern with how the individual might live *in relation to* society can be seen on the Weber side with respect to the latter's concern with the ethics of ultimate values in relation to the ethics of responsibility, his attitudes toward the Calvinist and the Lutheran conceptions of *vocational calling*, and the very explicit attention in his later years to the modes of individual existence implied by his typological array of forms of individual salvation. The significance of these latter forms of existence in Weber's larger sociology has been sadly overlooked. In particular their standing in a tradition of concern precipitated by Kierkegaard's departure from Hegel has not received sufficient attention. Kierkegaard's argument had been that 'the individual is in the process of becoming far too reflective to be able to be satisfied with merely being represented' and this is most appropriately seen against Hegel's conception of the individual in relation to society in the mode of particularity/generality (a view which is in part reproduced by Durkheim, as well as Simmel).

It was, however, Simmel who, in the classic period of sociology, addressed most explicitly and persistently the relation between the individual and society (and the individual and objective culture), an interest which was wrought quite consciously in relation to those nineteenth century German figures who had most acutely focused the importance of the study of individual modes of existence in the face of what was to them the drastically meaningless nature of societal life: namely, Schopenhauer and Nietzsche (Simmel 1912). It was Simmel who, of those who have subsequently become recognized as giants of the classical period, pursued these questions in sociological terms; who, as it were, translated philosophical into sociological issues and without ever abandoning the philosophical mode. In superficial terms Simmel's views on the relationship between individual and society bear quite a close resemblance to those of Durkheim, for both argued explicitly that societalization and individualization occurred in mutually amplifying tandem. For both, individuation was primarily a product of social differentiation and for both, the division of labour provided the grounds upon which the conception of the cult of individuality (to use Durkheim's phrase) was based. Simmel would have had no problem with Durkheim's contention that increasingly members of social groups have little in common other than their humanity. Indeed such an idea was central to Simmel's writing on modern urban life. It is, however, along such lines that Simmel probed almost incessantly the growth in the modern world of what nowadays is sometimes called 'deep subjectivity'. Simmel portrayed a modern situation in which the concern with the inner lives of individuals became increasingly evident. In a sense Simmel and Durkheim agree about those matters — for both replay many times the idea that collective life in modern societies is increasingly impersonal (although Simmel had more to say about the nuances and subtleties of that circumstance). But Simmel departs from Durkheim in mounting a scenario in which individualism can be at odds with the functioning of society. Again a caveat is in order, in that clearly for Durkheim there was an aspect of the individual which was ubiquitously at odds with societal life — but the crucial difference is that Simmel made that incongruity an absolutely central feature of his analyses of turn-of-the-century industrial societies; without — it must be emphasized — making it into an anthropological constant of the human condition, and without recourse to ideas concerning the profanity of 'antisocietal' individualism.

Thus both Simmel and Durkheim maintained that what we have here called societalization (namely the increasing sense of the autonomy and facticity of the societal dimension of human life) and individualization went hand-in-hand in a mutually amplificatory manner. But they disagreed in two major respects. Firstly, they diverged with respect to what we may call 'the authorship' question, namely, who or what was responsible for the mutual amplification. Secondly, they disagreed over certain implications of the amplificatory process.

In referring to what we have called the authorship question we find that whereas Simmel emphasized that the individuation and individualization of both society and individual person was to be conceived with reference to the epistemology of the everyday world — in other words on an ethnoepistemological basis — Durkheim argued (at least in his early work) that society *itself* acts. In fact that contention was made an explicit bone in Durkheim's early evaluation of Simmel's sociology. Thus in Durkheim's view the societalization process, exemplified in the development of the State as the core of the society, was an ontological matter. For Simmel societalization was most appropriately seen as a conception of individuals — as, to be more precise, a *form*. Simmel also argued that *the* individual, in the sense of what individual*ism* amounted to, was also a form of giving shape to the experiences of human entities. Thus the more finely grained and leaning-toward-the-subjective became the form of the individual, the more the individuals both in isolation and in interaction tended to *form* a conception of an 'out-there' entity. In contrast,

Durkheim, certainly in his most explicit comments on the relationship between societal 'Stateness' and individualism, paid attention to the *objective* relationship between State and individual, arguing that the one satisfied the growing needs of the other, but giving equal ontological weight to both, with the society having, as it were, more empirical sway in the course of social evolution. What the differences amount to, in succinct form, is that whereas Durkheim emphasized society as authority, with individual identities being wrought in relation to and in consolidation of the authoritativeness of the society, Simmel emphasized the 'authorship' *of individuals*, with the individual being given an identity relative to society (and *vice versa*).

The implications of such differences pivot upon the issue of the *synchronicity* of the relationship between individual and society. Durkheim was strongly committed to the view that human freedom resided in liberation from 'inner urges' and from the constraints of external nature. Thus the socialization—perhaps, more accurately the societalization—of men and women was the central ingredient of a rational, moral individualism. Simmel, pursuing another trajectory, was keen to add to the accumulation of 'freedom *froms*' which had been initiated by Kant in two major respects. On the one hand, Kant had in that perspective liberated man from nature, by awarding the form 'nature' to *man* rather than to external reality. On the other hand, Kant had in a sense liberated man from God by showing the moral basis of the belief in God. Subsequently in the nineteenth century Hegel and Marx had shown the possibilities for man's liberation from history and from culture. Simmel apparently wanted to pursue the programme of 'liberation' even further by liberating the individual from society and also in a sense from his psychology—a prospectus which had some quite remarkable overlaps with the work of Freud, and which had also gained selective inspiration from Schopenhauer and Nietzsche.[10] In that connection Simmel spoke of the continuing discovery of what he called the teleology of individual life. As far as the link with Durkheim is concerned we have seen that whereas Durkheim converted Kant's transcendental ego into such notions as the *conscience collective* and 'the consciousness of the consciousness', Simmel converted it into the concrete, historically grounded individual.

Simmel maintained that conceptions of individualism took different *forms* in different places and at different times. In the period in which he himself lived, he maintained that the *clash* between society and individual was formidable (Simmel 1959). This clash hinged on the thesis that both individuals and society—that is, the *form* of individualism and the *form* of societalism—were in a phase of exclusiveness. The form of society was one which required that each individual should play a role or series of roles such that the society could operate as an organic whole. On the other hand, the same requirement was encountered at the level of individuals. In other words, *both* society and individual tended towards *completion*. The tendency toward that condition at the societal level automatically diminished completion at the level of the individual, and *vice versa*. Clearly influenced by both Hegel and Marx in this respect Simmel nevertheless posited an avoidable tension. Simmel, however, hinted at a future state of affairs when society and individual would become sufficiently autonomous and differentiated from each other as to conflict less. In that prospect society would be regarded as a more or less autonomous realm, as would the life of individuals *qua* individuals. Simmel's writings on the relationship between individual and society as a social form (the master social form) were matched by his work on the relationship between individual and culture. As far as his own historical context was concerned he saw that the individual stood in relation to culture in like manner to his relationship with society. On the one hand, objective culture had the appearance of possessing its own logic — its own immanence of development. On the other hand, the individual's concern with his own ideational needs were at odds with 'out-there' objective culture. The latter offered, as it were, too much to select from relative to individual wholeness.

INDIVIDUAL, SOCIETY, OBJECTIVITY AND ABSOLUTENESS

There runs through Simmel's work a thread which needs further unravelling and which traces both the work of his fellow classical sociologists and very recent contributions to our theme. The long drawn-out crystallization of sociological analysis up to the classical period can fruitfully be seen as an attempt to locate the significance of society — both in the society-in-general and particular-society senses — with respect to the relationship between men and women as individuals, on the one hand, and what Simmel called 'objectivity', on the other. Written into the Judeo-Christian tradition is the problem of how to reconcile a conception of basic truth, and the lives that individuals live with that truth, with the contingency of *society*. The old Christian principle of rendering-unto-Caesar-that-which-is-Caesar's-and-unto-God-that-which-is-God's may be regarded as the paradigmatic expression of that dilemma as it has prevailed through much of the last two thousand years of Western history. The secularization of the concept of natural law in Hobbes' work, Machiavelli's concept of the State, and the Protestant attempts to synchronize the life of the individual-in-society relative to 'truth' constituted a crucial turning point during the sixteenth and seventeenth centuries. Thereafter 'society' became clearly recognized as an object of concern in its own right. Within Protestantism the primary distinct options became either the Lutheran path of separating society and individual as human realms, with the society being regarded as the immediate *context* in which the individual as subject can relate to pure objectivity (namely God), and the Calvinist path of attempting to *synthesize* individualism and societalism in terms of a covenantal relationship to supreme, distinctively personalized objectivity. In both cases the connection between subjectivity and objectivity was much clearer — more finely delineated — than that which had prevailed in traditional Catholicism. Moreover, it is no accident that whereas the connection between *tradition and authority* had been central to Catholicism, the notion of *identity* made a definite appearance during precisely the period to which we have just alluded. Lockes' concern with the identity of interests, Leibniz's talk of monads, Descartes' notion of individual, cognitive autonomy and Rousseau's pejorative concern with *amour propre* were invoked — but of course from different points of view — to deal with a dimension of social-human nature which would fill the vacuum created by the attenuation of a societally mediated, but transcendentally pivoted, sense of *certainty*.[11] The attribution to Rousseau in such a respect of having achieved a 'Copernican Revolution' in placing societal man — in the sense of man in *particular* societies, not merely *societé générale* — is particularly important (Cassirer 1945:1–60). For it was he who did indeed sketch in a particularly vivid form the image which was to be so salient among many nineteenth century and early twentieth century thinkers. That image, roughly described, consisted of the idea that society was situated between the individual in his or her own subjectivity, on the one hand, and an extra-terrestrial realm, on the other hand, and that society in its politicality formed a kind of triangle in conjunction with the other two. In other words society was rivaled by — in a sense inhibited by — the attachment of the individual to extra-societality (Colletti 1972, 1973; Cf Althusser 1972: 113–60).

Hegel and Marx, from different perspectives, were to attempt to achieve a resolution of this problem — Hegel by making the society in its Stateness the mode of synthetic consummation of subjectivity and objectivity, a resolution which had the effect of upgrading traditional authority in relation to the individual. (In terms of that kind of dialectical theory identity appears, as we have seen, in the form of the identity of subject and object.) Marx, on the other hand, sought what has been called a concrete form of freedom — freedom for both Hegel and Marx residing in a unification of subject and object, i.e. finding freedom *in a relationship* — a search which was based on the contention that the relationship between inner subjectivity and absolute objectivity was actually a *societal* product. The problem, therefore, for Marx was to identify and overcome the social circumstances which led to the positing of subject and object in asocietal terms (even though he readily conceded that the recognition of that idea was a necessary philosophical condition for changing the world).

A central motif of Simmel's work was that concerning the relationship between individuation and objectivation, a motif which he referred particularly to the relationship between the individual and nature as discussed by Kant. His basic idea in this respect was that there is an amplificatory relationship between the sense of being an individual and the sharpness of the delineation of external generality, an idea which Simmel developed particularly clearly in his essay on money (Simmel 1900). For Simmel, as for Marx, *money* was an exemplification of the principle of generality (although Marx drew different conclusions). As far as the relationship between individual and society was concerned Simmel argued that,

> as something psychologically concrete, society blends with the individual; but as something general, it blends with nature. It is the general, but it is not abstract. To be sure, every historical group is an individual, as is every historical human being; but it is this only in relation to other groups; for its members, it is super-individual . . . The group . . . is super-individual . . . in a specific manner of generality — similar to the organic body, which is 'general' above its organs, or to 'room furniture', which is 'general' above table, chair, chest, and mirror. And this specific generality coincides with the specific objectivity which society possesses for its members as subjects (Simmel, 1950:257).

Simmel went on to argue that the relationship between the individual and nature differs from the relationship between the individual and society in that the individual participates 'spiritually' in society. Even though society, like nature, confronts the individual with an 'imperative firmness', living a life of its own 'which follows its own laws', 'society's' 'in front of' the individual is, at the same time, a 'within'.

> The harsh indifference toward the individual also is an interest: social objectivity needs general individual subjectivity, although it does not need any particular individual subjectivity. It is these characteristics which make society a structure intermediate between subject and an absolutely impersonal generality and objectivity (Simmel, 1950:258).

As we will see later, these contentions of Simmel have an important bearing on more recent social-scientific debates about individualism, the autonomy of society, identity and authority. Let us, however, at this juncture emphasize that Simmel's perspicuous observations find their parallels in the work of Durkheim and Weber. Both of those sociologists were through the larger part of their writing lives deeply preoccupied with the status of the society relative to individualism and to 'objective principles'. Both focused in much of their work on the ways in which particularisms were transcended by more general, 'objective' and 'higher' principles — and both nagged at the problem of the implications of such for the viability of societies with particular reference to the capacity of the latter to provide what we might nowadays call *contextual* meaning for individuals within their domain. Durkheim spoke of the successive inclusion of societal commitment on the part of individuals in a developing 'international life' which stands at a 'higher' level than particular societies (Durkheim 1961:472-4). Weber, on the other hand, focused on the political resilience of national societies — *via* their monopoly of the means of coercion. Moreover, for Weber legal-rational 'authority' appears to have possessed the attributes of Simmel's 'specific generality'. In that view *society itself* takes on the character of 'objectivity'. In the Weberian perspective societies — certainly Western ones — increasingly exhibit objective impersonality in terms of their bureaucratic apparati.

There is little doubt that the freeing of economic life from subsumption by the State with the development of capitalist enterprise from the late eighteenth century onwards was a crucial condition of the growth of sociology during the nineteenth century. [12] Closely related to this was the development of political-philosophical ideas concerning the separation of civil society from the State. These two cognitive developments raised numerous problems concerning the terms in which societies operated (both synchronically and diachronically).

The conjunction of the perception of a civil-societal realm and the crystallization of the problem of economic autonomy highlighted the problem of the 'warrant' under which societies functioned. The conception of societies being split into civil-societal and State spheres placed into sharper focus the identity of the individual. Prior to the period of which we are speaking there had been a theoretical sense of much greater *contextuality* with respect to the individual's membership of a societal community, a circumstance most closely approximated when states were defined largely in religious terms, and membership of society — mediated by diffuse communality and *relatively* closed stratification systems — was primarily a religio-cultural matter. The crystallization of the idea of economic autonomy and of the cleavage between State and civil society thus threw both identification and authorization into a state of ambiguity and flux, particularly with the accentuation of enfranchisement issues during the nineteenth century.

As far as economic autonomy was concerned, the intellectually expressed options seemed to range from advocacy of adaptation of societies *to* the economic realm as a *condition* of societies, at one extreme, to the claim that economic processes were subject to conditioning by other factors, at the other extreme. Of course, within these two extreme options there was great variation, depending primarily upon the conception of the nature and real significance of those economic laws. (That circumstance accounts for the fact that Marxians and advocates of free-enterprise capitalism were *both* to be found at the first end of the spectrum.) The range of intellectual diagnosis concerning the relationship between civil society and the State cut across that which had to do with the problem of the independence of economic factors and the utilitarianism of everyday life. The two major opinion-sets in the former respect were, on the one hand, the liberal view of society (which upheld the differentiation of civil society from the State) and, on the other hand, the 'holistic' view (which sought to overcome that alleged cleavage). The first in effect upheld a differentiated form of societal identification—that is, the relationship to the State was regarded in terms of *citizenly* involvement, with other aspects of the individual's life being regarded as private. The holistic view, in contrast, sought to fuse the two realms, such that the individual was not split into two forms of identification.

The classical sociologists worked against the back-drop of two *major* social-scientific attitudes resulting from the possible mixture of cognitive choices *vis á vis* the State/civil-society issue, on the one hand, and the problem of the status of economic factors, on the other hand.[13] On the one hand, there were those who largely accepted ideas which heralded the separation between State and civil society, involving differentiated conceptions of individual identity in relation to the political State *and* who also tended to accept the need to adapt to relatively autonomous economic reality. On the other hand, there were those who denied the necessity of the separation between civil society and the State and who also tended to see in the relative autonomy of the economic realm the vehicle for overcoming that cleavage. Roughly speaking these clusters became manifest in salience, on the one hand, of Spencer and, on the other hand, of Marx in the work of the classical sociologists. Durkheim in his early effort to overcome economism used Spencer as his protagonist. Weber (and contemporaries such as Simmel, Troeltsch and Sombart) were less specific in their targets', but Marx and Marxists were clearly at the forefront of their thinking in such respects.

Durkheim was thus opposed to the (primarily British) liberal view of society on two grounds—namely, its economism, and its separation of civil society from the State. On the other hand, Weber was apparently opposed to totalistic views primarily on the ground that they fused civil society with the State. Related to Weber's view in this respect was his *tempered* opposition to economistic materialism. In the latter respect Weber did not deny that the modern world was conceived in terms of its materiality, measurability and manipulability. Indeed much of his work consisted in a quest for the origins and supports of that iron-cage circumstance. In effect Weber argued that practical-rational freedom at the level of individuals had, as it were, been bought at the price of orientation to—indeed a fixation upon—what we might call an 'object world' (including the self as object). The other side of the coin of instrumental rationality—which involved emphases upon knowledge of the best means with which to pursue chosen goals and the integration of means and goals—was the suitability of its application to a manipulable and calculable world of objects. In other words, without 'manipulables' and 'calculables' there would be no practical rationality—no release from the relatively blind adherence to a substantive rationality which enchanted the world. Nor could there have been a generalized sense of calculability without the development of a positive orientation to the 'world' in the mode of concern with practicality.

Thus Weber was more disposed than Durkheim to accept materialism as a fact of the modern world. The former's primary interest at the turn of the century was in tracing historically the 'irrational presuppositions' which supported the modern emphasis upon the economic factor. Simmel—in his *Philosophy of Money* and in other writings—had sought a psychological explanation for the materialist conceptions of the modern world. That endeavour broadly paralleled—perhaps in part inspired— Weber's interest in 'irrational presuppositions'. In fact Simmel's work provides a kind of bridge between Durkheim and Weber in this respect. Simmel put much emphasis upon the concomitance and mutual am- plification of, on the one hand, the sense on the part of individuals of an out-there domain of objective, socio-economic reality and, on the other hand, an increase in the sense of subjectivity and individuation. In that general development social differentiation—the division of labour—was, according to Simmel, a very important factor. There were traces of such a view in Durkheim's work.

But whereas Durkheim was concerned to subsume the economic under the moral-societal, Weber and Simmel were eager to account for, in psychological and historical as well as sociological terms, what they saw as the generalized sense of the subjective *belief in* the autonomy of the out- there world of modern reality, of which the economic dimension was paradigmatic. While there is no doubt that Durkheim and Weber (as well as Simmel) were highly critical of materialistic and/or utilitarian accounts of the crystallization of the modern world they differed in the situating of economic factors in the modern circumstance. Durkheim clearly sought to show the supremacy of the societal (moral) over the economic, while Weber was more interested in the derivation of the modern sense of materiality. There certainly was overlap between their views, an overlap which might be best emphasized by stating that while Durkheim asked the question how is society *in general* possible, Weber was much more in- terested in the more periodized question how is the *modern sense of the reality* of worldly societality possible? The former question received, as we have seen, an answer in terms of sacred, moral societality while the latter received an answer which pivoted upon the historical 'unfolding' of a modern circumstance in which 'irrational presuppositions' shared by individuals supported a particular conception of a worldly domain sublimated in terms of its own laws. Perhaps the differences may best be highlighted by pointing out that whereas Weber (and Simmel) worked broadly in terms of a 'Lutheran' problematic concerning the relationship between individual access to and choice in respect of ultimate values, on the one hand, and a worldly, out-there external domain on the other hand, Durkheim *literally* reversed the Lutheran conception of 'the two kingdoms' by making the societal domain the realm of the sacred and the individual domain the more natural repository of profanity. Nevertheless we must insist that on both the 'French' and the 'German' side the dialecticity of the relationship between objective generality and subjective particularity is evident.[14]

Each of the three major classical sociologists in their respective, but overlapping, ways thus made the relationship between individualism and societalism the crux of the development of their conceptions of the sociological enterprise. On the other hand they differed in the degree to which they then made the collective-societal domain the 'true' subject matter of sociology. Durkheim clearly went the furthest in that direction, while Weber attempted to maintain the centrality of (individual) action. In the latter respect what is of key importance in the present context is that Weber attempted during the last ten years of his life to ground that centrality in a notion of what in modern terminology we might call *codes* of the relationship between individual and society, of which the most fundamental were those issuing from the cross-tabulation of the asceticism/mysticism and inner-worldliness/other-worldliness forms of salvational orientation. Simmel again stands in the middle insofar as he saw the study of sociology as the study of (interactional) *forms* of sociation (of which society was the most general and exchange the most basic), while leaving the study of the individual as an *extra-sociological* perspective on the human condition. The study of social forms proceeded *as if* they were autonomous, but *really* they were seated in the minds of individuals.

SOCIOLOGISM AND THE INDIVIDUAL

The imperial claims which were made for the autonomy of professional sociology played a large part in the subsequent de-thematization of the individual as a topic of inquiry. Indeed — in Simmelian mode — it might be said that the irony of sociology has lain in its having developed around the problem of the relationship between individual and society and yet having become by the 1940s and 1950s a discipline which largely maintained the supremacy of society over the individual. Of course other schools of sociological thought had subsisted during the same period. The Frankfurt School stands out in this respect, since it was in that context that the issue of the 'oppression' of the individual by societal structure and process was given sustained attention — with particular reference to the relationship between the work of Freud and the work of Marx. However, until the late 1960s the impact of the Frankfurt School was slender, except in terms of the 'attenuated Frankfurtism' of Fromm (whose work in any case was regarded as being primarily of psychological as opposed to sociological significance) and the controversy surrounding the 'exilic Frankfurtism' of *The Authoritarian Personality.*[15] The latter — although quickly regarded as a sociological classic and thus inspiring much research — was influential primarily in the fields of social psychology and in the personality-and-politics approach to the study of political socialization (Greenstein, 1975). Its larger sociological significance was relatively unrecognized, in large part probably because, in spite of its empirical fruitfulness, it contributed to theoretical confusion by focusing only on the *pathology* of what we would call identity-and-authority relations. (Obviously a compelling reason for this concentration on the pathology of the identity-authority theme was the recent experience of Fascism. In fact that was the motor force of *The Authoritarian Personality.*) Indeed the Frankfurt School — as opposed to its Habermas-centred successor[16] — has been largely responsible in some sociological circles for the conflation of authority and authorit*arianism* (Friedrichs, 1972).

In mainstream American sociology (the dominant national sociology of the period early 1940s to mid-1960s) a realm of social psychology was 'allowed' to attend to what was left over after the social-structuration of the individual had been attended to, an area which overlapped with a rather more distinctively sociological (primarily, but not exclusively, *symbolic interactionist*) focus on reference-group theory, role-taking and the like.[17] In the work of Parsons and his associates the period in question involved an establishment of the concepts of *status-role* as the 'unit' of intersection of the individual with social system and *internalization* as the processual aspect of the acquisition of the social norms. As is well known, Parsons' idea of internalization drew initially on a trend which he discerned in Durkheim's thinking (*from* the external constraint of social facts *to* the internalization of social norms), to be strongly supplemented later by ideas on introjection and identification drawn from Freud (Parsons 1964). However, shortly after Wrong's celebrated attack on 'the over-socialized conception of man' a major step was taken within the Parsonian circle toward the re-thematization of the individual as a topic of sociological inquiry — namely, Bellah's (1964) conception of the differentiation of personality from social-structural and cultural realms.

The cost that was paid for the de-thematization of the individual was great, most notably with respect to the difficulties in treating the theme of authority without explicit attention to the 'phenomena' over which authority may be exercised. We might state the problem succinctly by arguing that much of mainstream sociology has since the classical period largely been a sociology without *a subject* (at least until very recently).[18] And one of the major manifestations of this has been the tendency to focus *on legitimate* authority as if all authority were legitimate (where legitimization has coalesced with socialization and internalization); *or* to treat, at the other extreme, authority in the mode of authoritarian*ism* or simply domination (where individualism has tended to be undefined). Lying somewhere between these two extremes falls the recent much-discussed work on Modern Man (Inkeles and Smith 1974), which regards the dominant form of modern individualism as simply an adaptive product of modern organizational forms and social-structural contingency—in effect 'Zweckrationalität' man (Baum 1977).

Thus in the reconstructed tradition of classical sociology the depth of the explicit concern with the individual displayed by Durkheim and Simmel—and the more implicit concern of Weber—was largely lost, an exception to this generalization being the work of the Frankfurt School (which was also until recently marginal) and its successor so-called critical theory. To some extent also the diffuse influence of Simmel on the symbolic interactionist tradition has been something of an exception to this, and it is important to note that it is within the symbolic interactionist tradition—broadly conceived—that the topic of identity has been most clearly thematized. But that in itself illustrates how the topic of identity has rarely been cast in terms that link it to wider, macro-sociological themes.[19]

The co-ordination of Freud with Durkheim (by Parsons) on the one hand and with Marx on the other hand (by some Frankfurt adherents)—in the respective modes of internalization and repression (or domination)—has assisted in the neglect of the relationship between the work of Simmel and the work of Freud. On occasion Simmel has been linked to Freud, but typically that has taken the form of suggesting that Simmel was 'sociology's Freud' in the sense that Simmel was concerned with hidden layers and 'dark corners' of everyday life. Rarely, on the other hand, has the *substance* of Simmel's work been connected constructively to that of Freud; in spite of the fact that Simmel was the classical sociologist who paid the most sustained attention to the individual.

We cannot undertake here the task of rectifying this situation. We can merely provide some pertinent indications relative to the theme in hand. The critical area of overlap between Freud and Simmel was the status of the ego and the ego-ideal. Simmel provided many clues as to the manner in which the ego became detached from the wider context — a context which had both societal and cultural dimensions. Simmel, like Freud, paid close attention to modes of relationship between the individual and what Freud called 'civilization' (Freud 1961). Both men maintained that at the time in which they were writing there was a great contradiction between society ('civilization') and the individual life — while both also suggested that that might not be the case in the future. Freud's contention was that the contradiction arose from 'a dispute within the economics of the libido, comparable to a context concerning the distribution of libido between ego and objects' (Freud 1961:88). Simmel argued that even though 'society lives only through individuals . . . that does not exclude a multiplicity of conflicts' (Simmel 1950:58). On the one hand, argued Simmel, 'individuals form this society out of elements which crystallize into this particular form of "society"; society in turn evokes its own representatives and organs, confronting the individual with demands and orders as if it were an extraneous part.' On the other hand, continued Simmel, 'conflict accrues from the invasions of the individual by society. For man's faculty of splitting himself into parts and then experiencing a particular part as his very ego, which collides with other parts and struggles to make a decision to act — this faculty of man often puts him, insofar as he is a social being and so recognized himself, into an antagonistic relation with the impulses and interests of his ego which are not part of his social character. The conflict between individual and society is transposed in the individual himself into a struggle between the antinomies of his nature' (Simmel, 1950:58).[20]

Our own claim is that in this passage Simmel highlights in his notion of the antagonistic relationship between individual and society, and the internalization of that antagonism, the very 'area' in which the concept of *identity* is sociologically most appropriately placed. Simmel incidentally provides a rationale for the location of identity as that which has to do with the *mediation of* personality and the societal realm. Identity constitutes the mode — in a sense it is a *code* — for dealing with the incipient tension which must surely characterize all circumstances in which there is any significant degree of differentiation between individual egos and a superordinate societal realm. Our use of the noun 'identity' and not identification is very deliberate in this connection. In Freud's terms, of course, it is *identification* in the sense of *identification with* — yielding ego to another — which is the more relevant term. Our use of the term identity is related to *the linking of* individual to 'society'. Following upon that conception it is necessary to see identification not so much in the mode of 'with' but rather in the mode of 'of'.

This is not to say that the notion of *identification-with* is unimportant.

There are indeed *two* senses in which this term remains valuable. First, there is the traditional-Freudian sense in which identification-with refers primarily to the strong psychic attachment of an individual to a superordinate object—generalized by Parsons to the mode of diffuse attachment of personalities to (superordinate) social systems (Parsons and Platt 1973:423–47).[21] In this sense the semantic relevance of identification lies in its conveying the idea of the individual (or group) being in situations of 'subordinate sameness' relative to another, individual or collective, actor. Second, *identification-with* remains important in that it may be used—as it were—horizontally, as opposed to in the vertical sense. Indeed this is really the base line for social-scientific talk about identity. Being in a state of identity-with is the very precondition for the establishment of specific identities. In other words, in order for a person or a group to have a specific identity *vis à vis others* there must be a sense that those others are in the same generic category.[22] The latter may be as broad as the category 'human being' or 'animate object' or it may be restricted to a particular ethnic, racial, sexual or caste category (these having historically been among the most salient forms of restriction), or even to narrow informal or organizational contexts. Clearly these two valuable senses of the notion of identification-with are empirically fused in the real world. For example, the tacit or explicit declaration of an ethnic identity in, say, modern America frequently involves both horizontal identification-with the wider category 'American', or even 'human being', *and* vertical identification-with—in the sense of subordination to—the relevant ethnic group.

In spite of the importance of identification-with, in *sociological* analysis the notion of identification-*of* selves and others (in both personal and collective respects) becomes particularly salient. That salience does indeed overlap with some of the conceptions of those neo-Freudians who have focused upon ego-identity, in the particular sense that the modern concern with ego-identity is obviously *rooted in* circumstances involving high degrees of individuation and individualization. This rooting has a number of different dimensions, including the differentiation of the individual from society and from culture, as well as differentiation within these realms.

It was precisely this differentiation which both Simmel and Freud—from somewhat different perspectives—addressed. Or at least this is a position which is quite clear in Freud's tentative attempt at quasi-sociological analysis, *Civilization and its Discontents* (1961). In the latter Freud presented an array of what we would call modes of individual existence in modern societies—ways in which individuals according to personality type might relate to modern societal circumstances. In this connection Freud drew attention to a mode of existence which he called 'the narcissism of minor differences'. Regardless of the pejorative sense in which Freud described this and some other modes of modern existence, the fact remains that in the modern world the concern with the cultivation of specific visible identities is very apparent. It is obvious that in modern societies there is an ongoing *production of* identities on a non-subjective basis—in the sense that 'identikits' are made available (in neo-capitalist societies on a commercial basis) for consumption and 'resale'. But the precondition for this is a high degree of differentiation of the individual from the domain of societality. Societies—and certainly not only capitalist ones—thus produce, in the most general sense of the word, both the need for identities and identikits and reservoirs of identity models.

Freud's preferred state of tough untrammeled egos has, as Rieff (1966) in particular has shown, been transformed—particularly in America—into the *therapeutic mode*. That circumstance involves individuals in the search for psychological methods of adapting to and coping with a situation in which the social-structural realm is regarded as increasingly *automatic* in its operation. Thus the therapeutic mode involves the adoption of personal policies and strategies for 'getting by'—for im-munizing selves from certain potential complications and for steering selves through unavoidable contingencies. In this respect Rieff speaks of the release of modern man from the *compulsions* of culture (Rieff 1966:21). However, Rieff's perceptive analysis was written in the mid-1960s before the so-called 'consciousness reformation' (Wuthnow 1968; Glock and Bellah 1977; Bell 1975). Even though it is too soon to judge whether there really has been a *massive* shift in emphasis in Western societies from utilitarian therapeuticism (or in Parsons' often-used phrase instrumental activism) to more eudaemonistic or self-realizational em-phases, there seems to be little doubt the latter *have* been *thematized* within Western societies during recent years (Robertson 1978:103–222).

It seems clear, in any case, that in modern Western societies—and almost certainly, although perhaps to a lesser degree, in European Communist societies—the individual is being *thematized* in everyday and in politico-administrative terms. Elsewhere the present author has discussed this issue in terms of the concepts of *tertiary mobilization*—involving a conjoining of individual-identity and political-societal-membership concerns (Robertson 1976); and *ascetic mysticism*—involving a *differentiated* conjunction of contribution to societal systemicity, on the one hand, and contribution to personal well-being, on the other hand (Robertson 1978:128–43). More diffusely, various developments—most conspicuously in the USA—in such respects have led to the emergence of demands for *dignity* and of the generalized insistence upon what amounts to *a right to identity*, to be safeguarded by the State. Of particular noteworthiness is the salience of legal constructions of 'the person'. In the USA such a focus has of course emerged within the general context of the concern with civil rights since the early 1960s. And although it may well be that that concern still pivots on its original, generative motif of the civil rights of blacks, the question of civil rights has in the 1970s been 'upgraded' to include matters of gender; sexual proclivity; ethnicity; age; rights to life and rights to death; and so on. Internationally and trans-nationally such concerns have become salient in terms of the human rights theme. Many of these developments actually seem to undermine the therapeutic emphasis on the 'tough, resilient ego' (able to cope with the demands of disciplined participation in the economic and bureaucratic affairs of society)—or at least to modify and re-shape such observance of the requirements of the self. (Of course, there is an important aspect of *consumerism* in this shift of emphasis at the level of the individual, as to be seen in the ideas of informed consent, and risk-sharing and risk-spreading.)

What is primarily at issue in the invocation of the convergence on some key points of Simmel and Freud is that of the differentiation of individual from what Freud called—rather amorphously—'civilization' and that which Simmel called society (with specific attention also being given to the differentiation of individuals from what Simmel called objective culture). As we shall shortly see there is in that respect further possibility of fruitful linking with other schools of thought. It is necessary at this juncture, however, to rehearse and elaborate certain points concerning the notion of differentiation and the relationship between individuation and 'objectivity'. As far as differentiation is concerned, it is important to emphasize that by this term we mean both increasing autonomy *and* increasing interdependence. Very superficially this appears to be a contradiction, but in fact it is not. To speak, for example, of the differentiation of individual from society (that is, differentiation of the sense of individual lives from the affairs of societies in the mode of societal continuity) is to say that, on the one hand, each domain specializes in 'being what it is', while, on the other hand, that for each to 'be what it is' the other is *required*, in selective respects. Inspired here by the lengthy writing of Simmel on this topic, it is nevertheless clear that such ideas are to be found in Durkheim, to a lesser extent in Weber, and in recent work by Parsons on the differentiation of action systems, and in many other modern essays. (One of the principal *variations* concerns whether analysts tend to see such differentiation in the form of positive complementarity *or* contradiction.)[23] In the work *inter alia*, of Simmel, Durkheim and Habermas we find variations upon the theme of particularity in relation to generality, that is, individual particularity in relationship both to objective generality in the abstract and more concretely to generality as manifest in the ideas of the laws of external nature: or what Habermas calls 'inner nature' and society in its systemness; Stateness (Durkheim); or organic wholeness (Simmel).

Durkheim had an image of a progressive interplay of particularization and universalization, with the latter being conditional upon the need to transcend the former. Individual identities form in relation to collective identities (in particular the concrete society). Collective identities are re-shaped in reference to the diversification of individual identities. Ideas about humanity-in-general lead to the relativization of societal identities, and so on, as a larger 'international life' develops.

Simmel, in different perspective, spoke more in the direction of the increasing *distancing* of individual particularism and societalism. He regarded the society as being interstitial in relation to the relationship between the individual and 'an absolutely impersonal generality'. In metaphysical mode Simmel argued that societies arose because 'man could not easily bear looking the object in the eye; as if he were equal neither to the rigidity of its lawfulness nor to the freedom which the object, in contrast to all coercion coming from men, gives him'. Simmel (1950:259) concludes the argument thus:

> By comparison, to bow to the authority of the many or their representatives, to traditional opinion, to socially accepted notions, is something intermediate. Traditional opinion, after all, is more modifiable than is the law of the object; in it, man can feel some psychological mediation; it transmits, as it were, something which is already digested psychologically. At the same time, it gives us a hold, a relief from responsibility—the compensation for the lack of that autonomy which we derive from the purely intrinsic relationship between ego and object.

Thus in this philosophical-sociological perspective we discover the general proposition that *the historical significance* of the relationship between individual and society largely resided in the *authoritativeness* of society, in mediating the relationship between individuals and the conception, however embryonic, of 'objective truth'. The notion of authority—or, as Weber put it, *traditional* authority—is thus very fruitfully seen in reference to the manner in which the agents of society (regardless of *the basis* of their being agents) rest their claim to legitimacy on their special relationship to that realm of truth. As we have seen, Simmel also coun-tenanced the idea that society *itself* may be regarded as a repository of 'objectivity'. And that kind of idea is to be seen with much more empirical and historical richness in Weber's account of the rise of the modern bureaucratized society. However, it may well be that such a circumstance was only a *phase* in the general differentiation of what Parsons calls the system of action, and that now we have moved to an even more dif-ferentiated circumstance.

In spite of Simmel's tendency to concentrate upon individualism in the sense of individualism of individual persons he addressed also the individualization of social categories and groups, in a manner which has some convergence with Durkheim. In this respect the basic argument is that the notion of individualization is not restricted to individuals as persons. Rather, with the development of very general categories and/or a sense of there being 'society out there', very distant from individuals as such, the principle of individuation may come to apply to groups and categories intermediate between the very general category and individuals as persons. As Simmel put it, 'on no account does this contradict the relationship of individual freedom to just the relatively *large* circle, for here the sense of individuality has permeated the *narrower* circle enclosing many individual persons, and thus the narrower circle serves here the same sociological function as the discrete individual would otherwise.' In such cases Simmel maintained that 'the sense of individuality has overstepped the boundary of the individual, as it were, and has absorbed the social aspect of the person that normally constitutes the antithesis to his individual aspect' (Simmel, 1971:256–7).

For all the differences in flavouring and normative intent the fact remains that there *is* a common ground of thinking as between Durkheim and Simmel on this point. Whereas Simmel seems to argue as if such mediation between the level of society and the level of individual is an inexorable consequence of the opening of a large gap between the two, Durkheim argues for *the necessity* of such mediation as a way of sustaining the mutual dependence of the two levels. Durkheim of course spoke with reference to professional groups and the like, whereas Simmel remained very open as to the nature of the intermediary forms of individuation of collectivities. That openness allows us in the modern period to get some analytic leverage upon a number of phenomena which may come close to the circumstance which Simmel described as involving the sense of individuality overstepping the boundary of the individual and absorbing the social aspect of the person which normally constitutes the antithesis of his individual aspect. For example in a number of modern societies, perhaps most notably the USA, ethnic identity seems to fit the Simmelian prospectus.

TOWARDS CONVERGENCE IN MODERN THEORY

It may seem odd in these days of sociological multi-paradigmicity to proclaim that there is wide agreement on matters pertaining to the relationship between identity and authority—or, more specifically, between individual and society. But, as we shall try briefly to show, there is indeed such wide agreement among scholars working from divergent perspectives and who may draw different conclusions from that which they diagnose. Actually proclamation of at least tacit agreement on these matters conforms closely to many of the substantive themes of the present essay. In other words, sociological multi-paradigmicity *itself* is a manifestation of the individuation process *vis à vis* 'objective knowledge' and, in the specific case of sociology, *vis à vis* the perception of society as 'out-there' and *overdetermined*. In that sense the 'overdetermination' of sociological paradigms is a kind of manifestation of *scientific individualization*. Perception of the overdetermination of society is amplified by the perception of the overdetermination of the sense of individuality. In a manner similar to that described by Simmel, paradigmatic *groups* of sociologists form, and individual sociologists in effect adopt, *identities* from elective attachment to those groups. The declining model of positivistic science is thus in large part *in decline* precisely because it was based upon the idea of the relative proximity of objective knowledge whose accessibility was guaranteed by the authority of tightly-knit communities of professionalistic scientists. Kuhn's (1970) model of the mono-paradigmicity of fields of normal science was thus a refraction of a crucial stage in modern science in the most general sense of the term 'science'. In Simmel's terms, Kuhn's image of the normal-scientific paradigmatic community is a good example of a circumstance in which 'society' is solidly 'inserted' between objective knowledge and the individual, paradigm groups thus becoming authoritative mediators of the relationship between the individual and that which he or she ostensibly pursues, namely scientific truth. It should quickly be added that in invoking Simmel previously in regard to this point and within this immediate context we are not thereby adhering to a philosophical position which suggests that the point of everyday life—or *even* everyday scientific life—is the pursuit of objective knowledge. What we *are* suggesting is that both in the case of everyday life and scientific life (but much more sharply in the latter) individuals are increasingly exposed both to the sense of an out-there realm of social-structuration and a realm, differentiated from the realm of social-structuration, of potential objectivity. All three realms have become differentiated from each other. (This, as we shall shortly see, relates to differences among sociological traditions in respect of the status of the sociologist as observer.)

The point which we have just made is not mere reflexive indulgence. For if it is indeed the case that we are right to make so much of processes of differentiation, then it would follow that we should *expect to find* disparity in sociological and other social-scientific paradigms precisely *because of* the common experience by sociologists as *individuals* of increasing overdetermination of society. We have, incidentally, used the term overdetermination at this juncture quite loosely. For present purposes we could as easily use a term such as self-production, or increasing automaticity (Rieff 1966), or increasing nature-likeness (Habermas 1975). And the examples could be compounded by drawing upon the works of other groups of equally diverse sociologists. As far as the *relationship* between individual and 'society' is concerned we find an equally impressive area of overlap of comprehension and terminology.

Touraine (1977:111) speaks of the *simultaneity of complementarity and opposition* between claims as to 'the rights of identity and expression', on the one hand, and 'the instrumentalism of the cultural model', on the other. In elaboration Touraine (1977:94) argues that while being

> oriented toward science and technique 'modern society' is also oriented toward expression, toward the rediscovery of mind and body, toward personal and collective identity. It is a society of movement and of organization by objectives, but it is also hierarchized and replaces old-style discriminations with new segregations [of a meritocratic nature].

Touraine (1977:95) clinches his point thus:

> At the same time as society's capacity for autotransformation increases, so it comes up more directly against 'human nature', defined not morally but scientifically as part of nature. The age of the One, of an entirely willed society or its contrary, a society reincorporated into nature, is an age that is never going to come . . . What is termed consumption cannot be reduced to the manipulation of demand by decision centers seeking to maximize their own advantages . . . What it brings out is man's resistance, with those natural characteristics being explored by anthropology . . . (M)an is no longer outside nature; he is nature itself and at the same time the organizer of nature.

Emphasizing, but not exploring here in detail, that there are very important differences in routes followed in order to reach destinations after having pitched camp on this spot, we can see many similar ideas produced in recent years, although not necessarily with Touraine's perspicuousness. Perhaps the most outstanding (and probably better known) such case is that of Habermas. Habermas addresses modern societies in terms of the uncoupling of a so-called socio-cultural domain from a domain of politico-economic systemicity, declaring in broad terms a diagnostic, but not a prognostic or normative agreement with Luhmann's idea of the differentiation of an administrative realm from the realm of meaningful interaction, where individuality is located. Habermas regards the two realms as mutually amplificatory, although in a pejorative sense of crisis. On the one hand, the politico-economic, systemic realm requires privatization and subjectivism on the part of societal members; on the other hand, privatization itself is fed by systematization. However, complete cleavage between the two realms is only conceivable unless we are on the brink of an entirely new mode of socialization (Habermas 1973:129), in which the new 'social eudaemonism' (operating according to the principles of 'strategic-utilitarian' ethics) overlaps with 'reactions, uncontrollable in the long run, against the continued violation of normative standards that are at odds with the growing steering needs of the politico-economic system.' From Habermas's point of view such a circumstance spells the 'end of the individual', since *for him* genuine individualism must involve meaningful interaction relative to the formation of collective identity centred upon the rational pursuit of truth. The modern search for identity is thus in effect seen by Habermas as basically a form of degradation of individualism and a mark of inadequate identity formation, in the Hegelian sense of the individual becoming 'a particular precisely only in its relation to the general' which was Adorno's phrase. Habermas approvingly invokes Adorno's contention that 'in the midst of standardized and administered human units, the individual lives on. He is even placed under protection and gains monopoly value. But he is in truth merely the function of his own uniqueness, a showpiece like the deformed who were stared at with astonishment and mocked by children' (Adorno in Habermas 1973:127). Adorno maintained that since the individual 'no longer leads an independent economic existence, his character falls into contradiction with his objective economic social role. Precisely for the sake of this contradiction, he is sheltered in a nature preserve, enjoyed in leisurely contemplation.'

Habermas maintains that modern societies are prone to motivation and legitimization crises largely because of the inevitability of there being tension between the systemic and the integrative dimensions of society. These tensions arise as follows. In the period of classical capitalism the economic realm was conceived as being 'nature-like', subject to its own 'out-there' laws of operation. That contrasted with a previous situation in which the economic domain was regarded as being within the societal realm, subject to legitimization in terms of tradition. However, gradually the economic domain — *via* processes of oligopolization, technification and bureaucratization — has come to be regarded as non-autonomous and thus subject to political steering. This amalgamation of economic and political matters poses problems of rationality and legitimization, since the effects of economic functioning can neither be 'legitimatized' with reference to the autonomous operation of economic forces nor to a received *tradition* of substantive rationality. The now partly amalgamated realm of economics and politics needs participation from the members of the society. On the one hand, it needs only partial participation to the extent of not being able to withstand fully legitimatizing participation; but, on the other hand, the

steering needs of modern societies require that attempts be made to co-
ordinate and manipulate some aspects of the cultural tradition and the
life-concerns of atomized individuals. Thus, in this view, while the steering
aspects of modern societies lack legitimatizing resources with respect to a
higher, non-instrumental rationality they also become embroiled in
matters pertaining to the identity concerns of individuals and groups and
to the realm of human nature. This situation amounts to one of contradiction between two major dimensions of human societies—made the
more acute by the global generalization of notions concerning human
nature and human rights.

Habermas's prescriptions (subsumed under his general commitment to
the unification of truth-directed theory and practice) are, as is rather well
known, centred upon the claim that it is only through guidance by a truth-
directed communicative rationality that the 'crises' and contradictions of
which he speaks can be overcome. We cannot here (unfortunately) digress
in order to add our own criticisms to those which have already been
mounted against Habermas's ideas in this respect. We do, however, wish to
underline a point of considerable importance which arises from Habermas's
work, and that concerns the inevitable complexity of identity matters in
modern societies and their contingent relationship to authority matters. It
is pivotal in Habermas's work that the authoritativeness of tradition has
been lost by virtue of, in the first place, the autonomization of the
economic realm and, subsequently, the conjoining of the economic and
political realms. The latter conjunction, characterized by instrumental
rationality, creates the impression that the fortunes of individuals and
groups are matters of decision, but the overall societal situation precludes
the provision of legitimate reasons for the fortunes of individuals, groups
and societies as wholes. At the same time privatization makes it inevitable
that the steering centre of the society will constantly be, as it were,
bumping into what we would call identity issues. In this respect, Habermas
points out two closely related issues. On the one hand, he shows the
inevitability of the public thematization of 'identity problems' in modern
societies. While we are by no means convinced that these can be accounted
for with as much reference to economic and political matters as that
garnered by Habermas, the fact remains that his analysis does provide a
vital historical, philosophical—as well as macro-sociological—setting for
the burgeoning concern with identity. Secondly, Habermas raises important issues which have very direct relevance to the theme of identity-in-
relation-to-authority. In that connection the crucial point is that, as we
interpret Habermas, the modern everyday concern with identity arises in
significant part as a filling of a vacuum left by the decline of con-
textualizing traditional-substantive rationality. In the latter respect
Habermas's conception of communicative rationality and communicative

ethics can be expressed in terms of *overcoming* blockages in communicative interaction which exist partly *because of* the pervasiveness of the concern with identity.

Gouldner (1976:147) has claimed that Habermas's image of the ideal speech situation has an affinity with the practices of 'the early "group dynamics" movement launched by Kurt Lewin, by the Bethel Laboratory with its training of "T" groups, by Moreno's psychodrama and sociodrama, and by their more recent derivatives, "encounter", "sensitivity-training" and "co-counselling" groups.' If there is something to this claim—and we believe that there is—then again we see the intimacy of identity and authority issues, particularly in the light of Swanson's arguments (*supra*: Chapter 6) concerning the link between the rise of such practices within the American business organization in the 1940s and the 'let-it-all-hang-out' styles of the so-called counter-culture of the late 1960s and 1970s. Seeking release from the constraints of bureaucratic rationality, business organizations—argues Swanson—developed a principle of *government by objectives*, involving circumscribed procedures for members to participate in the planning of goals and thereby commit themselves to the organization by injecting their identity and other diffuse concerns into the discussion groups (see also Touraine 1977:95). What such a situation involves is the sharing of identity concerns—in Habermas's phrase the everyday *thematization* of such concerns—in order that they should no longer be an impediment to effective interaction. (In a different, but very important sense, identity expression *becomes collectively authoritative*.) Acknowledging that Habermas has a lot to say about the conditions for and nature of his ideal speech communities, the fact remains that the thematization and reconstruction of identities is seen in part as a solution to the problem of authority in the sense of *decoding identities* in order that legitimate authoritativeness may be located. [24] In effect the obtaining of the latter constitutes the equivalent of the permanent establishment of 'tradition' that is, tradition is seen as ongoingly *shapeable*.

Habermas thus implicitly makes a good case for the inexorability of the thematization of identity both in the 'real' world and in social-scientific study of it. As is clear from other chapters in this volume, attempts to exercise authority in the modern world have increasingly to come to terms with identity matters. As we have indicated, something like the *right to identity* has emerged in recent years, most conspicuously in the USA—covering such matters as age, sex and ethnicity; while, at a 'deeper' level of identity, matters connected with 'self-realization', the definition of life and death, and so on have become matters for public debate. Many such developments relate closely to Durkheim's arguments about the mutual amplification of concern with, on the one hand, individual self-definition and, on the other hand, with activities of the State. More to the immediate point, however, is the degree to which the scientific study of processes of identification—for example in *attribution* theory—has come to the fore. Undoubtedly refracting everyday problems of 'doing identity', this problem-area may be fruitfully regarded as analytic-observer attempts to distill the codes of self- and other-identification. In a sense therefore, it may be said that the concern which many social scientists exhibit in identity and identification indirectly confirms Habermas's thematic insistence upon the ubiquity of *problems of* communicative rationality. For when all is said and done, identity and identification have to do with matters of both intra-individual and inter-individual (as well as intergroup) communication.

As we have intimated, the most explicit concern with identity *per se* within the sociological community has been in the American context—and that primarily within the symbolic interactionist domain. While eschewing a history of symbolic interactionist writing about identity in this essay we need, nevertheless, to note certain characteristics of that stance. The intellectual backdrop to the symbolic interactionist focus on identity has been the tradition of pragmatism, mediated to symbolic interactionism proper by Mead. The individuated and subjectivized version of the Hegelian dialectic presented by Mead is of particular relevance here—in that the aspect of *translation* of the issue of identity from the Hegelian sense of the synthetic resolution of the relationship between subjectivity and objectivity in relationship to the principle of generality has gone *relatively* unrecognized. *In the American context* the notion of identity has often been used in effect to suggest that it is out of what we might call 'identity work' that 'society' (as a processual notion) is constructed (that is out of *encounters* with others, and *via* others with self). Symbolic interactionist talk of authority has been rare—an outstanding candidate for exception being the use to which Gerth and Mills (1954) put the conception of *generalized other* in their *Character and Social Structure*. In general, it could be said that symbolic interactionists have conceived of identity formation as an ongoing activity relative to a posited, but unexplicated context. (In which connection our note—P. 278, n. 19—on Goffman should be re-consulted.)

The notion of the generalized other, so central to Mead's conception of the self, has an interesting connection with the character of American society. In particular that concept would seem to be linked to the specific features of American social democracy. Mead argued that 'it is in the form of the generalized other that the social process influences the behavior of the individuals involved in it and carrying it on, i.e., that the community exercises control over the conduct of its individual members; for it is in this form that the social process or community enters as a determinative factor into the individual's thinking' (Mead 1934:155). It has been noted that the generalized other is 'remarkably similar' to Durkheim's conception of collective representation, a notion which came in Durkheim's work to replace the notion of conscience collective (Stone and Farberman 1970). What is of particular interest is, however, not that the two concepts perform similar functions in the work of the two individuals, but rather the subtle differences between them once a loose similarity between them has been established. The most crucial of these subtle differences is surely that the notion of generalized other conveys the sense of *generality* in a very abstract way. In other words Mead's conception of the generalized other is a kind of 'populist' notion, while Durkheim's notions of conscience collective and collective representation have much more to do with societal entitivity.[25] Durkheim conveys a notion of 'otherness' as a transcendence of particularity—or, as in the case of the early view of the conscience collective, as a *fusion* of 'I-ness' and 'otherness'.

American conceptions of identity within the symbolic interactionist tradition are thus typically individualistic in reference to *a diffuse notion of otherness*, characteristics which following Simmel we can see as implicated in a vicious circle. This feature of American sociological conceptions of identity is of course bound-up with such attributes of American social theory (and, of course, American society) as the relative absence of attention to historically provided social niches. In this respect it is the absence of concern both sociologically and phenomenally with class stratification in the European sense which is very important. The cultural commitment to *equality* (within categories declared to be 'fully American') has amounted to a commitment to the identity of all men (in the sense of their sameness in human terms). Against such a backdrop the search for personal and group identity is therefore likely to be more intense than other societal circumstances where class stratification has been more crystallized.

This example only serves to re-emphasize the need to note differences with respect to the manner in which identity and/or authority *are studied* in different socio-cultural, social-scientific traditions—as well, of course, to the manner in which such studying is embedded in the *a priori*s of *different societies*. While we may generalize about the significance of differentiation of the individual from other dimensions of the human condition in such a way as to encompass many societies in the modern world, this neither means that such processes of differentiation have proceeded at the same pace in all societies nor, even more importantly, does it mean that the *modes of dealing with the individual-society relationship* will be the same in those societies which have been subject to such differentiation. In the latter connection it is essential to realize that notwithstanding possibly similar processes of differentiation across a large number of modern societies, within particular societies or within clusters of culturally contiguous societies, there will be relatively *unique* and long-persisting codings of the relationship between individual and society.[26]

In turn, it must be fully appreciated that in spite of the trans-nationalism of much sociological discussion sociological theorizing itself is subject to such centripetal pressures. It is, then, no accident that in order to discuss the relationship between individual and society—or between identity and authority—we have tended to draw *as sociologists* very disproportionately upon German, followed by French authors. In the German case the relevance derives primarily from an historical concern with the relationship—to put it a little crudely—between societal determinism and individual freedom. In Germany sociology has always been subject to a contextual pressure to take account of the relationship between individual freedom and societal structure. Because of that it is not at all surprising that the *sociological* study of individualism has been a vital topic of German sociology since the early development of the discipline in that society. In France, by way of contrast, sociology has in large part been developed *in defiance* of individualism, coming to a head in the structuralist concern for 'a science without men' (or women) and a vision of a society without individuals in the more classical senses of individualism. Durkheim's attempt to socialize the latter has been invoked and re-invoked in this essay—but he stood as a brilliant mediator of a tradition which began in the early modern era with Rousseau, passing—*inter alia*—through Comte, and culminating in the modern period with the emphasis among French sociologists on such notions as the over-determination, self-production and autotransformation of society. In general terms, French social thought has had a tendency to revolve around the dilemma of sociologistic collectivism or existentialism (Cf Tiryakian 1962; Poster 1975). That is certainly not to deny the significance of French psychology, but that—interestingly—has tended to move between the points of psychologizing collectivities and in the modern period concern with the deep-*structural* determination of personality. In other words French intellectuals have tended to *so* dichotomize the socio-cultural and the individual realms and from a sociological point of view to denigrate the significance of the individual level *per se* as to make individualism either *entirely social* or completely *a*social (that is, existential). The overall consequence is that *sociologists* have been under intellectual-contextual constraint either—first—to assimilate the individual to society; or—second—to seek underlying deep structures which would account for both what people in other culture areas might call individual *and* society, or the subjective and objective (Bourdieu 1977). (Or—third—to get the individual right out of the analytic picture, which may be done for existentialistic or anarchistic reasons.) Such differences between the German and the French traditions in large part help us to account for the particular difficulties which Parsons attempted to overcome by co-ordination of the theories of different cultural traditions. The respective emphases surely reflected differing conceptions of the relationship between individual and society. Marx had, of course, also attempted something similar with respect to German, French and British intellectual traditions.

One of the major shifts in Parsonian action theory during the past two decades has been, as we have indicated, the conception of the differentiation of action systems. Parsons and his adherents increasingly view the components of action system in relationships of autonomy-in-interdependence, a notion which we briefly touched on in a previous part of this discussion (and which in general terms is surely connected to Parsons' notion of the 'double contingency' of interaction). Unlike, however, those who regard this normatively as a disastrous circumstance Parsons takes this to be part-and-parcel of the process of modernization. Nevertheless, the 'loosening' of the Parsonian scheme makes for quite a lot of continuity with those who see a hiatus between the everyday lives of individuals and the relative autonomy of the social-organizational realm (notably in the political and economic aspects of the latter). It raises the problem of the relationship between individual and society to a higher analytic level. Indeed Habermas explicitly draws on Parsons' work in order to point-up the dimensions of what he, Habermas, regards as the present crisis potential, while Parsons himself has used his own scheme to analyse certain aspects of crisis (Parsons 1977; Parsons and Platt 1973).

We have emphasized, then, that there is a high degree of agreement of a descriptive kind about the differentiation of individual from society in its systemicity. This tacit neo-consensus is however expressed in different terms according not merely to obvious philosophical entry points and the sketching of consequences but also according to different *codings* in the conception of the identity-authority relationship. Much theoretical work needs to be done on the latter—and some of the preceding chapters (notably those of Baum, Kavolis and of Holzner and Robertson) take steps in that direction. For such an idea suggests that the problem of order to which the identity-authority relationship undoubtedly has reference may *itself* be subject to a 'higher' or 'deeper' form of constraint. The differences which we have indicated between German, French and American theorizing are related to that idea, although talking of the idea of identity-authority relationships being subject to constraint has more immediate relevance to the socio-cultural domain *per se* rather than theorizing about it. What is basically involved in our raising this idea is that although there is much to be said for the notion that authority basically has to do with the linking of the operation of social-structure to a substantive rationality, relationships between the political (or politico-economic) steering aspects of a society and its individual adherents will be subject to particular and different forms as one shifts one's focus from society to society. Thus *even if* there are crises of authority, even if 'the sacred canopy' (Berger 1967) no longer performs its traditional functions, there remains an aspect of the identity-authority link which may be subject to quite definite, indeed determinate patterns — a theme which Baum (Chapter 3) has explored in detail.

Ideally discussion of these matters ought to proceed simultaneously on two fronts — in a manner which has some similarity to Marx's simultaneous concern with, on the one hand, the comparison of 'national' theories and, on the other hand, the comparison of societies. Such a prospect is somewhat daunting in that it inevitably raises a host of issues about the different conceptions of the relationship between observer and domain-of-analysis across societies and intellectual traditions. In referring to the question of variation in observer/domain relationships what we have in mind is this: many debates have occurred in recent years concerning the relationship between the sociological observer and the domain of 'his' analysis; these controversies have pivoted around the options of treating the domain of analysis as consisting in subjects or objects; at the former extreme we find various schools of phenomenology, ethnomethodology, sociological Wittgensteinians, 'verstehen' Weberians and others; at the latter extreme we discover various types of positivists and structuralists, while in the middle — or trying to be in the middle — there have been various schools which have seen the domain of analysis in both subjective and objective terms: Parsons, Habermas and Bourdieu are prominent examples of that thrust, while disagreeing among themselves.

The point that we seek to make in this connection is that the questions usually raised in 'puritanical' terms of methodology, epistemology and ontology are actually at the same time *substantive sociological* problems. For images of the 'correct' relationship between observer and domain are intimately bound-up with what we have described as the quest for the ideal relationship between individual and society.[27] In other words, we see a significant parallel between the 'professional' observer/domain relationship, on the one hand, and the individual/society relationship, on the other hand. And this, in turn, means — quite obviously — that the conception of the correct relationship between observer and domain of analysis as espoused by professional sociologists stands in a problematic relationship to *everyday* (or lay, or folk) conceptions of the relationship between observer and domain. (None of this, it should be stressed, means that each society or civilization has the same degree of everyday concern with observerness/domainness. That *too* is certainly a matter of variation.) Such considerations — as we have just said — raise a vast number of issues, but issues which we think are of vital importance in the modern debate about the nature and practice of social science. Only a few may be tempted to take up the challenge of pursuing all of these questions as a research package. But on the other hand insensitivity to the procedural issues on the part of more substantively inclined sociologists will be costly in the long run, as will insensitivity to the substantive issues on the part of those more interested in 'the idea of social science'. What in effect is being asked for is a genuinely international or transnational social science—in the broadest frame, an intercivilizational science of society. Unfortunately at the present time—in spite of superficial evidence to the contrary—sociology is still largely pursued in terms of 'sociological nationalism'. Culturally based sociological traditions are pitted against each other simply at the level of 'logic', so betraying the very idea of comparativeness which was such a central feature of classical sociology.

Notes

CHAPTER 1

1. The interest of the Durkheimians—including, of course, Mauss—in the odyssey of individualism has often been overlooked. Aspects of Durkheim's own approach to individualism are explored in the final chapter of this volume.

2. On the other hand, as Mauss (1968), Ullman (1966) and Morris (1972)—among others—have shown, the concept of the individual was much longer in the making in the Western world than the period since the Reformation. The Renaissance period was crucial in this respect.

3. On the cleavage within the Frankfurt School on this kind of question see Weinstein and Platt (1973:1–33). For discussion of the school of culture-and-personality in relation to the Frankfurt School, see Lasch (1978).

4. For the conception of cultural sociology used here, see Robertson (1978).

5. The obvious significance of general processes of locating and identifying helps to throw the importance of the concept of ascription into a new light. On this see Mayhew (1968), Kemper (1974) and Guiot (1977).

6. For an interesting statement on the epistemological aspects of social order, see Imersheim (1977).

7. On folk in relation to analytic models and the types of mathematics appropriate to different types of folk models see Anderson and Moore (1960), Moore and Anderson (1969) and other works by those authors. (Simmel has exerted a great influence in the shaping of their theories.)

8. The image of social structure with which we are operating here is quite similar to that of S. F. Nadel (1957). Although Nadel works with the concept of role rather than identity in erecting his theory of social structure, his point in respect of roles is well taken: 'The role concept is not an invention of anthropologists or sociologists but is employed by the very people they study . . . It operates in that strategic area where individual *behaviour* becomes social conduct (p.20). See also Banton (1965). In any case Gregory Stone makes a very strong case for considering many 'roles' to be best described as identities, particularly those which are 'sticky'. Identities, *not* roles, persist across situations. See Travisano (1970).

9. For some of the difficulties in the anlaysis of the symbol/social-structure problem, see Robertson (1970:15–93). See also Firth (1973), Bellah (1970) and Douglas (1966, 1970). As we emphasize elsewhere in this chapter there are 'higher' levels of explicit culture in many societies, particularly in those with traditions of monotheistic religious culture; while the notion of an even more fundamental form of culture—i.e., culture-as-code—is important in the later stages of this chapter (and elsewhere in this volume as a whole).

10. This draws attention to the negotiational character of identity construction, particularly in American society. For two different perspectives see Scott and Lyman (1968) and Guiot (1977).

11. In this connection we note the idea in a neo-Meadian perspective of the generalized other standing for 'selective societal segments' (Gerth and Mills 1954:95). For cross-cultural variation in the identification of deviants, see Robertson and Taylor (1973:52–67).

12. These reflections upon the specific theme of status crystallization theory raise many problems of an inter-civilizational nature. In a review of Lyn H. Lofland, *A World of Strangers: Order and Action in Urban Public Space* (1973), Dean McCannell draws attention to the difference between *personally knowing*, and *categorically knowing* individuals. 'This capacity for highly developed categorical thought, which . . . is at the heart of modern urban-based social relations, is very like Kant's "future history" and identical to Claude Lévi Strauss' characterization of the primitive's relationship to nature. Is it possible that the city has become the "nature" of modern man, holding for him the same fascination, opportunity and terror that the forest held for our ancestors and requiring in us a rebirth of a primitive logic in which the categories are not filled by

parts of plants and animals but by different "types" of our fellowmen' (McCannel 1975:1026)? These comments lead directly to comparisons of civilizations with respect to the relationship between subject-centred and object-centred thought. For some insightful comparisons of Western and Buddhist thought in such respects, see Paz (1971:88–101). The notions of the socio-cultural *creation of* the category of 'nature' and the associated notion of nature-likeness *within* the human domain has received much attention in recent years—for example in Habermas (1975) and Sahlins (1976). Bordieu (1977:167) speaks of naturization as the product of a long labour of disenchantment. We are of the view that disenchantment generally is closely bound-up with the problem of individual identity. The disenchantment of identity *itself*—in the sense of attempting to unlock the code of identity—is also suggested by the present essay.

13. More recent Parsonian theory emphasizes the idea of behavioural system, rather than biological organism. This development goes some way to meeting part of the criticism of Parsons with respect to his presenting an 'over-socialized conception of man'. See Lidz and Lidz (1976).

14. Lofland's may well be a particularly American view, which is actually relativized somewhat at the end of the present chapter where American modes of identification are given a particular typological status (Type D). Compare the interpretation of Dilthey by Habermas (1972:140–60).

15. There is some overlap between these views and those of some ethnoscientists. See Spradley (1972). On the other hand, what distinguishes our view in this respect is our emphasis on cultural content and tradition.

16. See Parsons in Parsons *et al.* (1961:251). In discussing the salience of ethnicity in modern America, Parsons has alluded to that kind of identity concern as constituting a form of de-differentiation—presumably of the relationship between social structure and personality (Parsons, 1975:70).

17. For relevant anthropological perspectives on the attribution of responsibility, see Gluckman (1972).

18. In recent social science such questions have received technical-theoretical attention in the works of, *inter alia*, Olson (1964), Coleman (1971, 1973), Hirschman (1970), Gamson (1975). See also Etzioni (1968) and Touraine (1977).

19. See Wilson (1973) for discussion of the significance of the introduction of Western religious ideas in the Third World, with particular attention to the development of ideas about voluntary membership in organizations.

20. Generally on this see, *inter alia*, Gough (1957), Anderson (1974), Service (1975).

21. For interesting discussion of the problems which Marxists have had with nationalism, see Nairn (1975).

22. These issues are raised again in the last chapter. Habermas (1975) has discussed such features of modern societies at length.

23. Of course, many collectivities have agents and representatives, but they are not frequently required to '*be*' the collectivity in their external relationships. In contrast, there are cases where *external* 'members' (for example of soccer teams) identify so comprehensively with collectivities that they do seem to 'become the collectivity in their relationships with others.

24. For critical discussion of the applicability of the concept of charisma and its circumstances, see Wilson (1975).

25. On the decline of honour and the rise of identity, see Berger *et al.* (1973:83–96). For an attempt to connect sin and virtue to social-communicational variables, see Douglas (1970).

26. The thrust of our use of the concept *code* has much in common with Eisenstadt (1978). See also Baum (this volume).

CHAPTER 2

1. By *substantive coherence* I refer to an understandable integration among an individual's intra-psychic structures; by *methodological coherence*, to the presence in a life history of a distinctive manner of undergoing changes in mood and behaviour (e.g., Rousseau; *Rameau's Nephew*). While the 'self'—like lyrical poetry—is not necessarily circumscribed in time and space, personal and collective 'identities'—like the novel (and the narrative genre in general)—seem to require rooting in a particular, though conceivably imaginary, time and place.

2. When it is desired to distinguish the 'direction-of-action' aspect of a cultural logic from its 'interpretation-of-meaning' aspect, the former may be called a *cultural pragmatic*, the latter a *cultural hermeneutic*. It is of the essence of cultural logics, as here conceived of, that they contain both of these elements in a mutually pervasive, though perhaps tension-filled, bundle.

3. On the 'individualizing' effects of the 'military community' see Nisbet (1973:11–90). On the comparative lack of heroic self-assertion in traditional Chinese poetry—in contrast to the Greek—see Chan (1974): Chinese conventions of heroic poetry 'tend to illuminate human frailty rather than strength; . . . in contrast to the [Homeric] epic's interest in victories and joyful camaraderie in a sumptuous hall, the Chinese poems tend to dwell upon defeat and bitter loneliness in a harsh outdoor setting' (158–9).

4. Even the popular American proponents of the self-made man as late as 'in the age of Jackson and Lincoln sought above all to strike a balance between traditional social and religious ideals and the spirit of individual economic enterprise' (Cawelti 1965:47).

5. For the context of the individualism of Abelard and St. Bernard, see Morris (1972).

6. On the rise of the norm of moral self-reliance, 'sustained by the belief that a person's inner resources are generally adequate to guide him in a morally sensible way through life', without external guidance by authorities or the community, in English sixteenth- and seventeenth-century sectarian Protestantism, see Leites (1974:42–3).

7. 'Thus the ultimate message of the mystic about the nature of selfhood is that the self is *essentially* more than a mere self, that transcendence belongs to its nature as much as the act through which it is immanent to itself, and that a total failure on the mind's part to realize this transcendence reduces the self to *less* than itself' (Dupré 1974:511). In monotheistic religions, mysticism is capable of laying the foundations for a very powerful experience of individuation. This is no less true of the 'inner castle' or 'little castle' that St. Teresa and Eckhardt use for their image of the deeper self, as of God's statement to a ninth-century Ṣûfî mystic, Bâyazîd (Abû-Yazîd) Bisṭâmî, in the Islamic tradition in which individualism remained relatively undeveloped in the end: 'I am thine through thee; there is no god but Thou' (Hodgson 1974:404).

8. Rimbaud goes on: 'All the forms of love, of suffering, of madness; he himself looks for, he exhausts in himself all the poisons, in order to keep only their quintessences . . . For he arrives at the *Unknown!*' Cited from Bays (1964:251–2).

9. '. . . The trickster himself is something of a "chaos", with his uncontrollable appetites, his enormous sexual apparatus, his unsociability, his amorality, his ability to change shape at will, etc . . . acting customarily without apparent plan or forethought . . . He brings order out of the chaotic myth world, and in the process he becomes less chaotic himself . . . never takes himself too seriously . . . always comes up laughing' (Ricketts 1966:340–1, 343, 347).

10. For some accounts of such experiences, see Contag (1970). Confucius himself 'was enraptured by the music of Shao so that he lost his taste for anything else . . .' (de Bary, 1970:149).

11. From a Western-rationalist point of view, one of the paradoxes of the crisis personality is that, while it is frequently a seeker for the luminosity of the soul, the concrete sensations of the body seem to have particular identity-defining importance for it (since all sorts of certainty, except those of the body, have crumbled). But, precisely for overloading the body with psychocultural significance, the crisis personality might be expected to have a more vulnerable body.

12. Both Prometheus and Tristan, who became highly individualized rebels, began, in the more primitive layers of Greek and Welsh tradition, as powerful tricksters.

13. Consistently, while Misch (1973) lists 'self-glorification' and 'self-scrutiny' as the two main modalities in which the self manifests itself, Goffman, in the index of *Frame Analysis* (1974) lists only 'self-deception (delusion)', with all sorts of 'conditions facilitating the production of'.

14. Expressed in the most thorough-going way possible, this becomes the Buddhist conception of the *false* self. 'There is . . . nothing that can be called the self, if by that is meant an unchanging, abiding substance. There are only the.aggregates of existence, the flowing together of energy and matter into particular shapes or forms' (Bowker, 1970:242).

15. In this section I draw upon some materials presented in Kavolis (1974b), but with major conceptual revisions. Only under the coincidence logic of selfhood (among the four types discussed in the previous section) is the assumption necessarily made that internal and external orders are—or should be—organized in the same manner. Even in this case, the question arises whether the internal order is 'naturally' in alignment with the external order (or spontaneously inclines toward it, as in Confucianism), or has to be brought into such alignment by 'human artifice'—a conscious act of will (as in Marxism).

16. The established sociological equivalent of 'miraculous intrusion' is Weber's charisma. But the former concept is more appropriate for analysing the organization of subjective experiences, such as 'love', 'inspiration', or even 'play' in Huizinga's sense, whereas charisma is the type of miraculous intrusion that is relevant to the building of public institutions (Eisenstadt 1968).

17. In Western traditions, a strong tendency exists to perceive those who live outside of the dominant conception of order as existing in a state of 'meaningless chaos' (or 'corrupted chaos', if they have previously been a part of the sanctified order and have been deprived of its blessings) (White 1972). In India, however, where opposites tend to be 'conjoined' rather than 'disjointed', chaos seems to have been recognized as more intimately interdependent with order, the latter deriving some of its authority from being in intimate touch with the former, than is the case in the dominant traditions of other classical civilizations (Falk 1973). In Chinese Taoism, chaos is the ground of order, and the modes of operation of order and of chaos are, at the deepest level, indistinguishable (Opitz 1967). For an analysis of the Western tendency toward 'disjunction' and Indian and Chinese tendencies toward 'conjunction', see Paz (1974).

18. In China, 'Universal harmony comes about not by the celestial fiat of some King of Kings, but by the spontaneous co-operation of all beings in the universe brought about by their following the internal necessities of their own natures' (Needham 1969:323).

19. Scholem (1941:315) speaks of the 'doctrine of the holiness of sin' as 'a position which . . . occurs with a kind of tragic necessity in every great crisis of the religious mind'. One could similarly say that the doctrine of the necessity of coercion occurs in every fundamental crisis of liberation movements, that of the superior health of madness in corresponding crises of therapeutic movements and so on.

20. The notion of the contract may be rooted in the economics of reciprocity of the simplest hunting-and-gathering societies, in which the recipient of a gift incurs a moral obligation to reciprocate, not necessarily immediately, with a gift of equivalent value. This, however, is a type of 'contract' by which the established machinery of society is operated; *the 'contract' replicates the abstract, pre-existing design in a concrete relationship*, but does not transform the social order or establish a new type of moral responsibility (as Rousseau's notion of social contract does). The idea of contract in commercial transactions is known, in a form recognizable in the West, in civilizations, such as the Indian and the Islamic, in which there is no dynamic native conception of establishing a political or moral order on the basis of a contract between citizens or between the ruler and the ruled. *The contract by which a new type of shared moral obligation is established* comes in at least two versions: the Old Testament covenant between God and his chosen people, a pact binding upon both parties, but established in a 'lawful' monarch-subject

relationship and by the determination of the superior party (the 'manager-centred' contract, similar in its imbalance to the employment contract in the capitalist economy before the development of powerful trade unions); and the civic contract by which the democratic city states of classical Greece, the political order of republican Rome, the free cities of medieval Europe, and the English tradition of common law operated and which, at least in principle, took the form of a 'manager-free' contract between differentiated and mutually dependent parties ('free citizens') to operate and to modify a social order by joint determination. The latter type of contract is established, and continually reconstructed, through a process that sometimes (especially in the Greek *polis*) bears considerable resemblance to that of creation of a work of art over time. There are legends in some other traditions — outside Japan — which postulate a kind of 'social contract' between a 'culture-hero' and the people by which a state or a civilization has been founded. But this mode of operation has not, outside Western traditions, continued to exist as an active principle continuously capable of producing new moral obligations by joint determination to establish them. All these versions of contract tend to become replaced in nineteenth century Western Europe by a conception of contract as a *mutually built machinery for acquiring from another exactly what one specifies, to be used for one's own purposes* (in the determination of which neither the other party to the contract, nor any 'nature that must be respected', has a necessary part). This modern notion of contract is conceived within a social order comprehended as a factory for the production of immediately desired satisfactions.

21. John Locke, who thought of human nature as a morally inert mass to be shaped by organized education, 'has opened up, in principle, the possibility of perfecting men by the application of readily intelligible, humanly controlled, mechanisms' (Passmore 1970:163).

22. I have the concept of the 'discipline of beauty' from a public lecture by William E. Naff on 'The Japanese Tradition of Courtly Love'.

23. What the specific structure of order conceived as a work of art can be depends on the type of artistic culture which those who conceive of order as a work of art have in mind. For a typology of artistic cultures, see Kavolis (1974a).

24. I am talking of 'asceticism' and 'mysticism' not as salvation orientations (Weber 1964), but as modes of comprehending order — whether such comprehensions are stated in a religious or a secular language.

25. Cross-modality interactions are also possible. Thus Hobbes, in his design for ordering human appetites in society, represents the superimposition of a 'masculine' culture (seen as rational) on a 'feminine' spontaneous nature (seen as vicious). The Hobbesian interaction between culture and nature has the form of a 'justified rape' — a rape, moreover, the need for which must be recognized by the victim.

26. The world of witchcraft, as it appears in [African] tribal beliefs, is . . . a world of decay, where all that is normal, healthy, and ordered is reduced to chaos and "primordial slime"' (Turner 1967:125). Chaos is apparently perceived in the 'mystical' rather than in the 'ascetic' modality in Africa, as also in Taoism. But in Africa it tends to be threatening; in Taoism nurturing.

27. This classification of modes of order and disorder, being based on the dichotomizing principle, itself implies 'lawful nature' as its meta-framework. It is possible to look at order-disorder phenomena within other meta-frameworks. But, if one's purpose is to analyse (rather than merely interpret), the 'lawful-nature' framework is, at some point, and at least as a heuristic device, indispensable. The analyst differs from the normative thinker in not assuming that lawful nature is the *only* conceivable framework within which to see what he is concerned with.

28. The notion of the self as a well-constructed dream is suggested by three terms from the linguistic universe of Sanskrit: *svá*, 'one's own', *svápna*, 'sleep, dream', *sv-ápas*, 'doing good work, skilful, artistic, artificially fashioned' (Monier-Williams 1899: 1274, 1280, 1281). This notion has deeper roots in India than in Europe, where the Judeo-Christian tradition has given a substantiality to the 'self' which it lacks, particularly, in traditions influenced by Buddhism (thus also in Japan).

29. Coleridge's five attributes of the organic form still constitute its best definition. 'First, the origin of the whole precedes the differentiation of the parts . . . Second, the form manifests the process of growth by which it arose . . . Third, as it grows the plant assimilates diverse elements into its own substance . . . Fourth, the achieved form of the plant is directed from within . . . Fifth, the parts of the living whole are interdependent' (Ritterbush 1968:20-1).

CHAPTER 3

1. While a broader and later formulation than Durkheim's own which more narrowly focused on expansion of personal freedom and engagement of individuals with government, I treat his as essentially unproblematical and factually true, in part, because studies of daily life in totalitarian industrializing and industrialized countries have shown a heavy reliance on *institutionalized anxiety* rather than direct coercion; Cf. Inkeles (1950), Inkeles & Bauer (1959), Schoenbaum (1967).
2. He also used the term *invariance* to formulate the problem of societal identity: 'I am interested in life as a movement, a course, and direction — as something variable yet combined with an 'invariance' (to borrow a term from mathematics) that makes it possible to grasp an identity as it passes through one mutation after another' (Castro 1954:34).
3. For the present purposes the critical features of these stages are: (*i*) during the historical stage, the birth of the idea of 'self' as an acting, willing, autonomous, and responsible agency and the filtering down of that idea to the masses during the early modern stage; and (*ii*) the birth of hierocracy as well as its two possible outcomes, caesaropapism and theocracy, which put sacred and secular authority into tension everywhere also during the historical stage, and the spreading down into the masses of that tension during the early modern stage; Cf. Bellah (1964), Parsons (1964), and Weber (1922:1158-1211).
4. The best short way to communicate the nature of the present paper which only addresses a portion of the invariance argument may be to present, without much explanation, the functional typology of solidarities I have been working with. Shown in Diagram 1, this *locates* the main problem focus of the present effort: it is in the political realm with a minor theme devoted to the area of moral solidarities where I shall use some of Weber's findings as regards the generality of value systems that crystallized during the historical stage.

DIAGRAM 1

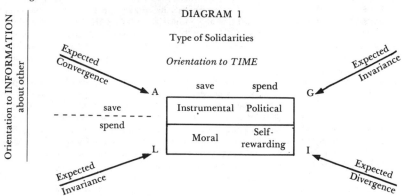

With political focus primary here, the following comment must suffice. Political solidarities require the spending of time in meeting the four conditions of Barnard lest authority relations evaporate. This is particularly evident in pursuit of long-range goals through political means rather than, say, through the operation of market mechanisms. But while thus attending to the maintenance of authority relations, participants may nevertheless engage in relative information saving because political process involves only the mobilization of those components of the identity of actors which are made up by their membership status in the cooperative system in question. Political process requires selective attention to the *relevant* membership identity, never to all aspects of the overall identity of actors. This is true precisely to the extent that political solidarities have been *differentiated out* from the matrix of a more diffuse identity-set which is a function of social evolution.

5. Whether this proposition is in fact a testable one requires a familiarity with available data in historical archives that I do not have, but indicating the two necessary steps of operationalizations is indeed simple. First, and following Almond and Coleman (1960), let the polity boundary maintenance stand for interest articulation and interest aggregation functions. Second, and deviating from Almond and Coleman (1960:33–8) who simply designate *associational* interest articulation as the only 'modern' form, let the focus be on what actually counts, viz. effectiveness and efficiency in articulating and aggregating interests. Then if the stored data permit it, Olsen's respective estimates could be used in testing for the permanence of those regimes that weathered the storms of social mobilization.

6. Stressing the unalterable substance of ethnics in their basic content ever-after the historical stage means parting company with Bellah's conception of religious modernity with its explicit emphasis on choice as regards ethics — 'life as an *infinite* possibility thing' and 'man's responsibility for the *choice* of his symbolism' — which presumably covers the very capacity to choose non-contingency on ultimate meaning, thus ending the human condition itself in Bellah's own terms (Bellah 1964:371–3).

7. To avoid misunderstanding, I am not taking a stand against Weber's Protestant Ethic thesis as regards the invention of free labour for the first time. But I seriously question the utility of exploiting that insight by indiscriminate extension to follower societies regardless of the degree of explicitness in doing so (McClelland 1961; Inkeles and Smith 1974). Whatever the utility of the facts generated for other uses, advancement of modernization theory with a focus on politics and problems of legitimation is not likely among them.

8. The managerial differences are of special import in light of Inkeles and Smith's correlations between education and individual overall modernity. When it comes to political life, Inkeles has been consistently wary about convergence, deeming it explicitly unlikely. On this point an absolute empiricist, he simply refers to the factual compatibility between variety in politics and industrialization on the one hand and industrialized society on the other (Inkeles and Bauer 1959:388–96; Inkeles 1975:493–5).

9. Far greater discontinuity in West German national politics has been stressed by Dahrendorf (1965). Probably due to occupation by democratic powers and more democratic regional traditions, the matter cannot be elaborated here.

10. The concepts of legitimacy, codes, and functionally specialized symbolic legitimatizing action do not belong to the strong points of sociological theory. 'Divine rights', 'rule through dei gratia' should not be confused with direct religious legitimization. On the contrary, these terms appeared at the tail end of the struggle between princes and the Pope, a conflict about the question whether priestly coronation *constituted* or merely affirmed temporal power, and one that sealed the differentiation of sacred and secular power. Ever after governmental power rested on a presumed commonality of interests of units organized in a state. Thus sovereignty of the people merely signals an extension of the size of the relevant units (Sternberger 1968). Furthermore, conceptions of political modernity remain muddled as can be seen in the fact that Huntington (1968) argues a case of 'societal modernity and political underdevelopment' for America while Almond and Verba (1963) take some of the very same elements designated as 'traditional' by Huntington as an indispensable ingredient of a 'civic political culture' which they designate as specifically 'modern'.

11. There are two readings of Swanson's explanation of the success or failure of the Reformation in Europe. A narrow constructionist reading assigning causal force to an authority code extant prior to the Reformation struggle and determining its outcome is definitely possible (Swanson 1967:23, 42, 232). As shown above, I decided on a correlational reading which suffices for my point, and relieves me of the need to confront the thorny causal question.

12. Whether these succeed anymore than Western advertising in the actual construction of an intended societal reality is, fortunately, unimportant here. This bombardment of interpretive messages may well be suffering from chronic inflation, hence constituting cheap currency for ordinary man.

13. While not as much industrialized as seems desirable for claiming polity compatibility with industrial society, one should note that when one defines a metro-city in terms of a population density of 100,000 or more *and* with a 65 per cent or more of the labour force in the non-agricultural sector of the economy, the metropolitan population of Latin America averaged 27.4 per cent in 1960 with a range of 48 per cent in Uruguay and 6 per cent in Haiti. Also during that year, of 20 Latin American countries one had a metro of 6.7 million, three countries a metro of 4 to 5 million, and six countries metros of 1 to 2 million inhabitants (Harris 1971:172–5, 179).

14. Such ideological 'mimicry' (Linz 1964) according to which such issues as fascism and communism 'amount to frivolous sideshows, in servile imitation of foreign models' (Castro 1954:127), pertains to political not necessarily other structures of society, such as education, economic relations, and foreign policy.

15. Typologies vary according to purpose. Mine here is to emphasize the variety of polity forms in industrial society, the theme of continuity in meaning codes, cross-historical universals, and hence a display of what modern types are extentions of prior forms. So I draw on empirical studies and provide the best distillate I can. Socialist polities are quite varied; but for my purpose here 'a dominant ideology' constitutes the one common element which makes of course East Germany's corporatist aspects quite distinct from the praetorianism of Latin American polities. Pursuing rather different goals, it is nevertheless gratifying to note that Fleron (1973) in his study of Soviet political leadership also finds a fourfold classification useful. Among his types of the monocratic, the adaptive-monocratic, the cooptative, and the pluralistic, the Soviet case displays characteristics of cooptation.

16. In American society for example, some findings show that governmental agencies have been captured by the interests they are supposed to regulate (Bernstein 1955); but that such interest representation in the administrative bureaucracy also carries a certain amount of legitimacy in a pluralist society has been stressed by Leiserson (1942).

17. There is one final aspect of this typology of polity types that can only be mentioned, not be given elaboration. Applying such concepts to the analysis of a given significant 'world system' as in Wallerstein's (1974) analysis of the capitalization of agriculture for the first time, may well shed considerable light on one of the dark spots in that study as well as others it is likely to spawn. For it seems to me exceedingly likely that there was a functional division of labour among the European polities at the time which made possible the invention and the experimental testing of the then wholly new idea of treating humans as just a factor of production as well as the ability to locate that experimentation abroad.

18. This formulation denies 'reality' to revolutions in one critical sense: capacity to change authority codes from internal resources alone. While a matter beyond the purview of this effort, another one under way examines the hypothesis that so-called successful revolutions as the French, the Russian, and the Dutch were successful in the non-political aspects of social structure and process *just because* they exhibited pre-post-revolutionary *continuity* in authority codes and individualisms; while the so-called unsuccessful cases, as those of 1848 Germany and Austria-Hungary, 'failed' because of a reliance on or widespread recourse to culturally foreign conceptions of authority and images of autonomous man among the rebellious forces.

19. Having relied on Inkeles and Bauer (1959) for relevant evidence above, it is necessary to stress that this interpretation departs wholly from theirs which stressed Soviet man's nagging doubt about the 'inner self' (Inkeles and Bauer 1959:286). But their formulation about doubt on 'inner', trust on 'outer self' derived apparently from the older guilt-shame dichotomy which is more concealing than revealing with respect to the relation per-sonality- and- social structure in modern complex society.

CHAPTER 4

1. I am aware that Durkheim was a liberal in his political commitments and occasionally made statements assigning ontological priority to individuals (Cf. Bellah, 1973:xx:xii–ff).
2. I have cited Parsons' definitions rather than Swanson's because I find the latter even more difficult to apply consistently to specific organizations and processes.

CHAPTER 5

1. Burkart Holzner has suggested to me that a meaningful typology of perspectives on identity, such as those represented in the present collection of essays, must include another dimension; namely, level of abstraction. He argues that a basic distinction can be made within each of the four types suggested in the above table between those per-spectives which are highly abstract and those which focus attention on concrete, mun-dane manifestations of psycho-social identity. From this standpoint, both this essay and Chapter 1 of this volume would be classified in the fourth type suggested by the table. However, the present discussion is couched in the more concrete terms of contemporary reality whereas the Holzner/Robertson analysis attempts to provide a far more abstract framework that transcends possibly transient and ephemarol, concrete manifestations of contemporary and emerging identity models and phenomena.

   While I accept the importance of this additional classificatory dimension, I believe it is of less significance than the two dimensions included in the above table. And at least one basis for this portion derives from the influence that both Holzner and Robertson have had on my own formulation. Indeed, it would be remiss to fail to acknowledge the fact that many, if not most of the ideas developed in this essay can be found in Robertson's writings on religious mysticism. For this reason, I am less impressed by the significance of the abstract-analytical versus concrete-empirical distinction than by the other two dimensions indicated above.
2. For example, Touraine (1972:3) argues:

   > A new type of society is now being formed. These new societies can be labeled post-industrial to stress how different they are from the industrial societies that proceeded them . . . They may also be called technotronic because of the power that dominates them. Or one can call them programmed societies to define them according to the nature of their production methods and economic organization.

   And Brzezinski (1967:18–21) observes that:

   > America is in the midst of a transition that is both unique and baffling . . . Ceasing to be an industrial society, it is being shaped to an ever increasing extent by technology and electronics and thus becoming the first *technotronic society*.
3. This conception of identity is almost identical with Anthony F. C. Wallace's (1961a, 1961b, 1962 and 1965) conception of 'mazeway', which he defines as the sum of all the culturally-derived '. . . cognitive maps which at any moment a person maintains, of self, of behavioural environment, and of those valued experiences or states of being which attract or repel him.' (Wallace 1965 in Spradley, 1972:310). Wallace (1965–72) suggests

that processes of selective attention to the total environment that have their roots in the cultural system are the basis for the unique 'behavioral environment' that each man creates for himself. Wallace's (1956, 1962, 1965) conception of 'mazeway' is extremely similar to the conceptions of identity that are implicit in Clifford Geertz's (1963, 1964, and 1966) work and the conceptions hinted at in Berger and Luckmann (1966).

4. In a perceptive review of this latest (1976) Bell prognostication, published in *The New Republic*, March 20, 1976, Frank E. Manuel (1976:22) observes:

> The nomenclature of the book is rather murky. I never learned what the author means by capitalism . . . his usage of 'contradiction' and 'the dialectical' is either a take-off on Marx-Hegel or derived from some private language of his own. 'Modern' is really baffling; it can signify anything from the Renaissance to the post-modern, which started sometime or other. Culture does get defined. For the 'meaning of culture' the reader can open to page 36 where he is enlightened by a series of dubious platitudes that capture the aromatic essence of the work.

5. An extremely conservative estimate argued that more than six million Americans had participated in some kind of sensitivity training, encounter, or 'personal growth' group (Maliver 1971). This essay cannot discuss the implications of intensive groups—either as a set of techniques or as a social movement. However, this subject has received some sociological treatment and the interested reader should consult Back (1970a and 1970b), Bottschalk and Pittison (1969), Lakin (1967 and 1970), Bart (1971), Jacobs (1971), Marx and Seldin (1973a and 1973b), and Marx and Ellison (1975) for analyses of sensitivity training-encounter as a social movement. Among the numerous works that treat the subject from a psychiatric-psychotherapeutic perspective, the most perceptive include Gornick (1970a and 1970b), Maliver (1971), and the comprehensive, balanced American Psychiatric Association Report (1971) on 'Encounter Groups and Psychiatry'.

6. This point seems of central importance in understanding the difference between primary, childhood socialization and secondary, adult socialization. That is, contrary to the general (psychoanalytically-influenced) assumption that permeates the social scientific literature, we are suggesting that the primary socialization of children is a far simpler achievement than the secondary socialization of adults—which requires a certain amount of de-socialization before re-socialization can even be initiated.

7. Sociological sceptics of contemporary movements deride ideological primary groups as 'group therapy for the masses'. This simply misses the point and ignores the most interesting aspects of current movements. It is not difficult to briefly indicate a few of the more obvious differences between therapeutic groups and ideological primary groups: the latter include no professional, 'impartial' therapist or certified leader; generally convene in members' homes on a rotating basis; involve no exchange of money for services; and are not connected to occupational or other organizational roles and responsibilities.

8. Underlying all these assumptions is an image of post-industrial, post-modern American society after 1960 with an affluent, new middle-class possessing considerable disposable purchasing power, leisure time, and educational attainments. Yet we see no reason why these assumptions, stated in slightly different form, would be less applicable in other post-modern, although not necessarily post-industrial, national contexts.

9. We believe that this ascribed homogeneity is one reason for the fecundity of feminist consciousness-raising rap groups' in proliferating new cultural identity models and expressive meanings in contrast to the paucity of new symbolic formulations generated by more conventional sensitivity training, encounter, and 'personal growth' groups. That is, feminist primary groups have a clearcut ascriptive criterion for defining inclusion and exclusion that is absent in intensive groups; the latter are more heterogeneous by virtue of the 'achieved' criterion for membership of 'ability to pay' the fee for participation.

CHAPTER 6

1. This is most obvious when we come to the source of a person's faith in the meaningfulness of his life taken as a whole and his sense of being empowered for it. I use 'meaning' in the sense of the relevance that something has for some goal or end.

My action gives relevance to material objects, ideas, feelings, people, particular acts of my own in short to anything that can have relevance for my goals. But my action cannot give meaning to the whole of my action, the whole of my life career. It cannot do this because the whole of my action is not a means, or an end, of the whole of my action but is necessarily identical with it. If my life career is to have a meaning, it must be in its relevance for the action of another: For another person's action, for God's action, for the action of some group. Either it has such relevance or it has not. If it has such relevance, this is a gift. It is a property given to the course of my life by its place in what the other is doing. It is something that I find and not something that I myself create or choose. I may accept it, reject it, ignore it, or try to change or escape it, but its existence is wholly objective.

Is this meaning also authoritative? Does it establish a meaning that seems to me rooted, and here I turn to some language of Clifford Geertz's (1966:4), in 'a general order of existence'? Does it clothe that meaning 'with such an aura of factuality' that it seems 'uniquely realistic'? Only, it seems, if the other has appropriate authority. Only if it acts from legitimatized standards and applies them in legitimate ways.

On methods in the search for identity, see Goffman (1967:149–270).

2. It has been of great importance for the development of modern styles of organization that skilled people have been in short supply and that some categories of such pepole are unionized or are otherwise protected in their rights on the job (Wilensky and Lebeaux 1965). The result has been a greater independence of employees, making it even more necessary that organizations afford them satisfactions in their work and motivate them to do their best.

3. The new styles of management were first articulated especially by Drucker (1954) and McGregor (1957, 1960). Jun and Storm (1973) and Biller (1973) provide exceptionally complete characterizations of the form they have come to take. Bennis and Slater (1968) describe the generalization of these patterns to the society as a whole. Empirical studies have shown that they have become widespread as the ideology of executives in Asia and Latin America as well as in Europe and North America (Haire, Ghiselli, and Porter 1966). Their actual implementation has been found more likely in organizations that confront a changeful but manageable environment and that are internally differentiated along functional lines (Lawrence and Lorsch 1967; Woodward 1965). They are also more likely to be used to guide horizontal than vertical relations in organizations (Leavitt 1965; Miles 1964, 1975; Miles and Ritchie 1968; Strauss 1972, 1974).

Of the major institutional sectors of modern societies, the one least affected by the new styles seems to be the political, especially those areas of government closest to the making of political decisions (Meade 1971; Mosher 1971; Scott 1969; White 1971; Waldo 1965, 1968). The usual explanation is that, in these areas of government, there is the greatest danger that the organization will become the servant of its employees rather than of the electorate to whom its chief officials are directly accountable.

Perhaps the single largest body of evidence on the consequences of the new methods in organizational life is found in the work of Likert and his colleagues (Likert 1967; Katz and Kahn 1966). Management by objectives as an operating procedure is described in detail in Ordione (1969) and Raia (1974). Schick (1970) examines its place in a society's political processes. Howard (1971) and Parker (1971) offer discussions of some specific techniques (e.g., planning-programming, budgeting) employed to implement it.

Related themes appear in efforts to reconstruct the foundations of jurisprudence (Nonet 1974; Selznick 1974).

4. The theological outlook that I describe appears to be more a development in the seminaries and the parishes than a direct descendent of the work of 'established'

theologians. Its expositors do see links to some ideas that have gone before: to the process theology of Hartshorne and Whitehead (Winter 1974; Cobb 1964; Hartshorne 1941, 1970; Rust 1969; Brown, James and Reeves 1971; Miller 1973), to the special form of the theology of hope found in Bloch (1959) and Moltmann (1969), to Bonhoeffer (Cox 1965; Weiland 1968), to the more communally-orientated varieties of existentialism (Macquarrie 1965; Keen 1966, 1969, 1974). For a discussion of ethical implications of the new theology, consult Sellers (1970). For a description of a set of social, political, and theological conceptions having some startling resemblances to the ones described in this paper but arising in the Italian Renaissance, see Bouwsma 1968:1–51.

CHAPTER 7

1. These are heavily ideal-typified attitudes towards the issue of social autonomy. In equally ideal-typical form they might be given names: sociologistic; idealistic; materialistic; utilitarian.
2. Of particular relevance here are the recent critiques of the utilitarian residue in the works of Marx offered by Dumont (1977) and Sahlins (1976). Understandably Parsons has seen in Dumont's analysis a confirmation and clarification of some of his own views (presumably those relating to Marx's social science, to utilitarianism in general and to Marx's utilitarian individualism). From very different angles sociologists have of course accused Parsons himself of utilitarianism. For example, see Gouldner (1970). Much more sympathetically, and on different grounds, Baum (1977) has made such an 'accusation'.
3. Oakes (1977) has raised a number of important issues in this respect in relation to Simmel's epistemology and methodology, including a tantalizing comparison of Simmel and Wittgenstein.
4. We use the latter term here—in contrast to Giddens' (1976) usage—in reference to the distinctively 'French use' of the term. In that perspective the dichotomies of individual and society, and subjectivity and objectivity are periodized, in the sense that as categories they *are produced by* societal circumstances. There is of course variation *within* the French productionist perspective—much of it pivoting upon the question of whether society *itself* is both subject and object or should be regarded in terms which transcend such categories.
5. Particularly illuminating on this issue is Tillich (1967). See also Robertson (1978:103–47) and Robertson (1980).
6. Habermas has made much of the importance of interaction relative to the emphasis upon action in the work of Marx. Although obviously standing himself in the tradition to which we here refer, Habermas has not—as far as we know—discussed the significance of interaction among the classical sociologists. His neglect of Simmel is particularly curious.
7. Bridges between Durkheim and Weber are built below with reference to Simmel, who discussed the relationship between forms of individualism and forms of the division of labour at length.
8. Ideas of a rather similar kind have been presented by Eisenstadt. See Eisenstadt and Curelaru (1976:347–86) and Eisenstadt (1978). Eisenstadt refers to *codes* 'which connect the contours of institutional order with basic answers to the symbolic problems of human and social existence' (Eisenstadt and Curelaru 1976:363). Weber's concept of *Wirtschaftsethik* is given as an example.
9. See Robertson (1978:128–43 and 176–81). Habermas does not use these terms. See Habermas (1973:117–43).
10. Arguing against those—notably Althusser—who see a move away from the individual-society antinomy in Marx's work, Dumont (1977) in effect argues that Marx tended to talk in terms of the release of the individual from societality.
11. A cognitive genealogy has been claimed by Althusserians with respect to this set of problems, in reference to Spinoza's attempt to link synthetically in a master process the realms of subjectivity, societality and absoluteness. (Althusser, 1972.) More generally, see Tillich (1967).

12. The next few paragraphs have roots in Nettl and Robertson (1968). See also Habermas (1974), Habermas (1975), Poggi (1973), and Dumont (1977).

13. In effect we are claiming here that two of the four main nineteenth-century attitudes toward the question of social autonomy were *particularly* worrisome to the classical sociologists.

14. The major attempts to co-ordinate Weber and Durkheim in this respect are Parsons (1937) and Berger and Luckmann (1966). It must also be acknowledged that Berger and Luckmann have for long stood out in recognizing the significance of identity as a pivotal sociological theme. In a sense the present essay underlines the importance of their recognition of that theme, although the perspective offered here differs in many respects. See also Luckmann (1967), Berger (1966), Berger (1967), and Berger *et al.* (1974). (In the latter — see especially p. 196 — Berger and his colleagues give particular attention to the emergence of the individual as a topic of modern sociological interest. See also in the same context, the emphasis upon the modern 'thematization of society'.)

15. Adorno *et al.* (1950). Fromm's early work, notably *Escape from Freedom* (1941), undoubtedly deserves more modern attention. See O'Brien (1976).

16. Particularly relevant here is Habermas' use of hermeneutical reflection in critical-theoretical perspective. In that respect Habermas draws upon Gadamer's (1975) 'rehabilitation of authority and tradition'. As Misgeld notes, Gadamer criticizes the Enlightenment 'for its abstract opposition of reason, authority and tradition, as if all tradition and all authority were unreasonable' (Misgeld 1976:165). However, Habermas' ambiguities about tradition and its authoritativeness lead to many difficulties, as Misgeld notes. (See also Bernstein 1976:219–36.) A major implication of the present essay is that the relationship between identity and authority is '*coded*' differently across the major contexts of civilizations and societies and that that in fact is the 'deep structure' *of tradition*.

17. As with all such generalizations there are bound to be exceptions. One of the most important such exceptions in this case is the work of Riesman (1950; 1954). However, although Riesman's work was clearly a case of the sociologist taking the individual seriously, the crucial factors of the *generalized* modern relationships between individual and social system were overlooked in his work. On the problems of identity in the case of a high degree of differentiation of the social system from the individual level (with specific reference to Riesman's work) see Parsons and White (in Parsons 1964:183–235).

18. At the same time the subjectlessness of much of 'mainstream' sociology in the post-World War II period never, of course, involved biting the bullet and going in for a philosophically-grounded sociology-without-a-subject on the French structuralist (and structuralism-related) model. (See the following footnote.)

19. This perhaps is the most appropriate point at which to say a few words about the thorny subject of Goffman's work on self, identity and interaction. Long regarded by many as a 'symbolic interactionist' with special concern for the everyday 'creativity' of the individual, Goffman's work has become increasingly distant from that perspective. In this respect we would agree with Gonos (1977:865): 'Far from grounding his analysis in the existence of everyday selves, as is gathered by many commentators from a reading of the *Presentation of Self* (1959), Goffman has almost singlehandedly among American micro-sociologists worked to undermine this possible grounding'. Gonos's argument is that Goffman is a *structuralist* — which specifically means in this context that Goffman sees *frames* as being prior to action and interaction. Goffman 'identifies well-defined worlds wherein action takes place' (857). Such frames are defined by the stable laws of their operation — Laws of which, as it were, individuals partake. While being persuaded of this feature of Goffman's analysis — notably in *Frame Analysis* (1974) — it is important to point-up the similarities between Gonos's interpretation of Goffman and the work of Simmel (to whom Goffman has of course paid tribute). For Simmel himself — in Kantian mode — emphasized that the individual always acts in terms of 'worlds', which have their own inner-laws of operation. Indeed Simmel's whole conception of *form* is built along these lines. And it is also important to note that for Simmel *the individual* is a form —

there being 'laws' of individualism. Moreover, even the structuralist interpretation of Goffman does not render inappropriate the more conventional view that Goffman seeks to make sociological space for the individual. For the more that the individual operates in terms of the 'laws' of framed activities the more room, so to speak, there is for the cultivation of an *inner* self. On the other hand, both Goffman and Simmel clearly show the possibilities of definite *sociological* analysis of the individual (which symbolic inter-actionists do not). On Simmel in this connection see his essay on 'Fashion', in Simmel (1971:294–323).

20. There is interesting overlap between Simmel's views and those of Durkheim in his essay 'The Dualism of Human Nature and its Social Conditions' (Durkheim *et al.* 1960:325–40). However, in spite of agreement on the dualistic nature of the individual Durkheim and Simmel depart with respect to the former's emphasis upon the spirituality of the social part of the individual.

21. Freud's notion of identification was in any case only loosely formed in his own work. The notorious fuzziness about Freud's meaning in this respect gives plenty of latitude for reformulation.

22. Freud addressed this problem indirectly in referring to what he called 'the psychological poverty of groups'. Freud maintained—in pejorative mode—that in modern America 'the bonds of society are chiefly constituted by the identification of its members with one another, while individuals of the leader type do not acquire the importance that should fall to them in the formation of a group' (Freud 1961:62–3). Our claim is that Freud was unintentionally pointing-up the American identity-authority code in these remarks. See Chapter One—pp. 31–39 of this volume and *infra.*, pp. 260ff.)

23. On this compare the emphasis upon contradiction in Bell (1975) and the simultaneous emphasis upon contradiction *and* complementarity in Touraine (1977:65–116).

24. For an interesting in-effect attempt to decipher the general code of identity construction, see Guiot (1977).

25. In this connection Freud's (1961:62–3) comment on 'the psychological problem' of American society—namely identification *with others*—is again relevant.

26. Of modern social scientists Dumont stands out as having contributed a great deal to this matter. See Dumont (1972; 1977) and works listed in the former: 244–5. We note again Swanson's many contributions to this theme.

27. Among recent essays which have implications for this issue: Ekeh's (1974) comparison of French and American approaches to the phenomenon of social exchange. This is also an appropriate point at which to mention that Etzioni's (1961; 1968) elaborate interest in patterns of *compliance* on a comparative basis has some relevance to the general concerns of the present essay.

References

CHAPTER 1

Adorno, T. W. *et al.* (1950) *The Authoritarian Personality*. New York: Harper.

Anderson, A. R. and Omar K. Moore (1969) 'Some Principles for the Design of Clarifying Educational Environments.' In David Goslin (ed.), *Handbook of Socialization Theory and Research*. Chicago: Rand McNally: 571–613.

Anderson, Perry (1974) *Lineages of the Absolutist State*. London: NLB.

Banton, Michael (1965) *Roles*. London: Tavistock.

Bellah, Robert (1970) *Beyond Belief*. New York: Harper and Row.

Berger, Peter *et al.* (1973) *The Homeless Mind*. New York: Random.

Binder, Leonard (1964) *The Ideological Revolution in the Middle East*. New York: Wiley.

Blau, Peter M. (1974) 'Presidential Address: Parameters of Social Structure.' *American Sociological Review* 39:615–35.

—— (1977) *Inequality and Heterogeneity: A Primitive Theory of Social Structure*. New York: Free Press.

Bourdieu, Pierre (1977, 1972) *Outline of a Theory of Practice*. Cambridge, England: Cambridge University Press.

Brittan, Arthur (1973) *Meanings and Situations*. Boston: Routledge.

Coleman, James S. (1971) 'Collective Decisions.' In Herman Turk and Richard Simpson (eds.), *Institutions and Social Exchange*. Indianapolis: Bobbs-Merrill: Ch. 17.

—— (1973) 'Loss of Power.' *American Sociological Review*, 38:1–17.

Cressey, Donald (1972) *Criminal Organization*. London: Heinemann.

Douglas, Mary (1966) *Purity and Danger*. London: Routledge.

—— (1970) *Natural Symbols*. London: Barrie and Rockliff.

Dumont, Louis (1970) *From Mandeville to Marx*. Chicago: Chicago University Press.

—— (1972, 1967) *Homo Hierarchicus*. London: Paladin.

Durkheim, Emile and Marcel Mauss (1963, 1903) *Primitive Classification*. Chicago: Chicago University Press.

Eisenstadt, S. N. (1978) *Revolution and the Transformation of Societies*. New York: Free Press.

Etzioni, Amitai (1961) *A Comparative Analysis of Complex Organizations*. New York: Free Press.

—— (1968) *The Active Society*. New York: Free Press.

Firth, Raymond (1973) *Symbols*. Ithaca: Cornell University Press.

Gamson, William A. (1975) *The Strategy of Protest*. Homewood, Illinois: Dorsey.

Gerth, Hans H. and C. Wright Mills (1954) *Character and Social Structure*. London: Routledge.

Gluckman, Max (ed.) (1972) *The Allocation of Responsibility*. Manchester: Manchester University Press.

Gonos, George (1977) '"Situation" versus "Frame"; The "Interactionist" and the "Structuralist" Analyses of Everyday Life.' *American Sociological Review* 42:833–53.

Gough, J. W. (1957) *The Social Contract Debate*. Oxford: Clarendon.

Guiot, Jean M. (1977) 'Attribution and Identity Construction: Some Comments.' *American Sociological Review* 42:692–704.

Habermas, Jürgen (1972, 1968) *Knowledge and Human Interests.* London: Heinemann.
—— (1975, 1973) *Legitimation Crisis.* Boston: Beacon Press.
Heap, James L. and Philip A. Roth (1973) 'On Phenomenological Sociology'. *American Sociological Review* 38:354–67.
Heidegger, Martin (1969) *Identity and Difference.* New York: Harper and Row.
Hirschman, Albert O. (1970) *Exit, Voice, and Loyalty.* Cambridge, Mass.: Harvard University Press.
Holzner, Burkart (1965) 'Observer and Agent in the Social Process.' *Archives of Social and Legal Philosophy* LIII.
—— (1972) *Reality Construction in Society.* Cambridge: Schenkman.
—— (1973) 'Sociological Reflections on Trust.' *Humanitas* IX:333–47.
—— (1974) 'Comments on Heap and Roth.' *American Sociological Review* 39:286–9.
Imersheim, Allen W. (1977) 'The Epistemological Bases of Social Order: Toward Ethnoparadigm Analysis.' *Sociological Methodology*: 1–51.
Kemper, Theodore D. (1974) 'On the Nature and Purpose of Ascription.' *American Sociological Review* 39:844–53.
Lasch, Christopher (1978) *Haven in a Heartless World.* New York: Basic Books.
Leach, Edmund (1965) *The Political Systems of Highland Burma.* London: Athlone Press.
Lévi-Strauss, Claude (1968, 1958) *Structural Anthropology.* New York: Basic Books.
Lidz, Charles W. and Victor M. Lidz (1976) 'Piaget's Psychology of Intelligence and the Theory of Action.' In Jan J. Loubser *et al.* (eds.), *Explorations in General Theory in Social Science.* New York: Free Press: Ch. 8.
Lofland, John (1969) *Deviance and Identity.* Englewood Cliffs: Prentice-Hall.
Lofland, Lyn H. (1973) *A World of Strangers.* New York: Basic Books.
MacIntyre, Alasdair (1967) *A Short History of Ethics.* London: Routledge.
Martins, Herminio (1972) 'The Kuhnian "Revolution" and Its Implications for Sociology.' In T. J. Nossiter *et al.* (eds.), *Imagination and Precision in the Social Sciences.* London: Faber: 13–58.
—— (1974) 'Time and Theory in Sociology.' In John Rex (ed.), *Approaches to Sociology.* Boston: Routledge: 246–94.
Mauss, Marcel (1968) 'A Category of the Human Spirit.' *Psychoanalytic Review* 55:457–81.
Mayhew, Leon (1968) 'Ascription in Modern Societies.' *Sociological Inquiry* 38:105–20.
McCannell, Dean (1975) Review of Lyn H. Lofland, *A World of Strangers. American Journal of Sociology* 80:1026.
McHugh, Peter *et al.* (1974) *On the Beginning of Social Inquiry.* London: Routledge.
Moore, Omar K. and A. R. Anderson (1960) 'Autotelic Folk Models.' *Sociological Quarterly* 1:203–16.
Morris, Colin (1972) *The Discovery of the Individual 1050–1200.* New York: Harper Torchbooks.
Nadel, S. F. (1957) *Theory of Social Structure.* Oxford: Clarendon Press.
Nairn, Tom (1975) 'The Modern Janus.' *New Left Review* 94:3–29.
Needham, Rodney (ed.) (1974) *Right and Left.* Chicago: Chicago University Press.

Nelson, Benjamin (1965) 'Self Images and Systems of Spiritual Direction in the History of European Civilization.' In Samuel Z. Klausner (ed.), *The Quest for Self-Control*. New York: Doubleday: 49–103.

— — (1973) 'Civilizational Complexes and Intercivilizational Encounters.' *Sociological Analysis* 34 (Summer):79–105.

Nettl, J. P. and Roland Robertson (1968) *International Systems and the Modernization of Societies*. New York: Basic Books and London: Faber.

Olson, Mancur Jr. (1965) *The Logic of Collective Action*. Cambridge, Mass.: Harvard University Press.

O'Neill, John (ed.) (1973) *Modes of Individualism and Collectivism*. London: Heinemann.

Parsons, Talcott (1951) *The Social System*. New York: Free Press.

— — (1968) 'The Position of Identity in the General Theory of Action.' In Chad Gordon and Kenneth J. Gergen (eds.), *The Self in Social Interaction*. New York: Wiley:11–24.

— — (1975) 'Some Theoretical Considerations on the Nature and Trends of Change of Ethnicity.' In Nathan Glazer and Daniel P. Moynihan (eds.), *Ethnicity: Theory and Experience*. Cambridge, Mass.: Harvard University Press: 53–83.

Parsons, Talcott *et al.* (eds.) (1961) *Theories of Society*. New York: Free Press.

Parsons, Talcott and Gerald M. Platt (1973) *The American University*. Cambridge, Mass.: Harvard University Press.

Paz, Octavio (1971, 1967) *Claude Lévi-Strauss: An Introduction*. London: Cape.

Poster, Mark (1975) *Existential Marxism in Postwar France*. Princeton: Princeton University Press.

Robertson, Roland (1968) 'Strategic Relations Between National Societies.' *Journal of Conflict Resolution* XII (March):16–33.

— — (1970) *The Sociological Interpretation of Religion*. Oxford: Blackwell; New York: Schocken.

— — (1974) 'Towards Identification of the Major Axes of Sociological Analysis'. In John Rex (ed.), *Approaches to Sociology*. London: Routledge: Ch. 5.

— — (1976) 'Societal Attributes and International Relations.' In Jan. J. Loubser *et al.* (eds.), *Explorations in General Theory in Social Science*. New York: Free Press: 713–35.

— — (1977) 'Individualism, Societalism, Worldliness, Universalism: Thematizing Theoretical Sociology of Religion.' *Sociological Analysis* 38:281–308.

— — (1978) *Meaning and Change: Explorations in the Cultural Sociology of Modern Societies*. Oxford: Blackwell and New York: New York University Press.

Robertson, Roland and Laurie Taylor (1973) *Deviance, Crime and Socio-Legal Control*. London: Martin Robertson.

Sahlins, Marshall (1976) *Culture and Practical Reason*. Chicago: Chicago University Press.

Schelling, Thomas (1963) *The Strategy of Conflict*. New York: Galaxy.

Schneider, David M. (1968) *American Kinship: A Cultural Account*. Englewood Cliffs: Prentice-Hall.

Schneider, David M. and Raymond T. Smith (1973) *Class Differences and Sex Roles in American Kinship and Family Structure*. Englewood Cliffs: Prentice-Hall.

Scott, Marvin B. and Stanford M. Lyman (1968) 'Accounts.' *American Sociological Review* 33:46–62.

Service, Elman R. (1975) *The Origins of the State and Civilization.* New York: Norton.

Spradley, James T. (ed.) (1972) *Culture and Cognition.* San Francisco: Chandler.

Swanson, Guy E. (1960) *The Birth of the Gods.* Ann Arbor: University of Michigan Press.

—— (1967) *Religion and Regime.* Ann Arbor: University of Michigan Press.

—— (1968) 'To Live in Concord with a Society.' In Albert Riess (ed.), *Cooley and Sociological Analysis.* Ann Arbor: University of Michigan Press: 87–150 and 165–72.

—— (1971) 'An Organizational Analysis of Collectivities.' *American Sociological Review* 36:607–24.

Tiryakian, Edward A. (1970) 'Structural Sociology.' In John C. McKinney and Edward A. Tiryakian (eds.), *Theoretical Sociology.* New York: Appleton-Century-Crofts: Ch. 4.

Torrance, John (1974) 'Max Weber: Methods and the Man.' *European Journal of Sociology* 15:127–65.

Touraine, Alain (1977, 1973) *The Self-Production of Society.* Chicago: Chicago University Press.

Travisano, Roland V. (1970) 'Alternation and Conversion as Qualitatively Different Transformations.' In Gregory P. Stone and Harvey A. Farberman (eds.), *Social Psychology Through Symbolic Interaction.* Waltham, Mass.: Ginn-Blaisdell: Ch. 59.

Turner, Victor (1969) *The Ritual Process.* Chicago: Chicago University Press.

Ullmann, Walter (1966) *The Individual and Society in the Middle Ages.* Baltimore: Johns Hopkins Press.

Wallace, Anthony F. C. (1956) 'Revitalization Movements: Some Theoretical Considerations for Their Comparative Study.' *American Anthropologist* 58:264–81.

Wallerstein, Immanuel (1975) *The Modern World System.* New York: Academic Press.

Warner, R. Stephen (1978) 'Toward a Redefinition of Action Theory.' *American Journal of Sociology* 83:1317–49.

Weber, Max (1948, 1920) 'The Protestant Sects and the Spirit of Capitalism.' In H. H. Gerth and C. Wright Mills (eds.), *From Max Weber.* London: Routledge: Ch. 12.

—— (1968, 1922) *Economy and Society.* Totowa: Bedminster Press.

Weinstein, Fred and Gerald M. Platt (1973) *Psychoanalytic Sociology.* Baltimore: Johns Hopkins University Press.

Wilson, Bryan (1973) *Magic and the Millenium.* New York: Harper and Row.

—— (1975) *The Noble Savages.* Berkeley, Los Angeles, London: University of California Press.

Wrong, Dennis (1977) *Skeptical Sociology.* New York: Columbia University Press.

CHAPTER 2

Abrams, M. H. (1971) *Natural Supernaturalism: Tradition and Revolution in Romantic Literature*. New York: Norton.

Balazs, Etienne (1964) *Chinese Civilization and Bureaucracy: Variations on a Theme*. New Haven: Yale University Press.

Barbu, Zevedei (1960) *Problems of Historical Psychology*. New York: Grove.

Barthelme, Donald (1972) *Sadness*. New York: Farrar, Straus and Giroux.

Bays, Gwendolyn (1964) *The Orphic Vision: Seer Poets from Novalis to Rimbaud*. Lincoln: University of Nebraska Press.

Bowker, John (1970) *Problems of Suffering in Religions of the World*. Cambridge, England: Cambridge University Press.

Bruford, W. H. (1975) *The German Tradition of Self-cultivation: 'Bildung' From Humboldt to Thomas Mann*. Cambridge, England: Cambridge University Press.

Burke, Peter (1972) *Culture and Society in Renaissance Italy 1420–1540*. London: B. T. Batsford Ltd.

Cawelti, John G. (1965) *Apostles of the Self-Made Man*. Chicago: The University of Chicago Press.

Chan, Marie (1974) 'Chinese Heroic Poems and European Epic.' *Comparative Literature* 26 (Spring): 142–168.

—— (1969) 'Nothingness and the Mother Principle in Early Chinese Taoism.' *International Philosophical Quarterly* 9 (September): 391–405.

Contag, Victoria (1970) *Chinese Masters of the 17th Century*. Rutland, Vt.: Charles E. Tuttle.

Craig, Albert M. and Donald H. Shively (eds.) (1970) *Personality in Japanese History*. Berkeley: University of California Press.

de Bary, Wm. Theodore and the Conference on Ming Thought (1970) *Self and Society in Ming Thought*. New York: Columbia University Press.

Dijksterhuis, E. J. (1961) *The Mechanization of the World Picture*. London: Oxford University Press.

Dodds, E. R. (1970) *Pagan and Christian in an Age of Anxiety: Some Aspects of Religious Experience from Marcus Aurelius to Constantine*. New York: Norton.

Dudley, Edward and Maximillian E. Novak (eds.) (1972) *The Wild Man Within: An Image in Western Thought from the Renaissance to Romanticism*. Pittsburgh: University of Pittsburgh Press.

Dumézil, Georges (1970) *The Destiny of the Warrior*. Chicago: The University of Chicago Press.

Dupré, Louis (1974) 'The Mystical Experience of the Self and Its Philosophical Significance.' *International Philosophical Quarterly* 14 (December): 495–511.

Durkheim, Emile (1947) *The Division of Labor in Society*. Glencoe, Ill.: Free Press.

Eisenstadt, S. N. (ed.) (1968) *Max Weber on Charisma and Institution Building*. Chicago: The University of Chicago Press.

Erikson, Erik H. (ed.) (1965) *The Challenge of Youth*. Garden City, N.Y.: Anchor Books.

—— (1962) *Young Man Luther: A Study in Psychoanalysis and History*. New York: Norton.

Falk, Nancy E. (1973) 'Wilderness and Kingship in Ancient South Asia.' *History of Religions* 13 (August): 1–15.

Gay, Peter (1970) *Weimar Germany: The Outsider as Insider.* New York: Harper & Row.

Gierke, Otto (1934) *Natural Law and the Theory of Society, 1500 to 1800. Vol I.* Cambridge, England: Cambridge University Press.

Goffman, Erving (1974) *Frame Analysis: An Essay on the Organization of Experience.* New York: Harper & Row.

—— (1967) *Interaction Ritual: Essays on Face-to-Face Behavior.* Garden City, N.Y.: Doubleday.

— — (1959) *The Presentation of Self in Everyday Life.* Garden City, N.Y.: Doubleday.

Gouldner, Alvin W. (1969) *The Hellenic World: A Sociological Analysis.* New York: Harper & Row.

Hauser, Arnold (1965) *Mannerism: The Crisis of the Renaissance and the Origins of Modern Art.* 2 Volumes. New York: Knopf.

Hodgson, Marshall G. S. (1974) *The Venture of Islam: Conscience and History in a World Civilization, Vol. I.* Chicago: The University of Chicago Press.

Huizinga, J. (1954) *The Waning of the Middle Ages.* Garden City, N.Y.: Doubleday.

Jung, G. and W. Pauli (1955) *The Interpretation of Nature and the Psyche.* New York: Pantheon.

Kavolis, Vytautas (1974a) 'Arts, Social and Economic Aspects of the.' Pp. 102–22 of the *Encyclopaedia Britannica*, 15th ed., Vol. 2.

—— (1974b) 'Paradigms of Order: Nature, the Factory, Art.' *Salmagundi* 26 (Spring): 69–84.

—— (1970) 'Post-modern Man: Psychocultural Responses to Social Trends.' *Social Problems* 17 (Spring): 435–48.

Klausner, Samuel Z. (ed.) (1965) *The Quest for Self-Control: Classical Philosophies and Scientific Research.* New York: Free Press.

Kohn, Melvin L. (1971) 'Bureaucratic Man: A Portrait and an Interpretation.' *American Sociological Review* 36 (June): 461–74.

Leites, Edmund (1974) 'Conscience, Casuistry, and Moral Decision: Some Historical Perspectives.' *Journal of Chinese Philosophy* 2 (December):41–58.

Lifton, Robert Jay (1970) *Boundaries: Psychological Man in Revolution.* New York: Vintage.

—— (1965) 'Youth and History: Individual Change in Postwar Japan.' Pp. 260–90 of *Erikson* (1965)

Martindale, Don (1962) *Social Life and Cultural Change.* Princeton, N.J.: D. Van Nostrand.

Maslow, Abraham H. (1961) 'Peak-Experiences as Acute Identity-Experiences.' *American Journal of Psychoanalysis* 21:254–60.

McIntosh, James (1976) 'Emerson's Unmoored Self.' *The Yale Review* 65 (Winter): 232–40.

Miller, Daniel R. and Guy E. Swanson (1958) *The Changing American Parent: A Study in the Detroit Area.* New York: Wiley.

Misch, Georg (1973) *A History of Autobiography in Antiquity.* Westport, Conn.: Greenwood Press, 1973.

Monier-Williams, Sir (1899) *A Sanskrit-English Dictionary, Etymologically and Philosophy Arranged with Special Reference to Cognate Indo-European Languages.* New Edition. Oxford: Clarendon Press.

Morris, Colin (1972) *The Discovery of the Individual 1050-1200.* New York: Harper Torchbooks.

Nakamura, Hajime (1964) *Ways of Thinking of Eastern Peoples: India/ China/Tibet/Japan, Revised Translation.* Honolulu, Hawaii: East-West Center Press.

Needham, Joseph (1969) *The Grand Titration: Science and Society in East and West.* London: George Allen and Unwin.

Nelson, Benjamin (1965) 'Self-Images and Systems of Spiritual Direction in The History of European Civilization.' Pp. 49–103 of *Klausner* (1965).

Nelson, Benjamin and Vytautas Kavolis (1973) 'The Civilization-Analytical Approach to Comparative Studies.' *Comparative Civilizations Bulletin* 5 (Spring): 13–14.

Nisbet, Robert (1973) *The Social Philosophers: Community and Conflict in Western Thought.* New York: Crowell.

Opitz, Peter-Joachim (1967) *Lao-tzu. Die Ordnungsspekulation in Tao-tê-ching.* München: Paul List Verlag.

Organ, Troy Wilson (1964) *The Self in Indian Philosophy.* The Hague: Mouton.

Otto, Walter F. (1965) *Dionysus: Myth and Cult.* Bloomington: Indiana University Press.

Passmore, John (1970) *The Perfectibility of Man.* New York: Charles Scribner's Sons.

Paz, Octavio (1974) *Conjunctions and Disjunctions.* New York: The Viking Press.

Pelzel, John C. (1970) 'Human Nature in the Japanese Myths.' Pp. 29–56 of *Craig and Shiveley* (1970).

Praz, Mario (1951) *The Romantic Agony*, 2nd Ed. London: Oxford University Press.

Ricketts, Mac Linscott (1966) 'The North American Indian Trickster.' *History of Religions* 5 (Winter): 327–50.

Ritterbush, Philip C. (1968) *The Art of Organic Forms.* City of Washington: Smithsonian Institution Press.

Scholem, Gershom G. (1941) *Major Trends in Jewish Mysticism*, Revised Edition. New York: Schocken Books.

Sorokin, Pitirim A. (1951) *Social Philosophies of an Age of Crisis.* Boston: Beacon Press.

Sprigge, Elizabeth (1949) *The Strange Life of August Strindberg.* New York: Macmillan.

Strauss, Leo (1953) *Natural Right and History.* Chicago. The University of Chicago Press.

Swanson, Guy E. (1973) 'The Search for a Guardian Spirit: A Process of Empowerment in Simpler Societies.' *Ethnology* 12 (July): 359–78.

Tiryakian, Edward A. (1972) 'Toward the Sociology of Esoteric Culture.' *American Journal of Sociology* 78 (November): 491–512.

Tocqueville, Alexis de (1957) *Democracy in America, Vol. II.* New York: Vintage Books.

Turner, Victor W. (1974) *Dramas, Fields, and Metaphors: Symbolic Action in Human Society.* Ithaca, N.Y.: Cornell University Press.

—— (1967) *The Forest of Symbols: Aspects of Ndembu Ritual.* Ithaca, N.Y.: Cornell University Press.

—— (1969) *The Ritual Process: Structure and Anti-Structure.* Chicago: Aldine Publishing Company.

Wallace, Anthony F. C. (1956) 'Revitalization Movements.' *American Anthropologist* 58 (April): 264–81.

Weber, Max (1964) *The Sociology of Religion.* Boston: Beacon Press.

—— (1968) *Economy and Society.* New York: Bedminster Press.

White, Hayden (1972) 'The Forms of Wildness: Archeology of an Idea.' Pp. 3–38 of *Dudley and Novak* (1972).

White, Lynn, Jr. (1971) 'Culture Climates and Technological Advance in the Middle Ages.' *Viator: Medieval and Renaissance Studies* 2: 171–201.

Wolff, Kurt H., ed. (1964) *The Sociology of Georg Simmel.* New York: The Free Press of Glencoe.

Zimmerman, Joe (1975) 'If It's Inside That Counts, Why Not Count It? I: Self-Recording of Feelings and Treatment by "Self-Implosion".' *The Psychological Record* 25 (Winter): 3–16.

CHAPTER 3

Almond, Gabriel A. and J. S. Coleman (eds.) (1960) *The Politics of Developing Areas.* Princeton, N.J.: Princeton University Press.

Almond, Gabriel A. and Sidney Verba (1963) *The Civic Culture.* Princeton, N.J.: Princeton University Press.

Avineri, Shlomo (1972) *Hegel's Theory of the Modern State.* Cambridge, U.K.: Cambridge University Press.

Barnard, Chester (1938) *The Functions of the Executive.* Cambridge, Mass.: Harvard University Press (1962 printing).

Bauer, Raymond A. (1955) *Nine Soviet Portraits.* New York: Technology Press & John Wiley & Sons.

Baum, Rainer C. (1962) 'Values and Organized Labor in Canada.' M.A. Thesis in Sociology, University of British Columbia.

—— (1969) 'Industrial Society and Democracy.' Pp. 594–607 in Gerson, Waltex M. (ed.), *Social Problems in a Changing World.* New York: Thomas Y. Crowell Company.

—— (1972) 'On Political Modernity: stratification and the generation of societal power.' Pp. 22–49 in Harvey, Edward B. (ed.), *Perspectives on Modernization: essays in memory of Ian Weinberg.* Toronto: University of Toronto Press.

—— (1974) 'Beyond Convergence: Toward Theoretical Relevance in Quantitative Modernization Research.' *Sociological Inquiry* 44 (4):225–40.

—— (1975) 'The System of Solidarities.' *Indian Journal of Social Research.* Vol. XVI, No. 1 & 2:306–53.

—— (1976) 'On Societal Media Dynamics.' Chapter 24 in Loubser, J. J., *et al.* (eds.), *Explorations in General Theory in Social Science.* New York: Free Press, especially section: The Nature of the Code and the Nature of Value Inflation and Value Deflation.

Baum, Rainer C. and Martha Baum (1975) 'The Aged and Diachronic Solidarity in Modern Society.' *Intl. Journal of Aging and Human Development.* Vol. 6, No. 4: 329–46.

Bellah, Robert N. (1960) 'Father and Son In Christianity and Confucianism.' Paper read at the annual meeting of the American Society for the Study of Religion, New York City; also Chapter 5 in Bellah, R.N., *Beyond Belief.* New York: Harper & Row, 1970.

—— (1964) 'Religious Evolution.' *American Sociological Review*, 29, 3 (June): 358–74.

—— (1967) 'Civil Religion in America.' *Daedalus* 96 (Winter): 1–21.

—— (1968) 'Response.' Pp. 388–93 in Cutler, Donald R. (ed.), *The Religious Situation: 1968*. Boston: Beacon Press.

Bendix, Reinhard (1947) 'Bureaucracy: The Problem and its Setting.' *American Sociological Review* 12 (October): 493–507.

—— (1956) *Work and Authority in Industry*. New York: John Wiley.

—— (1964) *Nation-Building and Citizenship*. New York: John Wiley.

—— (1967) 'Tradition and Modernity Reconsidered.' *Comparative Studies in Society and History* 9, 3:292–346.

Bernstein, Marver (1955) *Regulating Business by Independent Commission*. Princeton, N.J.: Princeton University Press.

Black, Cyril E. (1966) *The Dynamics of Modernization*. New York: Harper & Row.

Blau, Peter M. (1956) *Bureaucracy in Modern Society*. New York: Random House.

—— (1964) *The Dynamics of Bureaucracy*. Chicago: University of Chicago Press.

Bronfenbrenner, Urie (1962) Soviet Studies of Personality Development and Socialization. Ithaca, N.Y.: Cornell University, Cornell Soviet Studies Reprint No. 6.

—— (1970) *Two Worlds of Childhood US and USSR*. New York: Russell Sage Foundation.

Büsch, Otto (1962) *Militärsystem und Sozialleben im Alten Preussen*. Berlin: Walter de Gruyter & Company.

Castro, Americo (1954) *The Structure of Spanish History*. Princeton, N.J.: Princeton University Press.

Cooper vs. Roberts (1971–2) 45 *Temp. Law Quarterly*, 661.

Crozier, Michael (1964) *The Bureaucratic Phenomenon*. Chicago: University of Chicago Press.

Cutright, Phillips (1963) 'National Political Development.' *American Sociological Review* 28, 2 (April): 253–64.

—— (1965) 'Political Structure, Economic Development, and National Security Programs,' *American Journal of Sociology* LXX, 5 (March): 537–550.

—— (1967) 'Inequality: A Cross-National Analysis.' *American Sociological Review* 32, 4 (August): 562–78.

Dahrendorf, Ralf (1959) *Class and Class Conflict in Industrial Society*. Stanford, California: Stanford University Press.

—— (1965) *Gesellschaft und Demokratie in Deutschland*. München: R. Piper & Co.

De Schweinitz, Karl (1964) *Industrialization and Democracy*. New York: Free Press.

Deutsch, Karl W. (1970) *Politics and Government*. New York: Houghton Mifflin Co.

Dietrich, Richard (1966) *Kleine Geschichte Preussens*. Berlin: Haude & Spenersche Verlagsbuchhandlung.

Dore, Ronald (1973) *British Factory—Japanese Factory*. Berkeley, Calif.: University of California Press.

Eberhard, Wolfram (1967) *Guilt and Sin in Traditional China*. Berkeley, Calif.: University of California Press.

Eckstein, Harry (1961) *A Theory of Stable Democracy*. Princeton, N.J.: Princeton University Center of International Studies Research Monograph No. 10.
—— (1966) *Division and Cohesion in Democracy*. Princeton, N.J.: Princeton University Press.
Eisenstadt, S. N. (1963) *The Political System of Empires*. New York: Free Press.
—— (1968) (ed.) *The Protestant Ethic and Modernization*. New York: Basic Books.
—— (1971a) *Social Differentiation and Stratification*. Glenview, Ill.: Scott, Foresman & Co.
—— (1971b) *From Generation to Generation*. New York: Free Press.
—— (1973) 'Post Traditional Societies and the Continuity and Reconstruction of Tradition.' *Daedalus* (Winter): 1–27.
Erikson, Erik (1963) *Childhood and Society*. New York: W. W. Norton & Co.
—— (1964) 'Human Strength and the Cycle of Generations.' Pp. 111–57 in Erikson, Erik (ed.), *Insight and Responsibility*. New York: W. W. Norton & Co.
Fetscher, Irving (1970) *Hegel's Lehre vom Menschen*. Stuttgart: Friedrich Frommann Verlag.
Field, Mark G. (1957) *Doctor and Patient in Soviet Russia*. Cambridge, Mass.: Harvard University Press.
Fischer, George (1968) *The Soviet System and Modern Society*. New York: Atherton Press.
Flanigan, Wm. H. and E. Fogelman (1970) 'Patterns of Political Violence in Comparative Historical Perspective.' *Comparative Politics* 3, 1 (October): 1–20.
Fleron, Frederic J. (1973) 'System Attributes and Career Attributes: The Soviet Leadership System, 1952 to 1965.' Pp. 43–85 in Beck, Carl *et al.*, *Comparative Communist Political Leadership*. New York: David McKay Co., Inc.
Fox, Thomas and S. M. Miller (1966) 'Intra-Country Variations.' Pp. 574–81 in Bendix, R. and S. M. Lipset (eds.), *Class, Status, and Power*. New York: Free Press.
Geyl, P. (1964) *History of the Low Countries*. London: Macmillan.
Gilison, Jerome M. (1972) *British and Soviet Politics*. Baltimore: The Johns Hopkins University Press.
Gould, Mark (1976) 'Systems Analysis, Macrosociology and the Generalized Media of Social Action,' Pp. 470–506 in Loubser, Jan *et al.* (eds.), *Explorations in General Theory in Social Science*. New York: Free Press.
Gray vs. Grunnagle (1966–7) 28 *University of Pittsburgh Law Review*, 509.
Gurr, Ted R. (1974) 'Persistence and Change in Political Systems, 1800–1970.' *American Political Science Review* 63, 4 (December): 1482–1504.
Gurr, Ted R. and Muriel McClelland (1971) Political Performance: A Twelve Nation Study. *Sage Comparative Politics Series* Vol. 2, No. 01–018.
Gusfield, Joseph R. (1967) 'Tradition and Modernity.' *American Journal of Sociology* 72 (January): 351–62.
Hackett, J. and A. Hackett (1963) *Economic Planning in France*. Cambridge, Mass.: Harvard University Press.
Harris, Walter D., Jr. (1971) *The Growth of Latin American Cities*. Athens, Ohio: Ohio University Press.
Hartmann, H. *et al.* (1946) 'Comments on the Formation of Psychic Structure.' *The Psychoanalytic Study of the Child*, 2:11–38.

Hayward, Jack (1973) *The One and Indivisible French Republic.* New York: W.
     W. Norton & Co.
Hegel, Georg W. F. (1837) *Vorlesungen über die Philosophie der Geschichte.*
     Berlin: Edward Gans; translated quote from Loewenberg, J. (ed.) *Hegel
     Selections.* Chicago: Scribner's Sons, 1929.
Hintze, Otto (1941) 'Weltgeschichtliche Bedingungen der Representativ-
     verfassungen.' Pp. 130–76 in Hintze, Otto, *Staat und Verfassung,* Bd. I,
     Leipzig: Koehler & Amelang.
Hough, Jerry F. (1969) *The Soviet Prefects: The Local Party Organization in
     Industrial Decision-Making.* Cambridge, Mass.: Harvard University Press.
Huntington, Samuel P. (1968) *Political Order in Changing Societies.* New Haven,
     Conn.: Yale University Press.
Inkeles, Alex (1953) 'The Totalitarian Mystique: Some Impressions of the
     Dynamics of Totalitarian Society.' Pp. 87–108 in Friedrich, Carl J. (ed.)
     Totalitarianism. New York: Grosset & Dunlap.
——— (1975) 'The Emerging Social Structure of the World.' *World Politics* XXVII
     (July): 467–95.
Inkeles, Alex and Raymond A. Bauer (1959) *The Soviet Citizen.* Cambridge,
     Mass.: Harvard University Press.
Inkeles, Alex and David H. Smith (1974) *Becoming Modern.* Cambridge, Mass.:
     Harvard University Press.
Jacobson, W. D. (1972) *Power and Interpersonal Relation.* Belmont, California:
     Wadsworth Publishing Co.
Kerr, Clark *et al.* (1969) *Industrialism and Industrial Man.* New York: Oxford
     University Press.
Kolkowicz, Roman (1967) *The Soviet Military and the Communist Party.* Prin-
     ceton, N.J.: Princeton University Press.
Leiserson, Avery (1942) *Administrative Regulation.* Chicago, Ill.: University of
     Chicago Press.
Lijphart, Arend (1968a) *The Politics of Accommodation.* Berkeley, California:
     University of California Press.
——— (1968b) 'Typologies of Democratic Systems.' *Comparative Political Studies*
     (April): 3–44.
——— (1969) 'Consociational Democracy.' *World Politics* 21 (January): 207–25.
Linz, Juan (1964) 'An Authoritarian Regime: Spain.' Pp. 291–341 in Allardt, Erik
     and Y. Littunen (eds.), *Cleavages, Ideologies and Party Systems.* Helsinki:
     Academic Bookstore.
Lipset, Seymour M. (1960) *Political Man.* New York: Doubleday & Co.
Lipset, Seymour M. and S. Rokkan (1967) 'Cleavage Structures, Party Systems,
     and Voter Alignment: An Introduction.' Pp. 1–64 in Lipset, Seymour M. and
     S. Rokkan, *Party Systems and Voter Alignments.* New York: Free Press.
Luhmann, Niklas (1968) *Vertrauen,* Stuttgart: F. Enke.
Malloy, James (1974) 'Authoritarianism, Corporatism and Mobilization in Peru.'
     Pp. 52–84 in Pike, Frederick B. and T. Stritch (eds.), *The New Corporatism:
     Social-Political Structures in the Iberian World.* Notre Dame: University of
     Notre Dame Press.
Marshall, T. H. (1965) *Class, Citizenship and Social Development.* New York:
     Doubleday.
Mayhew, Leon (1968) *Law and Equal Opportunity.* Cambridge, Mass.: Harvard
     University.

—— (1971) *Society: Institutions and Activity.* Glenview, Ill.: Scott, Foresman & Co.

McClelland, David C. (1961) *The Achieving Society.* Princeton, N.J.: Van Nostrand.

—— (1964) 'The United States and Germany.' Pp. 62–92 in McClelland, David C., *The Roots of Consciousness.* Princeton, N.J.: Van Nostrand.

Meisel, Alan (1975) 'An Empirical Study of Informed Consent in Psychiatry.' Unpubl. Research Proposal with Roth, Lidz, and Walker, University of Pittsburgh, Western Psychiatric Institute and Clinic, Pittsburgh, Pa.,

Meyer, Alfred G. (1965) *The Soviet Political System.* New York: Random House.

Miller, Daniel and G. Swanson (1960) *Inner Conflict and Defense.* New York: Henry Holt.

Moore, Barrington, Jr. (1966) *The Social Origins of Dictatorship and Democracy* Boston: Beacon Press.

Naegele, Kaspar D. (1963) 'Youth and Society.' Pp. 43–63 in Erikson, Erik H. (ed.), *Youth: Change and Challenge.* New York: Basic Books.

Nettl, J. P. (1967) *Political Mobilization.* London: Faber & Faber Ltd.

Olsen, Marvin E. (1968) 'Multivariate Analysis of National Political Development.' *American Sociological Review* 33, 5 (October): 699–712.

Parsons, Talcott (1937) *The Structure of Social Action.* (Glencoe, Ill.: Free Press, 1949 edition).

—— (1945) 'The Problem of Controlled Institutional Change.' Pp. 238–74 in Parsons, T., *Essays in Sociological Theory.* Glencoe, Ill.: Free Press (1954 edition).

—— (1947) 'Certain Primary Sources and Patterns of Aggression in the Social Structure of the Western World.' Pp. 298–322 in Parsons, T. *Essays in Sociological Theory.* Glencoe, Ill.: Free Press (1954 edition).

—— (1951a) *The Social System.* Glencoe, Ill.: Free Press.

—— (1951b) *Toward a General Theory of Action.* Cambridge, Mass.: Harvard University Press (1959 edition).

—— (1953a) *Working Papers in the Theory of Action.* Glencoe, Ill.: Free Press.

—— (1953b) 'A Revised Analytical Approach to the Theory of Social Stratification.' Pp. 92–129 in Bendix, Reinhard and S. M. Lipset (eds.), *Class, Status, and Power.* Glencoe, Ill.: Free Press.

—— (1959) 'An Approach to Psychological Theory in Terms of the Theory of Action.' Pp. 612–711 in Koch, Sigmund (ed.), *Psychology: A Study of a Science.* Vol. III, New York: McGraw-Hill.

—— (1961) 'The Contribution of Psychoanalysis to Social Science.' *Psychoanalysis and Social Science* IV:28–38.

—— (1963a) 'On the Concept of Political Power.' *Proceedings of the American Philosophical Society* 107, 3:232–62.

—— (1963b) 'On the Concept of Influence.' *Public Opinion Quarterly* 27 (Spring): 37–62.

—— (1963c) 'Youth in the Context of American Society.' Pp. 93–119 in Erikson, Erik H. (ed.), *Youth: Change and Challenge.* New York: Basic Books.

—— (1964) 'Evolutionary Universals in Society. *American Sociological Review* 29, 3 (June): 339–57.

—— (1966) *Societies.* Englewood Cliffs, N.J.: Prentice Hall Inc.

—— (1968a) 'On the Concept of Value Commitments.' *Sociological Inquiry* 38 (Spring): 135–60.

—— (1968b) 'The Position of Identity in the General Theory of Action.' Pp. 11–23 in Gordon, Chad and K. Gergen (eds.), *The Self in Social Interaction*. New York: Wiley.

—— (1969a) 'Some Problems of General Theory in Sociology.' Pp. 27–68 in McKinney, John C. and E. Tiryakian (eds.), *Theoretical Sociology: Perspectives and Development*. New York: Appleton-Century-Crofts.

—— (1969b) *Politics and Social Structure*. New York: Free Press.

—— (1971) *The System of Modern Societies*. Englewood Cliffs, N.J.: Prentice Hall Inc.

Parsons, Talcott and R. F. Bales (1955) *Family, Socialization and Interaction Process*. Glencoe, Ill.: Free Press.

Parsons, Talcott and Neil J. Smelser (1956) *Economy and Society*. Glencoe, Ill.: Free Press.

Piers, Gerhard and M. D. Singer (1953) *Shame and Guilt*. Springfield, Ill.: Thomas Publ.

Ploss, Sidney (1965) *Conflict and Decision-Making in Soviet Russia*. Princeton, N.J.: Princeton University Press.

Pride, Richard A. (1970) Origins of Democracy. *Sage Comparative Politics Series* Vol. 1, No. 01–012.

Pye, Lucian W. (1966) *Aspects of Political Development*. Boston: Little, Brown & Co.

Riesman, David (1950) *The Lonely Crowd*. New Haven, Conn.: Yale University Press.

Riesman, David & Nathan Glazer (1952) *Faces in the Crowd*. New Haven: Yale.

Rogowski, Ronald and Lois Wasserspring (1971) 'Does Political Development Exist? Corporatism in Old and New Societies.' Sage Professional Paper, *Comparative Politics Series*, Vol. 2, No. 01–024.

Rokkan, Stein (1961) 'Mass suffrage, secret voting and political participation.' *European Journal of Sociology* 2 (1):132–54.

Rose, Arnold M. (1967) *The Power Structure*. New York: Oxford University Press.

Rose, R. and D. W. Urwin (1970) 'Persistence and Change in Western Party Systems Since 1945.' *Political Studies* 18:287–319.

Russell, Bertrand (1938) *Power*. London: G. Allen & Unwin.

Scheuch, Erwin K. (1972) 'Die Problematik der Freizeit in der Massengesellschaft.' Pp. 23–41 in Scheuch, Erwin K. and R. Meyerson (eds.), Soziologie der Freizeit. Köln Kiepenheuer & Witsch.

Schlottmann, Uwe (1968) *Primäre und Sekundäre Indivualität*. Stuttgart: F. Enke.

Schmitter, Phillipe C. (1971) *Interest Conflict and Political Change in Brazil*. Stanford: Stanford University Press.

Schneider, D. M. (1968) *American Kinship: A Cultural Account*. Englewood Cliffs, N.J.: Prentice Hall Inc.

Schoenbaum, David (1966) *Hitler's Social Revolution*. Garden City, N.Y.: Doubleday & Co., Inc.

Schoeps, Hans-Joachim (1966) *Preussen: Geschichte eines Staates*. Berlin: Propyläen Verlag.

Schonfeld, Wm. R. (1971) Youth and Authority in France. *Sage Comparative Politics Series* 2, No. 01–014.

Smelser, Neil J. (1959) *Social Change in the Industrial Revolution*. Chicago: University of Chicago Press.

—— (1962) *Theory of Collective Behavior.* (New York: Free Press paperback edition, 1971).

Sternberger, D. (1968) 'Legitimacy.' Pp. 244–8 in Sills, D. (ed.) *International Encyclopedia of the Social Sciences.* Vol. 9, New York: Free Press.

Stevens, Evelyn (1974) 'Mexico's PRI: The Institutionalization of Corporatism.' Paper read at the IPSA Convention, Chicago: September.

Stewart, Philip D. (1969) 'Soviet Interest Groups and the Policy Process: The Repeal of Production Education.' *World Politics* 22, 1 (October): 29–50.

Swanson, Guy (1967) *Religion and Regime.* Ann Arbor, Mich.: University of Michigan Press.

Tannenbaum, Frank (1965) *Ten Keys to Latin America.* New York: A. Knopf.

Wallerstein, Immanuel (1974) *The Modern World System: Origins of Capitalist Agriculture in the Sixteenth Century.* New York: Academic Press.

Weber, Max (1918) 'Science as a Vocation.' Pp. 129–56 in Gerth, H. H. and C. Wright Mills (eds. and translators), *From Max Weber.* New York: Oxford University Press (1964).

—— (1922) *Economy and Society* (Roth, G., translator and editor), New York: Bedminster Press (1968).

—— (1916–17) *The Religion of India.* New York: Free Press paperback edition (1968).

Whyte, Wm. F. (1961) *Men at Work.* Homewood, Ill.: Richard D. Irwin & Dorsey Press.

Wiarda, Howard J. (1971) 'Toward a Framework for the Study of Political Change in the Iberic-Latin Tradition: The Corporative Model.' Paper read at the Annual Meeting of the American Political Science Association, Chicago, Ill.: September 7–11 (1971).

Wilson, Richard (1974) *The Moral State.* New York: Free Press.

Wolfe, James H. (1974) 'Corporatism in German Political Life: Functional Representation in the GDR and Bavaria.' Pp. 323–40 in Heisler, Martin O. (ed.), *Politics in Europe.* New York: David McKay Co.

Wylie, Lawrence (1963) 'Youth in France and the United States.' Pp. 243–60 in Erikson, Erik H. (ed.), *Youth: Change and Challenge.* New York: Basic Books.

Zborowski, Mark (1969) *People in Pain.* San Francisco: Jossey Bass Inc.

CHAPTER 4

Adorno, T. *et al.* (1950) *The Authoritarian Personality.* New York: Harper.

Ahlstrom, Sidney E. (1972) *A Religious History of the American People.* New Haven and London: York University Press.

Baum, Rainer C. (1975) 'Authority and Identity: The Case for Evolutionary Invariance.' Paper presented at the Conference on Identity and Authority, University of Pittsburgh, April 1975 (mimeo.).

Bell, Daniel (1973) *The Coming of Post-Industrial Society: A Venture in Social Forecasting.* New York: Basic Books.

Bellah, Robert (1973) *Emile Durkheim on Morality and Society.* Chicago: The University of Chicago Press.

—— (1967) 'Civil Religion in America,' *Daedalus* 96 (Winter).

—— (1975) *The Broken Covenant*. New York: The Seabury Press.

Berger, Peter L. (1967) *The Sacred Canopy*. New York: Doubleday & Co.

Boguslaw, Robert (1965) *The New Utopians*. Englewood Cliffs, N.J.: Prentice-Hall.

Brzezinski, Zbigniew (1970) *Between Two Ages: America's Role in the Technotronic Era*. New York: Viking Press.

Burkholder, John R. (1974) 'The Law Knows No Heresy: Marginal Religious Movements and the Courts,' *Religious Movements in Contemporary American Society*, M. Leone and I. Zaretsky, (eds.) Princeton, N.J.: Princeton University Press.

Coleman, James (1974) *Power and the Structure of Society*. New York: W. W. Norton and Co.

Eliot, T. S. (1940) *Christianity and Culture*. New York: Harcourt, Brace & World.

Geertz, Clifford (1973) *The Interpretation of Cultures*. New York: Basic Books.

Gerth, H. H. and Mills, C. Wright, (eds.) (1958) Weber, Max, 'Science as a Vocation,' *From Max Weber: Essays in Sociology*. New York: Oxford University Press.

Greely, Andrew M. (1972) *The Denominational Society: A Sociological Approach to Religion in America*, Glenview, Ed.: Scott, Foresman.

Herberg, Will (1955) *Protestant—Catholic—Jew: An Essay in American Religious Sociology*. Garden City, N.Y.: Doubleday & Co.

Holzner, Burkart (1972) *Reality Construction in Society*. Revised edition. Cambridge, Mass.: Schenkman Publishing Co.

Jaspers, Karl (1964) *Three Essays: Leonardo, Descartes, Max Weber*, trans. by Ralph Mannheim. New York: Harcourt, Brace & World.

Klapp, Orrin (1969) *The Collective Search for Identity*. New York: Holt, Rinehart and Winston.

Lipset, Seymour M. (1967) *The First New Nation*. New York: Doubleday & Co.

Loewenstein, Karl (1966) *Max Weber's Political Ideas in the Perspective of Our Time*, The University of Massachusetts Press.

Lukes, Steven (1972) *Emile Durkheim*. New York: Harper & Row, Publishers.

Marty, Martin E. (1969) *The Modern Schism: Three Paths to the Secular*. New York: Harper & Row, Publishers.

Mitscherlich, Alexander (1970) *Society Without the Father*. New York: Schocken Books.

Mowinckel, Sigmund (1955) *He Who Cometh*, trans. by G. W. Anderson. Nashville: Abingdon.

Nash, Manning (1971) 'Buddhist Revitalization in the Nation States: The Burmese Experience,' in Robert F. Spencer, (ed.), *Religion and Change in Contemporary Asia*. Minneapolis: University of Minnesota Press.

Olson, M. (1971) *The Logic of Collective Action*. New York: Schocken Books.

Parsons, Talcott (1966) *Societies: Evolutionary and Comparative Perspectives*. Englewood Cliffs: Prentice-Hall.

Parsons, Talcott and Platt, Gerald (1973) *The American University*. Cambridge, Mass.: Harvard University Press.

Pfeffer, Leo (1974) 'The Legitimation of Marginal Religions in the United States,' *Religious Movements in Contemporary America*. Irving Zaretsky and M. Leone, (eds.) Princeton, N.J.: Princeton University Press.

Platt, Gerald and Weinstein, Fred (1969) *Psychoanalytic Sociology*. Baltimore: Johns Hopkins University Press.

Poggi, Gianfranco (1972) *Images of Society. Essays on the Sociological Theories of Toqueville, Marx, and Durkheim.* Stanford, California: Stanford University Press. London: Oxford University Press.

Simmel, Georg (1971) *On Individualistic and Social Forms: Selected Writings,* edited and introduced by Donald N. Levine. Chicago: University of Chicago Press.

Swanson, Guy (1967) *Religion and Regime: A Sociological Account of the Reformation.* Ann Arbor, Mich.: University of Michigan Press.

Tiryakian, Edward (1972) 'Toward the Sociology of Esoteric Culture,' *American Journal of Sociology* 78, 3:491–512.

Tussman, Joseph, (ed.) (1962) *The Supreme Court on Church and State.* New York: Oxford University Press.

Warner, W. Lloyd (1953) *American Life: Dream and Reality.* Chicago, Ill.: University of Chicago Press.

West, Charles C. (1966) 'Community — Authentic and Secular,' in J. F. Childress and David Harned, (eds.), *Secularization and the Protestant Prospect.* Philadelphia: Westminster.

Williams, Robin (1970) *American Society.* New York: Alfred Knopf.

Wilson, Bryan (1973) *Magic and the Millenium.* New York: Harper & Row.

CHAPTER 5

Allardt, Erik (1971) 'Culture, Structure, and Revolutionary Ideologies.' *International Journal of Comparative Sociology* XII: 24–40.

Allen, Pamela (1970) *Free Space.* New York: Times Change Press.

American Psychiatric Association (1970) 'Encounter Groups and Psychiatry' by the A.P.A. Task Force on Recent Developments in the Use of Small Groups. Washington, D.C., April.

Back, Kurt W. (1970a) 'Varieties of Sensitivity Training.' *The Sensitivity Training Movement.* New York: Russell Sage Foundation.

—— (1970b) 'Encounter Groups and Social Responsibility.' *The Sensitivity Training Movement.* New York: Russell Sage Foundation.

Bart, Pauline B. (1971) 'The Myth of a Value-Free Psychotherapy.' In Wendell Bell and James A. Mau (eds.) *Sociology and the Future.* New York: Sage.

Baum, Rainer C. (1974) 'Beyond Convergence.' *Sociological Inquiry* 44(4):225–40.

—— (1975) 'The System of Solidarities.' *Indian Journal of Social Research* 1 and 2: 305–53.

Bell, Daniel (1961) 'The End of Ideology in the West.' In Bell, *The End of Ideology.* New York: Crowell-Collier.

—— (1967a) 'Notes on the Post-Industrial Society (I).' *The Public Interest,* Winter.

—— (1967b) 'Notes on the Post-Industrial Society (II).' *The Public Interest,* Spring.

—— (1973) *The Coming of Post-Industrial Society.* New York: Basic Books.

—— (1976) *The Cultural Contradictions of Capitalism.* New York: Basic Books.

Bellah, Robert N. (1964) 'Religious Evolution.' *American Sociological Review* 29 (June): 358–74.

Bendix, Reinhard (1964) 'The Age of Ideology: Persistent and Changing.' In

David Apter (ed.), *Ideology and Discontent*. London: Collier-Macmillan Ltd., 294–327.

Berger, Peter L. (1965) 'Psychoanalysis and the Sociology of Knowledge.' *Social Research*.

—— (1976) 'The Cultural Contradictions of Capitalism by Daniel Bell.' Book Review in *Commentary*, Vol. 61, No. 4 (April): 82–3.

Berger, Peter L., Brigitte Berger, and Hansfried Kellner (1973) *The Homeless Mind: Modernization and Consciousness*. New York: Random House.

Berger, Peter L. and Thomas Luckmann (1967) *The Social Construction of Reality*. Garden City, New York: Doubleday Anchor Books.

Blum, Alan F. and Peter McHugh (1971) 'The Social Ascription of Motives.' *American Sociological Review* 36 (February): 98–109.

Blumer, Herbert (1957) 'Collective Behavior.' In Guttler, J. B. (ed.), *Review of Sociology: Analysis of a Decade*. New York: John Wiley and Sons, 127–58.

Brim, Orville (1966) 'Adult Socialization.' In Orville Brim and Stanton Wheeler (eds.), *Socialization After Childhood*. New York: Russell Sage Foundation.

Brzezinski, Zbigniew (1968) 'America in the Technotronic Age: New Questions of Our Time.' *Encounter* (January): 16–23.

Cherniss, Cary (1972) 'Personality and Ideology: A Personalogical Study of Women's Liberation. *Psychiatry* 35 (May): 109–25.

Deevey Jr., Edward S. (1960) 'The Human Population.' *Scientific American* (September): 2–9.

Denisoff, R. Serge (1974) *The Sociology of Dissent*. New York: Harcourt Brace Jovanovich.

De Solla Price, Derek J. (1963) *Little Science, Big Science*. New York: Columbia University Press.

Dreifus, Claudia (1973) *Woman's Fate: Raps From a Feminist Consciousness Raising Group*. New York: Bantam Books.

Erikson, Erik H. (1963) *Childhood and Society*. New York: Norton Books.

Flacks, Richard (1970) 'Young Intelligentsia in Revolt.' *Transaction* (June): 47–55.

Freeman, Jo (1972) 'The Women's Liberation Movement: Its Origins, Structures, and Ideas.' In *Recent Sociology No. 4: Family, Marriage, and the Struggle of the Sexes*, Hans Peter Dreitzel (ed.). New York: The Macmillan Co.

—— (1973) 'The Origins of the Women's Liberation Movement.' *American Journal of Sociology* 78 (No. 4): 792–811.

Geertz, Clifford (1964) 'Ideology as a Cultural System.' In David Apter (ed.), *Ideology and Discontent*. London: Collier-Macmillan Ltd., 44–77.

—— (1966) 'Religion as a Cultural System.' In Michael Banton (ed.), *Anthropological Approaches to the Study of Religion*. Tavistock Publications Ltd., 1–46.

Gehlen, Arnold (1969) *Moral and Hypermoral*. Frankfurt: Athenaum.

Goodenough, Ward H. (1957) 'Cultural Anthropology and Linguistics.' In *Report of the Seventh Annual Round Table Meeting on Linguistics and Language Study*, P. L. Garvin (ed.), Washington: Georgetown University Monograph Series on Languages and Linguistics No. 9.

Gornick, Vivian (1970a) 'The New Therapies: A Brief Encounter.' *The Village Voice*, January-February.

—— (1970b) 'Reflections on Collectivities.' *Vocations for Social Change* (November-December): 28–31 (reprinted from *Every Woman*).

—— (1971) 'Consciousness-Raising.' *The New York Times Magazine* (January 10).

Gottschalk, L. A. and E. Mansell Pattison (1969) 'Psychiatric Perspectives on T-Groups and the Laboratory Movement: An Overview.' *American Journal of Psychiatry* 126 (December): 823–39.

Gusfield, Joseph (1968) 'The Study of Social Movements.' In *The International Encyclopedia of the Social Sciences*. New York: Crowell, Collier and Macmillan.

Hayden, Tom (1970) Untitled. In the *San Francisco Chronicle* (September 15): 8.

Heberle, R. (1949) 'Observations on the Sociology of Social Movements.' *American Sociological Review* 14: 346–57.

Hole, Judith and Ellen Levine (1970) *Rebirth of Feminism*. New York: Quadrangle.

Holzner, Burkart (1968) *Reality Construction in Society*. Cambridge, Mass.: Schenkman Publishing Company.

Homans, George C. (1950) *The Human Group*. New York: Harcourt Brace & Co.

Jacobs, Ruth (1971) 'Emotive and Control Groups as Mutated New American Utopian Communities.' *Journal of Applied Behavioral Science* 7:2.

Kagan, J. (1969) 'Continuity in Development.' Paper presented at the meeting of the Society for Research in Child Development, March 27, 1969, Santa Monica, California.

Kanter, Rosabeth Moss (1968) 'Commitment in Social Organization: A Study of Commitment Mechanisms in Utopian Communities.' *American Sociological Review* 33 (August): 499–517.

—— (1970) 'Communes.' *Psychology Today* 4 (July): 53–8.

Kavolis, Vytautas (1968) *Artistic Expression: A Sociological Analysis*. Ithaca, New York: Cornell University Press.

—— (1969) 'Revolutionary Metaphors and Ambiguous Personalities: Notes Toward An Understanding of Post-Modern Revolutions.' *Soundings* 52 (Winter): 394–414.

—— (1970) 'Post-Modern Man: Psycho-Cultural Responses to Social Trends.' *Social Problems* 17 (Spring): 435–49.

—— (1974) 'Notes on Post-Industrial Culture.' *Arts in Society* 11 (Fall-Winter).

Keniston, Kenneth (1968-9) 'Heads and Seekers: Drugs on Campus, Counter-Cultures and American Society.' *The American Scholar* 38 (Winter): 97–112.

King, Richard (1972) 'The Eros Ethos Cult in the Counter-Culture.' *Psychology Today* (August): 35–70.

Kroeber, Alfred and Talcott Parsons (1958) 'The Concept of Culture and of Social System.' *American Sociological Review* 23: 582–3.

Lakin, Martin (1969) 'Some Ethical Issues in Sensitivity Training.' *American Psychologist* 24 (October): 923–8.

—— (1971) 'Group Sensitivity Training and Encounter — Time Out for Measurement.' Unpublished manuscript.

Lindesmith, A. R. and A. L. Strauss (1957) *Social Psychology* (revised edition). New York: The Dryden Press.

Maliver, Bruce L. (1971) 'Encounter Groups up Against the Wall.' *The New York Times Magazine* (January 3).

Mannheim, Karl (1936) *Ideology and Utopia*. New York: Harcourt Brace.

Manuel, Frank E. (1965) 'Toward a Psychological History of Utopias.'

—— (1976) 'The Cultural Contradictions of Capitalism by Daniel Bell.' Book Review in *The New Republic*, March 20, 1976.

Marin, Peter (1975) 'The New Narcissism.' *Harper's* (October): 45–56.

Marx, John H. (1969) 'A Multidimensional Conception of Ideologies in Professional Arenas: The Case of the Mental Health Field.' *Pacific Sociological Review* 12 (Fall): 75–85.

Marx, John H. and S. Lee Spray (1970) 'Marital Status and Occupational Success Among Mental Health Professionals.' *Journal of Marriage and the Family* 32 (February: 110–18.

—— (1972) 'Psychotherapeutic "Birds of a Feather": Social Class Status and Religio-Cultural Value Homophily in the Mental Health Field.' *Journal of Health and Social Behavior* 13 (December): 413–28.

Marx, John H. and Joseph H. Seldin (1973a) 'At the Crossroads of Crisis I: Therapeutic Sources and Quasi-therapeutic Functions of Post-Industrial Communes.' *Journal of Health and Social Behavior* 14 (March): 39–52.

—— (1973b) 'At the Crossroads of Crisis II: Organizational and Ideological Bases of Contemporary Communes.' *Journal of Health and Social Behavior* 14 (June).

Marx, John H. and David Ellison (1975) 'Sensitivity Training and Communes: Contemporary Quests for Community.' *Pacific Sociological Review.* Forthcoming.

Marx, John H., Patricia Rieker, and David L. Ellison (1974) 'The Sociology of Community Mental Health: Historical and Methodological Perspectives.' In *Sociological Perspectives on Community Mental Health*, Paul M. Roman and Harrison M. Trice (eds.). Philadelphia: F. A. Davis Company, pp. 9–41.

Marx, John H. and Burkart Holzner (1974) 'The Social Construction of Strain and Ideological Models of Grievance in Contemporary Movements.' Unpublished manuscript.

Mauss, Armand L. and Donald W. Peterson (1973) 'The Cross and the Commune: An Interpretation of the Jesus People.' In Charles Y. Glock (ed.), *Religion in Sociological Perspective.* Belmont, California: Wadsworth Publishing Co.

McLuhan, Marshall (1962) *The Guttenberg Galaxy.* Toronto, Ontario: University of Toronto Press.

—— (1967) *The Medium is the Message.* New York: Bantam Books.

Mischel, Walter (1969) 'Continuity and Change in Personality.' *American Psychologist*, Vol. 24, No. 11: 1013–18.

Mitchell, Juliet (1971) *Woman's Estate.* New York: Pantheon Books-Random House.

Moore, Omar K. (1973) 'The Science of Knowledge.' In 'The Sociological Implications of Sociological Change,' a four-part Cogar Foundation Series presented at Herkimer County Community College, first lecture, November.

Ms. Magazine A Guide to Consciousness Raising. New York: Ms. Magazine.

Nahirny, Vladimir C. (1963) 'Some Observations on Ideological Groups.' *The American Journal of Sociology* 68:173–81.

Nisbet, R. A. (1952) 'Conservatism and Sociology.' *American Journal of Sociology* 58:167–75.

Oberschall, Anthony (1973) *Social Conflict and Social Movements.* Englewood Cliffs, New Jersey: Prentice-Hall.

Parsons, Talcott (1950) *The Social System.* Glencoe, Illinois: The Free Press.

Parsons, Talcott and Renee Fox (1952) 'Illness and the Urban American Family.' *Journal of Social Issues* 8:31–44.

Reich, Charles (1970) *The Greening of America.* New York: Random House.

Rieff, Philip (1966) *The Triumph of the Therapeutic.* New York: Harper Torchbooks.

Roszak, Theodore (1969) *The Making of a Counter Culture*. New York: Random.

Ruitenbeek, Hendrik M. (1970) *The New Group Therapies*. New York: Discus Books.

Sherif, M. (1952) 'The Concept of Reference Groups in Human Relations.' In M. Sherif and M. O. Wilson (eds.), *Group Relations at the Crossroads*. New York: Harper and Brothers, 203–31.

Sisk, John P. (1976) 'Salvation Unlimited.' *Commentary*, Vol. 61, No. 4 (April): 52–6.

Slater, Philip E. (1970) *The Pursuit of Loneliness* Boston: Beacon Press.

Smelser, Neil J. (1963) *Theory of Collective Behavior*. New York: The Free Press.

Spradley, James P. (1972a) *Culture and Cognition: Rules, Maps, and Plans*. Chandler Publishing Co.: San Francisco and Toronto.

—— (1972b) 'Foundations of Cultural Knowledge.' In *Culture and Cognition*, James P. Spradley (ed.). San Francisco and Toronto: Chandler Publishing Co.: 3–38.

Strauss, A. (1947) 'Research in Collective Behavior: Neglect and Need.' *American Sociological Review* 12:352–4.

Tanner, Leslie B. (1970) *Voices From the Women's Liberation Movement*. New York: New American Library.

Toffler, Alvin W. (1970) *Future Shock*. New York: Random House.

Touraine, Alain (1972) *The Post-Industrial Society, Tomorrow's Social History: Classes, Conflicts, and Culture in the Programmed Society*. Translated by Leonard F. X. Mayhew. New York: Random House.

Turner, Ralph H. (1969) 'The Theme of Contemporary Social Movements.' *British Journal of Sociology* 20 (December): 586–99.

Wallace, Anthony F. C. (1956) 'Revitalization Movements.' *American Anthropologist* 58:264–81.

—— (1961a) *Culture and Personality*. New York: Random House.

—— (1961b) 'On Being Just Complicated Enough.' *Proceedings of National Academy of Sciences* 47:458–64.

—— (1962) 'Culture and Cognition.' *Science* 135:351–7.

—— (1972) 'Driving to Work.' In *Culture and Cognition*, James P. Spradley (ed.). San Francisco and Toronto: Chandler Publishing Co.: 310–26.

Wallace, Anthony F. C. and John Atkins (1960) 'The Meaning of Kinship Terms.' *American Anthropologist* 62:58–80.

Weller, Jack M. and E. L. Quarantelli (1973) 'Neglected Characteristics of Collective Behavior.' *American Journal of Sociology* 79:665–85.

Wheeler, Stanton (1966) 'Socialization in Institutions.' In Orville Brim and Stanton Wheeler (eds.), *Socialization After Childhood*. New York: Russell Sage Foundation.

Wheelis, Allen (1953) *The Quest for Identity*. New York: Norton.

CHAPTER 6

Back, Kurt W. (1972) *Beyond Words, The Story of Sensitivity Training and the Encounter Movement*. New York: Russell Sage.

Bell, Daniel (1973) *The Coming of Post-Industrial Society, A Venture in Social Forecasting*. New York, Basic Books.

—— (1976) *The Cultural Contradictions of Capitalism*. New York: Basic Books.

Bellah, Robert N. (1964) 'Religious evolution.' *American Sociological Review* 29 (June): 358–74.

Bennis, Warren G. and Philip E. Slater (1968) *The Temporary Society*. New York: Harper and Row.

Berger, Peter, Brigitte Berger, and Hansfried Kellner (1973) *The Homeless Mind: Modernization and Consciousness*. New York: Vintage.

Biller, Robert P. (1973) 'Converting knowledge into action: toward a post-industrial society.' Pp. 35–40 in Jong S. Jun and William B. Storm (eds.), *Tomorrow's Organizations*. Glenview: Scott Foresman.

Bloch, Ernst (1959) *Das Prinzip Hoffnung*. 2 vols. Frankfurt: Suhrkamp Verlag.

Block, Jack and Norma Haan (1971) *Lives through Time*. Berkeley: Bancroft Books.

Bouwsma, William J. (1966) *Venice and the Defense of Republican Liberty, Renaissance Values in the Age of the Counter Reformation*. Berkeley: University of California Press.

Brown, Delwin, Ralph E. James, Jr., and Gene Reeves (eds.) (1971) *Process Philosophy and Christian Thought*. Indianapolis: Bobbs-Merrill.

Cobb, John B., Jr. (1965) *A Christian Natural Theology Based on the Thought of Alfred North Whitehead*. Philadelphia: Westminster Press.

Cox, Harvey (1964) *The Secular City*. New York: Macmillan.

Crowne, Douglas P. (1966) 'Family orientation, level of aspiration, and interpersonal bargaining.' *Journal of Personality and Social Psychology* 3 (June): 641–5.

Cunningham, Robert L. (1970) *Situationism and the New Morality*. New York: Appleton-Century-Crofts.

Drucker, Peter (1954) *The Practice of Management*. New York: Harper.

Eisenstadt, Schmuel N. (1966) *Modernization: Protest and Change*. Englewood Cliffs: Prentice-Hall.

Elder, Glenn (1966) Oakland Growth Study, *Adolescent Face Sheet* (November). Dittoed coding instructions. Institute of Human Development, University of California, Berkeley.

—— (1974) *Children of the Great Depression*. Chicago: University of Chicago Press.

Galbraith, John K. (1971) *The New Industrial State*. Boston: Houghton Mifflin.

Gamson, William A. (1975) *The Strategy of Social Protest*. Homewood: Dorsey.

Geertz, Clifford (1966) 'Religion as a cultural system.' Pp. 1–46 in Michael Banton (ed.) *Anthropological Approaches to the Study of Religion*. New York: Praeger.

Goffman, Erving (1967) 'Where the action is.' Pp. 149–270 in his *Interaction Ritual, Essays on Face-to-Face Behavior*. Chicago: Aldine.

Haan, Norma (1969) 'A tripartite model of ego functioning values and clinical and research applications.' *The Journal of Nervous and Mental Disease*. 1948 (January): 14–30.

—— (1974) *The implications of family ego patterns for adolescent members*. Doctoral dissertation. California School of Professional Psychology.

Haire, Mason, Edwin E. Ghiselli, and Lyman W. Porter (1966) *Managerial Thinking: An International Study*. New York: Wiley.

Hartshorne, Charles (1941) *Man's Vision of God and the Logic of Theism*. Chicago: Willett, Clark.

—— (1970) *Creative Synthesis and Philosophic Method*. LaSalle: Open Court.

Hoge, Dean R. (1974) *Commitment on Campus: Changes in Religion and Values over Five Decades*. Philadelphia: Westminster Press.

Howard, S. Kenneth (1971) 'Analysis, rationality, and administrative decision making.' Pp. 285–301 in Frank Marini (ed.), *Toward a New Public Administration*. Scranton: Chandler.

Huehns, Gertrude (1951) *Antinomianism in English History*. London: Cresset.

Inkeles, Alex and David H. Smith (1974) *Becoming Modern: Individual Change in Six Developing Countries*. Cambridge: Harvard University Press.

Jun, Jong S. and William B. Storm (1973) *Tomorrow's Organizations*. Glenview: Scott Foresman.

Katz, Daniel and Robert L. Kahn (1966) *The Social Psychology of Organizations*. New York: Wiley.

Keen, Sam (1966) *Gabriel Marcel*. London: Carey Kingsgate Press.

—— (1969) *Apologies for Wonder*. New York: Harper and Row.

—— (1974) *Voices and Visions*. New York: Harper and Row.

Kohn, Melvin L. (1969) *Class and Conformity, A Study in Values*. Homewood: Dorsey.

—— (1971) 'Bureaucratic man: a portrait and an interpretation.' *American Sociological Review* 36 (June): 461–74.

Lawrence, Paul R. and Jay W. Lorsch (1967) *Organization and Environment: Managing Differentiation and Integration*. Boston: Graduate School of Business Administration, Harvard University.

Leavitt, Harold J. (1965) 'Applied organizational change in industry: structural, technological and humanistic approaches.' Pp. 1144–70 in James G. March (ed.), *Handbook of Organizations*. Chicago: Rand McNally.

Likert, Rensis (1967) *The Human Organization: Its Management and Value*. New York: McGraw-Hill.

Lippitt, Ronald (1949) *Training in Community Relations*. New York: Harper.

Lundborg, Louis (1974) *Future Without Shock*. New York: Norton.

Macquarrie, John (1965) *Studies in Christian Existentialism*. London, SCM.

McGregor, Douglas (1957) 'An uneasy look at performance appraisal.' *Harvard Business Review* 35 (May-June): 89–94.

—— (1960) *The Human Side of Enterprise*. New York: McGraw-Hill.

Meade, Marvin (1971) '"Participative" administration—emerging reality or wishful thinking?' Pp. 169–87 in Dwight Waldo (ed.), *Public Administration in a Time of Turbulence*. Scranton: Chandler.

Miles, Raymond E. (1964) 'Conflicting elements in managerial ideologies.' *Industrial Relations* 4 (October): 77–91.

—— (1975) *Theories of Management*. New York: McGraw-Hill.

Miles, Raymond E. and J. B. Ritchie (1968) 'Leadership attitudes among union officials.' *Industrial Relations* 8 (October): 108–17.

Miller, Daniel R. and Guy E. Swanson (1958) *The Changing American Parent, A Study in the Detroit Area*. New York: Wiley.

—— (1960) *Inner Conflict and Defense*. New York: Holt.

Miller, Delbert C. and William H. Form (1964) *Industrial Sociology, The Sociology of Work Organizations*. New York: Harper and Row.

Miller, Keith (1973) *The Becomers*. Waco: Word Books.

Moltmann, Jurgen (1969) *Religion, Revolution and the Future*. M. Douglas Meeks, Translator. New York: Scribner's.

Mosher, Frederick C. (1971) 'Public service in the temporary society.' *Public Administration Review* 31 (January): 47–61.

Newell, Allyn and Herbert A. Simon (1972) *Human Problem Solving*. Englewood Cliffs: Prentice-Hall.

Nonet, Philippe (1974) 'Law and institutional design: accountability vs responsiveness.' Mimeographed paper. Center for the Study of Law and Society, University of California, Berkeley.

Ordione, George S. (1969) *Management Decisions by Objectives*. Englewood Cliffs: Prentice-Hall.

Parker, David F. (1971) 'The inadequacy of traditional theories and the promise of PPB as a systems approach.' Pp. 301–8 in Frank Marini (ed.), *Toward a New Public Administration*. Scranton: Chandler.

Parsons, Talcott (1964) 'Evolutionary universals in society.' *American Sociological Review* 29 (June): 339–57.

Perrow, Charles (1965) 'Hospitals: technology, structure, and goals.' Pp. 910–71 in James March (ed.) *Handbook of Organizations*. Chicago: Rand McNally.

—— (1972) *Complex Organizations, A Critical Essay*. Glenview: Scott Foresman.

Raia, Anthony P. (1974) *Managing by Objectives*. Glenview: Scott Foresman.

Rieff, Philip (1966) *The Triumph of the Therapeutic, Uses of Faith after Freud*. New York: Harper and Row.

—— (1973) *Fellow Teachers*. New York: Harper and Row.

Rust, Eric C. (1969) *Evolutionary Philosophies and Contemporary Theology*. Philadelphia: Westminster.

Schick, Allen (1970) 'The cybernetic state.' *TransAction* 7 (February): 15–26.

Scott, William G. (1969) 'Organization government: the prospect for a truly participative system.' *Public Administration Review* 29 (January-February): 43–53.

Sellers, James E. (1970) *Public Ethics: American Morals and Manners*. New York: Harper and Row.

Selznick, Philip (1957) *Leadership in Administration*. Evanston: Row, Peterson.

—— (1974) 'The ethos of American law.' In Irving Kristol and Paul Weaver (eds.) *Politics and the Idea of Man*. Forthcoming.

Simmel, Georg (1890) 'Superordination and subordination.' Pp. 181–303 in Kurt Wolff (ed.) *The Sociology of Georg Simmel*. Glencoe: Free Press, 1950.

Strauss, George (1972) 'Management by objectives: a critical view.' *Training and Development Journal* 26 (April): 10–15.

—— (1974) 'Workers: attitudes and adjustments.' Pp. 73–98 in Jerome M. Rosow (ed.), *The Worker and the Job: Coping with Change*. Englewood Cliffs: Prentice-Hall.

Swanson, Guy E. (1971a) 'An organizational analysis of collectivities.' *American Sociological Review* 36 (August): 607–24.

—— (1971b) *Social Change*. Glenview: Scott, Foresman.

—— (1973) 'The search for a guardian spirit, a process of empowerment in simpler societies.' *Ethnology* 12 (July): 359–78.

—— (1974) 'Family structure and the reflective intelligence of children.' *Sociometry* 37 (December): 459–90.

Turner, Ralph H. (1969) 'The theme of contemporary social movements.' *The British Journal of Sociology* 20 (December): 390–405.

Vroom, Victor H. and Philip W. Yetton (1974) *Leadership and Decision-making*. Pittsburgh: University of Pittsburgh Press.
Waldo, Dwight (1965) 'The administrative state revisited.' *Public Administration Review* 25 (March): 5–30.
—— (1968) 'Public administration.' Pp. 145–56 in *Industrial Encyclopedia of the Social Sciences*. Vol. 13. New York: Macmillan and The Free Press.
Weiland, J. Sperna (1968) *New Ways in Theology*. Dublin: Gill and Macmillan.
White, Orion F., Jr. (1971) 'Social change and administrative adaptation.' Pp. 59–83 in Frank Marini (ed.), *Toward a New Public Administration*. Scranton: Chandler.
Wilensky, Harold L. (1964) 'Mass society and mass culture: interdependence or independence?' *American Sociological Review* 29 (April): 173–97.
—— (1965) *Industrial Society and Social Welfare*. New York: Free Press.
Winter, J. Alan (1974) 'Elective affinities between religious beliefs and ideologies of management in two eras.' *American Journal of Sociology* 79 (March): 1134–50.
Woodward, Joanne (1965) *Industrial Organization: Theory and Practice*. London: Oxford University Press.
Wuthnow, Robert (1975) *Consciousness and the Transformation of Society*. Unpublished doctoral dissertation. Department of Sociology. University of California, Berkeley.

CHAPTER 7

Adorno, Theodor W. *et al.* (1950) *The Authoritarian Personality*. New York: Harper.
Althusser, Louis (1972, 1959, 1970) *Politics and History*. London: NLB.
Baum, Rainer (1974) 'Beyond Convergence.' *Sociological Inquiry* 42:156–60.
—— (1977) 'Beyond the Iron Cage.' *Sociological Analysis* 38.
Bell, Daniel (1975) *The Cultural Contradictions of Capitalism*. New York: Basic Books.
Bellah, Robert (1964) 'Religious Evolution.' *American Sociological Review* 29:358–74.
Bellah, Robert N. (ed.) (1973) *Emile Durkheim on Morality and Society*. Chicago: Chicago University Press.
Berger, Peter (1966) 'Identity as a Problem in the Sociology of Knowledge.' *European Journal of Sociology* 7:105–15.
—— (1967) *The Sacred Canopy*. New York: Doubleday.
Berger, Peter and Thomas Luckmann (1966) *The Construction of Social Reality*. New York: Doubleday.
Berger, Peter *et al.* (1973) *The Homeless Mind*. New York: Random House.
Bershady, Harold (1973) *Ideology and Social Knowledge*. Oxford: Blackwell.
Bourdieu, Pierre (1977, 1972) *Outline of a Theory of Practice*. Cambridge: Cambridge Univeristy Press.
Cassirer, Ernest (1945) *Rousseau, Kant and Goethe*. Princeton: Princeton University Press.
Colletti, Lucio (1972, 1969) *From Rousseau to Lenin*. New York: Monthly Review Press.

—— (1973, 1969) *Marxism and Hegel*. London: NLB.

—— (1975) 'Introduction.' In Karl Marx, *Early Writings*. New York: Vintage: 7–56.

Dumont, Louis (1972, 1966) *Homo Hierarchicus*. London: Paladin.

—— (1977) *From Mandeville to Marx*. Chicago: Chicago University Press.

Durkheim, Emile (1961, 1912) *The Elementary Forms of the Religious Life*. New York: Collicr.

Durkheim, Emile *et al.* (1960, various dates) *Essays on Sociology and Philosophy*. New York: Harper.

Eisenstadt, S. N. (1978) *Revolution and the Transformation of Society*. New York: Free Press.

Eisenstadt, S. N. and M. Curelaru (1976) *The Form of Sociology*. New York: Wiley.

Ekeh, Peter (1974) *Social Exchange Theory*. London: Heinemann.

Etzioni, Amitai (1961) *The Comparative Analysis of Complex Organizations*. New York: Free Press.

—— (1968) *The Active Society*. New York: Free Press.

Feyerabend, P. K. (1975) *Against Method*. London: LNB.

Freud, Sigmund (1961, 1930) *Civilization and Its Discontents*. New York: Norton.

Friedrich, Carl J. (1972) *Tradition and Authority*. New York: Praeger.

Fromm, Erich (1941) *Escape From Freedom*. New York: Rinehart.

Gadamer, Hans-Georg (1975, 1972) *Truth and Method*. New York: Seabury Press.

Gellner, Ernest (1974) *The Legitimation of Belief*. Cambridge: Cambridge University Press.

Gerth, Hans H. and C. Wright Mills (1954) *Character and Social Structure*. London: Routledge.

Giddens, Anthony (1976) *New Rules of Sociological Method*. New York: Basic Books.

Glock, Charles Y. and Robert N. Bellah (1976) *The New Religious Consciousness*. Berkeley, Los Angeles: California University Press.

Goffman, Erving (1967) *Interaction Ritual*. New York: Anchor.

—— (1959) *The Presentation of Self in Everyday Life*. Garden City, N.Y.: Doubleday.

—— (1974) *Frame Analysis*. New York: Harper and Row.

Gonos, George (1977) '"Situation" versus "Frame"; the "Interactionist" and the "Structuralist" Analyses of Everyday Life.' *American Sociological Review* 42:833–53.

Gouldner, Alvin (1976) *The Dialectic of Ideology and Technology*. New York: Seabury.

—— (1970) *The Coming Crisis of Western Sociology*. New York: Basic Books.

Greenstein, Fred I. (1975) *Personality and Politics*. New York: Norton.

Guiot, Jean M. (1977) 'Attribution and Identity Construction: Some Comments.' *American Sociological Review* 42:692–703.

Habermas. Jürgen (1972, 1968) *Knowledge and Human Interests*. London: Heinemann.

—— (1974) 'On Social Identity.' *Telos* 19:91–103.

—— (1975, 1973) *Legitimation Crisis*. Boston: Beacon Press.

Hollis, Martin (1977) *Models of Man*. Cambridge: Cambridge University Press.

Inkeles, Alex and David H. Smith (1974) *Becoming Modern*. Cambridge, Mass.: Harvard University Press.

Kuhn, Thomas (1970) *The Structure of Scientific Revolutions.* Chicago: Chicago University Press.
Mead, George Herbert (1934) *Mind, Self and Society.* Chicago: Chicago University Press.
Misgeld, Dieter (1976) 'Critical Theory and Hermeneutics: The Debate Between Habermas and Gadamer.' In John O'Neill (ed.), *On Critical Theory.* New York: Seabury Press: Ch. 9.
Mommsen, Wolfgang (1974) *The Age of Bureaucracy.* Oxford: Blackwell.
Nelson, Benjamin (1969) *The Idea of Usury.* Chicago: Chicago University Press.
—— (1971) 'Discussion on Industrialization and Capitalism.' In Otto Stammler (ed.), *Max Weber and Sociology Today.* Oxford: Blackwell.
Nettl, J. P. and Roland Robertson (1968) *International Systems and the Modernization of Societies.* New York: Basic Books and London: Faber.
Oakes, Guy (1977) 'Introduction: Simmel's Problematic.' In Georg Simmel, *The Problems of the Philosophy of History.* New York: Free Press:1–38.
O'Brien, Ken (1976) 'Death and Revolution: A Reappraisal of Identity Theory.' In John O'Neill (ed.), *On Critical Theory.* New York: Seabury Press: Ch. 6.
Parsons, Talcott (1937) *The Structure of Social Action.* Glencoe: Free Press.
—— (1964) *Social Structure and Personality.* New York: Free Press.
—— (1968) *The Structure of Social Action.* New York: Free Press (paper edition).
Parsons, Talcott and Gerald M. Platt (1973) *The American University.* Cambridge, Mass.: Harvard University Press.
Poggi, Gianfranco (1972) *Images of Society.* Stanford: Stanford University Press.
Poster, Mark (1975) *Existential Marxism in Postwar France.* Princeton: Princeton University Press.
Rex, John (1974) 'Social Structure and Humanistic Sociology: The Legacy of the Classical European Tradition.' In John Rex (ed.), *Approaches to Sociology.* London: Routledge.
Rieff, Philip (1966) *The Triumph of the Therapeutic.* New York: Harper and Row.
Riesman, David *et al.* (1950) *The Lonely Crowd.* New Haven: Yale University Press.
Riesman, David (1954) *Individualism Reconsidered.* Glencoe: Free Press.
Robertson, Roland (1976) 'Societal Attributes and International Relations.' In Jan J. Loubser *et al.* (eds.), *Explorations in General Theory in Social Science.* New York: Free Press: 713–35.
—— (1977) 'Individualism, Societalism, Worldliness, Universalism: Thematizing Theoretical Sociology of Religion.' *Sociological Analysis* 38:281–308.
—— (1978a) *Meaning and Change: Explorations in the Cultural Sociology of Modern Societies.* Oxford: Blackwell and New York: New York University Press.
—— (1978b) 'Talcott Parsons.' In T. Raison (ed.), *Founders of Social Science.* London: Scolar:284–300.
—— (1980) 'Max Weber's Sociology of Religion: Nineteenth Century Background and Contemporary Intellectual Context.' In Ninian Smart *et al.* (eds.), *Religious Thought in the Nineteenth Century.* Cambridge: Cambridge University Press.
Sahlins, Marshall (1976) *Culture and Practical Reason.* Chicago: Chicago University Press.
Simmel, Georg (1900) *Philosophie des Geldes.* Leipzig: Duncker and Humblot.

—— (1912) *Schopenhauer und Nietzsche*. Leipzig: Duncker and Humblot.

—— (1950, 1908) Writings collected in Kurt Wolff (ed.), *The Sociology of Georg Simmel*. New York: Free Press.

—— (1955, 1908) *Conflict and the Web of Group-Affiliations*. New York: Free Press.

—— (1971, various dates) Writings in Donald Levine (ed.), *Georg Simmel on Individuality and Social Forms*. Chicago: Chicago University Press.

—— (1976, various dates) Writings collected in Peter Lawrence (ed.), *Georg Simmel: Sociologist and European*. New York: Barnes and Noble.

Stone, Gregory and Harvey A. Farberman (eds.) (1970) *Social Psychology Through Symbolic Interaction*. Waltham: Ginn-Blaisdell.

Tillich, Paul (1967) *Perspectives on 19th and 20th Century Theology*. New York: Harper and Row.

Tiryakian, Edward (1962) *Sociologism and Existentialism*. Englewood Cliffs: Prentice-Hall.

Touraine, Alain (1977, 1973) *The Self Production of Society*. Chicago: Chicago University Press.

Weber, Max (1968, 1920) *Economy and Society*. Totowa: Bedminster Press.

Wrong, Dennis (1977) *Skeptical Sociology*. New York: Columbia University Press.

Wuthnow, Robert (1976) *The Consciousness Reformation*. Berkeley, Los Angeles: California University Press.

Notes on Contributors

BURKART HOLZNER is Professor and Chairman of the Department of Sociology, University of Pittsburgh. His books include *Reality Construction in Society* and (as co-author) *Knowledge Application: The Knowledge System in Society*. His articles and essays have dealt with issues in sociological theory, the sociology of knowledge, knowledge application, research organizations and social movements.

ROLAND ROBERTSON is Professor of Sociology, University of Pittsburgh. He is author of *The Sociological Interpretation of Religion*, and of *Meaning and Change*; co-author of *International Systems and the Modernization of Societies* and of *Deviance, Crime and Socio-Legal Control*; and the editor of *Sociology of Religion*. His published articles and essays have dealt, *inter alia*, with issues in general sociological theory, social stratification, international relations, deviance, the history of sociological thought, civilizational analysis, religion, and modernization.

VYTAUTAS KAVOLIS is Charles A. Dana Professor of Comparative Civilizations and Professor of Sociology at Dickinson College. His major publications are *Artistic Expression: A Sociological Analysis* and *History on Art's Side: Social Dynamics in Artistic Efflorescences*. He has also edited *Comparative Perspectives on Social Problems* and published three books in Lithuanian: *Lithuanian Liberalism*, *The Genesis of Man—A Psychological Study of Vincas Kudirka*, and *A Generation Deprived of its Earth: Essays on the World-Feeling of Exile*.

RAINER C. BAUM is Professor of Sociology at the University of Pittsburgh. A general sociologist with interests in theory, comparative nation-building, and stratification, he is currently engaged in cross-national comparative work on modernization problems. He is co-editor of *Explorations in General Theory in Social Science*, author and co-author of papers therein as well as in *Sociological Inquiry*, *The Indian Journal of Social Research*, *International Journal of Aging and Human Development*, *Zeitschrift für Soziologie*, *Sociological Analysis*, and in collections of essays.

RICHARD K. FENN is Associate Professor of Sociology, University of Maine. He is the author of articles on theoretical problems in the sociology of religion, with particular reference to the secularization of American society. These have been published in such journals as *Review of Religious Research*, *Sociological Analysis* and *The Journal for the Scientific Study of Religion*, and in collections of essays.

JOHN H. MARX is Associate Professor of Sociology, university of Pittsburgh. He is the co-author of *Knowledge Application: The Knowledge System in Society* and of articles and essays on topics in medical sociology, the mental health professions, the sociology of identity and ideology, cultural movements, and the sociology of knowledge.

GUY E. SWANSON is Professor of Sociology, University of California, Berkeley. His books include *Birth of the Gods, Religion and Regime* and *Social Change*. He has co-authored other works, including *The Changing American Parent* and *Inner Conflict and Defense*. His articles and essays have dealt with a variety of topics including studies of complex organizations, religious belief and behaviour, secularization and the theory and methodology of comparative research.

Name Index

(Excludes citations in Reference section)

Subject Index